AS/400 Data Management Fundamentals

Robert W. Janson
Florida Community College at Jacksonville

boyd & fraser publishing company
I(T)P An International Thomson Publishing Company

Danvers • Albany • Bonn • Boston • Cincinnati • Detroit • London • Madrid • Melbourne
Mexico City • New York • Paris • San Francisco • Singapore • Tokyo • Toronto • Washington

Executive Editor: James H. Edwards
Editorial Assistant: Beth A. Sweet
Production Editor: Barbara Worth
Manufacturing Coordinator: Carol Chase
Marketing Director: William Lisowski
Composition: Gex, Inc.
Interior Design: Books By Design, Inc.
Cover Design: Kevin Meyers

boyd & fraser publishing company
A division of International Thomson Publishing Inc.

I(T)P The ITP™ logo is a trademark under license.

Printed in the United States of America

This book is printed on recycled, acid-free paper that meets Environmental Protection Agency standards.

For more information, contact boyd & fraser publishing company:

boyd & fraser publishing company
One Corporate Place • Ferncroft Village
Danvers, Massachusetts 01923, USA

International Thomson Publishing Europe
Berkshire House 168-173
High Holborn
London, WCIV 7AA, England

Thomas Nelson Australia
102 Dodds Street
South Melbourne 3205
Victoria, Australia

Nelson Canada
1120 Birchmount Road
Scarborough, Ontario
Canada M1K 5G4

International Thomson Editores
Campose Eliseos 385, Piso 7
Col. Polanco
11560 Mexico D.F. Mexico

International Thomson Publishing GmbH
Konigswinterer Strasse 418
53227 Bonn, Germany

International Thomson Publishing Asia
221 Henderson Road
#05-10 Henderson Building
Singapore 0315

International Thomson Publishing Japan
Hirakawacho Kyowa Building, 3F
2-2-1 Hirakawacho
Chiyoda-ku, Tokyo 102, Japan

1 2 3 4 5 6 7 8 9 10 BN 9 8 7 6 5

Library of Congress Cataloging-in-Publication Data

Janson, Robert W.
AS/400 data management fundamentals / Robert W. Janson.
p. cm
Includes index.
ISBN 0-7895-0045-0
1. IBM AS/400 (Computer)--Programming. 2. Data structures (Computer science). I. Title.
QA76.8. I25919J34 1995
005.74--dc20 95-2330
CIP

Contents

Chapter 6

Databases and Database Management Systems 96

Chapter 7

Logical Files 110

Preface

This book assumes that the reader has a basic understanding of the AS/400, such as the ability to execute CL commands and write CL programs, experience with a high-level programming language, and familiarity with common AS/400 utilities such as QUERY/400, DFU, SDA, and PDM. These utilities will be used to demonstrate various aspects of data management and will definitely be needed to perform the programming exercises. Instruction in how to use these utilities and commands will be brief (except for QUERY/400). If the required skills don't exist or a more in-depth treatment of these topics is desired, I suggest another book of mine, *An Introduction to the AS/400* also published by boyd & fraser.

Because the amount of data is small, some of the programming exercises can be simulated with DFU. However, functions such as commitment control or embedding SQL statements in programs can't be simulated. Knowledge of a high-level programming language is needed. All screens are for Version 2 Release 3 of OS/400 even though some functions of Version 3 are covered.

I'd like to thank my previous students for their continual feedback (requested or not) regarding each topic, its explanation, and associated exercises, as well as for their remarkable diligence (and seeming delight) in catching technical errors, spelling mistakes, and typos. They have made this and my other books better.

Many thanks also to my wife Brenda for her kind acceptance of the inconveniences and demands of this and all past books.

Robert W. Janson
Jacksonville, Florida

Introduction

1

Overview

Data is an essential component of all information systems. How data is stored and accessed will affect every user and customer of the system. This chapter will explore the growing importance of data and the need for timely access to accurate data. We will also explain the basic purpose of data management and database management systems. We will examine the difference between the physical and logical organization of files, as well as the purpose of each.

After finishing this chapter, you will understand

- The importance of data
- The purpose of data management
- The major features of a database management system
- The difference between the logical and physical organization of data

A Brief History of Data Storage

Information retention and access systems are not new. Mother nature has developed many storage and retrieval systems throughout evolution. An animal's "instinct" is a group of stored behavior patterns that result in a better chance of survival for the animal. The "information" is stored in each animal's DNA and passed on from parent to child. Nature, like computer manufacturers, has constantly improved the information storage and transmission capabilities of animals. A giant technological leap took place when human beings developed a larger information processing and storage unit (the brain) and learned to transfer information verbally. New information, like how to start a fire, could be transferred instantly through speech rather than through human DNA.

As human activity grew in complexity, information grew in quantity. Even early civilizations found human memory inadequate. It became necessary to record vital information externally in a safe and permanent manner. For instance, some of the earliest recorded information originated from Phoenician merchants. To keep track of their vast business dealings, the Phoenicians adopted a common character representation system, better known as an alphabet, to record debts and trade agreements. Like businesses today, the Phoenicians needed a recording method and media that was permanent and reliable. In addition, accessing and retrieving the data had to be very easy. Prior to this time (1200 B.C.), the medium of choice was a clay tablet. Though resembling some modern media such as a WORM (write-once read-many) disk and ROM chips in terms of updatability, clay tablets had some definite drawbacks in terms of portability and capacity. Meanwhile, the Egyptians had been making some technological improvements in storage media, and the Phoenicians soon adopted their "breakthrough" media of papyrus. Over time, paper was developed and became the most widely used storage media for thousands of years. Only in the last century have new technologies overtaken paper as the storage media of choice.

While improvements in storage media were being made, the method of recording data also improved. The movable type printing press created by Gutenberg around 1456 had a huge impact on recording and disseminating information (and modern history). Books were transformed from rare and costly items into commodities. Some people contend that the end of the Dark Ages and the rise of modern nation states were caused by the information and new ideas that were made so available by this cheap printing method. So, you could say that France, Germany, and all other nations are the result of an improved information storage method. (Of course, others might say this is a "techie" interpretation of history.)

Just as the storage media evolved from paper through punch cards, tape, and disk, the printing press was replaced as the primary information recording device. Key punch machines, tape and disk devices, as well as silicon-based memory and microprocessors have been the standards of the last 50 years.

In addition to continually improving the storage media and devices, there have been constant improvements in the organization of and access to information. Historically, as the amount of information grew, the time it took to access the information also increased. It became very clear that the organization of information directly affected ease of access. Some of the earliest efforts at recording all human knowledge resulted in the alphabetical ordering of each topic. Over time, the organization was changed such that the topics were grouped together by subject (history, philosophy, science, mathematics, and so on.) and an alphabetic index was created. A person could read the individual topics and learn more because they were in a logical order rather than alphabetical. The alphabetical index was an alternative method for the reader to locate (access) a specific topic. These alternative organizations and access methods made it easier and faster for a person to access and use information.

Information as an Asset

Information or knowledge has always been held in high regard. Adages such as "Knowledge is power" or "Fools rush in where wise men fear to tread" attest to the importance society places on information. However, this perception was not always universally held. An appreciation of the value of information has gradually spread to all human activities. For instance, "keeping track" of a business's activities was not done in an organized manner prior to the adoption of modern business practices. A stockroom attendant in a 1700's barrel-making shop would simply walk through a stockroom's aisles to find an item. As industry grew, a smart businessperson realized that if the locations of all inventory were written down, the item could be found faster. What's more, not as many stockroom attendants would be needed to manage inventory. Now that the items could be found immediately, less time was wasted wandering the aisles, and fewer people were needed. This decreased the cost of doing business and increased profits. Thus was born paperwork.

Over time, keeping track of certain information became a necessity in order to conduct business. Information became vital to the health of a business and grew in terms of volume and complexity. In some cases, the data regarding an item or event became as important as the item itself. For instance, a large grocery chain maintains a record of where its products are stored within the warehouse (just like the old barrel maker). Every time new products are received, a record is made of the date and time they are received as well as where they are placed. Just like the barrel maker, the grocery chain needs to know where each item is located in order to function efficiently. However, to see why information is vital, imagine what happens if the location information is lost. The warehouse for the grocery chain is the size of 10 football fields and has shelves 20 feet high. If a stockroom attendant puts 15 crates of fresh grapes on a shelf and records the wrong location—instead of aisle 753 and shelf 41, he records aisle 75 and shelf 41—how easy would it be to find those grapes? The grapes are as good as lost. Even if they could be found within several days, they would be spoiled (or raisins). Losing the location data is just as bad as losing the grapes themselves. In addition, the lack of information results in losing customers because their orders cannot be filled.

What this example implies is that the information about an asset has become as important as the asset itself. And just as businesses protect their physical assets, businesses came to realize that they needed to protect their information, both from loss and inaccuracy. The process of gathering and maintaining information was no longer regarded as a cost of doing business—it became viewed as a necessity in order to survive. Quick and reliable access to the information was also a requirement. Having the data but not being able to access it was just as bad as not having the data—or the asset—at all.

Recently, the perception of information has changed again. Information still provides efficiencies and enables the company to function; however, information can actually add value beyond the scope of a company's primary business function. For instance, in order to maintain the item's inventory quantity, the grocery chain also records each of their customer's purchases. They know that the Joneses purchased ten jars of baby food from one of their stores last week. One day, a marketing executive had the bright idea to customize advertising. When a sales flyer was sent to the Joneses, it included information about many other baby items—baby oil, disposable diapers, and so forth—rather than information on sport socks or leisure-time items. (The theory being that the Joneses are probably too busy with the baby to be playing racquetball or "enjoying" bungee jumping.) The Joneses were prime customers for these baby items, and by bringing these products to their attention, the store would probably sell more of them. As a matter of fact, the store discovers that by customizing advertising they get a 20 percent increase in sales. The store makes more money because of what they know. They have not offered the goods cheaper or provided them more conveniently. They have made more money from information. Information has become a resource that can be used to increase this company's sales and beat out their competition. As a matter of fact, a local children's day-care center would be willing to pay the grocery store for their list of customers who buy baby products. Information even has value beyond what it tells about the business and its assets.

Data Management

Since information is valuable, it must be protected and used wisely. The activities that ensure the safety and proper use of data are grouped into a general category called **data management**. Proper data management results in data that is accurate, safe, and easily accessible.

To ensure these results, data management organizations implement both manual and computer-based control procedures. These control procedures range from restricting physical access to DASD (direct access storage devices) by putting a badge lock on a door to installing specialized software that ensures the accurate storage and timely access to data. This specialized software is called a database management system (DBMS) and often comprises hundreds of programs.

All computer operating systems provide some data management functions. After all, few people would buy a computer if their data wasn't safe and accessible. Since the AS/400 is a very popular computer, you can probably guess that it has software that provides timely access to safe and accurate data. As a matter of fact, the AS/400's DBMS and operating system allow users to create, store, and control access to data in files and databases. (A database is a set of related files.) In addition, users can define individual data fields, group the related fields into files, and build relationships between these files. The AS/400 also provides a variety of user-friendly utilities to easily enter, change, and retrieve data.

Another key feature of the AS/400's DBMS is that it protects data. Programs in the DBMS can back up data (store duplicate copies) and, in the case of processing errors, reverse incorrect updates.

Physical Storage

Computers do a very good job at storing vast amounts of data. However, how computers actually store the data is not always as it seems. As a matter of fact, most computer makers try to hide how the computer actually stores information because it is not very user friendly. Or in other words, information as it is actually stored on the computer is not in a "human understandable form." Whenever information is retrieved from storage, it is translated from a machine-understandable form into a human-understandable form.

For instance, digital computers represent all numbers and characters with 0s and 1s. Every character and numeric digit has a corresponding unique combination of 0s and 1s. Another way of saying this is that the computer stores all data in binary equivalents. A human can learn these binary representations, but this definitely falls on the nonuser-friendly side of the computer interface fence. Since the physical organization and storage of information is not very user friendly and we know that the AS/400 is a very user-friendly computer, it probably won't surprise you to learn that the AS/400 buffers the user from many of the physical aspects of data storage. The user is removed from not only the binary representations of data but also other physical aspects of data storage such as the specific physical devices used for storage and the location of data on the media (for example, on PCs, which diskette and the track and sector location; on mainframes, the particular diskpack number, disk device location number, and byte offset).

On the AS/400, the user does not become involved in many of the mundane physical aspects of data management. (If you have ever had to search through 50 diskettes trying to find a particular file or tried to remember what storage locations were still available on a diskpack, you have had the misfortune of dealing with the physical side of data management.) The AS/400 has a unique approach to storing data called **single level storage**. When creating a file, single level storage requires the user only to name the file and identify a library to store it in. Conversely, when accessing a file, the file and library names are the only identification needed. The particular drive and path or device and volume serial numbers that physically identify where the file is located are not needed. The AS/400 handles physical storage space and many data management activities automatically.

Of course, there are some instances where the identification of a particular physical device or storage location is necessary. For instance, making copies of files to tapes or diskettes and transporting them to a safe location is considered a good data management procedure. In order to copy information to tape or disk, a particular external storage device would need to be identified. The AS/400 developers realized this need and, for certain functions, have provided the ability to control some aspects of physical storage.

Physical versus Logical Data Organization

The difference between the way the data is actually stored and the way it seems to be stored can take many forms. As mentioned earlier, a simple example of appearance versus reality is the fact that computers store all data as 0s and 1s, but users see data in character or numeric format. The impression is that the data is stored as characters and numbers, whereas in reality it is stored as 0s and 1s.

Another example of physical storage (how data is actually stored) versus logical storage (the way data appears to be stored) is record organization within files. Records can appear to be in a certain order within a file but actually be organized in a totally different manner. For instance, records in a file may appear to be in alphabetical order. If you request the first record in an employee file, the DBMS would return John Aaron's record (Aaron being the first employee record in the file alphabetically). In reality, the data records could be stored in an entirely different order, and the DBMS could be using an index to access the data.

A file index works the same as an index for a book. Normally, a textbook's topics are laid out in a logical order that makes the subject easier to understand. If the readers want to locate a specific topic or read the topics in alphabetical order, they would use the index.

Records within files and databases are also in a certain order but can be accessed individually or in a different order through an index. An index is said to give the file a different logical organization. The records appear to be in a certain order when accessed with the index, but in actuality they are not physically in that order.

Logical organizations, or views, are usually created to satisfy different user access requirements. If one user needs to access the employee file by social security number and another by date of birth, different indices can be built to satisfy both users. Files are usually physically organized to provide the fastest overall access, take up the least amount of space, and require the least amount of maintenance. Logical organizations are built to satisfy different user access needs.

Summary

Being able to store and access information has been a concern since the earliest civilizations. Mankind (as well as mother nature) has continually improved the storage media and devices that record and access information. Each improvement has resulted in an increase in the amount of data that can be stored and a decrease in the time to retrieve any single piece of data.

These advancements in storage and retrieval have also been achieved through better data management and organization. Data management is a general category for procedures that ensure the accuracy, safety, and timely access to data. Data organization is broken down into physical and logical organization. Physical organization is the way that data is actually stored on a storage media. The physical organization of data directly affects overall data access time. Logical organizations provide alternative accesses for users and a means to restrict access and protect data. It should always be remembered that the way data appears to be organized (logical) does not necessarily reflect how it is actually organized (physical). Indices can give files many different logical organizations that have no relationship to the physical organization of the data.

REVIEW QUESTIONS

1. Why are logical organizations created?
2. What is single level storage?
3. How do computers actually represent characters and numbers?
4. What is data management?
5. What are some features of most database management systems?

DISCUSSION QUESTIONS

1. Give other noncomputer examples of information storage and access. Describe how the data is physically organized, the storage media, and if there are any alternative logical organizations or alternative ways to access the data.
2. Compare logical to physical organization.

AS/400 Physical Storage

2

Overview

This chapter will cover how the AS/400 physically stores and organizes data in files. There are many different ways to store character and numeric information, and this chapter will cover the methods supported by the AS/400. The chapter will also demonstrate how to access the data and display it in as near to machine-understandable format as possible on the AS/400.

After finishing this chapter, you will understand

- EBCDIC
- Hexadecimal data representation
- The different methods of numeric data storage
- The difference between externally and internally defined data
- The tools available for data definition on the AS/400

After finishing this chapter, you will be able to

- Display the EBCDIC and hexadecimal representations of stored data
- Convert hexadecimal into EBCDIC characters

Physical Character Representation

As we mentioned in Chapter 1, specific 0 and 1 sequences are used to represent different characters. However, in the early days of computers (the 1940s and 1950s), the set of 0s and 1s was different not only between computer manufacturers but even between computers made by the same manufacturer. This confusion led IBM to create the first generally adopted binary character representation system. This system, which is still widely used today, is called EBCDIC (Extended Binary Coded Decimal Interchange Code).

Besides setting up standard 0 and 1 representations for each character, EBCDIC set a standard length for each character's binary representation. EBCDIC used 8 binary digits (or **bits**) to define each character. Prior to EBCDIC, other binary systems defined different characters with a different number of bits. For instance, an A was defined with 3 bits, a B with 6 bits, and a C with 5 bits. EBCDIC standardized characters at 8 bits or a **byte**. Figure 2.1 shows some of the characters supported by EBCDIC and their 8 bit binary representations.

FIGURE 2.1

Character	Binary	Character	Binary	Character	Binary
a	1000 0001	v	1010 0101	Q	1101 1000
b	1000 0010	w	1010 0110	R	1101 1001
c	1000 0011	x	1010 0111	S	1110 0010
d	1000 0100	y	1010 1000	T	1110 0011
e	1000 0101	z	1010 1001	U	1110 0100
f	1000 0110	A	1100 0001	V	1110 0101
g	1000 0111	B	1100 0010	W	1110 0110
h	1000 1000	C	1100 0011	X	1110 0111
i	1000 1001	D	1100 0100	Y	1110 1000
j	1001 0001	E	1100 0101	Z	1110 1001
k	1001 0010	F	1110 0110	0	1111 0000
l	1001 0011	G	1110 0111	1	1111 0001
m	1001 0100	H	1110 1000	2	1111 0010
n	1001 0101	I	1100 1001	3	1111 0011
o	1001 0110	J	1101 0001	4	1111 0100
p	1001 0111	K	1101 0010	5	1111 0101
q	1001 1000	L	1101 0011	6	1111 0110
r	1001 1001	M	1101 0100	7	1111 0111
s	1010 0010	N	1101 0101	8	1111 1000
t	1010 0011	O	1101 0110	9	1111 1001
u	1010 0100	P	1101 0111		

Another system of character representation that has been widely adopted is called ASCII (American Standard Code for Information Interchange). ASCII also represents each character in 1 byte, but the 0 and 1 combinations for each character are different from EBCDIC.

Generally, ASCII is used by PCs and EBCDIC by mainframe and mid-sized computers. The AS/400, being a mid-sized computer, uses EBCDIC. (When trying to access data that has been transferred between an AS/400 and a PC, this difference in character representation systems should be remembered. If there is a problem with access, it may be because the data is stored according to the nonsupported system, and a conversion is necessary.)

The AS/400 (and most other computers) allow users to view data as it is physically stored. The binary representation is never the level of detail needed or wanted by users or programmers. Instead, most EBCDIC computers show a two-digit, **hexadecimal** representation of each character.

Hexadecimal digits can have a value ranging from 0 to 9 and A through F. Each of these characters is used to represent the unique 0 and 1 combinations possible with 4 bits. Figure 2.2 shows the 4-bit binary combinations and their hexadecimal character equivalents.

FIGURE 2.2

Binary	Hexadecimal
0001	1
0010	2
0011	3
0100	4
0101	5
0110	6
0111	7
1000	8
1001	9
1010	A
1011	B
1100	C
1101	D
1110	E
1111	F

Besides being broken down into 8 bits, a byte is also said to comprise 2 nibbles (seriously!). Each nibble is 4 bits in length and, therefore, can be represented by one hexadecimal character. The hexadecimal character representation of stored data is usually the lowest level of physical storage that an operating system displays, and in this the AS/400 is no exception.

On the AS/400, file data is stored in a member. The user can display the data's EBCDIC and hexadecimal representations with the DSPPFM (display physical file member) command. To display the data, type the command at any command line and press F4. At the `Display Physical File Member (DSPPFM)` screen, specify the library, file, and member to be displayed (Figure 2.3) and press ENTER. The `Display Physical File Member` screen (Figure 2.4) will be shown.

Initially, only the EBCDIC characters are shown. To display the hexadecimal representations, press F10, and Figure 2.5 will be displayed. The hex characters are displayed on the left of the screen, and the EBCDIC characters on the right. Press F11 to arrange the two hexadecimal characters below the EBCDIC character (Figure 2.6). Notice that character 1 is represented by the two hex characters F and 1. If we translate the hex characters F1 into their binary equivalents of 1111 and 0001, notice that these 8 bits do indeed match up to the character 1 in Figure 2.1.

FIGURE 2.3

```
                  Display Physical File Member (DSPPFM)

Type choices, press Enter.
File . . . . . . . . . . . . . . > CHARDATA__      Name
  Library  . . . . . . . . . . . >   MYLIBXX___    Name, *LIBL, *CURLIB
Member . . . . . . . . . . . . . > *FIRST____      Name, *FIRST, *LAST
From record  . . . . . . . . . .   1_________      Number, *END

                                                                  Bottom
F3=Exit F4=Prompt  F5=Refresh F12=Cancel F13=How to use this display
F24=More keys
```

FIGURE 2.4

```
                     Display Physical File Member
File . . . . . . :   CHAR                Library  . . . . :   MYLIBXX
Member . . . . . :   DATA                Record . . . . . :   1
Control  . . . . .   __________          Column . . . . . :   1
Find . . . . . . .   ________________________________________
*...+....1....+....2....+....3....+....4....+....5
This was the first record entered       1 %
This was the second record entered      2 $
This was the third record entered       3 !
This was the fourth record entered      4 +
This was the fifth record entered       5 -
                        ****** END OF DATA ******

                                                                  Bottom
 F3=Exit   F12=Cancel     F19=Left    F20=Right    F24=More keys
```

From Figure 2.6, we can also figure out the EBCDIC binary representations of some characters not included in Figure 2.1. For instance, the character % is contained in the first record as the 43rd character. If you check the hexadecimal representation, you'll see that there is a 6 in the first nibble and a C in the second nibble. Translating the hex characters into binary gives 0110 1100, which is indeed EBCDIC's binary representation for the character %.

FIGURE 2.5

```
                       Display Physical File Member
File . . . . . . :   CHAR                Library  . . . . :   MYLIBXX
Member . . . . . :   DATA                Record . . . . . :   1
Control  . . . . .   _________           Column . . . . . :   1
Find . . . . . . .   ________________________________________
* . . . + . . . . 1 . . . . + . . . . 2     *...+....1....+....2
E38889A2 40A681A2 40A38885 40868999 A2A34099   *This was the first r*
E38889A2 40A681A2 40A38885 40A28583 96958440   *This was the second *
E38889A2 40A681A2 40A38885 40A38889 99844099   *This was the third r*
E38889A2 40A681A2 40A38885 408696A4 99A38840   *This was the fourth *
E38889A2 40A681A2 40A38885 40868986 A3884099   *This was the fifth r*
                        ****** END OF DATA ******

                                                                     Bottom
F3=Exit   F12=Cancel    F19=Left    F20=Right    F24=More keys
```

FIGURE 2.6

```
                       Display Physical File Member
File . . . . . . :   CHARDATA            Library  . . . . :   MYLIBXX
Member . . . . . :   CHARDATA            Record . . . . . :   1
Control  . . . . .   _________           Column . . . . . :   1
Find . . . . . . .   ________________________________________
*...+....1....+....2....+....3....+....4....+....5
This was the first record entered       1 %
E88A4A8A4A884889AA4988998489A8988444444F464444444
389206120385069923095369405535954000000010C0000000

This was the second record entered      2 $
E88A4A8A4A884A889984988998489A8988444444F454444444
38920612038502536540953694055359540000020B0000000

This was the third record entered       3 !
E88A4A8A4A884A88984988998489A89884444444F454444444
38920612038503899409536940553595400000030A0000000

This was the fourth record entered      4 +
E88A4A8A4A88489A9A84988998489A8988444444F444444444
38920612038506649380953694055359540000040E0000000

                                                                    More...
F3=Exit   F12=Cancel    F19=Left    F20=Right    F24=More keys
```

Numeric Representation

Computers treat characters and numbers differently. For instance, you can add and subtract numbers but not characters.

Since computers are so good at processing numbers, a great portion of all stored data is numeric. To save space, computer developers created several different ways to store numeric data more efficiently than with EBCDIC. Most computers support at least the following three methods:

Zoned decimal

Packed decimal

Binary

To clear up any possible confusion, yes, the characters 1, 2, 3, and so on can be stored in EBCDIC. However, when stored in EBCDIC, they are treated as characters and cannot be used in arithmetic computations. If numeric data is going to be used in calculations, it must be stored in one of the three methods.

Zoned Decimal

This method does not present a great savings in storage space over EBCDIC. Data defined as zoned decimal, however, is allowed to be used in calculations, and negative numbers can be stored in less space than EBCDIC.

Zoned decimal positive numbers are stored with the same combination of 0s and 1s as EBCDIC characters. That is, the first nibble is always 1111 (displayed as a hexadecimal F). The second nibble has the same 0s and 1s as in Figure 2.1. Negative numbers are where some storage space is saved. With zoned decimal, the sign of the number is denoted by the last digit's first nibble. For a negative number, the nibble is defined as 1101 and displayed as a hexadecimal D. All preceding nibbles follow the normal EBCDIC representation. So the number 123456 would appear as

```
F1F2F3F4F5F6
```

and –123456 would appear as

```
F1F2F3F4F5D6
```

Figure 2.7, the `Display Physical File Member` screen, confirms that those two numbers would be stored on the AS/400 as described. The first line is the EBCDIC interpretation of the bits, the second line is the hex representation of the first nibble of each byte, and the third line is the second nibble of each byte. The two numbers are separated by blank spaces, which are represented with the hex characters 40404040.

Packed Decimal

Packed decimal makes better use of each nibble than does zoned decimal. Zoned decimal sets each first nibble's bits to 1s (hexadecimal F), except for negative numbers, where the first nibble of the last digit is set to 1101 (hexadecimal D). Packed decimal doesn't waste all those first nibbles. It uses each nibble to represent a numeric digit. The very last nibble is used to denote the sign, F for positive numbers and D for negative numbers.

FIGURE 2.7

```
                         Display Physical File Member
File . . . . . . : ZONED                    Library  . . . . :    MYLIBXX
Member . . . . . : NUMBERS                  Record . . . . . :    1
Control  . . . . . __________               Column . . . . . :    1
Find . . . . . . . ________________________________________

*...+....1....+.
123456    123450
FFFFFF4444FFFFFD
1234560000123456

                        ****** END OF DATA ******

                                                                     Bottom
F3=Exit   F12=Cancel F19=Left   F20=Right    F24=More keys
```

So the number 123,456 stored in packed decimal would be represented in hex as

0123456F

–123,456 would be represented as

0123456D

Notice that it took only 4 bytes (8 nibbles) to store the number in packed decimal. With zoned decimal, it required 6 bytes—50 percent more space. Packed decimal is the default storage method on the AS/400. If the user defines a numeric field and does not specify the type, packed decimal is used. Figure 2.8 shows the AS/400 storage of the two numbers and the attempt by the system to convert the packed digits into EBCDIC characters.

Binary

Binary, like packed decimal, makes use of every nibble. Binary, however, makes better use of each bit in a nibble. To understand how binary is more efficient than packed decimal, we need to take a different look at our normal, everyday decimal numbers.

Decimal numbers are said to be based on 10. For instance, the number of characters used to represent numbers is 10 (the characters 0 through 9). In order to represent large numbers, a numeric

FIGURE 2.8

```
                    Display Physical File Member
File . . . . . . :  PACKED              Library . . . . :   MYLIBXX
Member . . . . . :  NUMBERS             Record . . . . . :  1
Control . . . . .   ___________         Column . . . . . :  1
Find . . . . . . .  _______________________________________

*...+....1..
■■á?    ■■á_
024644440246
135F0000135D

                     ****** END OF DATA ******

                                                                 Bottom
F3=Exit   F12=Cancel F19=Left   F20=Right   F24=More keys
```

character's position within the number has meaning. For instance, the character 5 in the number 531 means 500 and the character 5 in the number 153 means 50. Our number system is said to be positional. (I know this sounds very basic, but things will get very strange in a few sentences. It's important that you remember that number systems have a set number of characters according to the base of the system, for example, ten characters for decimal, and are positional.)

In a positional number system, the value of each position or digit within the number increases as you go from right to left. How much it increases again depends on the base of the system. With the decimal system, each time you move left one digit, that digit is ten times greater than the digit to the right. For instance, in a two-digit decimal number, the first digit (the leftmost digit) represents tens, and the second digit represents ones; in a three-digit number, the first digit represents hundreds; in a four-digit number, the first digit represents thousands.

In a binary number system, the base number is 2. There are only two characters (0 and 1), and each digit, as you go left through a number, is two times as large as the previous digit. In a two-digit binary number such as 10, the 0 stands for 1s and the 1 stands for 2s. In a three-digit binary number, the first digit is groups of 4; in a four-digit number, the first digit represents groups of 8; and in a five-digit number, the first digit is groups of 16s. Unlike the decimal system where each number to the left is 10 times greater than the previous number, in a binary system each number to the left is only two times as large.

As another example, think of the number 1111 in both decimal and binary. In the decimal number system, each position is ten times greater than the position to the right of it. (The rightmost position always represents ones.) So the first digit represents ones, the next digit tens, the next digit hundreds, and the leftmost digit thousands. With binary, the rightmost digit is also ones; however, the next digit to the left is only two times greater, so it represents twos. The next one represents fours, and the leftmost represents eights. So the binary number 1111 says there is one group of 1, one group of 2, one group of 4, and one group of 8 for a grand total of 15 in our decimal system.

Since computers think in terms of 0s and 1s, it only seems natural that they would store numbers in straight binary. In addition, we mentioned earlier, that the binary form can store more information because it better utilizes each bit. For instance, each nibble in packed decimal represents one digit of a decimal number. So the highest number that can be represented in a nibble is 9. If you were to try to store the decimal number 15 it would require 2 nibbles in packed decimal. But as we just showed, binary can store the decimal number 15 in 4 bits or 1 nibble.

To see how powerful this becomes, let's use our previous example of 123,456. To store the number 123,456 in packed decimal would require 1 nibble for each digit and 1 nibble for the sign. Since most computers allocate an entire byte at a time, 123,456 would actually take up 4 bytes when stored in packed decimal. If we chose binary, the number would be represented as follows:

```
11110001001000000
```

The leftmost digit represents one group of 65,536, the next digit represents one group of 32,768, the next one group of 16,384, all the way down to the last digit, which represents zero groups of 1. Computers allocate an entire byte at a time, so the binary number would be stored as follows:

```
0000 0001 1110 0010 0100 0000
```

and would be displayed in hexadecimal as

```
01 E2 40
```

In this case, binary is able to store the number in 3 bytes. With packed decimal, it would require 4 bytes—25 percent more space—and with zoned decimal, 6 bytes—100 percent more space. Binary can store more numeric data because it gets a compounding (or positional) effect with each bit, whereas packed decimal gets the compounding with only every 4 bits.

Binary uses the first bit to denote the sign of the number. However, binary negative numbers also have a unique format called **two's complement.**

Two's Complement

To find the binary representation of a negative number, there are two simple steps. Starting with the positive number's binary representation:

1. Switch each bit (from 1 to 0 or 0 to 1).
2. Add 1 to the number.

So for the number –1, we would take the positive number binary representation, which is

```
0000 0000 0000 0001
```

switch each bit

```
1111 1111 1111 1110
```

and add 1

```
1111 1111 1111 1111
```

The hexadecimal representation of –1 is FFFF. For our example of 123,456, it's a little more complicated. The binary representation (with the hex representation shown above) is

```
 0    0    0    1    E    2    4    0
0000 0000 0000 0001 1110 0010 0100 0000
```

switch each bit

```
 F    F    F    E    1    D    B    F
1111 1111 1111 1110 0001 1101 1011 1111
```

and add 1

```
 F    F    F    E    1    D    C    0
1111 1111 1111 1110 0001 1101 1100 0000
```

Figure 2.9 shows the AS/400 `Display Physical File Member` screen with these two numbers in hexadecimal format with the nonsensical EBCDIC interpretation.

FIGURE 2.9

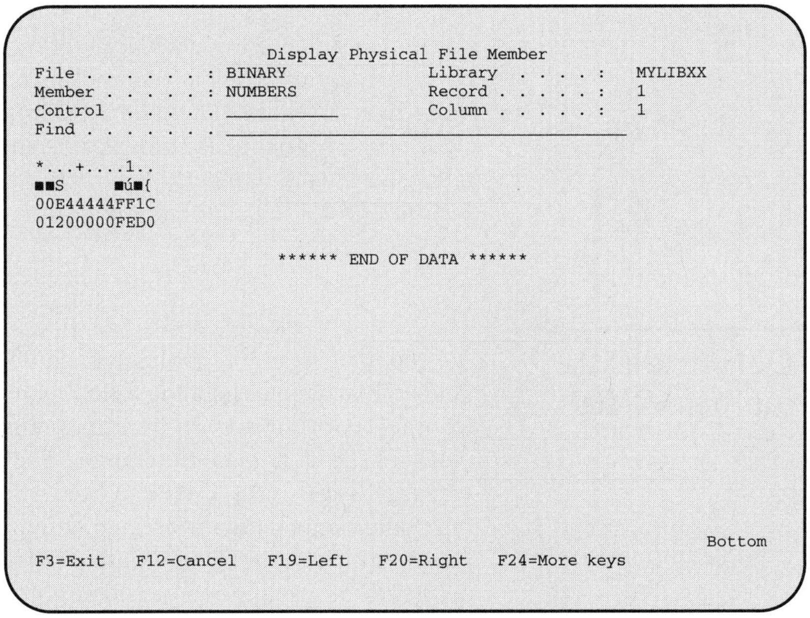

```
                    Display Physical File Member
File . . . . . . : BINARY           Library . . . . :   MYLIBXX
Member . . . . . : NUMBERS          Record . . . . . :   1
Control  . . . . . __________       Column . . . . . :   1
Find . . . . . . . ________________________________________

*...+....1..
■■S     ■ú■{
00E44444FF1C
01200000FED0

                     ****** END OF DATA ******

                                                             Bottom
F3=Exit   F12=Cancel   F19=Left   F20=Right   F24=More keys
```

Field Space Allocation on the AS/400

The preceding explanations used the theoretical number of bytes or bits needed to represent a number in a particular format. In reality, the AS/400 (and all computers) allocates a certain number of bytes for each number based on the storage method and number of digits. For zoned decimal, the AS/400 allocates 1 byte for each digit. In packed decimal, it's 1 byte for every two digits and an extra nibble for the sign. Binary's rules for space allocation are a litte more complicated. The system automatically allocates 2 bytes for any number up to four digits and 4 bytes for any number up to nine digits. This means that for one-digit numbers, packed decimal uses only 1 byte, but binary uses 2. (Figure 2.10 shows a comparison of binary and packed decimal.)

FIGURE 2.10

Number of Digits	Number of Bytes Allocated When Storing with: Binary	Packed Decimal
1	2	1
2	2	2
3	2	2
4	2	3
5	4	3
6	4	4
7	4	4
8	4	5
9	4	5

Notice that for one- and five-digit numbers, packed decimal actually uses less space than binary. However, for four-, eight- and nine-digit numbers, binary uses one less byte.

Before choosing a numeric format, the user should also be aware that binary storage on the AS/400 is limited to 9-digit numbers; zoned decimal and packed decimal, however, can store up to 31-digit numbers. In addition, the packed and zoned decimal numbers are much more user friendly. Their hexadecimal character representations closely resemble the decimal representations. Hexadecimal representations of binary numbers, especially negative numbers (as you were torturously made aware), are not human readable and are very difficult to decipher.

Defining Data on the AS/400

To store data, it must first be defined. Defining data includes creating fields. This means assigning a field name, specifying the type of data (character or numeric) to be stored, and defining the length of each field and the storage method to use. The AS/400 provides two general ways to define data. Data can be defined **internally** or **externally**. Internally defined data is defined within application programs using a programming language's data definition commands. Externally defined files are defined outside application programs using a DDL (data definition language).

Generally, the advantage of external over internal data definition is that externally defining data creates one definition. With internal data definition, each program that uses that data must contain a definition for the data. Therefore, any change to an internally defined data field would require changing definitions in every program that uses it. This can become a logistical headache with large complex applications. Of course, tools and techniques can be employed to make these changes easier; however, the maintenance is less with externally defined files.

On the AS/400, a file can be defined internally using RPG, COBOL, or any of the other supported programming languages. Files can be defined externally using **SQL**, **IDDU** (interactive data definition utility), or **DDS** (data definition specifications).

Data can be defined externally with SQL either by using the interactive SQL utility or through SQL "programs" called Query Management (QM) queries. SQL, however, also has the capability to manipulate data; that is, in addition to commands that define data structures, there are commands to load, view, and modify data. These manipulation commands can be used within application programs, through the interactive SQL utility, or in QM queries.

IDDU is a menu-driven data definition utility. Through a series of menus and screens, IDDU provides data definition options and prompts the user for information necessary to define data on the AS/400. After the information has been gathered, IDDU generates and compiles DDS source code to create the file.

DDS is strictly a data definition language. It contains commands that allow a user to define

File structures

Individual field characteristics

Field edits and audits

Most organizations use DDS to define data. Even though IDDU has a user-friendly menu interface, it is limited in the data definition functions it offers. Moreover, because IDDU is menu driven, it does not offer the flexibility of PDM and SEU in terms of updating the generated DDS code. For these reasons, most programmers use DDS.

SQL is also not usually used to define data because of the extra space and processing required to store and maintain data. However, it is often used as a manipulation or query tool on files defined with DDS. We will cover DDS in the next several chapters and SQL in a later chapter.

Summary

Data can be stored in many different ways. The format in which data appears or is presented has no connection to how it is actually stored. On the AS/400, character data is stored in EBCDIC. For numeric data, programmers have several options. These numeric storage methods differ in how efficiently they store the data. The options (in order of increasing efficiency but decreasing user friendliness) are zoned decimal, packed decimal, and binary. The user can select the storage method when the data fields are defined.

Data on the AS/400 can be defined either internally within a program using the programming language's native commands or externally using DDS, SQL, or IDDU. DDS is the predominant method because of the greater control it offers overs IDDU and its advantage in efficiency over SQL.

REVIEW QUESTIONS

1. What are the numeric data storage methods supported on the AS/400?
2. What are the two general ways data can be defined on the AS/400? What is the difference between the methods?
3. What is two's complement?
4. What is the default method of storage for numeric data?
5. What tools or utilities can be used to externally define data on the AS/400?
6. What is EBCDIC?
7. What is ASCII?
8. What are the EBCDIC characters that match up with the following 0s and 1s:

   1110 1000 1100 0101 1101 0011 1101 0011 1101 0110

DISCUSSION QUESTIONS

1. What are the advantages and disadvantages between packed decimal, zoned decimal, and binary?
2. Discuss the advantages and disadvantages of SQL, IDDU, and DDS for data definition.

Creating Data Physical Files

3

Overview

In this chapter, the focus changes from the physical storage of data to its logical organization. We will start by defining the smallest units of logical data—fields and records—and then show how to specify fields and records on the AS/400 with DDS. In this discussion, we will highlight the AS/400's unique data storage structures and the utilities that allow information to be stored and accessed.

After finishing this chapter, you will understand

- More of the differences between logical and physical organizations
- What a field and a record format are
- The purpose of AS/400 libraries, physical files, and members
- Some of the functions of DDS

After finishing this chapter, you will be able to

- Create a library, source physical file, and member with either PDM or CL commands
- Define fields and records with DDS
- Compile source code and create a data physical file
- Load data into a data physical file member with DFU

Physical versus Logical Data Organization on the AS/400

The previous chapter described the physical organization of data on the AS/400. Physical organization is the way that data is actually stored, such as the particular 0s and 1s that represent different characters and numbers. There is another level of organization called the logical organization. Files can have many different logical organizations. For instance, say we have the numeric information shown in Figure 3.1.

FIGURE 3.1

102367093050122552

Physically, this data could be stored in any of the previous discussed numeric methods. However, in order for this information to have any meaning, there must be a logical organization. In other words, the individual digits must be organized in some manner that gives them meaning, for example, they could be telephone numbers, social security numbers, dates, or salaries. A logical organization defines how the data is grouped so that the data has meaning.

Just as bits, nibbles, and bytes are units of physical organization, fields, records, and files are units of logical organization. Unlike bits, nibbles, and bytes, logical units have no fixed length. For instance, a field is the smallest logical unit of information, but it can comprise any number of characters or digits. A field, by definition, is any number of related characters or digits that represent one piece of information. For instance, the individual numbers listed in Figure 3.1 could be the number of dependents for each employee of a company. In this case, each digit would be a separate field. However, this series of numbers could also be a list of each employee's weekly salary. For example, there are three employees, the first makes $1,023.67 a week, the second $930.50, and the third $1,225.52. In this case, each field is made up of six digits.

A logical organization is concerned not only with the length of each field but also with the type of data. A field could be six digits but still be interpreted in two entirely different ways. For instance, the numeric data in Figure 3.1 could have a different logical organization even if the field length were still six. Each six digits could represent the date of birth for each employee rather than a salary; for example, the first employee date of birth was October 23, 1967 (10/23/67), the second 09/30/50, and the third 12/25/52.

Besides field length and type, information is further logically organized into records and files. A record is a group of logically related fields, and a file is a group of logically related records.

For instance, a school has information about each student. Each student's information would be stored in individual fields such as student last name, first name, address, student id number, number of credits taken, and grade point average. Each field is a single piece of information, and each field has a length and type. Student last and first name are 10 and 8 characters in length, address is 32 characters, student id number is 11 characters, number of credits is 3 digits, and grade point average is 3 digits with 2 decimal places. Each student's fields make up a single record. For instance, the fields that contain information regarding Larry Smith (his name, address, student id, and so on) are one record.

Every student has a record, and all these records together make up the STUDENT file. As far as physical storage is concerned, these characters and digits are simply a continuous string of 0s and 1s. However, with a logical organization, these 0s and 1s can be interpreted and displayed in the human-understandable form of fields, records, and files.

Before data can be stored, both the logical and physical organization of data must be specified. As mentioned in Chapter 2, the AS/400 has several methods to define data. The most popular is DDS (data definition specifications). When a user defines a file with DDS, it is called the **source code** definition of that file. Computers do not understand source code. Source code file definitions must be translated into machine code. This is accomplished by **compiling** the source code.

Libraries, Objects, and Members

The AS/400 stores source code, machine language definitions, and data in libraries, objects, and members. Libraries are used to group related objects (PC-oriented users find comfort in comparing libraries to directories), and objects are used to group related members. The two types of objects we are concerned with are **source physical files** and **data physical files**.

Objects are classified by a type and an attribute. An object is called a source physical file when it has a type of *FILE and an attribute of PF-SRC. Data physical files are objects with a type of *FILE and an attribute of PF-DTA (Figure 3.2).

FIGURE 3.2

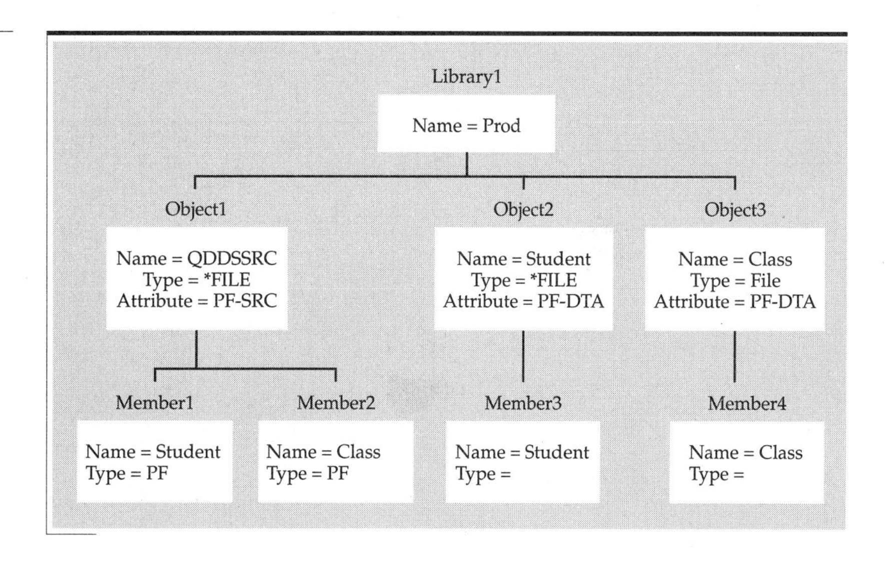

Members belonging to a source physical file contain **source code**. This source code can be DDS file definitions. (Source physical file members can also contain program source code. Program source code members contain programs written in languages such as RPG, COBOL, or C.) Members that contain DDS source code are defined with a type equal to PF. In Figure 3.2, members 1 and 2 both have a type of PF.

Data physical files (objects 2 and 3 in Figure 3.2) contain machine-language definitions of files. The members underneath each data physical file hold the raw data. In other words, the member contains the 0s and 1s and the file object has the machine-understandable explanation of how the bits should be interpreted for humans and application programs.

Data physical files and their members are created by compiling the source code definition contained in source physical file members. For instance, object2 and member3 are the result of compiling member1 (Figure 3.3). To compile a member, the user invokes the operating system (either through a CL command or PDM, for instance) and identifies the member to be compiled. In this case, member1 contains the DDS source code for the STUDENT file. When member1 is compiled, a data physical file object is created, and the machine-language version of the file definition is placed in the object. Compiling a source code member also creates a member (with a blank type) under the data physical file. This new member will eventually hold the 0s and 1s that make up the STUDENT file data. Initially, the data physical file member is empty. Data must be loaded into the member with either a data manipulation utility (like DFU or SQL) or a specialized application program.

FIGURE 3.3

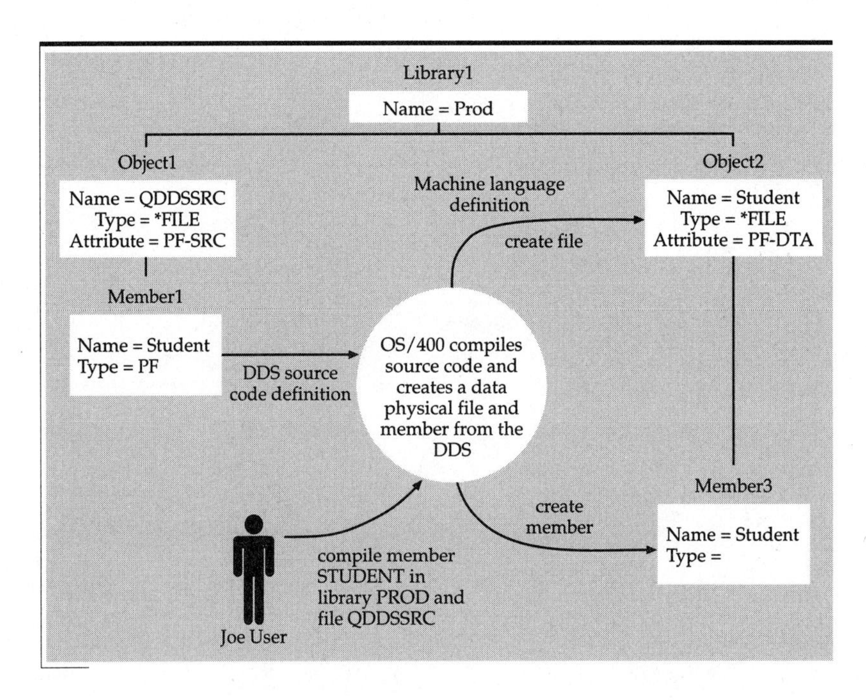

Defining Fields and Records

DDS is a data definition language that allows a user to define fields and records. By "definition," we mean the ability to assign a name, length, and type to each field and record format. This definition is stored in a source physical file member. Before a data physical file and member (which will hold the machine-language file definition and data) can be created, the user must create a library, source physical file, and member to hold the DDS source code definition. Once entered into a source physical file member, the source code can be compiled to create the data physical file and member.

Creating a Library, Physical File, and Member

PDM (Program Development Manager) or CL (Control Language) commands can be used to create a library, a source physical file, and a member with a type of PF. To create a library with PDM, first issue the STRPDM command. The `AS/400 Programming Development Manager (PDM)` screen (Figure 3.4) will be displayed. At this screen, choose option 1, `Work with libraries`. The `Specify Libraries to Work With` screen (Figure 3.5) will be displayed. Leave the default prompt value, *ALL, and press ENTER. A list of all the libraries that the user can access is displayed (Figure 3.6). Notice on the `Work with Libraries Using PDM` screen that options can be entered next to the libraries' names. These options direct the AS/400 to perform various functions, such as delete the library or display the library description. (The function keys are another way to perform library tasks. Each key along with its definition is listed at the bottom of the screen.)

FIGURE 3.4

```
                AS/400 Programming Development Manager (PDM)

Select one of the following:

     1. Work with libraries
     2. Work with objects
     3. Work with members

     9. Work with user-defined options




 Selection or command
 ===>____________________________________________________________________
___________________________________________________________________________
F3=Exit       F4=Prompt        F9=Retrieve        F10=Command entry
F12=Cancel    F18=Change defaults
```

FIGURE 3.5

```
                    Specify Libraries to Work With

Type choice, press Enter.

  Library . . . . . . . . . . .     *ALL______     *LIBL, name, *generic*, *ALL,
                                                   *ALLUSR, *USRLIBL, *CURLIB

F3=Exit      F5=Refresh      F12=Cancel
```

FIGURE 3.6

```
                    Work with Libraries Using PDM

List type  . . . . . . .  *ALL____          Position to . . . . .    __________

Type options, press Enter.
  2=Change          3=Copy                       4=Delete      5=Display
  7=Rename          8=Display description        9=Save        10=Restore ...

Opt  Library        Type        Text
__   QGPL           *PROD

                                                                     More...
Parameters or command
===> ____________________________________________________________________________
F3=Exit             F4=Prompt             F5=Refresh         F6=Create
F9=Retrieve         F10=Command entry     F23=More options   F24=More keys
```

Press F6 to create a library. This will result in the `Create Library (CRTLIB)` screen being displayed (Figure 3.7). At this screen, the name of the new library should be specified.

For all examples in this book, it is assumed that each user has a userid, where the last two digits are a unique number, such as DATAB99. For the new library name, enter the text MYLIB followed by the unique two-digit number. For userid DATAB99, the library name would be MYLIB99. (The library name used in all examples will be MYLIBXX, where XX is assumed to be the unique two-digit userid number.)

FIGURE 3.7

```
                         Create Library (CRTLIB)

 Type choices, press Enter.

 Library . . . . . . . . . . . . . MYLIBXX___      Name
 Library type . . . . . . . . . . *PROD           *PROD, *TEST
 Text 'description' . . . . . . . Joe User's personal library____________
 ______

                                                                     Bottom
 F3=Exit   F4=Prompt   F5=Refresh   F10=Additional parameters   F12=Cancel
 F13=How to use this display        F24=More keys
```

At the Create Library screen, descriptive text for the library can also be entered. After specifying the new library, press **ENTER**. Pressing **ENTER** tells the system to start creating the new library. When the library is created, the Work with Libraries Using PDM screen will be redisplayed with a message on the second to last line saying Library MYLIBXX created, and MYLIBXX will be included in the list of libraries (Figure 3.8).

FIGURE 3.8

```
                         Work with Libraries Using PDM

 List type . . . . . . .    *ALL______        Position to . . . . .  _________

 Type options, press Enter.
   2=Change          3=Copy                          4=Delete     5=Display
   7=Rename          8=Display description           9=Save       10=Restore ...

 Opt  Library       Type        Text
 __   QGPL          *PROD
 __   MYLIBXX       *PROD

                                                                    More...

 Parameters or command
 ===> __________________________________________________________________
 F3=Exit          F4=Prompt               F5=Refresh        F6=Create
 F9=Retrieve      F10=Command entry       F23=More options  F24=More keys
 Library MYLIBXX created.
```

The library could also have been created with the CL command CRTLIB. The syntax and parameters would have been as follows:

```
CRTLIB LIB(MYLIBXX)
```

Now that a library exists, a source physical file (an object) can be created. From the AS/400 Programming Development Manager (PDM) menu (see Figure 3.4) choose option 2, Work with objects. This time the Specify Objects to Work With screen (Figure 3.9) will be displayed. On this screen, specify the library under which the new object will reside. For our example, we would type **MYLIBXX** at the prompt and press **ENTER**. This will bring up all objects contained in the specified library (Figure 3.10). Since the library was just created, no objects will be listed.

To create the source physical file begin by pressing **F6**, the Create option. The Create Commands screen (Figure 3.11) will be displayed. This screen lists options to create a multitude of different types of objects. To decide which type to create, remember that the file we want to create will eventually hold DDS source code. The previous section on object types stated that all source code members must reside under an object with a type of *FILE and an attribute of PF-SRC (source physical). Given these conditions, option 126 will create the type of object we want. (Paging down through the list of options will eventually result in Figure 3.12 being displayed.)

Type **147** at the command line, and press **ENTER**. The Create Source Physical File (CRTSRCPF) screen (Figure 3.13) will be displayed. On this screen, enter the name of the new object—DDSSRC, the library it will reside under—MYLIBXX, and any descriptive text. After this is done, press **ENTER**. The system will start creating the new object. When it is complete, the Create Commands screen will reappear with a message at the bottom of the screen that says

FIGURE 3.9

```
                         Specify Objects to Work With

Type choices, press Enter.

  Library . . . . . . . . .   MYLIBXX___    *CURLIB, name

  Object:
    Name . . . . . . . . . .  *ALL______    *ALL, name, *generic*
    Type . . . . . . . . . .  *ALL______    *ALL, *type
    Attribute  . . . . . . .  *ALL______    *ALL, attribute, *generic*,
                                            *BLANK

F3=Exit      F5=Refresh      F12=Cancel
```

FIGURE 3.10

```
                     Work with Objects Using PDM

Library . . . . .    MYLIBXX___        Position to . . . . . . . .   _____
                                       Position to type  . . . . .   _____

Type options, press Enter.
  2=Change        3=Copy         4=Delete       5=Display  7=Rename
  8=Display description          9=Save         10=Restore 11=Move ...

Opt  Object       Type         Attribute    Text

  (No objects in library)


Parameters or command
===> ____________________________________________________________________
F3=Exit           F4=Prompt            F5=Refresh        F6=Create
F9=Retrieve       F10=Command entry    F23=More options F24=More keys
```

FIGURE 3.11

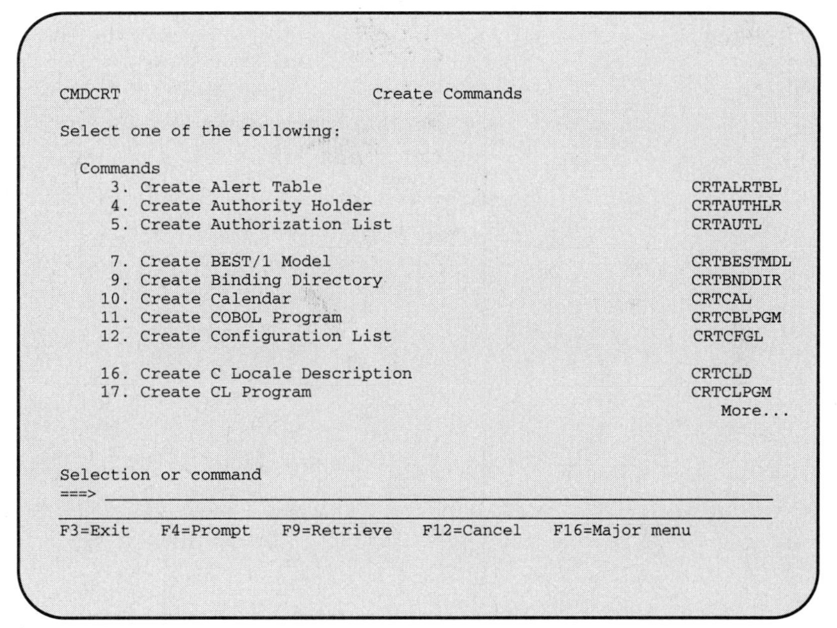

CMDCRT
Create Commands
Select one of the following:
Commands
3. Create Alert Table CRTALRTBL
4. Create Authority Holder CRTAUTHLR
5. Create Authorization List CRTAUTL
7. Create BEST/1 Model CRTBESTMDL
9. Create Binding Directory CRTBNDDIR
10. Create Calendar CRTCAL
11. Create COBOL Program CRTCBLPGM
12. Create Configuration List CRTCFGL
16. Create C Locale Description CRTCLD
17. Create CL Program CRTCLPGM
More...
Selection or command
===>
F3=Exit F4=Prompt F9=Retrieve F12=Cancel F16=Major menu

`File DDSSRC created in library` MYLIBXX. To verify that the object was created, go through PDM and get to the `Work with Objects Using PDM` screen for MYLIBXX. It should display one object in that library, DDSSRC (Figure 3.14), with an attribute of PF-SRC and a type of *FILE.

FIGURE 3.12

```
CMDCRT                            Create Commands

Select one of the following:

   136. Create Save File                                          CRTSAVF
   137. Create Subsystem Description                              CRTSBSD
   138. Create Search Index                                       CRTSCHIDX
   139. Create Spelling Aid Dictionary                            CRTSPADCT
   140. Create SQL C Program                                      CRTSQLC
   141. Create SQL ILE C Object                                   CRTSQLCI
   142. Create SQL COBOL Program                                  CRTSQLCBL
   143. Create SQL FORTRAN Program                                CRTSQLFTN
   144. Create SQL Package                                        CRTSQLPKG
   145. Create SQL PL/I Program                                   CRTSQLPLI
   146. Create SQL RPG Program                                    CRTSQLRPG
   147. Create Source Physical File                               CRTSRCPF
   148. Create Service Program                                    CRTSRVPGM
   149. Create Session Description                                CRTSSND
                                                                     More...

Selection or command
===> ________________________________________________________________________

F3=Exit   F4=Prompt   F9=Retrieve   F12=Cancel   F16=Major menu
```

FIGURE 3.13

```
                 Create Source Physical File (CRTSRCPF)

Type choices, press Enter.

File . . . . . . . . . . . . . . .   DDSSRC____    Name
  Library  . . . . . . . . . . .       MYLIBXX___    Name, *CURLIB
Record length  . . . . . . . . .   92____        Number
Member, if desired . . . . . . .   *NONE_____    Name, *NONE, *FILE
Text 'description' . . . . . . .   A DDS SOURCE PHYSICAL FILE EXAMPLE
____________________

                                                                     Bottom
F3=Exit   F4=Prompt   F5=Refresh   F10=Additional parameters   F12=Cancel
F13=How to use this display        F24=More keys
```

The source physical file could also have been created with the single CL command—CRTSRCPF. The syntax and parameters would have been as follows:

```
CRTSRCPF FILE(MYLIBXX/DDSSRC)
```

We are now ready to (finally!) create a member. To create a member, choose option 3, `Work with members`, from the `AS/400 Programming Development Manager (PDM)` menu. The `Specify`

FIGURE 3.14

```
                    Work with Objects Using PDM

Library . . . . .   MYLIBXX___        Position to . . . . . . _________
                                        Position to type  . . . . .
__________

Type options, press Enter.
  2=Change        3=Copy          4=Delete        5=Display  7=Rename
  8=Display description           9=Save          10=Restore 11=Move ...

Opt  Object       Type           Attribute   Text
__   DDSSRC       *FILE          PF-SRC      A DDS SOURCE PHYSICAL FILE EXAMPLE

                                                                        Bottom
Parameters or command
===> ____________________________________________________________________
F3=Exit           F4=Prompt           F5=Refresh        F6=Create
F9=Retrieve       F10=Command entry   F23=More options  F24=More keys
```

Members to Work With screen (Figure 3.15) will be displayed. This screen prompts for the library and source physical file to which the member will belong. Type the previously created library and object names, and press ENTER.

FIGURE 3.15

```
                     Specify Members to Work With

Type choices, press Enter.

  File  . . . . . . . . . .    DDSSRC____      Name, F4 for list

    Library . . . . . . . .     MYLIBXX___   *LIBL, *CURLIB, name

  Member:
    Name  . . . . . . . . .    *ALL______      *ALL, name, *generic*
    Type  . . . . . . . . .    *ALL______      *ALL, type, *generic*, *BLANK

F3=Exit      F4=Prompt      F5=Refresh      F12=Cancel
```

The Work with Members Using PDM screen (Figure 3.16) will be displayed. This screen lists all the current members within the file. To create a member, press F6. The Start Source Entry Utility (STRSEU) screen (Figure 3.17) will be displayed. At this screen, the member name and type to be created should be specified. For our example, create a member called STUDENT. Since DDS code is going to be entered, the member type would have to be PF.

FIGURE 3.16

```
                     Work with Members Using PDM

File  . . . . . . DDSSRC____
  Library . . . .    MYLIBXX___            Position to  . . . . .  ________

 Type options, press Enter.
   2=Edit        3=Copy       4=Delete     5=Display   6=Print
   7=Rename      8=Display description     9=Save      13=Change text ...

 Opt  Member      Type        Text

   (No members in file)

 Parameters or command
 ===> ____________________________________________________________________
F3=Exit             F4=Prompt            F5=Refresh          F6=Create
F9=Retrieve         F10=Command entry    F23=More options    F24=More keys
```

FIGURE 3.17

```
                    Start Source Entry Utility (STRSEU)

Type choices, press Enter.

Source file . . . . . . . . . .>  DDSSRC__       Name, *PRV
  Library , . . . . . . . . . .>   MYLIBXX__     Name, *LIBL, *CURLIB, *PRV
Source member . . . . . . . . .   STUDENT___     Name, *PRV, *SELECT
Source type . . . . . . . . . .   PF________     Name, *SAME, BAS, BASP, C...
Text 'description' . . . . . . .  *BLANK______________________________
_____

                                                                   Bottom
 F3=Exit  F4=Prompt  F5=Refresh  F12=Cancel  F13=How to use this display
 F24=More keys
```

After the member type has been specified and descriptive text has been entered, press **ENTER.** This will automatically invoke SEU, and the `Edit` screen (Figure 3.18) will be displayed. This screen allows the user to enter the DDS source code using SEU editing commands.

FIGURE 3.18

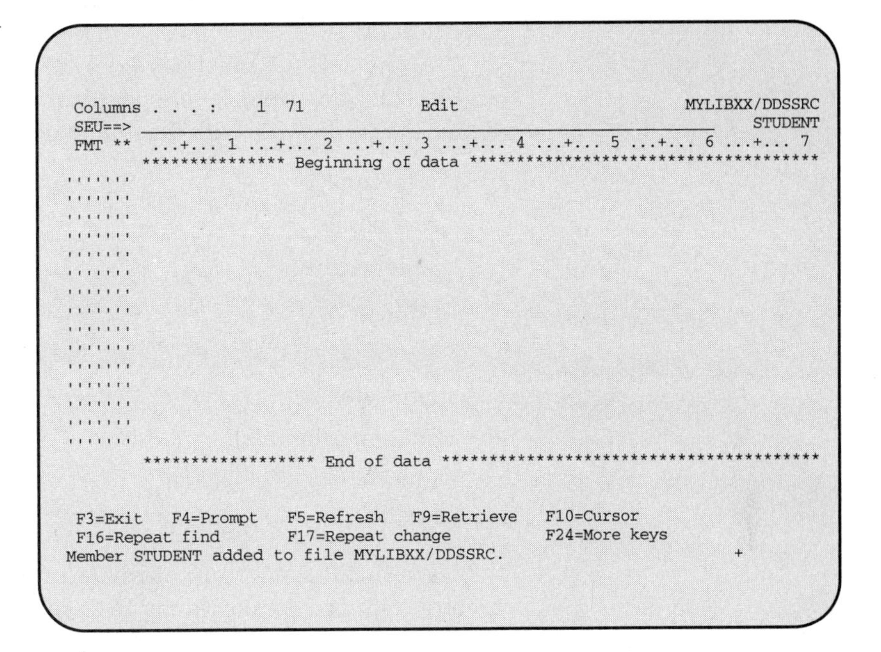

The member could also have been created using the CL command STRSEU. The syntax and parameters to create the member with the STRSEU command are as follows:

```
STRSEU SRCFILE(MYLIBXX/DDSSRC) SRCMBR(STUDENT) TYPE(PF)
```

Defining Fields and Record Formats with DDS

DDS field and record specifications are entered into a source physical file member and can span one or more lines. DDS is a semipositional language, meaning that many commands and values must be entered in certain locations on the line. For instance, when defining a field, the name of the field must be entered in columns 19 through 28. Not all keywords and parameters are positional. Many functions can be specified anywhere within columns 45 through 80, which leads us to the general rule that *all positional entries are specified between columns 1 and 44*. Columns 45 to 80 of each specification are the keyword/function area, and this area is not positional. Commands specified in the keyword/function area are said to be "free format."

There are three levels of specifications—file, record, and field. When a function or keyword is specified, the level that it applies to must also be defined. In other words, the scope that is affected by the keyword or function must be clearly defined. Therefore, each data definition specification can be classified as a file, record, or field level specification.

A physical file must have only one record format specification and at least one field level specification. For an example, we will define the student file with the following fields:

last name

first name

street address

city

state

zip code

student id number

number of credits taken

grade point average

We'll call this group of related fields STUDREC (for student record). Figure 3.19 shows the DDS specifications that would define this file.

Line 4 is an example of a record level specification. An R in column 17 signifies that the specification is for a record. In record specifications the name of the record format is entered in columns 19 through 28 and in the function area, the keyword TEXT can be specified. TEXT allows the user to specify descriptive information about the record format. When the record format is used in a program, the text will be included in the program as documentation. The syntax of the TEXT command requires enclosing the description with single quotes and parentheses. The TEXT keyword can also be used for field level specifications.

The remaining entries in Figure 3.19 are examples of field level specifications. Leaving column 17 blank marks the specification as a field level specification. The field name is specified in the same column positions as the record name. Field specifications, however, are a little more complicated than record specifications. For instance, field level specifications must include a length. Positions 30 through 34 are reserved for length entries. The user must also specify the data type. Column 35 is reserved for this purpose. A blank or A indicates

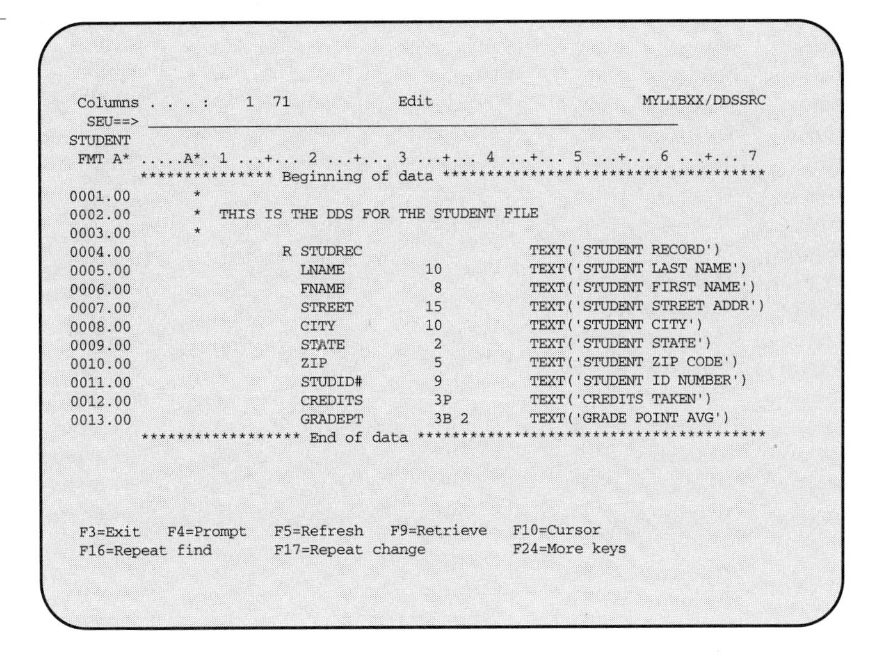
Columns . . . : 1 71 Edit MYLIBXX/DDSSRC
SEU==>
STUDENT
FMT A* .....A*. 1 ...+... 2 ...+... 3 ...+... 4 ...+... 5 ...+... 6 ...+... 7
*************** Beginning of data ***************************************
0001.00 *
0002.00 * THIS IS THE DDS FOR THE STUDENT FILE
0003.00 *
0004.00 R STUDREC TEXT('STUDENT RECORD')
0005.00 LNAME 10 TEXT('STUDENT LAST NAME')
0006.00 FNAME 8 TEXT('STUDENT FIRST NAME')
0007.00 STREET 15 TEXT('STUDENT STREET ADDR')
0008.00 CITY 10 TEXT('STUDENT CITY')
0009.00 STATE 2 TEXT('STUDENT STATE')
0010.00 ZIP 5 TEXT('STUDENT ZIP CODE')
0011.00 STUDID# 9 TEXT('STUDENT ID NUMBER')
0012.00 CREDITS 3P TEXT('CREDITS TAKEN')
0013.00 GRADEPT 3B 2 TEXT('GRADE POINT AVG')
****************** End of data **
F3=Exit F4=Prompt F5=Refresh F9=Retrieve F10=Cursor
F16=Repeat find F17=Repeat change F24=More keys

FIGURE 3.19

that field will contain character data. If the field will contain numeric data, several values—P, S, B—can be specified. These values correspond to the packed decimal, zoned decimal, and binary methods of storage. In the example, notice that CREDITS is defined as packed decimal and GRADEPT as binary. If decimal places are needed, the number of places required is entered in positions 36 and 37. GRADEPT requires two decimal places, so 2 was entered in column 37.

While typing in the DDS specifications, positioning the cursor at the correct column and entering the data can become a nuisance. SEU supplies a DDS input prompt that will easily position entries in the correct columns. Pressing the **F4** key tells the system to display the input prompt. Because this is a physical file member, the DDS prompt will be displayed in the bottom portion of the screen. The user can simply fill in the blanks, and SEU will correctly enter the specification.

Once all the DDS has been entered, press **F3** to exit SEU. The `Exit` screen will be displayed (Figure 3.20). You can save the source code from this screen by entering **Y** at the `Change/create member` prompt and pressing **ENTER.** The `Work with Members Using PDM` screen will be displayed, and the newly created STUDENT member with a type of PF will be listed (Figure 3.21).

FIGURE 3.20

```
                              Exit

Type choices, press Enter.

  Change/create member . . . . . . .   N              Y=Yes, N=No
    Member . . . . . . . . . . . . .   STUDENT___     Name, F4 for list
    File . . . . . . . . . . . . . .   DDSSRC____     Name, F4 for list
      Library . . . . . . . . . . .      MYLIBXX___   Name
    Text . . . . . . . . . . . . . .   SOURCE CODE FOR STUDENT FILE____

    Resequence member . . . . . . . .  Y              Y=Yes, N=No
      Start . . . . . . . . . . . . .  0001.00   0000.01-9999.99
      Increment . . . . . . . . . . .  01.00          00.01-99.99

  Print member . . . . . . . . . . .   N              Y=Yes, N=No

  Return to editing . . . . . . . . .  N              Y=Yes, N=No

  Go to member list . . . . . . . . .  N              Y=Yes, N=No


F3=Exit   F4=Prompt   F5=Refresh   F12=Cancel
```

FIGURE 3.21

```
                     Work with Members Using PDM

File . . . . . .   DDSSRC____
  Library . . . .    MYLIBXX___          Position to . . . . .  ______

Type options, press Enter.
  2=Edit          3=Copy       4=Delete       5=Display   6=Print
  7=Rename        8=Display description       9=Save      13=Change text ...

Opt  Member       Type         Text
__   STUDENT      PF_______    SOURCE CODE FOR STUDENT FILE______________



                                                                     Bottom
Parameters or command
===> ______________________________________________________________________
F3=Exit           F4=Prompt              F5=Refresh        F6=Create
F9=Retrieve       F10=Command entry      F23=More options  F24=More keys
Member STUDENT added to file MYLIBXX/DDSSRC.                          +
```

Field Reference Files

A common practice in most information systems organizations is to create a single source physical file to hold all field definitions. This file is called a field reference file.

Field reference files do not contain any data. They are simply built to hold field definitions and are referenced by other files. These other files will actually contain data. The advantage of the field reference file is that all field definitions are in one place and, therefore, can be easily located. In this sense, the field reference file acts as a data dictionary. Field reference files also make the programmer's job easier because all data fields have to be defined only once. If other files want to use the same field, they can simply reference the definition in the field reference file. A single location for all field definitions also makes for easy updating. If a field needs to be changed, only the definition in the field reference file is updated. (Some other steps need to be taken to change a field definition, but we will cover these steps in later chapters.) For instance, if an organization goes to nine-digit zip codes, instead of changing multiple file's zip code definition, the one definition in the field reference file can be modified.

We will create a field reference file for all of our examples. The field specifications from STUDENT will be copied to a member called FRF (field reference file) in the source physical file DDSSRC within MYLIBXX (Figure 3.22). Notice that the fields are in alphabetical order. This makes finding a particular field definition easier. In addition, most organizations require text that clearly defines a field (if the field name is not sufficient), and there are usually standards regarding field names and keywords/functions that should or should not be used. For instance, many organizations that use RPG restrict field names to six characters since this is the maximum field name size that can be placed in an RPG command specification.

Using FRF to hold all field specifications would mean changing the source definition of STUDENT to reference FRF. The DDS code to do this can be seen in Figure 3.23. Notice the new keyword REF on line 4. This identifies the file that contains all referenced field definitions.

FIGURE 3.22

```
               *************** Beginning of data ***************************************
0001.00            ***************************************************************
0002.00            *   THIS IS A FIELD REFERENCE FILE FOR ALL SCHOOL INFORMATION
0003.00            ***************************************************************
0004.00                  R FRFFMT                    TEXT('FIELD REFERENCE')
0005.00                    CITY          10          TEXT('CITY ADDR')
0006.00            *****************************************************************
0007.00            *   CREDITS IS THE TOTAL NUMBER OF CREDITS COMPLETED BY A STUDENT
0008.00            *   GRADES OF INCOMPLETE, F OR WITHDRAWN ARE NOT INCLUDED IN
0009.00            *   THIS TOTAL
0010.00            *****************************************************************
0011.00                    CREDITS        3P         TEXT('CREDITS TAKEN')
0012.00                    FNAME          8          TEXT('FIRST NAME')
0013.00            *****************************************************************
0014.00            *   GRADEPT IS THE AVERAGE GRADE FOR ALL CLASSES COMPLETED. ONLY
0015.00            *   THOSE CLASSES INCLUDED IN CREDITS ARE USED TO CALCULATE
0016.00            *   GRADEPT.
0017.00            ***************************************************************
0018.00                    GRADEPT        3B 2       TEXT('GRADE POINT AVG')
0019.00                    LNAME         10          TEXT('LAST NAME')
0020.00                    STATE          2          TEXT('STATE ADDR')
0021.00                    STREET        15          TEXT('STREET ADDR')
0022.00                    STUDID#        9          TEXT('STUDENT ID NUMBER')
0023.00                    ZIP            5          TEXT('ZIP CODE')
               ****************** End of data *************************************
```

FIGURE 3.23

```
Columns . . . :    1  71            Edit                          MYLIBXX/DDSSRC
SEU==> ___________________________________________________________  STUDENT
FMT A* .....A*. 1 ...+... 2 ...+... 3 ...+... 4 ...+... 5 ...+... 6 ...+... 7
       *************** Beginning of data *************************************
0001.00      *
0002.00      * THIS IS THE DDS FOR THE STUDENT FILE
0003.00      *
0004.00                                            REF(MYLIBXX/FRF)
0005.00             R STUDREC                      TEXT('STUDENT RECORD')
0006.00               LNAME     R                  TEXT('STUDENT LAST NAME')
0007.00               FNAME     R                  TEXT('STUDENT FIRST NAME')
0008.00               STREET    R                  TEXT('STUDENT STREET ADDR')
0009.00               CITY      R                  TEXT('STUDENT CITY')
0010.00               STATE     R                  TEXT('STUDENT STATE')
0011.00               ZIP       R                  TEXT('STUDENT ZIP CODE')
0012.00               STUDID#   R
0013.00               CREDITS   R
0014.00               GRADEPT   R
       ****************** End of data ****************************************

F3=Exit   F4=Prompt   F5=Refresh   F9=Retrieve   F10=Cursor
F16=Repeat find       F17=Repeat change          F24=More keys
```

(The keyword REF is also a file level keyword, meaning the function defined affects the entire file.) Each field definition is then marked with an R in column 29. This means that the field definition should be retrieved from the file specified in the REF keyword.

Any referenced definition can be overridden by specifying the desired definition in the field specification. For instance, we have changed the text associated with the student fields by simply specifying new text definitions in several of the STUDENT field definitions.

Compiling

The final step in creating a data physical file is to compile the DDS member. Compiling the source member translates the file's source code definition into machine language and creates the data physical file object to hold the machine-language file definition. In addition, a member is created under the data physical file that will hold the data.

To compile from the `Work with Members Using PDM` screen, type **14** in the option field to the left of the member name, and press **ENTER.** When using a field reference file, the field reference file must exist before any files that reference it can be compiled. Therefore, always compile the FRF file first and ensure that it was successfully compiled. You can verify that the compile was successful and that the data physical file was created by going to the `Work with Objects` screen and checking that an object named FRF with a type of *FILE and attribute of PF-DTA is listed. After this has been done, STUDENT can be compiled.

Compiling a DDS member can also be performed with the CL command CRTPF. The syntax would be as follows:

```
CRTPF FILE(MYLIBXX/FRF) SRCFILE(MYLIBXX/DDSSRC) SRCMBR(FRF)

CRTPF FILE(MYLIBXX/STUDENT) SRCFILE(MYLIBXX/DDSSRC) SRCMBR(STUDENT)
```

Loading Data with DFU

DFU is a system utility that allows users to quickly load small amounts of data into files. The user can invoke DFU by typing option 18 next to the filename on the `Work with Objects Using PDM` screen. DFU creates a temporary program and a display screen that allows data to be entered, changed, or deleted from the file one record at a time. Since the file has just been created, the temporary program will automatically default to entry mode (Figure 3.24). The mode can be changed by pressing the appropriate function key. (See the bottom of the screen for each function key's definition.)

To load data, simply move the cursor to the underlined area next to the field name, and type the values to be entered. To input the record into the file, press ENTER when you finish entering all the data. (Move the cursor out of any data entry field before pressing ENTER; otherwise, DFU displays a ridiculous error message stating that Enter is an invalid entry. This is one of the not-so-user-friendly features of DFU). For our example, we'll load some data regarding a few fictional students. We can display the newly entered data by issuing the DSPPFM command. Figure 3.25 shows the data that was entered.

FIGURE 3.24

```
WORK WITH DATA IN A FILE                          Mode . . . . :   ENTRY
Format . . . . :   STUDREC___                     File . . . . :   STUDENT


LNAME:    __________
FNAME:    ________
STREET:   _______________
CITY:     __________
STATE:    __
ZIP:      _____
STUDID#:  _________
CREDITS:  ___
GRADEPT:  ___





F3=Exit               F5=Refresh               F6=Select format
F9=Insert             F10=Entry                F11=Change
```

FIGURE 3.25

```
                        Display Physical File Member
File . . . . . . :   STUDENT              Library . . . . :   MYLIBXX
Member . . . . . :   STUDENT              Record . . . . . :   1
Control  . . . . .   ___________          Column . . . . . :   1
Find . . . . . . .   ________________________________________
*...+....1....+....2....+....3....+....4....+....5....+....6...
FlintstoneFred     11 Limestone DrBedrock   AZ88888-11111111 ¤ H
FlintstoneWilma    11 Limestone DrBedrock     88888123456789   °
Rubble    Barnard 15 Limestone DrBedrock   AZ88888          ¬
Rubble    Betty   15 Limestone DrBedrock   AZ88888444444444 ± ±
                         ****** END OF DATA ******








                                                                  Bottom

F3=Exit   F12=Cancel   F19=Left   F20=Right   F24=More keys
```

Summary

The AS/400 has unique storage structures such as libraries, source physical files, data physical files, and members. These structures are used to organize and store raw data (the 0s and 1s) and the data definitions that make the raw data intelligible.

A source physical file is a directory of members that contains source code file definitions. A data physical file contains a machine-language file definition and acts as a directory of data members that share the same definition. Libraries act as directories for either data or source files.

DDS is a data definition language that allows users to define the logical and physical organization of their data. DDS is entered into source physical file members and compiled. Compiling DDS source code encompasses

Translating the source code into machine language

Creating a data physical file

Loading the machine-language definition into the data physical file

Creating a member beneath the data physical file that will eventually hold the raw data

Compiling is done by simply specifying an option on the `Work with Members Using PDM` screen or issuing the CL command CRTPF from any command line.

Most organizations use field reference files to store all field definitions. This single location for all field definitions makes modifying field definitions faster and cuts down on the chance of error.

After a data physical file and member have been created, application programs or data manipulation utilities (such as DFU and SQL) can be used to load data into the physical file member.

EXERCISE

In this exercise, we are going to create two files for a local video rental store. They have just bought an AS/400 and are planning to write a video-tracking application system. It's been determined that initially two files are needed: one file to contain information about each of the different titles in stock and another to keep track of each copy and its status. The fields and their definitions are as follows (define all numeric fields as packed decimal):

TITLES

Field	Text	Type of Data	Length
TNUM	Title number	Character	7
TNAME	Title name	Character	20
TYPE	Type of show	Character	10
MEDIA	Media	Character	3
RPRICE	Rental price	Numeric	3.2
SPRICE	Sales price	Numeric	5.2

PRODUCT

Field	Text	Type of Data	Length
SNUM	Serial number	Character	7
TNUM	Title number	Character	7
STATUS	Status	Character	1
RENT#	Number of times rented	Numeric	3

The media field tells what type of media the show has been recorded on (for instance, video disk, beta, VHS, cartridge). The status of the individual product signifies whether it is available or out on rental. The number of times rented is used by the store owner to determine when it is time to "retire" a particular tape or disk.

1. Create three new members called FRF, TITLES, and PRODUCT with types equal to PF in MYLIBXX and DDSSRC. (If you have not already created MYLIBXX and DDSSRC, create them at this time by issuing the CRTLIB and CRTSRCPF commands, substituting your unique two-digit number for the characters XX in MYLIBXX. After creating the library and file, create the members FRF, TITLES, and PRODUCT.)
2. Enter the DDS to define the fields and the appropriate text in FRF. Then enter the DDS for TITLES and PRODUCT, referencing the definitions in FRF.
3. Create the data physical files by issuing the correct CRTPF commands.

4. Enter the following data for the TITLES file by specifying option 18 on the `Work with Objects Using PDM` screen:

TNUM	1	2
TNAME	Gone With the Wind	Gone With the Wind
TYPE	Romance	Romance
MEDIA	VD	B
RPRICE	2.50	1.00
SPRICE	89.95	19.95

TNUM	3	4
TNAME	Super Mario Bros III	E.T.
TYPE	Game	Sci-Fi
MEDIA	CRT	VHS
RPRICE	3.50	2.00
SPRICE	95.95	29.95

TNUM	5	6
TNAME	Duck Hunt	Nightmare on Elm St
TYPE	Game	Horror
MEDIA	CRT	VHS
RPRICE	1.50	3.00
SPRICE	10.00	79.95

5. Enter the following data for the PRODUCT file:

SNUM	1	2	3	4	5	6
TNUM	6	6	4	2	1	3
STATUS	A	O	A	A	O	O
RENT#	470	356	777	6	123	545

SNUM	7	8	9	10	11	12
TNUM	5	3	3	4	1	7
STATUS	A	O	O	O	A	T
RENT#	21	467	321	444	77	3

6. Display the data using the DSPPFM command, and verify that the data was entered correctly. The results from issuing the two DSPPFM commands should be as follows (the EBCDIC character displayed for RENT# data will be different on different workstations):

```
                          Display Physical File Member
File . . . . . . :   PRODUCT              Library  . . . . :   MYLIBXX
Member . . . . . :   PRODUCT              Record . . . . . :   1
Control  . . . . .                        Column . . . . . :   1
Find . . . . . . .
*...+....1....+..
1       6      Aå
2       6      O ?
3       4      AÏ"
4       2      A ?
5       1      O
6       3      Oè¬
7       5      A
8       3      Oã"
9       3      O
10      4      Oà|
11      1      A "
12      7      T






                        ****** END OF DATA ******
```

```
                          Display Physical File Member
File . . . . . . :   TITLES               Library  . . . . :   MYLIBXX
Member . . . . . :   TITLES               Record . . . . . :   1
Control  . . . . .                        Column . . . . . :   1
Find . . . . . . .
*...+....1....+....2....+....3....+....4....+
1       Gone With the Wind  Romance   VD     r¬
2       Gone With the Wind  Romance   B      r¬
3       Super Mario Bros IIIGame      CRT    ß¬
4       E.T.                SciFi     VHS    r¬
5       Duck Hunt           Game      CRT
6       Nightmare on Elm St Horror    VHS    r¬
                        ****** END OF DATA ******










                                                              Bottom
F3=Exit   F12=Cancel   F19=Left   F20=Right   F24=More keys
```

REVIEW QUESTIONS

1. What is the smallest logical unit of data?
2. What is the physical size of the smallest logical unit?
3. What type of information is stored in source physical file members?
4. Explain what is meant by the term *semipositional* when describing DDS.
5. What information is stored in a data physical file and its members?
6. How are data physical files created?
7. What function does DFU perform?
8. What are the three levels of data specification provided by DDS?

DISCUSSION QUESTIONS

1. What are the actions taken and results of compiling source code file definitions?
2. Why are field reference files used?

Changing Data Physical Files

4

Overview

In this chapter, we will explore DDS functions that help ensure that accurate and complete data is entered into a database. The new specifications to define these functions will be added to already existing file definitions, and the impact of changing a file's definition will be examined. We will also discuss several procedures to safely make changes to already existing files, and we will create a general utility program for changing file definitions.

After finishing this chapter, you will understand

- The importance of editing and auditing data
- How DDS supports edits and audits
- Trigger programs
- Data independence
- The effect of recompiling a file definition on data and application programs
- Level checking

After finishing this chapter, you will be able to

- Define DDS edits in the field specification function area
- Copy and rename files
- Change a file definition without loss of data
- Locate all programs that use a file

Editing Data

Before data is written to a file, an editing or auditing process usually occurs to ensure that the data is correct. For instance, whenever a date is entered, a common data management practice is to verify that the date is valid. Some very easy checks can be made to verify this. If the data is being entered in MM/DD/YY format, an edit can be specified to make sure that the month is a number between 1 and 12 and that the day is a number between 1 and 31. These types of simple edits help stop erroneous data from being entered into a file.

These simple edits, however, are not perfect. For instance, if the date 2/30/96 (an invalid date because February can never have 30 days) were entered, it would pass the edits. We can perform a more sophisticated edit by creating a file of each month's valid range of days and check the file whenever a date is entered. This would ensure that valid dates are entered; however, it still does not guarantee that the information is correct. (For instance, 2/5/58 is a valid date, but it is probably incorrect if it pertains to a carton of milk currently on a grocer's shelf.) Edits do not guarantee correct data but can greatly decrease the amount of incorrect data that is entered.

Traditionally, edits and data definition have been performed inside application programs. Programs that receive data from a user contain the logic to initially "screen" the data. However, there has been a trend in file management and database management systems to provide greater **data independence**, meaning that any information or activity concerning data storage should occur independently or outside application programs. As discussed earlier, DDS is a means to define files outside application programs. DDS also provides the capability to define simple edits and audits of data. These edits and audits will be "picked up" by any screens and utilities that use the database field definitions as the basis for screen field definitions. For instance, DFU is a utility that creates a data entry screen. Any edits defined in a DDS field specification will be in force when data is entered on the DFU entry screen. This happens because DFU uses that DDS field definition to build the entry screens' fields.

Using DDS to define edits is not foolproof. An application program can still insert any information into a physical file regardless of the edits specified in the DDS. Fortunately, the AS/400 developers are continuing to improve the AS/400 DBMS. They have announced that with Version 3 of OS/400, the DBMS will be called DB2/400 and will support **trigger programs**, user-defined programs that are automatically executed whenever a record is inserted, deleted, or updated. Trigger programs are particularly useful for edits.

Defining Edits with DDS

Editing keywords are placed in the function area (columns 45 through 80) of the field specification. The edit keywords have a wide range of functions, and unlike many other keywords and values, they are not as rigid in format. You have already seen one keyword, TEXT. The editing keywords use the same format as TEXT, a single command followed by a value within parentheses. As our first example, we will implement the date edits previously described using the keyword RANGE.

RANGE allows users to specify a range of values that are valid for a field. For the month field, the RANGE command would be entered as RANGE(1 12). Values entered into a screen's month field would be checked against this range. If the value entered was not from 1 to 12, the entry would be highlighted and a message displayed stating that the value was invalid.

An edit can also be specified for discrete values rather than just a range. The VALUES keyword allows the user to list the specific values that an entry will be checked against. Using the month example again, month could also be defined as a character field. This field should contain only the discrete values of January, February, and so on. To specify this edit, the VALUES keyword would be used as follows:

```
VALUES('January' 'February' 'March' 'April'
'May' 'June' 'July' 'August' 'September'
'October' 'November' 'December').
```

When entering new records into a file, it is often desirable to define some fields as mandatory entry fields. In other words, certain fields must be filled in order to enter a record into the file. An example might be an address field. No new student record should be allowed into the database unless an address is entered. The DDS keyword CHECK provides this function. Three parameters can be specified with the CHECK keyword: ME, MF, AB.

ME (mandatory entry) specifies that at least one character or number must be entered in the field. A single blank or zero is a valid entry. This specification would be used for the address field example. Notice how this doesn't guarantee accurate addresses, but it does prevent an oversight.

MF (mandatory fill) specifies that a field must be totally filled in. If a field is defined as five in length, five characters or numbers must be supplied whenever the field is being entered. An example of a mandatory fill data field is a zip code. All zip codes must fill the entire length of the field. There are no three- or four-digit zip codes.

The last value AB (allow blank) means that no data entry is required for this field—blanks are allowed. If no data is entered, blanks and zeros are substituted for character and numeric fields, respectively. If no parameters are specified with the CHECK keyword, AB is the default.

Another commonly used editing keyword is COMP (compare). COMP allows the user to specify a test for the value. The value will be accepted only if the result of the test is true. For instance, an example of a comparison test for a quantity-in-stock field would be

```
COMP(GT 0)
```

This test ensures that all values entered for quantity in stock are *g*reater *t*han zero. Several operands can be used to define the tests, including

EQ—Equal

NE—Not equal

LT—Less than

LE—Less than or equal

GE—Greater than or equal

For our previous date example, we might specify that no year entered can be less than 95. This would prevent dates such as 02/05/58 from being entered as an expiration date for a carton of milk.

Limitations to DDS-Defined Edits

DDS edits do not solve our data integrity problem. The edits defined do not affect the physical file. Edits are picked up only by screens that use the DDS field definitions as the basis for a screen field. For instance, a programmer can use SDA and define a screen to accept student information for the STUDENT file. If the screen's fields are not based on the DDS field definitions containing the edits, the program will process unedited data. The database management system will not stop the program from entering data that does not pass the DDS edits. In other words, the DDS keywords do not stop incorrect data from being entered into files. As a matter of fact, DDS edits are not picked up by all system utilities that allow file modifications. For instance, with DFU you can execute temporary update programs in CHANGE mode, and not all the edits will be enforced.

DDS edit keywords help with data integrity. However, to ensure accurate data, application programs would have to include edits. (In OS/400 Version 3, separate programs called trigger programs can contain these edits.) Also system security and manual procedures should be created and implemented to restrict users' capability to input data or input incorrect data. For instance, a manual procedure to stop incorrect data might require that all screen fields be based on database field definitions. In this way, all application screens would contain the correct edits. To stop users from entering data, the AS/400 security system can be used to restrict access to system utilities, like DFU, that allow data to be entered into physical files.

Trigger Programs

As mentioned, trigger programs are also used to edit data. Trigger programs are user-written application programs. A **trigger** is created that identifies an application program as a trigger program for a file. When a trigger is defined, besides identifying the program and file, the user must specify when the trigger program should be called. When a trigger program should be called is defined by the type of file transaction (insert, delete, or update) that should "kick off" the program and the time in relation to the transaction (before or after the transaction). For instance, a trigger can be defined to occur before an insert to a file, or after an update, or before a delete. There are actually six unique combinations for defining when a trigger program should be executed, and six also happens to be the maximum number of triggers that can be defined for a file (isn't it funny how that just so happened?).

In our date example from before, we would define a trigger (with the OS/400 Version 3 CL command ADDPFTRG, add physical file trigger) to execute the trigger program before an insert to the file is performed. When the trigger program is called, the information to be inserted is passed to the trigger program. The trigger program can then edit the data. As a matter of fact, for our date edit, a common data checking program should probably be written. All trigger programs that are checking dates could simply call this date check program.

For instance, another file may contain employees' date of birth. The trigger program for that file would also call the date check program and pass the date of birth. A common date check would avoid duplicating program code in many trigger programs. The common date check program, however, doesn't absolve the trigger program from date editing. Each trigger program would still have to perform unique audits for the particular data being entered.

For instance, earlier we mentioned that the expiration year for a carton of milk should not be before 1995. This is a unique edit for the expiration date. We would not want that edit performed on an employee's date of birth. This type of check would be done in the trigger program, not the common date check.

When a trigger program runs before a transaction and finds an error, no changes will be made to the file. When a trigger program finds an error but the program is running after the transaction, the transactions' changes to the file are reversed. Further, when a trigger program finds an error, a message can be sent to the original program modifying the file. It is the modifying programs' responsibility to fix the incorrect data.

Trigger programs can also be used to enforce even more complex data integrity rules such as ensuring that data is entered in a field or that data between files are "in synch." For instance, another file called OVERFLOW also contains student names and addresses. OVERFLOW contains students who have been placed on a class waiting list. Whenever an update to a student's address in the STUDENT file occurs, if that student is in the OVERFLOW file, the student's address should be changed there also. We could do this by creating a trigger program for the STUDENT file to check if the student's address was being changed. If the address were being changed, the trigger program would check if the student was in the OVERFLOW file and, if so, modify the address in OVERFLOW. This dual updating of addresses would occur no matter what program or utility tried to update the student's address in STUDENT.

We will discuss keeping data accurate and safe in much greater detail later in the book.

Modifying an Existing File Definition

Based on these new editing functions, the file definitions from Chapter 3 can be improved on. In case you didn't notice, some data was missing from the last chapter's STUDENT file and STUDENT contained incorrect data. (Notice in Figure 3.25 that state and student id number are missing from two of the records and that one of the student id numbers is negative.) We need to fix the already existing data, as well as add the new DDS keywords so that these types of mistakes will be caught in the future.

Changing the files can be done by simply adding the keywords to the source and recompiling. The problem with recompiling the source code is that the old file object (with the machine language file definition) and member are deleted, and a new file definition and empty member are created. In other words, the data in the old file is

FIGURE 4.1

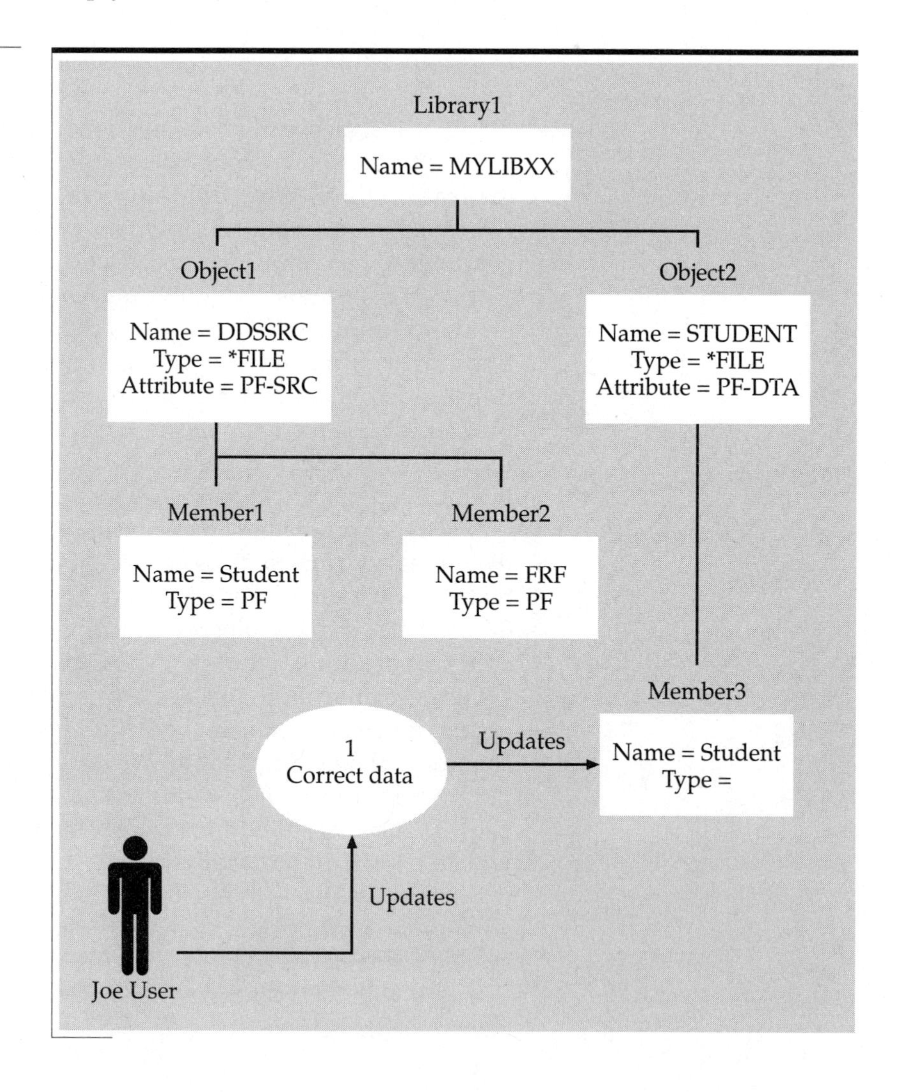

erased. To change the file and save the data, we need to store the data in a temporary file, recompile the new definition, and then copy the data from the temporary file to the new file.

The steps we would take when changing a file definition are as follows: First, fix any incorrect data in the already existing file (Figure 4.1). This can be done using a utility such as DFU or an application program. After the data is corrected, the DDS field definition can be updated using SEU (process 2 in Figure 4.2). After the source code is changed, the data must be copied to a temporary file(process 3, Figure 4.2). After the data is successfully copied, the new field definitions can be generated by compiling the DDS (process 4, Figure 4.3). The new field definitions need to be incorporated into the data files. This is done by recompiling STUDENT (process 5, Figure 4.4). Finally, the data is copied from the temporary file to the new STUDENT file (process 6, Figure 4.5).

FIGURE 4.2

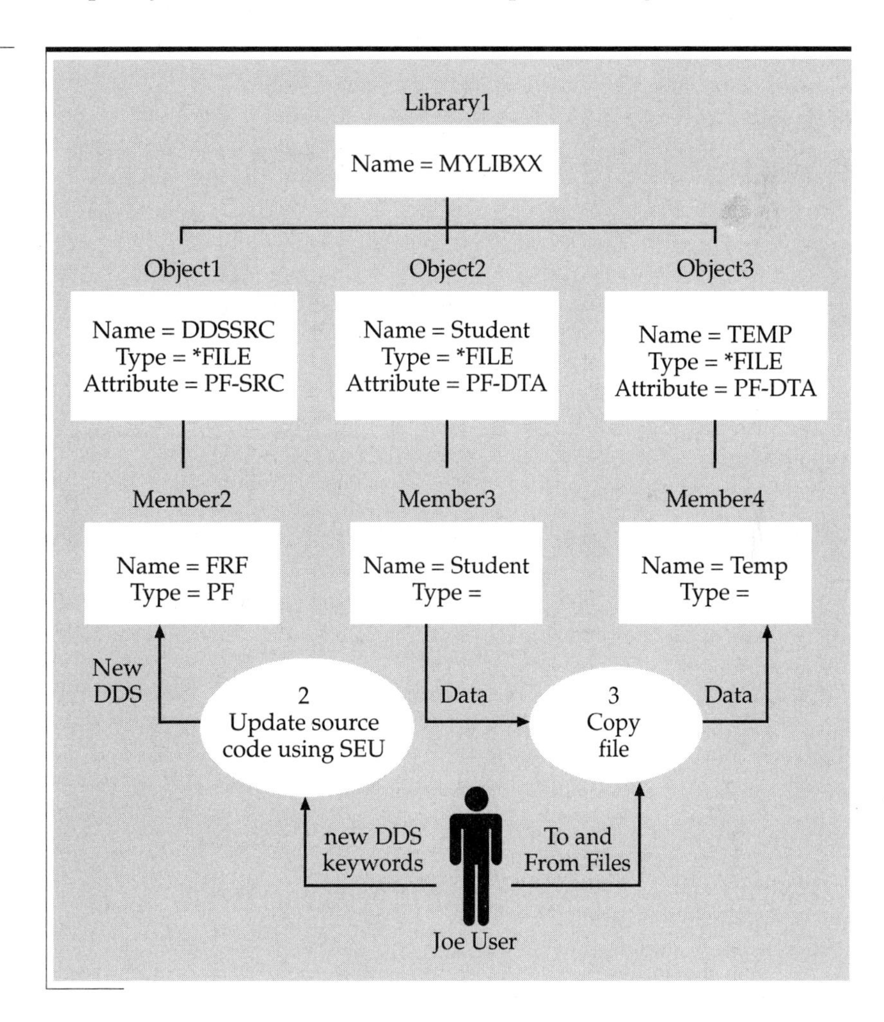

FIGURE 4.3

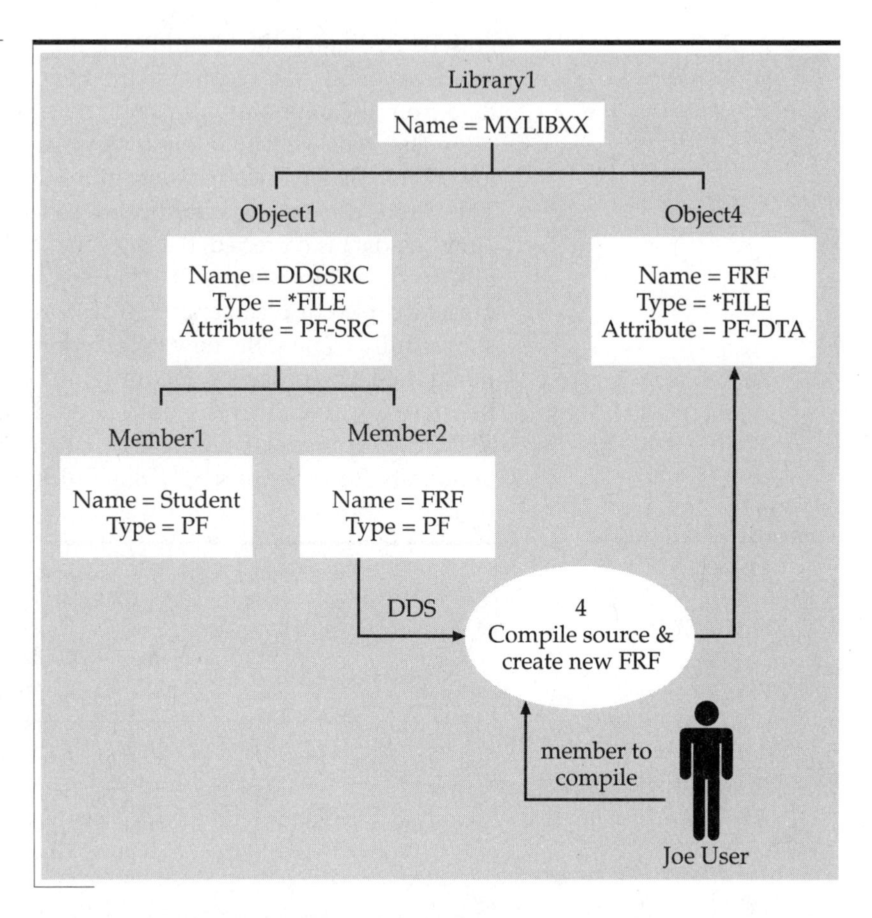

FIGURE 4.4

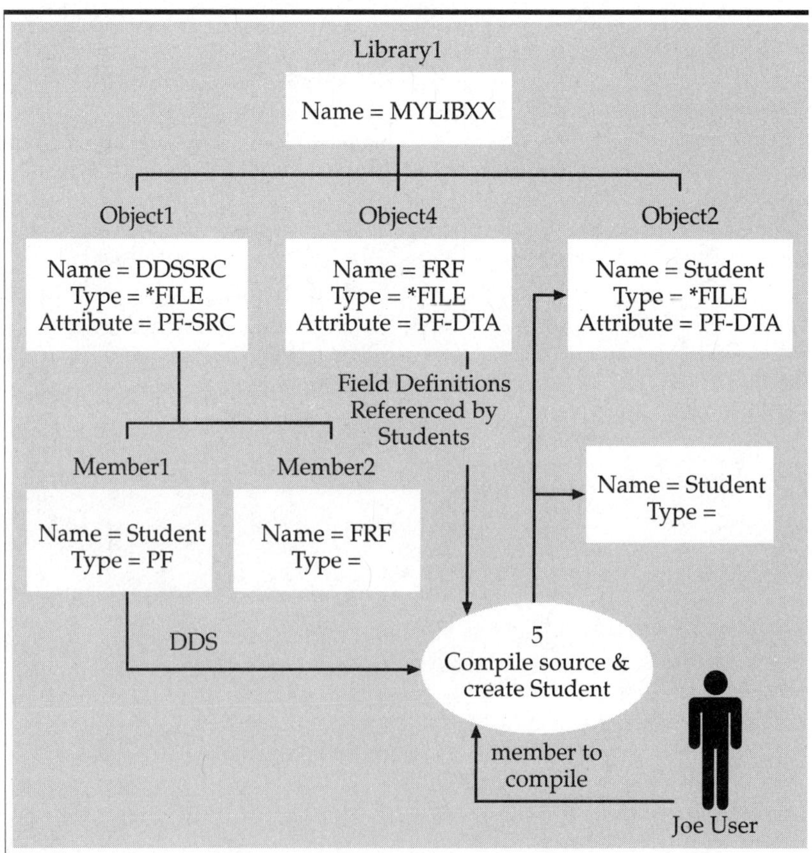

FIGURE 4.5

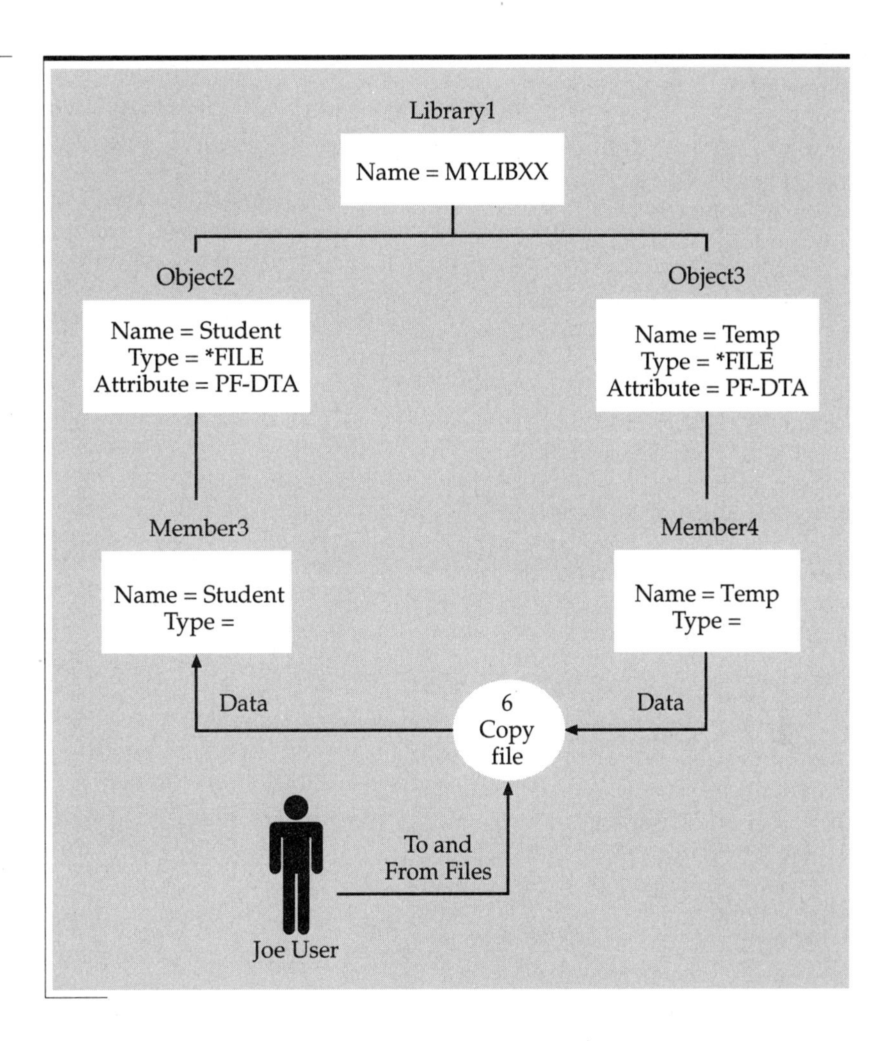

From our previous example, we would make the following modifications to the data in STUDENT:

Change Fred's student number from –11111111 to 111111111

Add AZ to Wilma's state field

Add student number 999999999 to Barney's record

These modifications can be made with DFU by typing **18** next to the STUDENT file on the `Work with Objects Using DFU` screen. DFU will prompt for the record number you wish to change. Type **1** and press **ENTER** to display Fred's record. Modify Fred's record and then records 2 and 3.

After the data has been corrected, the DDS can be updated. We will add CHECK keywords to the FRF file that will make several fields mandatory entry, and the student id and zip codes will be defined as mandatory fill. We will also define two other checks that ensure that the number of credits taken is a positive number and that any grade point averages entered are between 0 and 4.00. See Figure 4.6 for the DDS.

FIGURE 4.6

```
              ****************************Beginning of data******************************
0001.00       ***************************************************************************
0002.00       *        THIS IS A FIELD REFERENCE FILE FOR ALL SCHOOL INFORMATION
0003.00       ***************************************************************
0004.00                 R FRFFMT                          TEXT('FIELD REFERENCE')
0005.00                   CITY         10                 TEXT('CITY ADDR')
0006.00                                                   CHECK(ME)
0007.00       ***************************************************************
0008.00       *     CREDITS IS THE TOTAL NUMBER OF CREDITS COMPLETED BY STUDENT.
0009.00       *     GRADES OF INCOMPLETE, F, OR WITHDRAWN ARE NOT INCLUDED IN
0010.00       *     THIS TOTAL
0011.00       ***************************************************************
0012.00                   CREDITS        3P               TEXT('CREDITS TAKEN')
0013.00                                                   CHECK(ME)
0014.00                                                   COMP(GE 0)
0015.00                   FNAME          8                TEXT('FIRST NAME')
0016.00                                                   CHECK(ME)
0017.00       ***************************************************************
0018.00       *    GRADEPT IS THE AVERAGE GRADE FOR ALL CLASSES COMPLETED. ONLY
0019.00       *    THOSE CLASSES INCLUDED IN CREDITS ARE USED TO CALCULATE
0020.00       *    GRADEPT.
0021.00       ***************************************************************
0022.00                   GRADEPT        3B 2             TEXT('GRADE POINT AVG')
0023.00                                                   RANGE(0 4)
0024.00                                                   CHECK(ME)
0025.00                   LNAME         10                TEXT('LAST NAME')
0026.00                                                   CHECK(ME)
0027.00                   STATE          2                TEXT('STATE ADDR')
0028.00                                                   CHECK(ME)
0029.00                                                   CHECK(MF)
0030.00                   STREET        15                TEXT('STREET ADDR')
0031.00                                                   CHECK(ME)
0032.00                   STUDID#        9                TEXT('STUDENT ID NUMBER)
0033.00                                                   CHECK(ME)
0034.00                                                   CHECK(MF)
0035.00                   ZIP            5                TEXT('ZIP CODE')
0036.00                                                   CHECK(ME)
0037.00                                                   CHECK(MF)
              ***************** End of data ***************************************
```

Now that the first two steps are complete, we copy the data into a temporary file. This can be accomplished with the CPYF command. The syntax and parameters are as follows:

```
CPYF FROMFILE(MYLIBXX/STUDENT) TOFILE(MYLIBXX/TEMP) CRTFILE(*YES)
```

Verify that the data was successfully copied by displaying the member with the DSPPFM command as follows:

```
DSPPFM MYLIBXX/TEMP
```

This should result in Figure 4.7.

After correctly copying the data into the temporary file, recompile the DDS in member FRF, and then create the new STUDENT file and member by recompiling the DDS in member STUDENT. Recompiling can be done by typing **14** next to member name on the `Work with Members Using PDM` screen. Specify yes to the prompt that asks if you wish to delete the already existing file. Verify

FIGURE 4.7

```
                     Display Physical File Member
File . . . . . . :   STUDENT                Library . . . . :   MYLIBXX
Member . . . . . :   STUDENT                Record . . . . . :   1
Control  . . . . .   __________             Column . . . . . :   1
Find . . . . . . .   ___________________________________
*...+....1....+....2....+....3....+....4....+....5....+....6...
FlintstoneFred     11 Limestone DrBedrock   AZ88888111111111 ¤ H
FlintstoneWilma    11 Limestone DrBedrock   AZ88888123456789   °
Rubble    Barnard 15 Limestone DrBedrock   AZ88888999999999 ¬
Rubble    Betty   15 Limestone DrBedrock   AZ88888444444444 ± ±
                     ****** END OF DATA ******

                                                                  Bottom
F3=Exit   F12=Cancel   F19=Left   F20=Right   F24=More keys
```

that the compiles were successful with the DSPMSG command. If the compile was good, copy the data back from the temporary file with the CPYF command as follows:

```
CPYF FROMFILE(MYLIBXX/TEMP) TOFILE(MYLIBXX/STUDENT) MBROPT(*REPLACE)
```

Again verify the data was copied correctly with the following command:

```
DSPPFM MYLIBXX/STUDENT
```

If the data is correct, we can now delete the temporary file with the DLTF command.

```
DLTF MYLIBXX/TEMP
```

As an alternative, we could have used the rename object (RNMOBJ) command instead of the first copy command. The rename object command would eliminate the need to delete the old STUDENT file. Instead of copying, recompiling, and then answering the prompt to delete the file, we can simply issue the rename command (as follows) and then recompile:

```
RNMOBJ OBJ(MYLIBXX/STUDENT) OBJTYPE(*FILE) NEWOBJ(TEMP)
```

For physical files, the rename object command is preferable to the copy command because it eliminates one step in the process. However, when it comes to logical files that have dependencies on the physical file, the rename object command has some side effects that need to be taken into consideration. (We will discuss these contingencies in future chapters on logical files.)

Creating a File Modification Utility Program

Did the preceding procedure seem like a long way to go just to change a file? Six different steps and checking to verify that each command executes successfully seems a little excessive. There should be and there is an easier way.

With our knowledge of CL, we can create a program and automate the last four steps of the procedure (the first copy/rename, the compiles, and the recopy). The first two steps (correcting the data and changing the DDS) are unique to each file modification, but the last four steps (and deleting the temporary file) are the same.

We'll write the program so that the person modifying the file passes the library, file, and member to be compiled. The utility program will rename the file, recompile FRF and the specified member, copy the data back, and delete the temporary file.

The program will require three variables to hold the user-supplied library, file, and member names. All the commands we covered in the preceding section will be used in the program. Figure 4.8 shows the program.

The user would enter the program into a member called CHGF with a type of CLP (the member should reside in a file called CLSRC within MYLIBXX), compile the member, and verify that the compile was successful with the DSPMSG command. We can test the program by making one more change to the STUDENT file. The state field should be defined as mandatory fill since there are no one-character state abbreviations. Change the DDS in FRF by adding a CHECK(MF) to the STATE field specification; then call the new program, CHGF, with the following command:

```
CALL MYLIBXX/CHGF ('MYLIBXX' 'DDSSRC' 'STUDENT')
```

We can verify that the utility program worked (and modified the file definition) by starting DFU against the STUDENT file. Enter the data in Figure 4.9, and press ENTER. If the program is correct, the cursor will be placed in the STATE entry area, and the error message `Mandatory fill field. Must fill to exit` will be displayed. You can verify the other field edits by typing erroneous data in the data fields. For instance, try to give Dino a 6.52 grade point average or –12 credits. Each time an error message will be shown that paraphrases the violated edit condition.

FIGURE 4.8

```
Columns . . . :    1  71            Edit                        MYLIBXX/CLSRC
SEU==> ____________________________________________________________    CHGF
FMT **  ...+... 1 ...+... 2 ...+... 3 ...+... 4 ...+... 5 ...+... 6 ...+... 7
        *************** Beginning of data ************************************
0001.00 /***************************************************************/
0002.00 /* DEFINES VARIABLES THAT WILL BE SUPPLIED TO THE PROGRAM      */
0003.00 /***************************************************************/
0004.00
0005.00 CHGFPGM:  PGM         PARM(&LIB &FILE &MEM)
0006.00
0007.00 /***************************************************************/
0008.00 /* DEFINES THE VARIABLES THAT WILL BE USED IN THE PROGRAM      */
0009.00 /***************************************************************/
0010.00
0011.00 DCL       VAR(&LIB)   TYPE(*CHAR)  LEN(8)
0012.00 DCL       VAR(&FILE)  TYPE(*CHAR)  LEN(8)
0013.00 DCL       VAR(&MEM)   TYPE(*CHAR)  LEN(8)
0014.00
0015.00 /***************************************************************/
0016.00 /* RENAMES THE FILE AS TEMPORARY FILE                          */
0017.00 /***************************************************************/
0018.00
0019.00              RNMOBJ     OBJ(&LIB/&MEM) OBJTYPE(*FILE) NEWOBJ(TEMP)
0020.00
0021.00 /***************************************************************/
0022.00 /* CREATES NEW FIELD DEFINITIONS (IN FRF), RECREATES DATA FILE */
0023.00 /***************************************************************/
0024.00              DLTF       FILE(&LIB/FRF)
0025.00              CRTPF      FILE(&LIB/FRF) SRCFILE(&LIB/&FILE) +
0026.00                           SRCMBR(FRF)
0027.00              CRTPF      FILE(&LIB/&MEM) SRCFILE(&LIB/&FILE) +
0028.00                           SRCMBR(&MEM)
0029.00
0030.00 /***************************************************************/
0031.00 /* COPIES THE DATA FROM THE TEMPORARY FILE TO THE NEW MEMBER   */
0032.00 /***************************************************************/
0033.00
0034.00              CPYF       FROMFILE(&LIB/TEMP) TOFILE(&LIB/&MEM) +
0035.00                           MBROPT(*REPLACE)
0036.00
0037.00 /***************************************************************/
0038.00 /* DELETES THE TEMPORARY FILE                                  */
0039.00 /***************************************************************/
0040.00
0041.00              DLTF       FILE(&LIB/TEMP)
0042.00              ENDPGM
        ****************** End of data ***************************************

F3=Exit  F4=Prompt  F5=Refresh  F9=Retrieve  F10=Cursor
F16=Repeat find     F17=Repeat change        F24=More keys
```

FIGURE 4.9

```
WORK WITH DATA IN A FILE                         Mode . . . . :  ENTRY
Format . . . . :  STUDREC___                     File . . . . :  STUDENT


LNAME:    Flintstone
FNAME:    Dino____
STREET:   15 Limestone Dr
CITY:     Bedrock___
STATE:    A_
ZIP:      _____
STUDID#:  _________
CREDITS:  ___
GRADEPT:  ___


F3=Exit              F5=Refresh            F6=Select format
F9=Insert            F10=Entry             F11=Change
```

Structural Modifications to Files

The previous changes to the file STUDENT were minor. To save the data when major structural changes are being made, an application program will usually have to be written to perform the recopying. In addition, a more complicated procedure to save and restore the data will have to be followed. However, some structural changes can still be handled with the CPYF command.

For instance, if we had changed a date field from three separate two-character fields of day, month, and year to one six-character field, a simple recopy would not have been possible. Even something as simple as a name change would prevent a copy because the CPYF command does not have the capability to convert the three fields to one field, nor can the CPYF command correlate an old field name to a new name. However, the FMTOPT (format options) parameter allows the copy to take place even if field names do not match between the two files.

Specifying FMTOPT(*NOCHK) within CPYF tells the operating system to ignore the formats of the two files and simply copy the file bit for bit to the new file. In the case of the date going from three separate fields to one field, as long as the six characters occupied the same positions in both record formats, the *NOCHK option would work. The same is true for new field names. As long as the fields share the same position within the records, the copy will be successfully completed.

The real problems arise when new fields are defined for a file. The CPYF command does have some features that enable a new field to be initialized to a set value or to drop fields that aren't included in the new file. However, these functions will help with only a small fraction of the structural changes that will occur over the lifetime of most files and databases. In many cases, an application is needed to correctly convert the data to the new structure. Most users prefer that an application program load the data rather than use a utility like DFU to enter the data by hand. In our CHGF, this would mean replacing the CPYF command with a CALL command to invoke a conversion program.

The Effect of File Modifications on Programs

As if changing a file weren't complicated enough, there are also some serious ramifications to application programs when files are modified. To grasp the problem, we'll have to explain what happens with file definitions when a program is compiled.

If a program is going to use externally defined files, all programming languages require that the file be identified in the source code. This is done because during the compiling of the program source code the compiled file definition is included in the compiled program object (Figure 4.10). If a file is changed, all programs that use the file need to be recompiled so that the new file definition is incorporated. If the program is not recompiled and a user attempts to run the program, the operating system will stop program execution and issue an error message.

The operating system can tell when a file has been changed by comparing **record format level identifiers**. When a file is created, a record format level identifier is generated. The record format level identifier is included in the file's definition, therefore, it is also in any program that uses the file. (You can display the file definition and the identifier with the DSPFD—display file definition—command or by choosing option 5, `Display`, from the `Work with Objects Using PDM` screen. You'll need to page down several screens to display the identifier as in Figure 4.11.) Recompiling a file definition generates a new file and a new identifier. When an application program that contains the old file definition is run, the operating system checks the program's file format level identifier against the current format level identifier. If the identifiers don't match, a message is sent to the program, and the program is stopped. This process is called **level checking**.

FIGURE 4.10

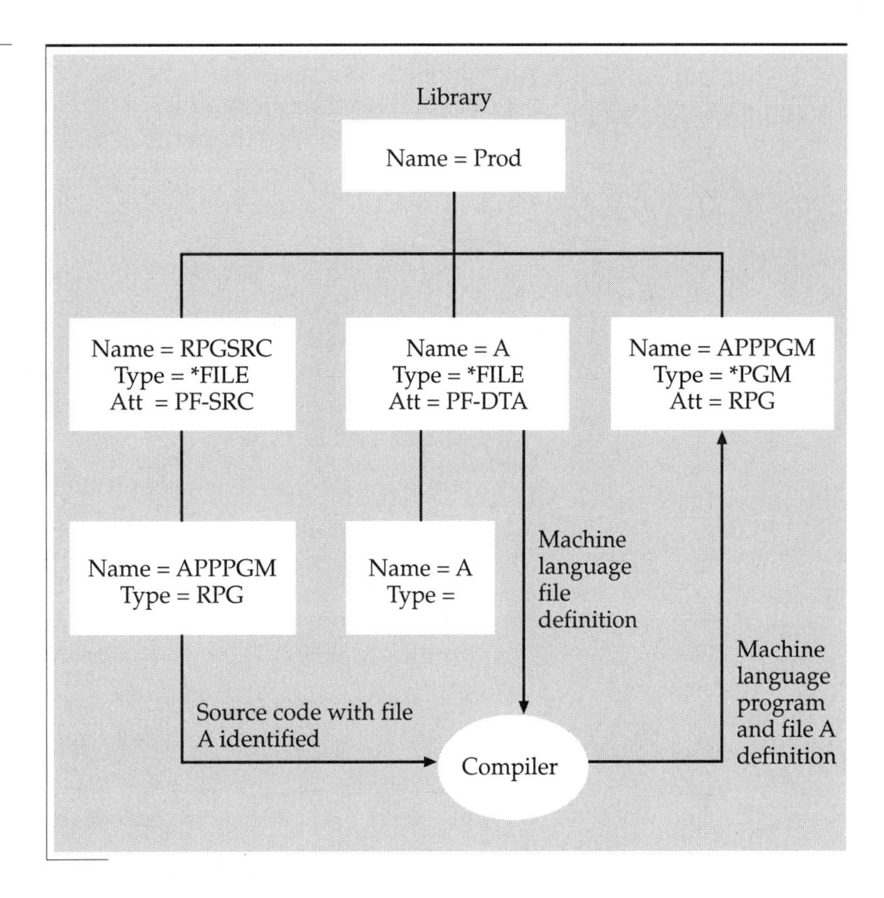

FIGURE 4.11

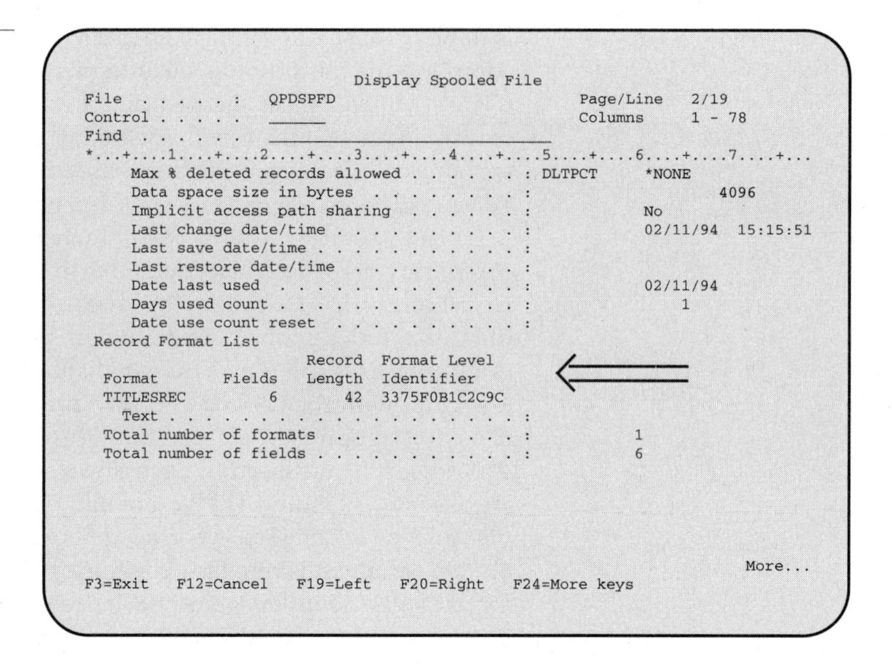

```
                                 Display Spooled File
File  . . . . . :   QPDSPFD                                  Page/Line    2/19
Control . . . . .   ______                                   Columns      1 - 78
Find  . . . . . .   ____________________________
*...+....1....+....2....+....3....+....4....+....5....+....6....+....7....+...
    Max % deleted records allowed . . . . . . . : DLTPCT      *NONE
    Data space size in bytes  . . . . . . . . . :                      4096
    Implicit access path sharing  . . . . . . . :             No
    Last change date/time . . . . . . . . . . . :             02/11/94  15:15:51
    Last save date/time . . . . . . . . . . . . :
    Last restore date/time  . . . . . . . . . . :
    Date last used  . . . . . . . . . . . . . . :             02/11/94
    Days used count . . . . . . . . . . . . . . :                 1
    Date use count reset  . . . . . . . . . . . :
Record Format List
                        Record  Format Level
 Format       Fields    Length  Identifier
 TITLESREC         6        42  3375F0B1C2C9C
   Text . . . . . . . . . . . . . . . . . . . . :
 Total number of formats  . . . . . . . . . . . :             1
 Total number of fields . . . . . . . . . . . . :             6

                                                                          More...
F3=Exit   F12=Cancel   F19=Left   F20=Right   F24=More keys
```

Since level checking is done whenever an application program is run, any program that uses a changed file must be recompiled. If there are hundreds of programs, how can the programmer find all the programs that use a particular file?

Fortunately, changing files is a common event. The AS/400 developers have foreseen the need to find all the programs that use a particular file and have supplied the CL command FNDSTRPDM (find string using PDM) to provide this function and more. The programmer specifies a character string, such as a data physical filename, and a source physical file to be searched. When the command is executed, all the source members within that physical file that contain the filename will be located. FNDSTRPDM also allows the programmer to specify functions to take place when each source member is found. These functions include

Printing the source member names

Automatically recompiling the members

Starting an SEU edit session for each member

For instance, assume two programs, DEANSLIST and ROSTER, access the file STUDENT. If the following command were submitted:

```
FNDSTRPDM STRING(STUDENT) FILE(MYLIBXX/CLSRC) MBR(*ALL)
          OPTION(*CMPL) PRTMBRLIST(*YES)
```

a report would be generated that lists the two source code members (Figure 4.12), and both source code members would be recompiled.

FIGURE 4.12

```
                              Display Spooled File
File . . . . . :   QPUOPRTF                          Page/Line   1/2
Control . . . . .                                    Columns     1 - 78
Find  . . . . . .
*...+....1....+....2....+....3....+....4....+....5....+....6....+....7....+...
5738PW1 V2R2M0  920925                 Programming Development Manager - Member
File  . . . . . . . . :   CLSRC
  Library . . . . . . :     MYLIBXX
Member  . . . . . . . :   *ALL
Type  . . . . . . . . :   *ALL
Find  . . . . . . . . :   STUDENT
From column . . . . . :   1
To column . . . . . . :   *RCDLEN
Kind of match . . . . :   2       1=Same case, 2=Ignore case
Number of matches . . :   2
                          Creation  Last Changed                   Deleted
 Member      Type         Date      Date      Time      Records  Records  Text
 ----------  ----------   --------  --------  --------  -------  -------  -----
 DEANSLIST   CLP          03/30/94  05/13/95  16:49:56  0000008  0000000
 ROSTER      CLP          04/23/94  02/05/95  13:18:28  0000011  0000000
                                        * * * * *   E N D   O F   L I S T I N G
```

Structural changes to files will also affect the CHGF in another, more subtle way. We talked about the need for a conversion program to replace the CPYF command in CHGF. This conversion program must access both the TEMP file and the file being changed. Therefore, it must also contain the correct level identifier when it is called from CHGF. Notice that CHGF recompiles the file definition of the changed file. This means that the file will have a new level identifier. When our conversion program attempts to copy the data from the TEMP file to the new file, the operating system will perform a level check. Since the conversion program does not contain the new level identifier, the operating system will stop the program from executing. To get the new level identifier into the conversion program, the conversion program must also be recompiled. The best way to ensure that we have the correct level identifier is to recompile the conversion program just before we call it. So, in addition to replacing the CPYF statement with a conversion program, we need to insert the CL command to recompile the conversion program's source code member.

Summary

DDS has many capabilities besides simply defining records and fields. This chapter demonstrated how edits can be specified for fields. These edits, however, do not affect the physical file. Field edits will be picked up by screen fields that use the database field as the basis of their definition.

Changing an already existing file with data is also more complicated than it first appears. Any changes to a file definition require a recompile. Recompiling deletes the old file definition and any members within the file. To preserve existing data, a procedure for temporarily copying and storing the data must be followed. With CL, a utility program can be created to automate most of this process and thereby decrease the chances of errors when making changes.

The CL commands available to help make file changes, however, are limited. Some simple changes (such as changing a field name) can be handled through the CPYF command's FMTOPT parameter, but any complex file restructuring will require an application program to transfer the data to the newly created file.

File changes can also affect application programs. During program compilation, file definitions are incorporated into the program. If major changes are made to a file definition, all application programs using the file must be recompiled to include the new definition. If the programs are not recompiled, the system will stop execution when it performs a level check. The CL command FNDSTRPDM can be used to both locate the affected programs and recompile the source code members.

EXERCISE

There were several errors with the data entered in the last chapters' exercise. We will follow the procedure laid out in this chapter to correct the data and change the file definition (to help prevent any future errors). To change the file definition, we will also create and run the file modification program described in the chapter.

1. Correct the data in PRODUCT (entered during the previous chapter's exercise) by changing serial number 12's

   STATUS to A

   TNUM to 2

2. Change the DDS in FRF by making the field STATUS mandatory fill.

   Make the following fields mandatory entry:

   TNUM

   TNAME

   TYPE

   MEDIA

   SNUM

   Create edits such that the following fields can contain only the specified values:

   STATUS can have values of only A or O.

RENTNUM and RPRICE can have values only greater than or equal to zero.

SPRICE can have values only greater than zero.

3. Create a new source physical file called CLSRC within library MYLIBXX.
4. Create a new member called CHGF with a type of CLP in CLSRC.
5. Enter the CL program in Figure 4.8 into member CHGF.
6. Compile member CHGF.
7. Execute CHGF for the PRODUCT and TITLES files by issuing the following commands:

```
CALL MYLIBXX/CHGF ('MYLIBXX' 'DDSSRC' 'PRODUCT')

CALL MYLIBXX/CHGF ('MYLIBXX' 'DDSSRC' 'TITLES')
```

8. Verify that the modifications were made by trying to enter the following data into the TITLE file from a DFU entry screen:

TNUM	7
TNAME	Sonic
TYPE	Game
MEDIA	CRT
RPRICE	0
SPRICE	0

Try to enter the following data for the PRODUCT file:

SNUM	13
TNUM	
STATUS	R
RENT#	70

9. Enter the following data into TITLES:

TNUM	7	8
TNAME	Popcorn	Jujubes
TYPE	CONSUMABLE	CONSUMABLE
MEDIA	X	X
RPRICE		
SPRICE	275	150

PROGRAMMING EXERCISE

There have been some changes in our customer's business. The video store will sell candy and popcorn, as well as offer VCRs for rental. This will necessitate some modifications to our files.

The term TITLE is no longer appropriate for all the items that are sold and rented. We need to make the following changes to the DDS for the FRF, PRODUCT, and TITLES files:

Change the field names of our TNUM and TNAME to INUM and INAME (the I standing for ITEM).

Change the TEXT definitions for the fields.

The new items are not videos, therefore the field MEDIA should no longer be a mandatory entry field.

Rename the file TITLES and the source member TITLES to ITEM.

Another change in business is that the new items don't have individual serialized products. For instance, each candy bar does not have a unique serial number. Therefore, a new field in the ITEM file will be SERIAL. SERIAL indicates whether a particular item has a serialized product or not. SERIAL is a mandatory fill field and can have only a value of Y or N.

Change FRF and ITEM to add the new field SERIAL and specify the correct edits and audits.

Because the names of the fields are being modified, the copy command in CHGF will not be able to recopy the data from the temporary file back to the new file. Therefore, to change the PRODUCT file, we will have to

Change the copy command in CHGF to include the value *NOCHK for the FMTOPT parameter

Because a new field is being added to ITEM, a high-level language (for example, RPG, C, COBOL) program will have to be created that will

- Read each ITEM record in the temporary file
- Read the file PRODUCT to see if a product record exists for the ITEM being copied
- If no PRODUCT record exists, set the new field SERIAL to N, else set SERIAL to Y
- Write each field's content to the correct field in the new ITEM file

The pseudocode for the conversion program is as follows:

Read TEMP file

Do while TEMP read is successful

Move TEMP.TNUM to ITEM.INUM

Move TEMP.TNAME to ITEM.INAME

Move TEMP.TYPE to ITEM.TYPE

Move TEMP.MEDIA to ITEM.MEDIA

Move TEMP.RPRICE to ITEM.RPRICE

Move TEMP.SPRICE to ITEM.SPRICE

Move 'N' to ITEM.SERIAL

Read PRODUCT file

Do while PRODUCT read is successful and ITEM.SERIAL = 'N'

If PRODUCT.INUM = ITEM.INUM

THEN Move 'Y' to ITEM.SERIAL

Else Read PRODUCT file

Enddo

Write ITEM

Read TEMP

Enddo

There are a couple of complications for the new conversion program and our original CHGF program.

1. Because the conversion program reads the file TEMP, TEMP must already exist to successfully compile the conversion source code. You will have to create a TEMP file in order to compile the conversion program source code and test the conversion program. Then, before running the CHGF program, the TEMP file will have to be deleted so that the change file program can execute.
2. Because the change file program recompiles the data file definition, a new format level identifier will be generated for the ITEM file. This means the conversion program will also have to be recompiled so that the format level identifier in the conversion program will match the ITEM file's format level identifier when the level check is performed. The CL command to recompile the conversion program source code (CRTRPGPGM, CRTCBLPGM, and so on) has to be inserted into CHGF before the CALL of the conversion program.
3. Because different conversion programs need to be run (depending on the file being updated), the CL program needs two new parameters passed. These two parameters will identify

   The source physical file containing the conversion program source code (&PGMSPF)

   The conversion program/member name (&PGMNME)

   The CRTXXXPGM (compile) and CALL commands will use these program variables to compile the correct program source code member and run the correct program.

After the conversion program has been created and tested, perform the following steps:

1. Using DFU, update the ITEM file by erasing the MEDIA field data for items 7 and 8. (Since these items were entered when MEDIA was a mandatory entry field, "dummy" information—an X—was supplied so that the records could be added to the file.)
2. Change the copy command in CHGF to include FMTOPT(*NOCHK), and recompile CHGF.
3. Run the CHGF program for the file PRODUCT.

4. Create a new CL member COMCHGF (for complex change file) in file CLSRC within library MYLIBXX.
5. Copy the CL source code from CHGF into COMCHGF.
6. Change the CL source as follows:
   a. Add DCL statements for &PGMSPF and &PGMNME.
   b. Add &PGMSPF and &PGMNME to the parameter statement at the beginning of the program.
   c. Replace the copy command in COMCHGF with a CALL command that invokes the application program &PGMNME.
   d. Add the appropriate CRTXXXPGM command (CRTRPGPGM, CRTCBLPGM, and so on) just before the CALL command that invokes the conversion program. Don't forget to use the variables &PGMSPF and &PGMNME.
7. Recompile COMCHGF, and run COMCHGF for ITEM. (Remember to also pass the conversion program name and the name of the source physical file that holds the conversion program's source code.)
8. Verify that the program ran correctly by starting DFU for each file. The screen field names should reflect the new names, all the data should be intact, and the new field SERIAL should be displayed with a value of Y or N.

REVIEW QUESTIONS

1. What is an edit?
2. What is data independence?
3. Why must recompiling be performed in order to change a file definition?
4. Do DDS edit keywords modify file definitions?
5. What function does the copy command perform when changing a file definition?
6. What limitations does the copy command have that will require an application program to be written for some file modifications?
7. What is level checking?
8. What does the command FNDSTRPDM do, and how does it help with file modifications?

DISCUSSION QUESTIONS

1. Explain why recompiling complicates the modification of already existing files.
2. Explain the advantages and limitations of the DDS editing keywords—CHECK, COMP, and RANGE.
3. How does DDS support data independence?

File Organization

5

Overview

This chapter explores several different methods of organizing and accessing data within a file. After explaining generally how each method works, we will demonstrate how to specify these with DDS and explore how the AS/400 implements the methods through internal objects called access paths. We will then change an existing file's organization and create a procedure to ensure all the data is preserved. Finally, we will discuss the different methods to handle deleted records and reclaim space, and we will demonstrate how to specify these methods on the AS/400.

After finishing this chapter, you will understand

- File organization and access methods
- Primary and secondary keys
- Sequential, indexed sequential, and random organizations
- Relative record numbers
- Access paths
- Arrival sequence
- Multilevel indices
- Dynamic space reclamation versus reorganization

After finishing this chapter, you will be able to

- Define a key field using DDS
- Create a hashing routine
- Specify a file's space reclamation method
- Reorganize a file

File Organization and Access

The manner in which data records are stored within a file is called the file's organization. There are three types of file organization: **sequential**, **indexed sequential**, and **random**. Each organization stores data records differently and has a unique procedure for accessing the data records. To understand the advantages and disadvantages of each organization method, the access procedure needs to be fully understood. The key to access procedures is understanding the way storage devices physically access the storage media and how individual records are identified.

Storage devices physically access the storage media either directly or sequentially. **Direct access** means the storage device can go directly to any storage location and read the information stored there. **Sequential access** means the storage device must go through all storage locations that physically precede the storage location being sought.

The difference between the two access methods is very similar to the difference between how a tape deck and a CD player play a particular song. If your stereo system's "music storage device" is a tape deck (bet you've never heard a tape deck called that before), the tape deck has to fast forward through any preceding songs to get to your favorite Box Car Willy tune. The tape deck accesses the storage media sequentially. However, if you're lucky enough to own the CD box set of Willy's greatest hits, the CD player can access the song directly. Access to the song is greatly sped up because the preceding songs are bypassed. CD players can also access the media sequentially, playing the songs in the order they are on the CD. The tape player, however, is limited to accessing the songs sequentially.

The same procedures are followed by computer disk and tape devices to access data records. However, when accessing a particular data record, there needs to be a way to identify that record. The CD player identifies each song with a number. Computers can also use this method, but database developers have given this number the impressive title of **relative record number**. Each record is given a number based on its relative position within the file. (The first record in a file has a relative record number equal to one, the second record's relative record number is two, and so on.)

Relative record numbers may work fine for CDs with small numbers of songs, but with data files that contain thousands or millions of records, it is very difficult to keep track of each record's individual record number. A more common method of identifying records is with a **primary key**. A primary key is a field (or collection of fields) whose value is unique for each record. For instance, in a file that contains a record for each student at a school, the social security number field could serve as the file's primary key. Since each student (and therefore each record) has a unique value for social security number, social security number is a good field for identification. However, if the school has foreign students (who do not have social security numbers), then social security number would not work. In that case, the multiple fields of name and phone number could be used to uniquely identify each student. (The values of these fields together would uniquely identify each record as long as there weren't two phoneless students with the same name or two same-named students sharing a phone.) These two fields, concatenated together, would be the primary key for the file.

Files can also have **secondary keys**. These fields do not necessarily have a unique value for each record. For instance, the student file could have the field "eye color" as a secondary key. Searching the file based on a particular eye color (such as brown) will not result in finding a single record. The search would return multiple student records that have a value of brown. Therefore, nonunique secondary keys cannot be used to locate a particular record.

Sequential File Organization

Sequential files store data records one after another in key order. Access to a sequential file is limited to the sequential access method, meaning that each record is processed in the order it is in the file. Processing an entire sequential file is like listening to a song. The song's notes are recorded (stored) in sequential order by time. When a music lover listens to the song, the notes are replayed (processed) in sequential order.

Sequential files are processed in the same manner. Unlike music, however, computer users often want to process data in a different order. For instance, to generate the dean's list, it would be easiest if the student file were in grade point order. However, when mailing out grades, the school wants to generate the grade reports in student zip code order because the post office gives a discount for presorted mass mailings. A sequential file can support access to the file in only one key order. This is one reason sequential organization is not always used.

The real drawback to sequential organization is its access method for retrieving a particular record. Many applications rely on fast retrieval of individual records. Keyed sequential files allow each record to be uniquely identified; however, retrieving a particular record means that each record is read (in sequential order) and the key field's value is checked. When the key value matches the value being searched for, the computer knows it has the correct record. For files of any magnitude, this is a very slow method to retrieve a single record.

Sequential files also do not require that a key be defined. Sequential files can be nonkeyed. Our song is an example of a nonkeyed file. The notes are stored in order by time, but the actual time is not stored with the note. (Telling the difference between two B-flats played at different times is impossible.)

Data records can also be organized by time, and the time does not have to be recorded. This type of file is called a nonkeyed sequential file. Identifying a particular record, like the note, is not possible. Until now, this is the type of file we have been using in our examples and you have been creating in the exercises.

Indexed Sequential Files

The characteristics of an indexed sequential file are

Each record contains a unique value for the key.

Records are grouped into blocks.

Each block contains records for a certain range of key values.

Within the block, the records are stored sequentially in key order.

Blocks do not have to be in key order.

For instance, the student file mentioned earlier could be grouped into blocks of 100 records each. The first 100 names (by name and phone number) would be in one block, the second 100 names would be in another block, and so on. The first 100 names, however, do not have to be stored in the first 100 locations within the file (Figure 5.1). Notice how each group of 100 records contains a certain range of last names and that the records are in order by name and phone number within that group.

FIGURE 5.1

Data Record #	Name	Phone	Other Student Fields
1	NETTLES, DIANE	454-8226	other student data
2	NETTLES, DIANE	562-7861	: : :
:	: :	: :	: : :
:	: :	: :	: : :
100	NEWCOMB, JEAN	982-0253	: : :
101	FOUTS, JOHN	653-4472	: : :
102	FOUTZ, ANNA	371-2901	: : :
:	: :	: :	: : :
:	: :	: :	: : :
200	FRALEY, TERRENCE	545-3672	: : :
201	AARON, ARTHUR	371-8823	: : :
202	AARON, BETTY	371-8823	: : :
203	AARON, RALPH	562-1986	: : :
204	ABARNO, WENDY	989-1648	: : :
205	ABBEY, ROBERTA	732-3110	: : :
:	: :	: :	: : :
:	: :	: :	: : :
300	ABERNATHY, THOMAS	260-2243	: : :
:	: :	: :	: : :
:	: :	: :	: : :
27101	ZINKL, CAROL	223-5096	: : :
27102	ZINO, FREDERICK	452-0987	: : :
:	: :	: :	: : :
:	: :	: :	: : :
27200	ZYUNG, ERIC	232-6529	: : :
:	: :	: :	: : :
79901	FRALEY, VICTOR	545-3672	: : :
:	: :	: :	: : :
79937	FRANKEN, AL	545-3672	: : :
:	: :	: :	: : :
80000	FRASER, MARY	887-3452	: : :

You're probably wondering why anyone would ever store information in this manner. The secret (and real power) of this organization is the index. An index is a file that contains an index record for each block of data records. The index record contains

The highest key value contained within the block

The starting storage location/address of the block

The index records are **stored in key order**. For the data in Figure 5.1, the index records would look like Figure 5.2.

Notice that there are only 800 index records. Since each index record represents one block of 100 data records, there are only one hundredth as many index records as there are data records. Since the index is much smaller, searching the entire index would take less time than searching all the data records.

FIGURE 5.2

Index Record #	Name	Phone	Block Storage Location
1	ABERNATHY, THOMAS	260-2243	201
:	: :	: :	:
:	: :	: :	:
253	FRALEY, TERRENCE	545-3672	101
254	FRASER, MARY	887-3452	79001
:	: :	: :	:
:	: :	: :	:
616	NEWCOMB, JEAN	982-0253	1
:	: :	: :	:
:	: :	: :	:
800	ZYUNG, ERIC	232-6529	27101

In addition, the index contains only the key field(s) and the storage location. None of the other student data is included in the index; therefore, index records are much smaller than the data records. Because of the difference in size, searching 100 index records is much faster than searching 100 data records. These two size facts (the number of records and record length) are particularly important in regard to access time in indexed sequential files.

When accessing an indexed sequential file for a particular record, the first step is to search the index sequentially. Each index record's key value is checked against the key value being searched for. When the index value is greater than the value being searched for, the block that contains the data record has been found. The system then goes directly to the block (as specified by the storage location in the index record) and sequentially reads each data record in the block, looking for the correct key value.

As an example, let's look at the procedure that would be followed to find the student Al Franken. The system would begin searching the index and read 254 index records before finally finding Mary

Fraser in an index record. The computer can recognize that Fraser comes after Franken in the alphabet; therefore, the computer knows that the Al Franken data record is stored in the block of data records that begins at storage location 79901 (the storage location designated in the Mary Fraser index record). The system then goes directly to location 79901 and reads the data records one at a time until it locates the Al Franken record in storage location 79937.

In locating the Franken record, the system had to read 254 index records and 37 data records. This is considerably fewer records than if the system had tried to find the Al Franken record with a sequential search of all the data records. With a sequential search, the system would have read 79,937 data records compared to the 37 data records and 254 index records that were read when searching with the index.

Imagine the difference in time needed to search using the two methods. On average, a sequential search for a particular record would require reading 40,000 data records (one half the total number of records). Using indexed sequential organization would result in reading an average of 400 index records (half the number of index records) and 50 data records (half the number of data records in each block). Since index records are smaller than data records, the amount of data searched with a sequential student file is over 100 times greater than with an indexed sequential file. (If you are thinking "big deal," next time you're getting money at an ATM, ask yourself if you'd like to wait 100 times longer for the computer to find your account balance.)

Indexed sequential, of course, has some disadvantages. First, because it requires that the storage device be able to go to the block directly, indexed sequential files cannot be stored on tape. Tape devices support only sequential access. Second, indexed sequential files take up more space. Not only is storage space required for the data, but extra space is required for the index. A good analogy is that organizing a file indexed sequentially is like putting shelves in a closet. Without shelves (sequential organization), you can fit 40 boxes in the closet, but getting at most of the boxes (the ones not on top and in front) is a real ordeal. With shelves (indexed sequential), you can fit only 36 boxes, but getting at the boxes is faster and easier. In file organizations, there is always a tradeoff between storage space and access time. This is not the last time we'll be faced with this dilemma.

Another feature of indexed sequential organization is that the entire file can still be processed sequentially by key. To process the indexed sequential file in key order, the system would simply read the first index record, go directly to the storage location indicated, and process the 100 data records stored there. The system would then read the second index record, go to the location specified, and process the 100 records there. This would continue for all 800 index records and all 80,000 data records.

Though indexed sequential files provide the capability to process an entire file in key order, processing data in an indexed sequential file this way would be slower than if the data was simply in a sequential file. Here is another tradeoff between sequential and indexed sequential organizations. Sequential processing of a file will be slower with indexed sequential files, but individual record retrieval will be much faster.

Random Organization

Random organization also provides fast retrieval of individual records. However, it does not use an index to record the storage location of data. Rather, random organization uses an algorithm to calculate a storage address and then places the data in that location. When there is a request for a particular record, the algorithm is performed, and the resulting location is accessed directly.

As a simple example, let's use a company's employee file. Each employee record is 80 bytes in length and has a primary key of employee number. Employee number is a unique four-digit number ranging from 0000 to 9999. A simple algorithm that could be used would be to multiply the employee number by 80. This would yield the relative byte address of the record within the file. In other words, employee number 0000 would result in the relative byte address of 0 (0000 * 80), meaning that this record will be placed in the first 80 bytes of the file. We then need to take the starting address of the file and add this to the relative byte address to give us the storage location. For our example, if the file started at storage location 72345, we would add our relative byte location of 0, which would result in storage location 72345. For employee 9999, the algorithm would result in storage location 872265 ((9999 * 80) + 72345). Figure 5.3 shows some of the records and their locations.

When a request for a particular employee record is made, the algorithm is performed against the employee number, and the resulting address is read directly by the storage device. For instance, a request for employee 1111 would result in storage location 161225. The storage device would go directly to that location and retrieve the data.

FIGURE 5.3

Storage Location	Employee Number	Other Employee Fields
72345	0000	employee 0000 data
72425		
72505	0002	employee 0002 data
72585		
: :	: :	: : :
: :	: :	: : :
161225	1111	employee 1111 data
: :	: :	: : :
: :	: :	: : :
872265	9999	employee 9999 data

The advantage to random organization is that, theoretically, no unnecessary data records are read. With index sequential organization, to find a particular record, any preceding data records in the block had to be read. With random organization, all unnecessary reads are eliminated because a storage address is generated by the algorithm. Another advantage is that no extra space is needed for an index.

Access to a record within a random file is not, however, instantaneous. There is some delay when accessing a particular record because of the time needed to perform the algorithm that yields the storage location. However, usually much less time is spent calculating than would be spent sequentially searching an index and data records.

There are, however, some problems with using a calculation to generate a storage location. In our employee file example, the amount of space allocated to the employee file was 800,000 bytes. (We needed room for 10,000 possible employee records of 80 bytes each.) What if our company had only 500 employees? We would be using only 40,000 out of the allocated 800,000 bytes, a utilization rate of only 5 percent! (In Figure 5.3, notice that the second and fourth records are blank, meaning that there are no employee numbers 1 and 3.) Our algorithm is obviously not very efficient because it requires too many empty record locations.

Hashing Routines

Space utilization can be improved by using a more complicated calculation called a **hashing routine**. There are many different hashing routines. What characterizes them all is that they generate a smaller range of addresses. A classic example is the division/remainder method (also referred to as the quotient/remainder method).

With the division/remainder method, you first determine how many storage locations will be in the file; in our previous example, it was 500. You then choose the largest prime number that is less than the number of records to be stored. (Choosing a prime number results in less chance of duplicate addresses being generated.) In the case of 500, the largest prime less than 500 is 499.

The division/remainder method plays on the fact that the number of possible remainders generated by division is equal to the divisor. For instance, if you divide any number by 2, there are only two possible remainders, 0 or 1. Dividing any number by 3 will result in only three possible remainders, 0, 1, or 2. Dividing by 4 will result in only four possible remainders, 0, 1, 2, or 3. Continuing this will result in the conclusion that dividing by 499 will result in 499 possible remainders ranging from 0 to 498.

As applied to the employee file example, this means that any employee number divided by 499 will result in a number from 0 to 498. This result plus 1 could be used as a relative record number for the employee record. (We need to add 1 in case the division results in a 0 remainder; there is no 0 relative record location. For the remainder of the chapter, we will forgo calculating the byte offset within the file and simply reference storage locations by the relative record number. Most computers support referencing records by relative record number.)

From our example, employee number 9999 would be stored in location 20. (9999 divided by 499 yields a remainder of 19. We then add 1 to get the relative record number of 20.) Employee 1111 would be stored in location 114. Figure 5.4 shows a look at storage and where some employee records would be placed.

FIGURE 5.4

Relative Record #	Employee Number	Other Employee Fields
1	0000	employee 0000 data
2	6987	employee 6987 data
3	0002	employee 0002 data
4	4494	employee 4494 data
:	: :	: : :
:	: :	: : :
19	3511	employee 3511 data
20	9999	employee 9999 data
21	8004	employee 8004 data
:	: :	: : :
:	: :	: : :
114	1111	employee 1111 data
:	: :	: : :
:	: :	: : :
499	1995	employee 1995 data

Figure 5.4 also illustrates why random storage got its name. After looking at the records in storage, most people would say that there is no organization and that the records are stored randomly.

There are a couple of problems with our new hashing routine. For instance, we allocated only 499 locations for our 500 employee records. Right away we know we are going to need at least one more storage location. A second problem is what to do if hashing two employee numbers result in the same location? When this happens, it is called a collision, and the two employee numbers are said to be synonyms.

Handling Collisions and Synonyms

One of the easiest solutions to a collision is to allocate more storage locations. For instance, for our employee file, we could allocate space for 1,000 records and divide by the largest prime number less than 1,000. Of course, allocating 1,000 records means 500 will be empty (thereby decreasing our space utilization), and collisions are still possible.

Consecutive spill (also sometimes referred to as **open addressing**) is an alternative method that simply places the record in the next empty storage location. For instance, if we tried to store employee number 8483 in its proper location of relative record number 1, we wouldn't be able to because employee number 0000 is already there. However, if locations 5 and 7 were empty (as in Figure 5.5), consecutive spill would dictate to search each succeeding storage location until an empty one was found—in this case, location 5. Employee record 8483 would then be written to location 5. Later, if another record also hashed out to location 1, it would be placed in the next empty location, location 7.

FIGURE 5.5

Relative Record #	Employee Number	Other Employee Fields
1	0000	employee 0000 data
2	6987	employee 6987 data
3	0002	employee 0002 data
4	4494	employee 4494 data
5		
6	3997	employee 3997 data
7		
:	: :	: : :
:	: :	: : :
:	: :	: : :
499	1995	employee 1995 data

The problem with consecutive spill is that when accessing a record, more than one data record may have to be read to find the correct record. One of the alleged advantages of random organization was that the only delay in retrieving a record was the time it took to calculate the storage location. Yet, when a hashing routing is employed to minimize unused space, there can be an added sequential search of data records after the initial location is accessed. With files that have very high space utilization, this can become a performance problem.

There are, of course, other ways to handle this **overflow** condition. One method is to set up an overflow area within the file. For instance, we could expand our employee file to 550 locations and consider locations 500 through 550 the overflow area. Whenever there is a collision, the synonym would be written to the first available space in the overflow area. When accessing the file, if hashing produced a location that did not contain the sought-after record, the overflow area would be searched sequentially.

Of course, this solution also adds extra space to our simple and efficient random file. (The tradeoff between space and performance once again rears its ugly head.) Allocating more space is a waste of valuable system resources, but without the extra space, performance suffers. These problems with random organization tend to "muddy the water" when trying to decide how to organize your files. If extra empty space is needed to make random files work, why not use index sequential organization?

To further discourage anyone from adopting random file organization, most computer systems do not fully support random organization. They usually offer only direct access by relative record number. The programmer is responsible for the hashing routine and collision resolution. The AS/400 is not an exception.

AS/400 Arrival Sequence

The explanations just given of three file organizations and their associated access procedures were generic. Each operating system or file management system uniquely implements these organizations and access procedures. In addition, they normally have their own naming conventions. For instance, the AS/400 supports access to files in **arrival sequence** order. In other words, a user or program can access records in the order in which they arrived into (were written to) a file. As for access, arrival sequence is similar to sequential access. For instance, look back at Figure 2.4. The records were written to the file in the order shown. The DSPPFM command accessed and displayed the records in the order they were written. If another record were written to the file, it would appear after the fifth record.

The AS/400 does not, however, store the records in arrival order. The AS/400 has sophisticated algorithms that calculate the most efficient utilization of available space and may even scatter records across physical storage devices. Since the records are not physically stored in arrival sequence order, the question is how does the AS/400 provide arrival sequence access?

Access to all files is provided through an **access path.** You can think of the access path as an index. (The exact contents of the access path, however, is proprietary information that IBM does not divulge. All the following examples are meant to illustrate access path functions and demonstrate how access path characteristics, such as size, can be affected by the functions provided. In addition, all examples of the content and workings of access paths are very elementary and by no means the most efficient way they could be implemented.) For instance, an arrival sequence access path, which supports only sequential access to a file, could simply consist of a list of storage locations. If the five records in Figure 2.4 were stored in locations A, B, C, D, and E, the access path could simply consist of a list of the storage locations as follows:

Arrival Sequence
Access Path

A
B
C
D
E

If two new records were added to the file and stored in locations P and J, the access path would be updated as follows:

Arrival Sequence
Access Path

A
B
C
D
E
P
J

In the case of arrival sequence access paths, only a list of the storage locations in arrival order would be necessary. When accessing the file, the access path would be searched sequentially and the records read directly. As the file is processed, the operating system keeps track of various file information such as location of the data records, the last record processed, and updates. All this various information is stored in internal objects that the user cannot access. These internal objects are referenced by the data physical file object. In Chapter 3, we said that the data physical file object contained the machine-language definition of the data. This was a small white lie. In actuality, the data physical file acts as an index to

Data member information (like field definitions)

The access path

File-processing control information

Position within the file

This type of information is pretty standard. Even long-established operating systems like MVS (for mainframes) use DSCBs (data set control blocks) and VTOCs (volume table of contents) to keep track of file-processing information. The secret, of course, is exactly what information is stored and how it is used to enhance access. And, as mentioned, IBM isn't talking.

Accessing Records Using Arrival Sequence Access Paths

An arrival sequence access path allows users to access records in sequential order or retrieve individual records by relative record number. All programming languages provide commands to access files in arrival sequence order. For instance, in RPG, the CHAIN command provides sequential access. In addition, RPG supports direct access by relative record number. (To retrieve by relative record number, the programmer must specify a program variable name with the RECNO option on the file description specification. The program variable is then set to the desired record number, and the CHAIN command is used.)

Retrieving a record for a specific key value (using an arrival sequence access path) can be done only by either sequentially searching the records or using a hashing routine to yield a relative record number. In other words, to access a specific record, you can either read each record (in arrival sequence order) and check for the value or derive the relative record number through a hashing routine and access the record directly. In most cases, a sequential search will take too long, and implementing a hashing routine requires expensive programming and testing time. Because many applications require individual record retrieval by key, arrival sequence access paths have limited usefulness. For record retrieval by key, the AS/400 programmer will want to define a **keyed sequence access path**.

Keyed Sequence Access Paths

DDS allows users to define key fields within a record (and all programming languages provide commands to access records by value.) When the file's source code is compiled, a keyed sequence access path (KSAP) is created. This access path is different from the arrival sequence access path in several important ways.

First, the keyed sequence access path (KSAP) allows users to access the records in both arrival sequence and keyed sequence. In addition, it allows the user to retrieve individual records according to key value. The complexity of an index to provide all these functions is best shown through a multilevel index example.

Multilevel Index

Sometimes files get so large that even the time to access the index becomes a problem. For example, say the census bureau had a file containing a record for each person in the United States (250 million records). Even if the index was only one hundredth the size of the data file, the index would contain 2.5 million records. A search of the index would on average require reading 1.25 million index records.

A way to decrease the number of index records read is to build an index for the index. For simplicity sake, assume that the original index for the file contained 25 index records as shown in Figure 5.6.

FIGURE 5.6

Index Record Storage Location	Name	Block Storage Location
101	AZZOR, FRANK	78901
102	BZYTINE, GENA	54378
103	CZXOT, PAULA	88932
104	DZZATI, CARLA	23178
105	EZZEL, WAYNE	15490
:	: :	:
110	JYUWEL, DENISE	:
:	: :	:
115	OZZOLLO, REKIA	:
:	: :	:
120	TZITIS, INEZ	:
:	: :	:
123	WZURTY, ZENO	19648
124	YZONI, LENARD	34258
125	ZZUNG, KRIS	45404

On average, 13 index records would be read for any record retrieval. To decrease the number of index records read, a higher level index could be built. The higher level index would look like Figure 5.7.

FIGURE 5.7

Index Record Storage Location	Name	Lower Level Index Storage Location
11	EZZEL,WAYNE	101
12	JYUWEL, DENISE	106
13	OZZOLLO, REKIA	111
14	TZITIS, INEZ	116
15	ZZUNG, KRIS	121

When a particular record is sought, the higher level index would be searched first. On average, three records would be read. The lower level index would then be accessed, and on average three lower level index records would be read. The two level index cuts the number of index records read from 13 to 6. Again, there is an increase in space used due to the second level of the index, but we have cut our number of reads in half and increased our index size by only 20 percent. (There are now a total of 30 index records versus 25 with the single level index.)

Multilevel indices can also be used to change the access order. Let's apply a multilevel index to the arrival sequence access path. We will build an index over the arrival sequence access path, and that index will allow access according to a key field. Let's take the earlier simpler example, as shown in Figure 5.8.

FIGURE 5.8

Storage Location	Data Records		
A	This was the first record entered	1	%
B	This was the second record entered	2	$
C	This was the third record entered	3	!
D	This was the fourth record entered	4	+
E	This was the fifth record entered	5	-
:	: : : : : :	:	:
J	This was the seventh record entered	7	)
:	: : : : : :	:	:
P	This was the sixth record entered	6	(

If the data was stored as in Figure 5.8, the arrival sequence access path would look as shown in Figure 5.9.

FIGURE 5.9

Storage Location	Arrival Sequence Access Path Records
1001	A
1002	B
1003	C
1004	D
1005	E
1006	P
1007	J

If we were to define the fourth word in each sentence as the key of the file, the logical order would be as shown in Figure 5.10.

FIGURE 5.10

Storage Location	Data Records		
E	This was the fifth record entered	5	-
A	This was the first record entered	1	%
D	This was the fourth record entered	4	+
B	This was the second record entered	2	$
J	This was the seventh record entered	7	)
P	This was the sixth record entered	6	(
C	This was the third record entered	3	!

To build a higher level index according to the key, the higher level index would contain the key field value and the location of the arrival sequence access path record. (Read the previous sentence carefully. The higher level index points to the arrival sequence access path, *not* the data record.) The higher level index would look like Figure 5.11.

FIGURE 5.11

Key Value	Arrival Sequence Record Location
fifth	1005
first	1007
fourth	1004
second	1002
seventh	1007
sixth	1006
third	1003

To retrieve a record for a particular key value (for example, sixth):

1. Search the high-level index for the key value. When the value is found, read the arrival sequence access path record location. (For the sixth record, this would be 1006.)
2. Go directly to the indicated storage location of the arrival sequence access path record (1006), and read the data record storage location. (This would be location P.)
3. Go directly to storage location P, and read the sixth data record.

To process the file in keyed order, simply read the higher level index sequentially, and perform steps 2 and 3 for each higher level index record. If a program wanted to access the file in arrival sequence, the arrival sequence access path could simply be read. This type of higher level index is also called an **indirect secondary index**. It is an index, but it does not point directly to the data records. It uses the primary index (the arrival sequence access path) to point to the data records.

Another way to look at the relationship between the access paths, data records, and the user is that the higher level index and the arrival sequence access path together are the keyed sequence access path (Figure 5.12). The user never accesses the data records directly. Users access the file either through the keyed index (which uses the arrival sequence to locate the data records), or they can process the records in arrival sequence by going through the arrival sequence access path.

FIGURE 5.12

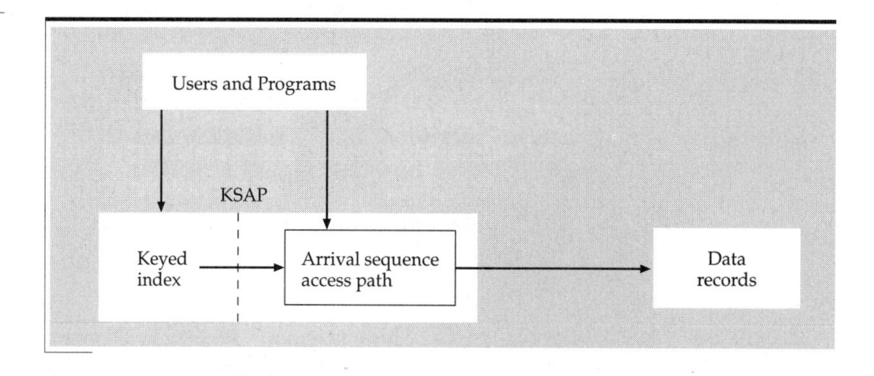

Another nice feature of the KSAP is that multiple keys can be defined for a file. As the example showed, a higher level index can be built according to any field, and creating the keyed index does not duplicate any data. The AS/400 supports multiple keyed sequenced access paths through objects called logical files, as well as with SQL views and the OPNQRYF command. (We will explore all these in detail in the next several chapters.)

Defining Keys with DDS

Defining a key with DDS is easy compared to understanding how key sequence access paths work. A key field specification is used to define a key. Key field specifications come after all field level specifications and are defined by entering a K in column 17 and the key field name in columns 19 through 28. In addition, there must be a separate field level specification already defined for the key field.

To define STUDID# as the key for the STUDENT file, add the specification on line 16 as seen in Figure 5.13.

Using a key specification alone defines the key as a secondary key. In other words, the database will allow records with duplicate key field values to be entered. To prevent duplicate records, a primary key needs to be defined. Primary keys are defined with a file level specification using the keyword UNIQUE.

A specification is interpreted as a file level specification based on its location within the DDS source code. Any specification that precedes the record and field level specifications is considered a file level specification, meaning that anything defined in that specification is true for the entire file. Entering the keyword UNIQUE (before the REF file level keyword on line 5) places it before the record level specifications. This means that every record in the file must have a unique value for the defined key. (Notice that there are no parameters required for the UNIQUE keyword.) The field STUDID# is now defined as a primary key.

To create the KSAP, we would follow the procedure developed in the previous chapter that saves the data and recompiles, in this case, only the STUDENT file definition member. No changes to FRF are needed, so FRF doesn't have to be recompiled.

FIGURE 5.13

```
 Columns . . . :    1  71           Edit                          MYLIBXX/DDSSRC
 SEU==> ____________________________________________________________ STUDENT
 FMT A* .....A*. 1 ...+... 2 ...+... 3 ...+... 4 ...+... 5 ...+... 6 ...+... 7
        *************** Beginning of data *************************************
0001.00       *
0002.00       *  THIS IS THE DDS FOR THE STUDENT FILE
0003.00       *
0004.00                                            UNIQUE
0005.00                                            REF(MYLIBXX/FRF)
0006.00                R STUDREC                   TEXT('STUDENT RECORD')
0007.00                  LNAME     R               TEXT('STUDENT LAST NAME')
0008.00                  FNAME     R               TEXT('STUDENT FIRST NAME')
0009.00                  STREET    R               TEXT('STUDENT STREET ADDR')
0010.00                  CITY      R               TEXT('STUDENT CITY')
0011.00                  STATE     R               TEXT('STUDENT STATE')
0012.00                  ZIP       R               TEXT('STUDENT ZIP CODE')
0013.00                  STUDID#   R
0014.00                  CREDITS   R
0015.00                  GRADEPT   R
0016.00                K STUDID#
       ****************** End of data ****************************************

 F3=Exit   F12=Cancel   F19=Left   F20=Right   F24=More keys
```

Using Keyed Sequence Access Paths

All programming languages provide commands that allow access by key value, and many system utilities, such as DFU and QUERY, allow users to manipulate records by key value. Another nice feature of keyed files is that they can still be accessed in arrival sequence order. As a matter of fact, you will find that the operating system functions access the files differently. Some will access by key; others will use the arrival sequence access path.

For instance, if we defined STUDID# as the key for STUDENT file and displayed the contents with the DSPPFM command, the records would appear as in Figure 5.14. Notice that the records are in arrival sequence order, not STUDID# order. The DSPPFM command accessed the records through the arrival sequence access path.

The CPYF command, on the other hand, uses the KSAP. Copying the records from STUDENT to a nonkeyed file called TEMP and then displaying TEMP with the DSPPFM command would result in Figure 5.15. Notice that the records in Figure 5.15 are in STUDID# order. This is because the copy program accessed STUDENT through the KSAP and wrote them to TEMP in the order they were retrieved from STUDENT.

Deleting Records and Space Reclamation

There is more to deleting data records from a member than one would think. The REUSEDLT parameter determines whether deleted record space will be reused when an insert is done. This parameter is defined when the file is created (the default is *NO) or can be changed with the CHGPF command. Figure 5.16 shows the REUSEDLT parameter on the `Create Physical File (CRTPF)` screen.

We can demonstrate that the space is not reclaimed by using DFU to access and delete records by relative record number. If REUSEDLT is defined as *YES, the inserted records should take the place of the

FIGURE 5.14

```
                         Display Physical File Member

 File . . . . . . :   STUDENT              Library  . . . . :   MYLIBXX
 Member . . . . . :   STUDENT              Record . . . . . :   1
 Control  . . . . .   __________           Column . . . . . :   1
 Find . . . . . . .   ________________________________________
 *...+....1....+....2....+....3....+....4....+....5....+....6...
 FlintstoneFred     11 Limestone DrBedrock   AZ88888111111111 ¤ H
 FlintstoneWilma    11 Limestone DrBedrock   AZ88888123456789   °
 Rubble     Barnard 15 Limestone DrBedrock   AZ88888999999999 ¬ .
 Rubble     Betty   15 Limestone DrBedrock   AZ88888444444444 ± ±
                           ****** END OF DATA ******




                                                                    Bottom
 F3=Exit   F12=Cancel   F19=Left   F20=Right   F24=More keys
```

FIGURE 5.15

```
                        Display Physical File Member

File . . . . . . :   TEMP                Library  . . . . :   MYLIBXX
Member . . . . . :   TEMP                Record . . . . . :   1
Control  . . . . .   __________          Column . . . . . :   1
Find . . . . . . .   _______________________________________
*...+....1....+....2....+....3....+....4....+....5....+....6...
FlintstoneFred     11 Limestone DrBedrock   AZ888888111111111 ¤ H
FlintstoneWilma    11 Limestone DrBedrock   AZ88888123456789   ·
Rubble    Betty    15 Limestone DrBedrock   AZ88888444444444 ± ±
Rubble    Barnard  15 Limestone DrBedrock   AZ88888999999999 ¬
                           ****** END OF DATA ******

                                                                    Bottom
F3=Exit    F12=Cancel    F19=Left    F20=Right    F24=More keys
```

deleted records. If the file's parameter is defined as *NO, added records should be placed at the end of file in arrival sequence order. We will use the nonkeyed file TEMP that was created in the previous section. It has been defined to not reuse deleted record space.

FIGURE 5.16

```
                       Create Physical File (CRTPF)

Type choices, press Enter.

Contiguous storage . . . . . . .   *NO_          *NO, *YES
Preferred storage unit . . . . .   *ANY__        1-255, *ANY
Records to force a write . . . .   *NONE_        Number, *NONE
Maximum file wait time . . . . .   *IMMED        Seconds, *IMMED, *CLS
Maximum record wait time . . . .   60____        Seconds, *NOMAX, *IMMED
Share open data path . . . . . .   *NO_          *NO, *YES
Max % deleted records allowed  .   *NONE_        1-100, *NONE
Reuse deleted records  . . . . .   *NO_          *YES, *NO
Sort sequence  . . . . . . . . .   *SRC          NAME, *SRC, *JOB...
  Library  . . . . . . . . . . .     __________  Name, *LIBL, *CURLIB
Language ID  . . . . . . . . . .   *JOB          Character value, *JOB
Coded character set ID . . . . .   *JOB_______   *JOB, *HEX...
Allow update operation . . . . .   *YES          *YES, *NO
Allow delete operation . . . . .   *YES          *YES, *NO
Record format level check  . . .   *YES          *YES, *NO
Authority  . . . . . . . . . . .   *LIBCRTAUT    Name, *LIBCRTAUT, *ALL...

                                                                     Bottom
F3=Exit   F4=Prompt   F5=Refresh   F12=Cancel   F13=How to use this display
F24=More keys
```

Start by deleting record number **1**. This is done by entering **1** in the *RECNBR field (as shown in Figure 5.17) and pressing **F23**. The system will ask to confirm the deletion. Do this by pressing **F23** again.

We will then enter another record by pressing **F9** and entering the data as shown in Figure 5.18. Before exiting DFU, try to display the first relative record by typing **1** in the *RECNBR field and pressing **ENTER**.

FIGURE 5.17

```
WORK WITH DATA IN A FILE                                  Mode . . . . :   CHANGE
Format . . . . :   STUDREC___                             File . . . . :   TEMP

*RECNBR: 1_______











F3=Exit                     F5=Refresh                  F6=Select format
F9=Insert                   F10=Entry                   F11=Change
```

FIGURE 5.18

```
WORK WITH DATA IN A FILE                                  Mode . . . . :   INSERT
Format . . . . :   STUDREC___                             File . . . . :   TEMP


LNAME:    Flintstone_
FNAME:    Dino____
STREET:   1 Dog House La.
CITY:     Bedrock___
STATE:    AZ
ZIP:      88888
STUDID#:  121212121
CREDITS:  __3
GRADEPT:  400








F3=Exit                     F5=Refresh                  F6=Select format
F9=Insert                   F10=Entry                   F11=Change
```

The result is an error message (shown in Figure 5.19) saying that the record was not found. To definitely prove that the first record location was not reclaimed, use the DSPPFM command to display the data (Figure 5.20). Notice that the DINO record was placed at the end of the data records, not at the beginning where space was available.

FIGURE 5.19

```
WORK WITH DATA IN A FILE                          Mode . . . . :   CHANGE
Format . . . . :    STUDREC___                    File . . . . :   TEMP

*RECNBR: _______1

F3=Exit                   F5=Refresh                F6=Select format
F9=Insert                 F10=Entry                 F11=Change
The record was not found in member TEMP.
```

FIGURE 5.20

```
                         Display Physical File Member
File . . . . . . :    TEMP                Library . . . . :    MYLIBXX
Member . . . . . :    TEMP                Record . . . . . :   2
Control . . . . .     ___________         Column . . . . . :   1
Find . . . . . . .    ________________________________________
*...+....1....+....2....+....3....+....4....+....5....+....6...
FlintstoneWilma    11 Limestone DrBedrock    AZ88888123456789   ·
Rubble     Betty   15 Limestone DrBedrock    AZ88888444444444 ± ±
Rubble     Barnard 15 Limestone DrBedrock    AZ88888999999999 ¬
FlintstoneDino     1 Dog House La.Bedrock    AZ88888121212121   ·
                          ****** END OF DATA ******

                                                                   Bottom
F3=Exit    F12=Cancel    F19=Left    F20=Right    F24=More keys
```

Now change TEMP's REUSEDLT parameter to *YES with the CHGPF command. The command would be entered as follows:

```
CHGPF FILE(MYLIBXX/TEMP) REUSEDLT(*YES)
```

We'll go back into DFU and add a new record to the file (as shown in Figure 5.21). Display the data records using DSPPFM (see Figure 5.22) to see where the record was added in the member. Notice that the newest record was placed at the beginning of the records. Because we changed the REUSEDLT parameter for the file, the system automatically began to reclaim space.

FIGURE 5.21

```
WORK WITH DATA IN A FILE                              Mode . . . . :   INSERT
Format . . . . :   STUDREC___                         File . . . . :   TEMP

LNAME:    Einstein__
FNAME:    Albert__
STREET:   Energy St______
CITY:     Mass
STATE:    CT
ZIP:      00002
STUDID#:  565656565
CREDITS:  999
GRADEPT:  400

F3=Exit                  F5=Refresh               F6=Select format
F9=Insert                F10=Entry                F11=Change
```

FIGURE 5.22

```
                    Display Physical File Member
File . . . . . . :   TEMP               Library . . . . :   MYLIBXX
Member . . . . . :   TEMP               Record . . . . . :   1
Control . . . . .    __________         Column . . . . . :   1
Find . . . . . . .   ____________________________________
*...+....1....+....2....+....3....+....4....+....5....+....6...
Einstein  Albert  Energy St     Mass      CT00002565656565r¤ ˙
FlintstoneWilma   11 Limestone DrBedrock  AZ88888123456789   ˙
Rubble    Betty   15 Limestone DrBedrock  AZ88888444444444 ± ±
Rubble    Barnard 15 Limestone DrBedrock  AZ88888999999999 ¬
FlintstoneDino    1 Dog House La.Bedrock  AZ88888121212121   ˙
                     ****** END OF DATA ******

                                                                Bottom
F3=Exit   F12=Cancel   F19=Left   F20=Right   F24=More keys
```

Reclaiming deleted record space will cut down on the size of files. However, there are some repercussions to defining files this way. First, records can no longer be accessed in arrival sequence order. Any processing that assumed arrival sequence order will be in error. Second, extra processing is needed for each update of the file. The system must check for deleted space before an addition is made. This, of course, means that additions to the file will take slightly longer. You may not notice the difference on a single transaction, but if a program is performing a large number of additions or deletions, the extra processing time may be noticeable. What's more, this dynamic reclamation does not ensure 100 percent space utilization. Periodically, these files will have to be reorganized to eliminate empty space.

If your system can't afford any further performance degradation, the best procedure is not to reclaim the space dynamically but on a periodic basis to reorganize the files. Periodically reorganizing files does allow empty space to build up; however, if reorganization is done frequently, the amount of wasted space is kept to a minimum. In addition, when a file is reorganized, the remaining records are kept in arrival sequence order. To demonstrate how the reorganization keeps the records in arrival sequence order, we'll delete two records, add one, and then reorganize. If we were using dynamic reclamation, the added record would be placed in one of the deleted records locations, and the file would no longer be in arrival sequence. If we set REUSEDLT to *NO and do the deletions, the added record will simply be put at the end of the file.

For our example, we will delete records 2 and 4 (Wilma and Barney) from the file and add a new record for Steve Winwood. Displaying the member would result in Figure 5.23.

FIGURE 5.23

```
                         Display Physical File Member
File . . . . . . :   TEMP                      Library  . . . . :   MYLIBXX
  Member . . . . . :   TEMP                      Record . . . . . :    1
Control  . . . . .   ___________               Column . . . . . :   1
Find . . . . . . .   ________________________________________
*...+....1....+....2....+....3....+....4....+....5....+....6 . . .
Einstein  Albert  Energy St       Mass        C000002565656565r *■ ˙
Rubble    Betty   15 Limestone DrBedrock      AZ88888444444444■ ±■ ±
Flinstone Dino    1 Dog House La.Bedrock      AZ88888121212121■■■ ˙
Winwood   Steve   1 Higher GroundHollywood CA90821123456789■■■ ˙

                                                                    Bottom
F3=Exit   F12=Cancel   F19=Left   F20=Right   F24=More keys
```

The `Display Physical File Member` screen could lead you to believe that the Winwood record is in location 4. The Winwood record is actually in relative record location 6. (You can prove this by starting

DFU and retrieving record 6.) Try to remember that the DSPPFM command shows records in arrival sequence order. It does not show each storage location. Further, there is no record 2 or 4. Betty's record is actually in the third record location.

We now want to reorganize the file. The command to reorganize a file is RGZPFM. We would reorganize the TEMP file by issuing the following command:

```
RGZPFM FILE(MYLIBXX/TEMP)
```

After reorganizing TEMP, if we start DFU and retrieve record number 2, the result would be Figure 5.24. The RGZPFM command filled in the empty locations and maintained the arrival sequence order. Winwood is still the last record, but now it is in location 4.

Reorganizing files can also be used to speed up sequential processing of keyed files. In our earlier discussion of index sequential files, we pointed out that processing an entire index sequential file in key order takes longer than processing the same data in a sequential file. This same problem is encountered by files using keyed sequence access paths. We can improve our KSAP performance by reorganizing the records by key. This can be done by using the KEYFILE parameter in the RGZPFM command. To reorganize TEMP by the key field, issue the following command:

```
RGZPFM FILE(MYLIBXX/TEMP) KEYFILE(*FILE)
```

FIGURE 5.24

```
WORK WITH DATA IN A FILE                         Mode . . . . :   CHANGE
Format . . . . :    STUDREC___                   File . . . . :   TEMP

*RECNBR:        2
LNAME:    Rubble____
FNAME:    Betty___
STREET:   15 Limestone Dr
CITY:     Bedrock___
STATE:    AZ
ZIP:      88888
STUDID#:  444444444
CREDITS:  _18
GRADEPT:  399


F3=Exit                  F5=Refresh                F6=Select format
F9=Insert                F10=Entry                 F11=Change
```

Summary

There are three primary data organization methods: sequential, index sequential, and random. Each method can be measured by the amount of space required, type of access provided, and record retrieval speed. Sequential uses the least amount of space, but for individual record retrieval, it is the slowest method. Both index sequential and random files take up more space but give considerable performance advantages.

The AS/400 has its own unique brand of organizations. Every file can be accessed in arrival sequence order. Arrival sequence files are not sequential files because the records are not physically written in sequential order. There is an arrival sequence access path that allows access to the records in the order they are written. There is also another type of access path called a keyed sequence access path. The KSAP is similar to an index. It allows sequential access by key order or arrival sequence order, as well as individual record retrieval by key value. All programming languages support both sequential and keyed access to AS/400 files.

AS/400 files also have two methods of handling empty space generated by record deletions. Free space from deletions can be reused when the next addition occurs, or it can accumulate until a reorganization is initiated. A reorganization eliminates all empty space and maintains the arrival sequence of the records. Reclaiming deleted space dynamically prevents arrival sequence access and may have an adverse affect on performance. In addition, it does not guarantee 100 percent space utilization. However, by reclaiming space immediately, file size is kept to a minimum.

PROGRAMMING EXERCISE

The video store is continuing to do well. However, with the addition of the new items (candy, VCRs, and so forth.), some problems were found with the system. People were entering new items (like a VCR) but forgetting to enter a serial number record for each new VCR. The management has asked that you write a program (ADD) that requires the entry of at least one serial number whenever a new item with SERIAL = Y is added.

Another problem has been that employees have been mistyping item numbers on the serial records when a new serial record is entered. The video store owners would like the ADD program to verify that the item number entered is valid.

Furthermore, with the addition of the consumable items, the DDS field definition for MEDIA was changed so that MEDIA is no longer mandatory. However, for nonconsumables, MEDIA information must be entered. Checking that MEDIA is filled for nonconsumable items will have to be done inside the program ADD.

The assignment consists of

1. Changing the files to keyed files with ITEM having a key of INUM and PRODUCT having a key of SNUM. This means the ITEM and PRODUCT files source code must be changed and recompiled. After updating the DDS source definitions, use CHGF to recompile the file definitions and save the data.

2. Create the following screens with SDA. Use the file field definitions as the basis for the screen fields.

```
ADDIS                        Add Items and Serials menu

Select one of the following:

      1. Add an item

      2. Add a serial

      3. Exit




 Selection
 ===>_
```

```
                               Add New Serial screen


        Serial number: _______

          Item number: _______




Fill in serial number and item number and press Enter
```

```
                Add New Item screen

       Item number: XXXXXXX

         Item name: ____________________

      Type of item: __________

             Media: ___

     Rental price: __________

       Sales price: ___

            Serial: _


                Change item number and press Enter

                                 or

                Enter item data and press Enter
```

3. Write a program called ADD that allows the customer to add items and serialized product. In the program, make sure to check that an item number exists for any product records that are entered. (You can do this by making a keyed retrieval with the item number supplied by the user.) If the retrieval is successful, the item exists. If the retrieval fails (the item number does not exist), make the customer enter new item information or change the item number to one that already exists. The pseudocode for the program is as follows:

ADD

```
Start: Display "Add Items and Serials" menu
       If option 1
       Then Call AddItm
       Else If option 2
            Then Call AddSer
            Else If option 3
                 Then End program
       Goto Start


AddItm

Disp:  Display "Add New Item" screen
       Read ITEM file using screen.item number as the key
       If item number in ITEM file
       Then Send message "Item already exists."
            Goto Start
       If Type not equal "CONSUMABLE" and MEDIA is blank
```

```
        Then Send message "Must fill in MEDIA."
             Goto Disp
        Move screen data to ITEM record
        Write to ITEM file
        If Serial = Y
        Then fill in item number on "Add New Serial" screen
             Call AddSer

EndAddItm


AddSer

        Display "Add New Serial" screen
        Read ITEM file using screen.item number as the key
        If item number in ITEM file
        Then Move screen data to PRODUCT record
             Set Status = A
             Set Rent# = 0
             Write to PRODUCT file
        Else fill in item number on "Add New Item" screen
             Call AddItm

EndAddSer
```

4. Enter the following data for the ITEM file with the newly created program:

INUM	9	10	11	12
INAME	MilkDuds	Citizen Kane	Fireball	VCR
TYPE	CONSUMABLE	Drama	CONSUMABLE	Sony
MEDIA		VD		VHS
RPRICE		300		700
SPRICE	275	11995	50	29900
SERIAL	N	Y	N	Y

INUM	13	14	15	16
INAME	VCR	Citizen Kane	Licorice	Peanuts
TYPE	RCA	Drama	CONSUMABLE	CONSUMABLE
MEDIA	VHS	VHS		
RPRICE	700	250		
SPRICE	29900	8895	250	325
SERIAL	Y	Y	N	N

5. Enter the following data for the PRODUCT file:

SNUM	13	14	15	16	17	18	19
INUM	10	12	13	14	12	13	14
STATUS	A	A	A	A	A	A	A
RENT#	0	0	0	0	0	0	0

REVIEW QUESTIONS

1. What is the effect of dynamic space reclamation on the arrival sequence of data records?
2. What is the difference between primary and secondary keys?
3. Which organization method uses hashing routines, and what is the purpose of a hashing routine?
4. Which organization method best supports sequential file processing in a single key order?
5. What is a collision?
6. What is the function of access paths? What two types of access paths are there?
7. Does the AS/400 support multiple keyed sequence access paths for a file? If so, how?
8. Where are key specifications located in a DDS source member?
9. Where are file level specifications located in a DDS source member?
10. What are two advantages to multilevel indices?

DISCUSSION QUESTIONS

1. What are the advantages and disadvantages to dynamically reclaiming space versus periodically reorganizing data?
2. Compare sequential and index sequential organization in regard to storage space and access time.
3. What are the advantages and disadvantages of random organization?

Databases and Database Management Systems

6

Overview

This chapter covers how database management systems (DBMSs) enhance data retrieval and update performance, provide greater access flexibility, and decrease data redundancy. We will explore several different database models and evaluate each on how well they accomplish these goals.

We will then cover the relational database model in greater detail and explore several key functions provided by a relational DBMS. We will also explain how the AS/400's DBMS provides these functions through logical files.

After finishing this chapter, you will understand

- The three primary data models and their differences
- The major features of database management systems
- The difference between logical and physical files

What Is a Database?

A database comprises related "groups of data." A database management system (DBMS) is a collection of programs that allows users to create, maintain, and relate these groups of data. All database management systems provide some method to define and access data. Many allow users to define data with a data definition language (like DDS) or with a utility that has easy-to-use menus (like IDDU). In addition, most DBMS have programs that allow users to retrieve or write data to the database. These programs are often called the DBMS's "access method services." Each DBMS names its groups of data differently—files, tables, segments, and so on—and supports different types of relationships between the groups.

There are three types of databases: hierarchical, network, and relational. To understand each, we must first explore how data can be related.

Data Relationships

Relationships between groups of data records can be described two ways. The first is the number of relationships a record has with records from another group. For instance, if we had a class file and an instructor file, we would say that there is a **one-to-many relationship** between instructor and class. An instructor record can be associated with many class records, but each class has only one instructor. We could depict the relationship as in Figure 6.1. (The double-headed arrow means that there are many class records related to each instructor record.) There can also be one-to-one or many-to-many relationships between data groups.

FIGURE 6.1

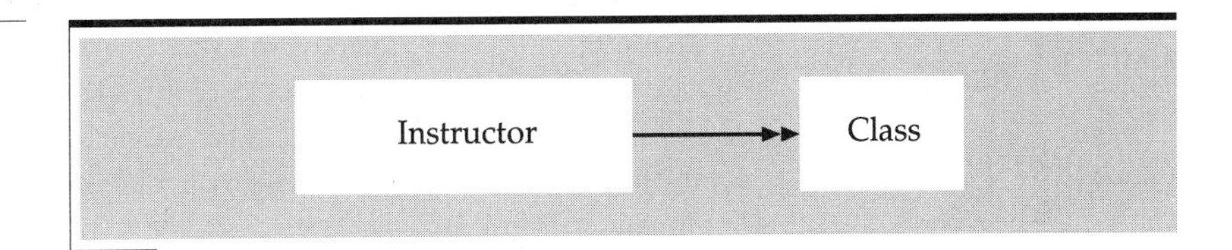

The second way to describe a relationship is the direction of access required. For example, if a school employee only accessed the database to find each instructor's classes, he or she needs a unidirectional relationship. In other words, the access between instructor and class needs to go in only one direction, from instructor to class (the employee supplies the instructor record key, and the associated class records are retrieved). If the employee also needed to be able to look up who is teaching a particular class (the employee has the class number and wants the associated instructor record), the relationship required between these two groups is said to be bidirectional. We would depict a bidirectional relationship by placing arrowheads on each end of the line connecting the two groups of data (as in Figure 6.2.) This relationship would be called a bidirectional, one-to-many relationship.

FIGURE 6.2

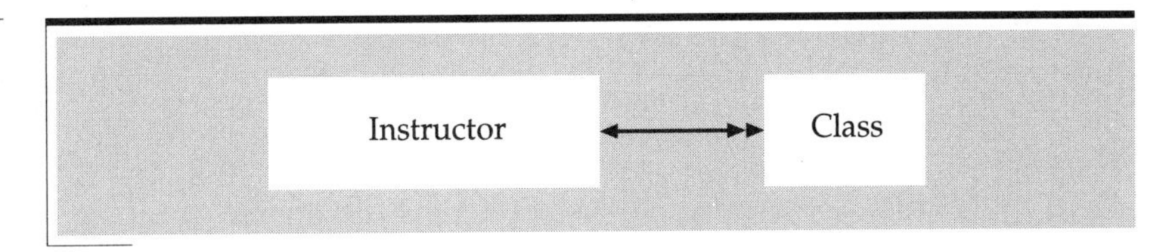

As mentioned, there can also be one-to-one and many-to-many relationships. These relationships can also be characterized by their direction. For instance, if our student file were in the database, it would also have a relationship with class. Each student can have many classes, and each class has many students. Class and student have a many-to-many relationship. If access was required in both directions, it would be a bidirectional, many-to-many relationship. We would depict the bidirectional, many-to-many relationship between class and student as seen in Figure 6.3.

FIGURE 6.3

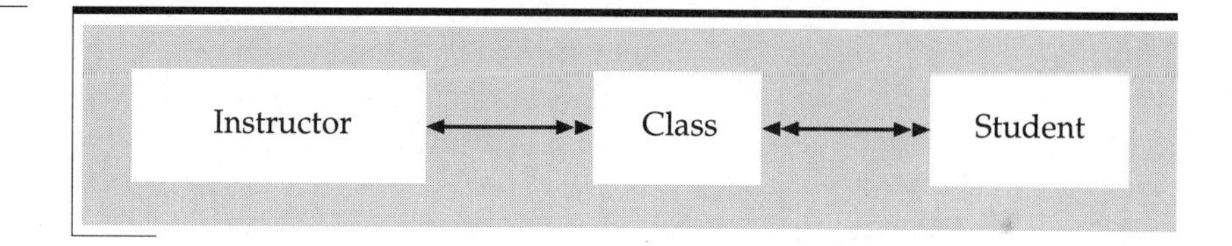

Each of the database models supports these types of relationships to a different degree, in a different manner, and with different costs and efficiencies.

Hierarchical Database

The most complex data relationship that a **hierarchical** database can support is a parent–child relationship. A parent–child relationship is a one-to-many, unidirectional relationship. In addition, the hierarchical database has restrictions regarding how the data groups can be accessed. A hierarchical database has one root "segment" (data group). The root segment has no "parent" and is the only entry point into the database. Access to any other data group in the database must be through the root. To access a record in a data group other than the root, you must supply the key to the record, as well as the key of the parent root record.

Another rule is that access to a data group must be through all its parents, grandparents, great-grandparents, and so on. This may sound strange, but here's an example to the rescue. Figure 6.4 shows a hierarchical database with the previously discussed school information. If an employee wanted to access information about a particular instructor (the root node), he or she would simply supply the key value for the instructor record wanted. For instance, if instructor was keyed by social security number, supplying social security number to the database's access method services would result in the appropriate instructor record being returned. If a particular class record was desired, not only is the correct key for the class record needed but also the key of the root instructor record. In other words, you would have to supply the appropriate class number and instructor social security number. To get a student record, you have to supply the student's key, a class key, and an instructor key.

As you can imagine, this can quickly become complicated and cumbersome. To get a particular child record, all its parents keys must be specified. The user must keep track of and specify a large amount of data whenever a data record is requested. A single point of entry to the database and, therefore, the need to specify all parent record keys is one of the drawbacks to the hierarchical model.

Somewhat offsetting this drawback is the fact that the hierarchical model permanently stores and maintains the relationships between records. A parent record "points" to its child records. When a particular record is specified—by specifying its parent, grandparent, great-grandparent, and so on—the DBMS only has to read the "family tree" records and very quickly retrieve the record.

FIGURE 6.4

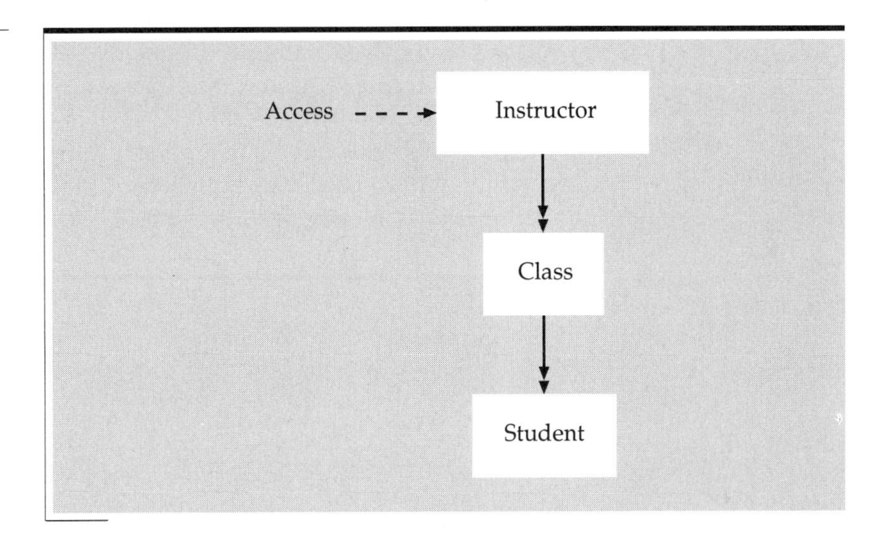

The downside to stored relationships is that the relationships must be constantly updated to reflect record additions and deletions. This means that updating data takes a little longer because the "pointers" between records also have to be updated. In addition, the stored relationships take up storage space. The total space occupied by the database is comprised of what is needed to store the data and what is required to store the pointers.

Another shortcoming of the hierarchical model is that not all data is related hierarchically. Some data does not relate in a one-to-many or one-to-one manner, and users often wish to access data bidirectionally. For instance, what if school employees also wanted to access student schedules? In database terminology, they want to access CLASS by STUDENT. (In English, the request would be to see all class records associated with a particular student.) To accomplish this, a bidirectional relationship between STUDENT and CLASS is needed, as is access to the database through a segment other than the root. This second requirement phrased in "databas-ese" would be the users are requesting multiple entry point access to the database. Hierarchical databases cannot support either of these requests.

Network Database

Network databases, like hierarchical databases, also maintain permanent relationships between data records. Networks, however, allow multiple entry points into the database and support more complex relationships. For instance, the bidirectional, multiple entry point requirements described earlier can be supported in a network database. Figure 6.5 depicts the bidirectional relationship between student and class and the multiple entry points.

Network databases can also support many-to-many relationships between data groups. In terms of access, the relationship between CLASS and STUDENT became more complex when the employees requested a bidirectional access. However, an added complication was that the relationship between the groups was many-to-many. When the relationship between data is many-to-many but the access required is unidirectional, the relationship is a relatively simple one to implement and maintain one-to-many. When bidirectional access is requested, the pointer system to maintain the many-to-many relationship becomes much more complex. Remember, just like the hierarchical database, the network database must update the stored relationships whenever the data is changed. Since networks support

FIGURE 6.5

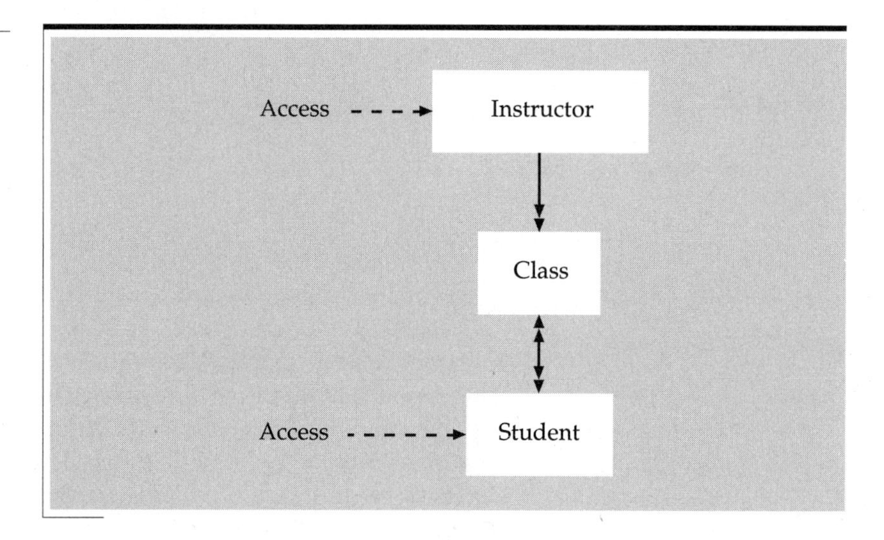

more complex relationships, the time required to maintain the relationships is greater. Further, because of the complexity of the network model, the DBMS packages tend to be very complicated and require specialized personnel or training in order to set them up and use them. This, of course, means that more time and money are required to store and maintain the data.

For all the advantages and flexibility of network databases, their performance and maintenance drawbacks limit their usefulness.

Relational Database

Relational databases are the easiest of the three models to understand. In general, the relational DBMSs are also the most user friendly and easiest to learn. You'll be pleased to hear that the AS/400 employs a relational database to store data.

The two major characteristics of the relational model are that groups of data are viewed as tables (also called relations), and permanent data relationships are not kept between tables. Compared to the organization and access rules of network and hierarchical data models, those of the relational model are simple. Each row in a table is comparable to a record, and each column is a field. The tables can have a key, and each row can be referenced by the value contained in the key field. Users can access any table by the key. Therefore, access points to the relational database are not limited, nor do they have to be defined.

Each group of school information would be considered a table in a relational database. If class information were needed, the user would simply supply the class number, and the class record would be returned. No parent record's key value is needed—as in a hierarchical database—nor would a new entry point into the database for CLASS need to be set up—as in a network model. With a relational database, CLASS is simply created as a table and accessed by the defined key.

To relate information between different tables, the relational model uses duplicate data fields. For instance, if the employee wanted to retrieve the class meeting times for a particular instructor, the Class and Instructor tables would have to share a common field. One way this could be done is to define an instructor SS# in the Class table (Figure 6.6). When data from the two tables is required, a join using the shared field of SS# and ISS# from both tables would be specified. The relational DBMS would search through the Instructor and Class records and join the rows that have the same value for SS# and ISS#. The results of the join can be saved, but the relationship between each of the records in the two groups is not saved.

FIGURE 6.6

Instructor

SS#	Iname

Class

Clnum	Sttime	Etime	Room	Iss#

Student

SS#	Name	Phone	Address

This approach has its advantages and disadvantages. Certainly the concept of tables with shared fields is easier to understand than database entry points, parent–child relationships, and multidirectional access paths. Therefore, most users of relational databases do not need any extensive data processing background. This saves on training and personnel costs. What's more, most relational DBMSs provide a menu- or icon-driven user-friendly interface and extensive help.

One of the disadvantages of the relational model is the required **data redundancy**. Implementing many-to-many relationships or joining multiple tables requires extensive duplication of data. Besides the cost associated with the required extra space, coordinating the maintenance of data that is stored multiple times becomes a complex and time-consuming task. In addition, this maintenance work is usually handled by user-developed programs outside the DBMS. This means extra time and money to develop the programs and extra processing time when the data is updated. (We will explore this area in much greater detail in later chapters and show how the AS/400 DBMS helps overcome this problem.)

Another disadvantage of the relational model is that by not using predefined relationships, retrieval performance suffers. Since the relationship must be created each time the data is accessed, retrievals are slower in the relational model than in the previous two models. However, because table changes do not require updating any stored relationships, relational databases provide faster updating of nonredundant data.

Database Management System Features

As mentioned earlier, all database management systems offer some capability to define data structures and manipulate the data contained in those structures. Depending on the individual software purchased, these functions can take many forms; they do not necessarily have to take the form of traditional commands. Data could be managed through screens, menus, or even a graphical interface.

DBMSs also provide **data access controls**. All users want to protect their data. One way to safeguard data is to make sure that only authorized people have access. This will help prevent malicious damage, as well as cut down on erroneous data by ensuring that only properly trained people have access and update capability to the information.

Another DBMS feature is the ability to provide **backup and recovery**. These utilities (when used properly) ensure that data can be recreated in the event of accident or disaster.

Enhanced **data integrity** is another DBMS advantage. Most systems provide programs and procedures to ensure that data is accurate and maintained correctly. The DDS editing keywords are an example of a data integrity tool supplied by the AS/400 DBMS.

Furthermore, all DBMSs provide some access method for programs and users. Programs can use specialized **data manipulation language** (DML) commands supplied by the DBMS, or the DBMS will support a program language's input and output commands. Many database systems also supply a command-based **query language** and a menu-driven or graphical interface that allow nonprogrammers easy access to the data. The AS/400 is not an exception here either. Interactive SQL and QUERY/400 provide these functions.

DBMSs also provide the ability to create **alternative views** of the data. These views are used to tailor the data to individual program and user needs.

Most important, a DBMS cuts down on **data redundancy**. By providing a single repository for data, information is not duplicated across the system. This saves on both space and the need to coordinate updates of the duplicated data. Of course, different database management systems provide these functions to different degrees and with varying effectiveness. We will explore how the AS/400 database provides all these functions. The remainder of this chapter and Chapter 7 will explore how logical files provide alternative views of data and reduce data redundancy. Chapters 8 and 9 will cover the primary data manipulation tools on the AS/400—QUERY/400, OPNQRYF, and SQL/400. Chapters 11 and 12 will cover data security, backup, and recovery.

Logical Files

A DBMS will usually offer three ways to view a database: a physical view, a global view, and the capability to build multiple user views of the data. What is traditionally called the "physical view of data" is mostly hidden from the AS/400 user because of the AS/400's single level approach to storage. The user does not have to know the disk, track, or sector on which data is stored. In addition, any indices or specific location addresses are used internally by the DBMS and are not readily available to the user. However, the AS/400 does provide a limited physical view of the data (with the DSPPFM command), as well as some capability to manipulate the physical organization of the data (for instance, with the RGZPFM command).

DDS does, however, provide a global view of all the data as files and allows construction of individual views. This is achieved through both physical and logical files.

As mentioned earlier, physical files contain the definition of individual fields within the file. In addition, physical files include an access path to the data (a key) and the data itself. These physical file definition "pieces" taken as a whole provide the global view of all data on the AS/400.

Customers often want to see data in a form other than how it is organized. In our student example, an employee may wish to see data from many files at one time. Maybe they would like to see a class's meeting times, the instructor teaching the class, and a list of all the students in the class. This requires combining information from three different files. Traditionally, an application program would have to be written to do this.

The AS/400, however, has another type of object called a logical file that allows data to be accessed differently from how it is organized in the physical files. (The AS/400 query tool, QUERY/400, can also be used to create unique views of the physical files. See Chapter 8 for a full explanation of QUERY/400's ability to join files.) Logical files, like physical files, contain file definitions. However, logical files contain only field definitions and an access path; no data is stored in a logical file. Because logical files contain no data, they must reference data that has already been defined in a physical file. An added feature is that a logical file can reference fields from many physical files. Through logical files, unique combinations of the data seem to exist without duplicating any data. Before we explain how to create these combinations, we need to explore some general relational functions.

Relational Algebra

All relational databases provide some means to:

Limit the fields and records that can be accessed

Access separately stored data at one time

These functions can be explained with the industry standard relational algebra operands of select, project, and join. Each of these operands results (or, as in the case of the DDS, appears to result) in a new table being created.

Select

A **Select** retrieves certain rows from a relational table, based on a condition. Generally, conditions are based on field values, for instance, QUANTITY > 0 or LASTNAME = "Jones". The rows selected are the ones that satisfy the condition. The general syntax of a SELECT is as follows:

```
SELECT FROM table name WHERE condition.
```

Performing a select such as

```
SELECT FROM Table 1 WHERE SS# > 200000000
```

against Table 1, as it appears in Figure 6.7, would result in the following records being returned:

Name	Address	SS#
Baker	22 2nd St	222222222
Zebra	99 9th St	999999999

FIGURE 6.7

Table 1

Name	Address	SS#
Able	11 1st St	111111111
Baker	22 2nd St	222222222
Zebra	99 9th St	999999999

Project

A **project** returns all rows from a table but only specified columns. The columns must be explicitly specified in the PROJECT, and the general syntax is as follows:

```
PROJECT table name ON column1 column2 ...... columnN
```

For instance, executing the following project:

```
PROJECT Table 1 ON Name SS#
```

would result in the following:

Name	SS#
Able	111111111
Baker	222222222
Zebra	999999999

Projects and selects can also be performed together. For instance, we may want to see just the employee names and social security numbers for people with social security numbers greater than 200000000. To perform this, we would issue the following relational algebra command:

```
PROJECT (SELECT FROM Table 1 WHERE SS# > 200000000) ON Name SS#
```

with the resulting table

Name	SS#
Baker	222222222
Zebra	999999999

A select when used with another relational command is called a subselect.

Joins

Joins let users combine data from different tables. There are several different types of joins.

A **general join** of two tables matches every row in the first table with every row in the second table. If the first table had two rows and the second table had three rows, the general join of these two tables would result in a six-row table. Issuing a general join on the two tables, as in the following:

```
GJOIN TableA TableB
```

would result in

```
TableA row1 + TableB row1
TableA row1 + TableB row2
TableA row1 + TableB row3
TableA row2 + TableB row1
TableA row2 + TableB row2
TableA row2 + TableB row3
```

As another example, if we had a Table 2, shown in Figure 6.8, and we performed the general join

FIGURE 6.8

Table 2

Name	Employer	SS#
Able	1st National Bank	111111111
Baker	Avis	222222222
Candy	Trinity Broadcasting	333333333
Zebra	New York Mets	999999999

```
GJOIN Table 1 Table 2
```

the resulting table would look like the following:

Name	Address	SS#	Name	Employer	SS#
Able	11 1st St	111111111	Able	1st National Bank	111111111
Able	11 1st St	111111111	Baker	Avis	222222222
Able	11 1st St	111111111	Candy	Trinity Broadcasting	333333333
Able	11 1st St	111111111	Zebra	New York Mets	999999999
Baker	22 2nd St	222222222	Able	1st National Bank	111111111
Baker	22 2nd St	222222222	Baker	Avis	222222222
Baker	22 2nd St	222222222	Candy	Trinity Broadcasting	333333333
Baker	22 2nd St	222222222	Zebra	New York Mets	999999999
Zebra	99 9th St	999999999	Able	1st National Bank	111111111
Zebra	99 9th St	999999999	Baker	Avis	222222222
Zebra	99 9th St	999999999	Candy	Trinity Broadcasting	333333333
Zebra	99 9th St	999999999	Zebra	New York Mets	999999999

Notice the extreme duplication of data. Not only is each table 1 row repeated four times and each table 2 row repeated three times, but the names and social security numbers are repeated within each row of the resulting table. An **equijoin** will eliminate some of that duplication.

An equijoin matches rows between tables that have the same values in a column. Tables 1 and 2 have common columns of Name and SS#. If an equijoin was performed, each row in table 1 and table 2 that shared the same values for social security number and name would be joined and placed in the resulting table. For instance, issuing the equijoin as

```
EJOIN Table 1 Table 2
```

would result in the following table:

Name	Address	SS#	Name	Employer	SS#
Able	11 1st St	111111111	Able	1st National Bank	111111111
Baker	22 2nd St	222222222	Baker	Avis	222222222
Zebra	99 9th St	999999999	Zebra	New York Mets	999999999

Notice that all the repeating records are eliminated. However, equijoins still repeat the shared column information. A **natural join** will eliminate the duplicate columns.

A natural join issued as

```
NJOIN table1 table2
```

results in the following table:

Name	Address	SS#	Employer
Able	11 1st St	111111111	1st National Bank
Baker	22 2nd St	222222222	Avis
Zebra	99 9th St	999999999	New York Mets

The AS/400 supports all these functions through logical files, SQL/400 and the query tool, QUERY/400. Simple logical files allow users to specify the select and project functions, whereas joined logical files and multiformat logical files provide the various join capabilities.

Summary

A database is a collection of related data, and a database management system is a set of programs that enable users to create, maintain, and manipulate databases. There are three types of databases: hierarchical, network, and relational. Each can be judged based on:

The speed of access and update

The data relationships supported

The amount of data redundancy employed

Ease of use

Hierarchical and network databases use stored data relationships that provide fast retrieval. However, these same relationships require maintenance and therefore slow down updating. Hierarchical databases support a more limited range of data relationships than the other two. However, network and relational databases handle complex relationships differently. Relational databases employ duplicate data and require the programmer to maintain the data. Network databases take care of the complex relationships, but the processing required to maintain these relationships will often drastically affect performance.

In terms of user friendliness, the concept of tables, rows, and columns does not require any advanced computer knowledge and is a clear favorite with users.

The AS/400 employs a relational database. Through logical files, users can seemingly create as many customized files as they want. In reality, logical files provide a different access path to physical file records and fields. Logical files appear to contain:

A rearrangement of physical file fields

A subset of fields from a single physical file

Information from multiple files

In reality, they do not contain any data.

All relational DBMSs provide the functional capability to perform select, project and joins on the tables. Through these relational operands the user is able to create the various user views of data.

REVIEW QUESTIONS

1. What is a database? What is a database management system?
2. What is a parent–child relationship?
3. Which type of database is the most user friendly?
4. Which database model(s) employ stored data relationships, and what is the impact on database performance?
5. What relational functions do logical files provide on the AS/400?
6. What database model(s) can implement many-to-many relationships?
7. Can relational databases support multiple access point entry?
8. What are groups of data called in relational databases?

DISCUSSION QUESTIONS

1. Discuss some of the advantages and features of a DBMS.
2. Describe the different types of relational joins.
3. How are logical files different from and similar to physical files?

Logical Files

7

Overview

This chapter will explain how to define AS/400 logical files and show how logical files provide user views of data with a minimum of data redundancy. We will also explore the complex and unique relationship between physical and logical files and pay special attention to the effects of physical file modification on logical files.

After finishing this chapter, you will understand

- The difference between logical and physical files
- The relationship between logical and physical files
- The differences between simple, join, and multiple format logical files
- How logical files can simplify program logic

After finishing this chapter, you will be able to

- Define and create simple, join, and multiple format logical files using DDS
- Identify a physical file's dependent logical files
- Modify physical files and ensure logical file integrity

Creating Logical Files

Logical files are defined with DDS and are created by compiling the source physical file member that contains the logical file's DDS definition (just like physical files). One difference between a logical and physical file definition is that the source physical file member containing the logical file's DDS definition has a type of LF rather than PF. For instance, to implement our previous student example, we would create three members with types of PF, load the DDS definitions, and compile the members, thereby creating three file objects with attributes of *PF-DTA (Figure 7.1). If our users also request that class rosters be available, one way to satisfy the request is with a logical file, ROSTER, that points to the three data members (Figure 7.2). To create a logical file, we first must create a member with a type of LF (using PDM or CL) and then enter the logical file's DDS source definition. (See Member7 in Figure 7.3.) Compiling the DDS will create the logical file.

Logical files do not contain any data; they simply point to data contained in physical files. When a user accesses ROSTER, he or she will actually be looking at the data contained in the STUDENT, GRADE, and INSTRUCTOR files. Notice also that the compile creates only a logical file object; there are no members. Since the logical file does not contain any data, there is no need for data members.

Logical files provide several benefits to the programmer. First of all, logical files and QUERY/400 can be used to easily generate customer reports. This, of course, relieves the programmer of having

FIGURE 7.1

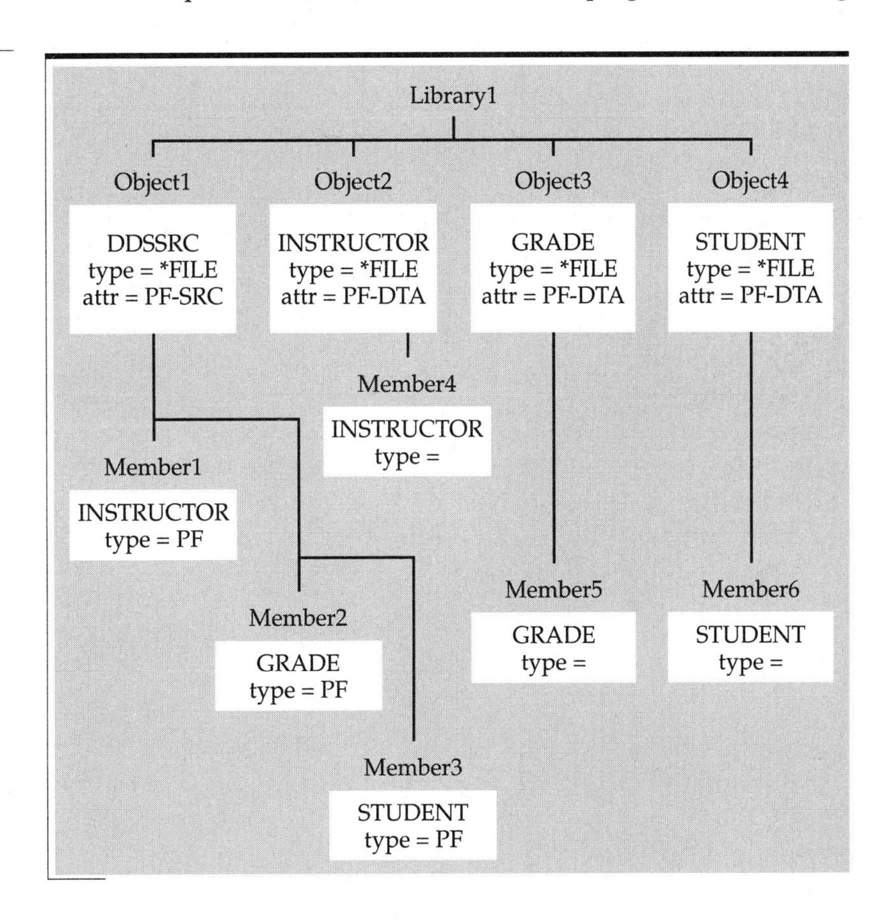

FIGURE 7.2

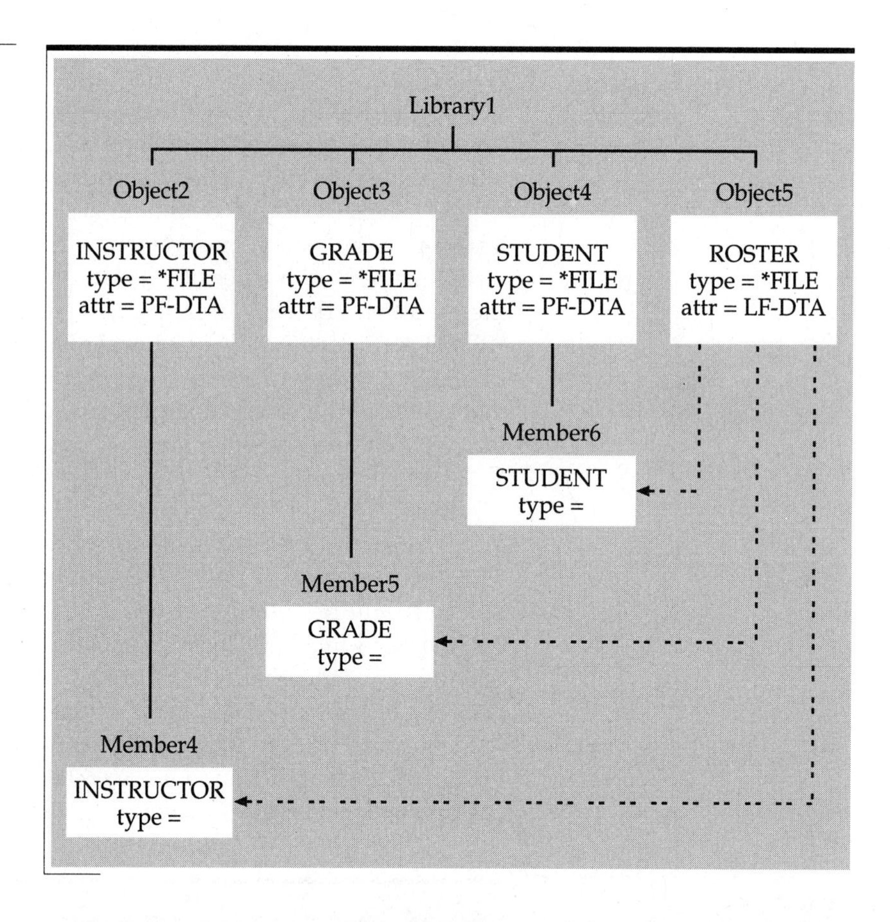

FIGURE 7.3

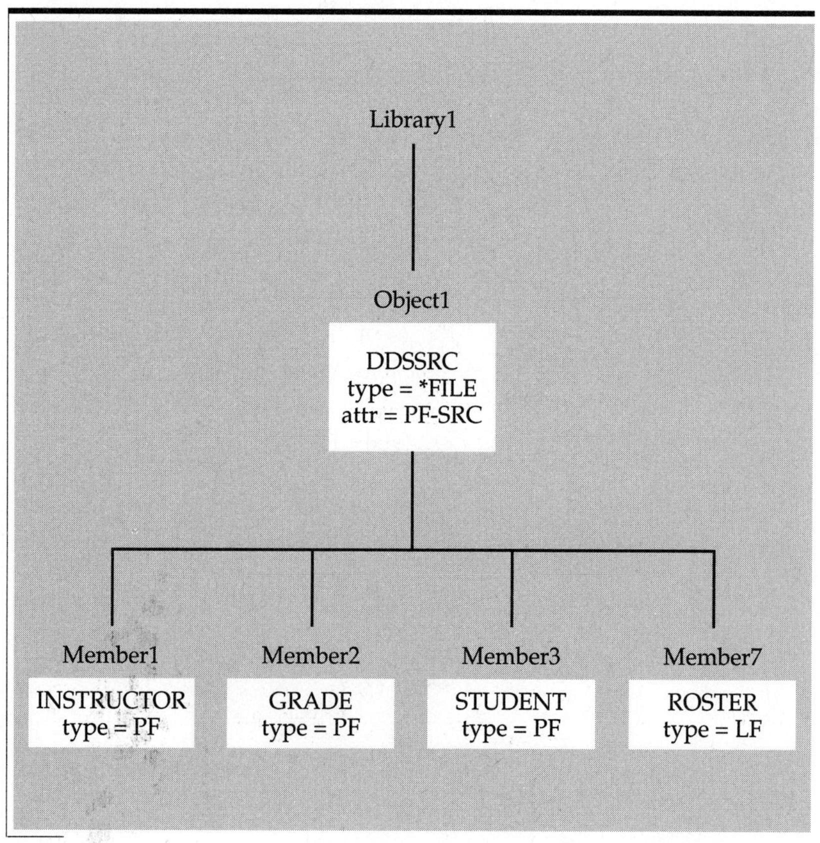

to write and maintain a large reporting system. Certainly, some report programs will still have to be written, but the number can be greatly reduced through logical files. The specialized access to physical files provided by logical files also simplifies program input and output logic. For instance, if an application program needed information from STUDENT, CLASS, and INSTRUCTOR, the program code to access ROSTER would be much simpler than what would be needed to search and access the three separate files. Logical files, because they are defined externally, can also be used by many programs. Without logical files, each program would have to contain the duplicate program code to access the separate physical files. Finally, logical files do not create any duplicate data. Many relational database systems create new tables of data when relational functions are performed. This means the programmer (or user) must maintain the data. In addition, extra storage space is needed for the duplicate data. This in not the case with logical files.

Logical files, however, do not come without cost. Remember how creating a KSAP required extra space for the higher level index? Well, the higher level index required to support the logical file's access path can take up even more space than the physical file KSAP. As a matter of fact, the join logical file index makes the physical files KSAP look like a TONKA toy. Not only do you need pointers to the correct records in multiple files, but information regarding the particular fields must also be stored.

Rather than concentrating on the internal workings of logical files (which the programmer has little control over), the remainder of our discussion will explore the different types of logical files that can be created, their uses, and how to define them with DDS.

Defining Simple Logical Files with DDS

Simple logical files allow users to perform the SELECT and PROJECT functions described in the previous chapter. These functions are defined with DDS field level specifications. Many of the keywords and procedures to create and define a logical file are the same as for a physical file. There are, however, special keywords needed to identify the fields in physical files and two new specifications for performing the SELECT function.

As a simple logical file example, we will define a logical file, DEANSLIST, for the STUDENT file. This logical file would be used by school employees to generate the dean's list at the end of each semester. Currently, the STUDENT file contains the following data:

LNAME	FNAME	STREET	CITY	STATE	ZIP	STUDID#	CREDITS	GRADEPT
Flintstone	Fred	11 Limestone Dr	Bedrock	AZ	88888	1111111	9	2.00
Flintstone	Wilma	11 Limestone Dr	Bedrock	AZ	88888	1234567	12	4.00
Rubble	Barnard	15 Limestone Dr	Bedrock	AZ	88888	9999999	15	3.00
Rubble	Betty	15 Limestone Dr	Bedrock	AZ	88888	4444444	18	3.99

We want to define a logical file that contains the student name, id #, and grade point of those students that have a grade point greater than or equal to 3.50. In addition, we would like the file's records ordered by grade point. That way when the file is printed, the 4.00

students will be first. (In relational algebra, this would translate into performing a SELECT based on the condition that GRADEPT > 3.50 and a PROJECT FNAME LNAME STUDID# GRADEPT.)

To create a logical file, the user must first create a physical file member in which to store the logical file definition. For the dean's list example, the user would create a physical file member within DDSSRC called DEANSLIST with a type of LF. The DDS specifications shown in Figure 7.4 would then be entered.

Notice that the logical file DDS definition contains record and field level specifications. As mentioned, logical file definitions contain many of the same keywords as physical files. For instance, in (Figure 7.4) the TEXT keyword defines the logical file's record format text. Keywords or field definitions in a logical file will override the physical file specification. If a logical file does not use a keyword or redefine a field's characteristics, the physical file's field definition is used.

FIGURE 7.4

```
 Columns . . . :    1  71              Edit                      MYLIBXX/DDSSRC
 SEU==>_________________________________________________________DEANSLIST
 FMT A*.....A*. 1 ...+... 2 ...+... 3...+... 4 ...+... 5...+...6 ...+... 7
        ***************Beginning of data*************************************
0001.00        *
0002.00        * THIS IS THE LOGICAL FILE THAT DEFINES THE DEANSLIST
0003.00        *
0004.00                   R DLFMT                       PFILE(MYLIBXX/STUDENT)
0005.00                                                 TEXT('DEANSLIST FORMAT')
0006.00                     FNAME
0007.00                     LNAME
0008.00                     STUDID#
0009.00                     GRADEPT
0010.00                   K GRADEPT                     DESCEND
0011.00                   S GRADEPT                     COMP(GE 3.5)
        ****************** End of data****************************************

 F3=Exit   F4=Prompt   F5=Refresh   F9=Retrieve   F10=Cursor
 F16=Repeat find       F17=Repeat change          F24=More keys
```

Several important differences between logical and physical file definitions need to be highlighted. The first is that the record level keyword PFILE is required in a simple logical file (see line 4, Figure 7.4). Since a logical file provides a different view of a physical file(s), the physical file(s) must be specified. In the case of a single physical file, this is done with the PFILE keyword.

A new field level specification is also shown in Figure 7.4. Line 11 is a **select specification**. The keyword COMP was used in an earlier chapter to check the validity of data entered into a field. In a logical file, however, COMP can also be used to "select" or "omit" physical file records from the logical file. In reality, no records are selected or omitted. The COMP specification is simply used to build the access path (index) to the correct records. Select specifications have an S in position 17. Line 11 selects physical file records that have a quantity greater than or equal to 3.5. The access path created will only point to the data records in the physical file with grade point values greater than 3.5.

Defining DEANSLIST could also have been accomplished with an omit specification. To define a field level specification as an omit, enter an O in position 17, and change the COMP condition to GRADEPT LT 3.5. All the COMP operands covered previously for physical files are valid for logical files.

To create the logical file, exit the SEU `Edit` screen, save the DDS, and compile the member. The school employee responsible for generating the dean's list can be told that the information is stored in the file DEANSLIST. He or she would not even have to know that STUDENT exists. Whenever the logical file DEANSLIST is requested, the AS/400 DBMS will retrieve data from the associated physical file defined in the PFILE keyword, STUDENT. The data would appear as in Figure 7.5.

FIGURE 7.5

```
                              Display Report
                                        Report width . . . ... :   40
Position to line  . . . . .  ______    Shift to column . . ... . _____
Line   ....+....1....+....2....+....3....+....4

       FNAME      LNAME       STUDID#    GRADEPT
000001 Wilma      Flintstone  123456789    4.00
000002 Betty      Rubble      444444444    3.99
****** ********   End of report  ********

                                                                Bottom
F3=Exit        F12=Cancel       F19=Left       F20=Right      F21=Split
```

Notice that the records are in grade point average from highest to lowest. The default order for a keyed file is ascending—smallest to largest. For files with character fields as their keys, ascending results in an alphabetic record listing. With numeric key fields, there may be times (such as with the dean's list) when the larger numbers should be listed first. In this case, the keyword DESCEND must be specified. DESCEND would be entered in the keyword area of the key field specification as seen in line 10 of Figure 7.4.

Modifying Data Using Simple Logical Files

Simple logical files can be used to modify the physical files they are based on. For instance, we could load the information as shown in Figure 7.6 using DFU. Notice that the screen says that the file being updated is the logical file DEANSLIST. Since logical files do not contain any data, in reality the new "Joe User" record will be inserted into the physical file STUDENT. Figure 7.7 shows the STUDENT data member after the update.

The "problem" with updating the physical file using the logical file format is that the fields not included in the logical file definition are given blank and zero values in the physical file. If all fields in the physical file should have a value, updating using the logical file

FIGURE 7.6

```
DL                                                Mode . . . . :   INSERT
Format . . . . :    DLFMT_____                    File . . . . :   DEANSLIST

FNAME:    Joe_____
LNAME:    User______
STUDID#: 231231231
GRADEPT: 3.25

F3=Exit                  F5=Refresh                F6=Select format
F9=Insert                F10=Entry                 F11=Change
```

FIGURE 7.7

```
                           Display Physical File Member
File . . . . . . :    STUDENT                Library . . . . :    MYLIBXX
Member . . . . . :    STUDENT                Record . . . . . :   1
Control . . . . .     __________             Column . . . . . :   1
Find . . . . . . .    ________________________________________
*...+....1....+....2....+....3....+....4....+....5....+....6...
FlintstoneFred     11 Limestone DrBedrock    AZ88888111111111 ¤ H
FlintstoneWilma    11 Limestone DrBedrock    AZ88888123456789   °
Rubble    Betty    15 Limestone DrBedrock    AZ88888444444444 ± ±
Rubble    Barnard 15 Limestone DrBedrock     AZ88888999999999 ¬
User      Joe                                       231231231   á

                         ****** END OF DATA ******

                                                                    Bottom
F3=Exit   F12=Cancel   F19=Left   F20=Right   F24=More keys
```

should not be allowed. (This can be accomplished with AS/400 object security and will be covered in Chapter 11.)

Another problem is that the omitted fields could be the key (or part of the key) of the physical file or another logical file. For instance, we could have easily not included STUDID# in DEANSLIST. When the Joe User record was entered, spaces would have been placed in the student id field. If we wanted to retrieve Joe User's student record, spaces would have to be specified for student id, not Joe User's actual id.

Even though the database will accept spaces as a value for the key, a second data record entered using the logical file would not have been accepted. Since the second record's STUDID# would be blank also, allowing a second record with a blank student id number would result in the file containing records with duplicate key values. The DBMS will not allow this to occur for files defined as UNIQUE.

When updating with logical files, the bottom line is to be careful. The fact that logical files do not have to contain all the physical file fields can lead to major data integrity problems.

The Logical–Physical File Relationship

The relationship between logical and physical files is simple: Logical files are based on physical files. The repercussions of this relationship are not so simple. The previous section covered the effect of updating data using the logical file. As demonstrated, the effects on the physical file are varied depending on the fields defined in the logical file and the physical file field definition (keyed or nonkeyed) itself.

The effects of changing the physical file, in both its data and structure, on the logical file are also very complex and dependent on the type of change and the file definitions. For simple changes, such as adding or deleting a record from the physical file, the physical–logical file relationship is very useful and user friendly. Record updates to the physical file are automatically reflected in the logical file. In general, this is a good feature. Users usually want to see physical file changes immediately reflected in all the logical files. With this in mind, the AS/400 developers made "immediate updating" the default for all logical files. (There is a logical file parameter that controls when updating will occur. However, there are performance considerations that are well beyond the scope of this book that need to be examined before you would update any other way than immediately.) Remember that a logical file contains no data. When we say that the logical file is updated, we're actually talking about changing the access path.

Logical files are automatically updated by the DBMS whenever there are physical file record insertions or deletions. Deleting an entire physical file, however, is much more complicated because of logical files. The AS/400 will not allow a physical file to be deleted if any logical files are based on that physical file. If a physical file could be deleted without regard to the dependent files, logical files could exist that were based on nonexistent physical files. If a user requested to view data through a logical file and the physical file it was based on did not exist, the DBMS would not know what to do. The AS/400 protects the logical files and the database by not allowing a physical file to be deleted until all the dependencies are removed. For instance, if we tried to delete the STUDENT file, the AS/400 DBMS would return the error message `Cannot delete file or member of file STUDENT in MYLIBXX` because DEANSLIST is dependent on STUDENT.

To erase a physical file, all dependent logical files must be deleted or modified to reference a different physical file. If you were given the task to erase a physical file, how would you find the dependent logical files? Certainly searching every library and logical file's DDS source code is an option, but not a pleasant one.

There is a tool (program) supplied by IBM called DLTDEPLGL (Delete Dependent Logicals) that can help. Issuing the DLTDEPLGL command and specifying the physical filename will result in the deletion of all dependent logical files.

The fact that logical files are dependent on physical files also affects the procedure for modifying a physical file's structure. When a simple change to a physical file (such as changing the name of a field) is made, the update procedure requires that we recompile the physical file definition. Since recompiling the physical file definition means the old physical file will be deleted, we must delete all dependent logical files before we can recompile the physical file definition. (Yikes!)

The problem with DLTDEPLGL, in this case, is that the logical files must be recreated after the new physical file is created. DLTDEPLGL doesn't help identify logical files or recreate them.

Fortunately, the AS/400 has a CL command called DSPDBR (display database relations) that displays all dependent files for a specified file. (As a matter of fact, the DLTDEPLGL program uses DSPDBR to locate the dependent logical files to delete.) For instance, issuing the following command:

```
DSPDBR MYLIBXX/STUDENT
```

would result in Figure 7.8. Notice the list of dependent files at the bottom of Figure 7.8. With this information, the programmer could delete the dependent logical files, delete the physical file, and then be able to identify the logical files to be recreated.

FIGURE 7.8

```
                              Display Spooled File
File . . . . . :  QPDSPDBR                              Page/Line   1/1
Control . . . . .  _____                                Columns     1 - 78
Find . . . . . .   ______________________________
*...+....1....+....2....+....3....+....4....+....5....+....6....+....7....+...
    2/22/94               Display Database Relations
 DSPDBR Command Input
   File . . . . . . . . . . . . . . . . . . : FILE        STUDENT
     Library . . . . . . . . . . . . . . . :             MYLIBXX
   Member . . . . . . . . . . . . . . . . . : MBR         *NONE
   Record format . . . . . . . . . . . . . : RCDFMT      *NONE
   Output . . . . . . . . . . . . . . . . . : OUTPUT      *
 Specifications
   Type of file . . . . . . . . . . . . . . :             Physical
   File . . . . . . . . . . . . . . . . . . :             STUDENT
     Library . . . . . . . . . . . . . . . :             MYLIBXX
     Member . . . . . . . . . . . . . . . . :             *NONE
     Record format . . . . . . . . . . . . :             *NONE
     Number of dependent files . . . . . . . :                 1
 Files Dependent On Specified File
   Dependent File        Library       Sharing      JREF
     DEANSLIST           MYLIBXX       Data

                                                                      Bottom
F3=Exit   F12=Cancel   F19=Left   F20=Right   F24=More keys
```

This complication with recompiling has a drastic effect on CHGF (and COMCHGF). Our wonderful CHGF program will no longer work for physical files with dependent logical files. It stands to reason that when the operating system attempts to delete the physical file (during the recompile), the DBMS will stop the deletion because there are logical files dependent on the physical file—or will it?

Closer inspection of the CHGF program shows that line 19 (see Figure 4.4) renames the physical file to TEMP. When a physical file is renamed, the dependent logical files are updated to reflect the renaming! In other words, if we were changing the physical file STUDENT and STUDENT was renamed to TEMP, all logical files that were dependent on STUDENT would now be dependent on TEMP. To prove this, look at the file description for DEANSLIST with the DSPFD (display file description) command. The file description would show that DEANSLIST is now based on TEMP, not STUDENT. (You would need to page down several screens to display the portion of DEANSLIST's description as seen in Figure 7.9.)

FIGURE 7.9

```
                              Display Spooled File
File . . . . . :   QPDSPFD                              Page/Line   2/51
Control . . . . .   _____                               Columns     1 - 78
Find . . . . . .   ______________________________
*...+....1....+....2....+....3....+....4....+....5....+....6....+....7....+...
    Number of data members . . . . . . . . . :          1
    Based on file . . . . . . . . . . . . . . :          TEMP       <===
      Library . . . . . . . . . . . . . . . . :          MYLIBXX
      Member . . . . . . . . . . . . . . . . . :          STUDENT
      Logical file format . . . . . . . . . . :          DLFMT
      Number of index entries . . . . . . . . :                  3
      Number of member accesses . . . . . . . :                  0
  Record Format List
                          Record  Format Level
   Format        Fields   Length  Identifier
   DLFMT             4        29  358B716E2A5AE
    Text . . . . . . . . . . . . . . . . . . :          DEANS LIST FORMAT
   Total number of formats . . . . . . . . . :         1
   Total number of fields . . . . . . . . . . :         4
   Total record length . . . . . . . . . . . :        29
  Member List

                                                                    More...
F3=Exit   F12=Cancel   F19=Left   F20=Right   F24=More keys
```

You could also prove that the logical file has been changed by executing the DSPDBR command for TEMP. The resulting display would show that DEANSLIST is now a dependent file of TEMP.

After renaming STUDENT, CHGF recompiles FRF and the STUDENT file's source code and copies the data back to the new STUDENT file from TEMP. None of this processing will be affected by the presence of the logical file since the logical file DEANSLIST is now dependent on TEMP, not STUDENT.

However, when we try to delete the temporary file on line 41, we will have a problem. Since, TEMP now has a dependent logical file, the DBMS will not allow TEMP to be deleted until the logical file is deleted. In addition, after TEMP and its dependent logical file DEANSLIST are deleted, we must recompile DEANSLIST's source code definition to recreate the DEANSLIST logical file for our users. (Yikes! again.)

Therefore, within the program we have to somehow find all the dependent logical files, delete the logical files, delete TEMP, and recreate all the logical files by recompiling their source code definitions. Fortunately for us, the DSPDBR command has some added parameters that will make all this possible.

The DSPDBR command (and many other CL commands) can be instructed to write out the command's results to a file. In this case, the DSPDBR command would write all the dependent logical filenames to a file. The information that is written (and, therefore, the file being written to) will have the following format and field names:

CL VARIABLE	TYPE	LENGTH	VARIABLE DESCRIPTION
&WHRTYP	*CHAR	1	Type of file: P=Physical, L=Logical
&WHRFI	*CHAR	10	File
&WHRLI	*CHAR	10	Library
&WHRMB	*CHAR	10	Member
&WHRRD	*CHAR	10	Record format
&WHNO	*DEC	5	Number of dependencies
&WHDTM	*CHAR	13	Retrieval date: century/date/time
&WHREFI	*CHAR	10	Dependent file
&WHRELI	*CHAR	10	Dependent library
&WHREMB	*CHAR	10	Dependent member
&WHTYPE	*CHAR	1	D=Data,I=Access path,O=Acc path owner,V=SQL VIEW
&WHJDIL	*DEC	2	Ordinal number of position in the JFILE list
&WHJREF	*DEC	2	Join reference number
&WHSYSN	*CHAR	8	System Name (Source System, if file is DDM)

Creating this file structure with PDM and SEU, though not intolerable, certainly is not user friendly. That is why those far-thinking AS/400 developers have already created and loaded this format on all AS/400s. (There is a file QADSPDBR in library QSYS with a record format called QWHDRDBR that matches this layout.) You can instruct the system (through DSPDBR options) to create a file with this format and write the DSPDBR results to the specified file. The system will automatically use the QWHDRDBR format when creating the specified file.

For instance, inside CHGF let's have the results go to a file called DEPFILES (dependent files). In the DSPDBR command, we will have to specify *OUTFILE as the output and MYLIBXX/DEPFILES as the file to write to. (We will also have to specify the name of the file that is changing.) The names of the dependent files will then be written to DEPFILES. CHGF will then read DEPFILES, delete each dependent file, and recompile each dependent file's source code. After all the dependent files have been deleted and recompiled, TEMP will be deleted.

For CHGF to access DEPFILES, it needs to be declared in the program. When program source code is compiled, file definitions are incorporated into the program object. Therefore, any file declared in the source code must exist when the source code is compiled. In other words, DEPFILES must be created before the new CHGF can be compiled. Do this by simply executing DSPDBR against any file and directing the output to MYLIBXX/DEPFILES. Figure 7.10 shows the new CHGF source code.

After entering the new source code, we would create DEPFILES (as described earlier) and then recompile CHGF. Make a small

FIGURE 7.10

```
         *************** Beginning of data ************************************
0001.00 /****************************************************************/
0002.00 /* IDENTIFIES THE VARIABLES THAT WILL BE SUPPLIED TO THE PROGRAM*/
0003.00 /****************************************************************/
0004.00
0005.00 CHGFPGM:  PGM         PARM(&LIB &FILE &MEM)
0006.00
0007.00 /****************************************************************/
0008.00 /* DEFINES THE VARIABLES THAT WILL BE USED IN THE PROGRAM.      */
0009.00 /****************************************************************/
0010.00
0011.00 DCL       VAR(&LIB)   TYPE(*CHAR)  LEN(8)
0012.00 DCL       VAR(&FILE)  TYPE(*CHAR)  LEN(8)
0013.00 DCL       VAR(&MEM)   TYPE(*CHAR)  LEN(8)
0014.00
0015.00 /****************************************************************/
0016.00 /* IDENTIFIES DEPFILES, WHICH WILL HOLD THE DEPENDENT LOGICAL   */
0017.00 /* FILENAMES                                                    */
0018.00 /****************************************************************/
0019.00
0020.00 DCLF      FILE(MYLIBXX/DEPFILES) RCDFMT(QWHDRDBR)
0021.00
0022.00 /****************************************************************/
0023.00 /* COPIES THE DATA TO THE TEMPORARY FILE                        */
0024.00 /****************************************************************/
0025.00
0026.00              RNMOBJ     OBJ(&LIB/&MEM) OBJTYPE(*FILE) NEWOBJ(TEMP)
0027.00
0028.00 /****************************************************************/
0029.00 /* CREATES NEW FIELD DEFINITIONS (IN FRF), RECREATES DATA FILE  */
0030.00 /****************************************************************/
0031.00              DLTF       FILE(&LIB/FRF)
0032.00              CRTPF      FILE(&LIB/FRF) SRCFILE(&LIB/&FILE) +
0033.00                           SRCMBR(FRF)
0034.00              CRTPF      FILE(&LIB/&MEM) SRCFILE(&LIB/&FILE) +
0035.00                           SRCMBR(&MEM)
0036.00
0037.00 /****************************************************************/
0038.00 /* COPIES THE DATA FROM THE TEMPORARY FILE TO THE NEW MEMBER    */
0039.00 /****************************************************************/
0040.00
0041.00              CPYF       FROMFILE(&LIB/TEMP) TOFILE(&LIB/&MEM) +
0042.00                           MBROPT(*REPLACE)
0043.00
0044.00
0045.00 /****************************************************************/
0046.00 /* FINDS ALL THE DEPENDENT LOGICAL FILES AND WRITES THEM TO     */
0047.00 /* DEPFILES IN THE USER'S LIBRARY.                              */
0048.00 /****************************************************************/
0049.00
0050.00              DSPDBR     FILE(&LIB/TEMP) OUTPUT(*OUTFILE) +
0051.00                           OUTFILE(&LIB/DEPFILES)
0052.00
0053.00
0054.00 /****************************************************************/
0055.00 /* READS THE DEPENDENT LOGICAL FILES FROM DEPFILES.  MONMSG     */
0056.00 /* CHECKS IF THE END OF THE FILE HAS BEEN REACHED.  IF IT IS    */
0057.00 /* THE END OF THE FILE THEN THE PROGRAM BRANCHES AND DELETES    */
0058.00 /* TEMP.  IF IT IS NOT THE END OF THE FILE THEN THE DEPENDENT   */
0059.00 /* FILE IS DELETED AND RECREATED FROM ITS DDS SOURCE.  THEN THE */
0060.00 /* NEXT DEPENDENT FILE IS READ FROM DEPFILES.                   */
0061.00 /****************************************************************/
0062.00
0063.00 READ:        RCVF       RCDFMT(QWHDRDBR)
0064.00              MONMSG     MSGID(CPF0864) EXEC(GOTO DELTEMP)
0065.00              DLTF       FILE(&WHRELI/&WHREFI)
0066.00              CRTLF      FILE(&WHRELI/&WHREFI) SRCFILE(&WHRELI/DDSSRC) +
0067.00                           SRCMBR(&WHREFI)
0068.00              GOTO       READ
0069.00
0070.00 /****************************************************************/
0071.00 /* DELETES THE TEMPORARY FILE AND ERASES ALL RECORDS IN DEPFILES*/
0072.00 /****************************************************************/
0073.00
0074.00 DELTEMP:     DLTF       FILE(&LIB/TEMP)
0075.00              CLRPFM     FILE(&LIB/DEPFILES)
0076.00              ENDPGM
         ****************** End of data **************************************
```

change to the student file, such as changing the name of the record format to STEWRECFMT. Then run CHGF.

To verify that CHGF ran correctly

1. Display the STUDENT file description (DSPFD), and see if the format record name has been changed.
2. Display the data in member STUDENT, and verify that it was saved and copied correctly.
3. Verify that TEMP has been deleted. (Use PDM to display all files in MYLIBXX.)
4. Verify that DEANSLIST exists.
5. Display STUDENT's database relations with the DSPDBR command, and verify that DEANSLIST is a dependent file.

Changing Logical Files and the Effect on Programs

Changing logical files is much easier than changing physical files. Since logical files do not contain any data, modifications to the structure of the logical file (such as adding fields) does not require any special procedure to save and recopy data. However, structural changes will change the logical file's record format level identifier. Therefore, any programs that use the logical file must be recompiled, or they will be stopped by the level check procedure. The FNDSTRPDM command can be used to locate all programs that use a particular logical file.

One method to avoid recompiling all the programs that use a changed logical file is to create a new logical file with the structural change. For instance, if a new field were being added to a logical file but only one in ten programs were going to use the new field, it might be easier to simply create a new logical file with the change and modify the programs using the new field to reflect the new logical filename. In this way, only a small number of programs need to be recompiled.

Joining Files

A more complicated logical file is a **join logical file**, which can contain information from multiple physical files. Join logical files give the AS/400 user much more control over the results of a join than the three relational joins covered in Chapter 6. Essentially, DDS provides the capability to select and join any physical file fields and records into one logical file. To demonstrate this capability, the CLASS and INSTRUCTOR files discussed earlier need to be created. Assuming that the physical file members called CLASS and INSTRUCTOR have already been created, enter the DDS in Figure 7.11 into FRF. Then enter the DDS in Figures 7.12 and 7.13 into members CLASS and INSTRUCTOR; save the members; and compile FRF, CLASS, and INSTRUCTOR. Don't forget that FRF must be compiled first if CLASS and INSTRUCTOR are to compile successfully.

Assuming that the logical file member called LOAD in DDSSRC and MYLIBXX already exists, enter the DDS in Figure 7.14.

Notice that there are several new keywords in the join logical file. For instance, the JFILE keyword (line 3, in Figure 7.14) identifies the files to be joined. Up to 32 files can be specified. (Don't try this, unless your goal is to annoy the systems support department and all the users. The resources needed to perform that large of a join could be considerable, and overall system performance might be drastically affected.)

FIGURE 7.11

```
               *************** Beginning of data *************************************
0001.00                  CL#          6          COLHDG('CLASS' 'NUMBER')
0002.00                                          TEXT('CLASS NUMBER')
0003.00                                          CHECK(ME)
0004.00                  IID          3          COLHDG('INSTRUCTOR' 'ID')
0005.00                                          TEXT('INSTRUCTOR ID')
0006.00                                          CHECK(ME)
0007.00                  INSTR       12          COLHDG('INSTRUCTOR' 'NAME')
0008.00                                          TEXT('INSTRUCTOR NAME')
0009.00                                          CHECK(ME)
0010.00                  SECT#        5          COLHDG('SECTION' 'NUMBER')
0011.00                                          TEXT('SECTION NUMBER')
0012.00                                          CHECK(ME)
               ****************** End of data ****************************************
```

FIGURE 7.12

```
               *************** Beginning of data *************************************
0001.00         *    THIS PHYSICAL FILE IS THE CLASS FILE DDS DEFINITION
0002.00         *
0003.00                                          UNIQUE
0004.00                                          REF(MYLIBXX/FRF)
0005.00                R CLFMT                   TEXT('CLASS FORMAT')
0006.00                  CL#        R
0007.00                  SECT#      R
0008.00                  IID        R
0009.00                K CL#
0010.00                K SECT#
               ****************** End of data ****************************************
```

FIGURE 7.13

```
               *************** Beginning of data *************************************
0001.00         *    THIS PHYSICAL FILE IS THE INSTRUCTOR FILE DDS DEFINITION
0002.00         *
0003.00                                          UNIQUE
0004.00                                          REF(MYLIBXX/FRF)
0005.00                R INSTRFMT                TEXT('INSTRUCTOR FORMAT')
0006.00                  IID        R
0007.00                  INSTR      R
0008.00                K IID
               ****************** End of data ****************************************
```

FIGURE 7.14

```
               *************** Beginning of data *************************************
0001.00         * THIS LOGICAL FILE JOINS THE INSTRUCTOR AND CLASS FILES
0002.00         *
0003.00                R LOADFMT                 JFILE(MYLIBXX/INSTRUCTOR +
0004.00                                                MYLIBXX/CLASS)
0005.00                                          TEXT('LOAD FORMAT')
0006.00                J                         JOIN(1 2)
0007.00                                          JFLD(IID IID)
0008.00                  INSTR
0009.00                  CL#
               ****************** End of data ****************************************
```

The logical file must also have a **join specification**. The join specification must follow the record specification and is indicated by placing a J in column 17 (line 6 in Figure 7.14). The join specification identifies which files are to be joined and the basis for the join. The keyword JOIN (entered in the keyword area of the join specification) identifies the files to be joined. The JOIN keyword is not required if only two files are specified in the JFILE keyword since they are the only possible files that can be joined. (We have entered the JOIN keyword for example purposes.) Further, library names and filenames do not have to be used to identify files in the join specification. When files are listed in the JFILE keyword, they are assigned a relative file number. The first file is 1, the next is 2, the file specified after the second is 3, and so forth. Whenever the file needs to be identified, the relative file number can be used instead of the longer file and library names. The join specification on line 6 uses the relative file numbers.

The JFLD keyword identifies the field(s) that will be used to join the records. In this case, line 7 specifies that records in the INSTRUCTOR and CLASS files that share the same value in their IID fields will be joined. More than one field can be defined as the join condition. This might be necessary if more than one field is needed to uniquely identify a record. For instance, the only way to absolutely distinguish each record in a file may be to check the last name, first name, and phone number fields. If this were the case, any records being joined from two different files should have matching data in all these fields. This could be done by using three JFLD keywords.

The last new keyword (which is not shown in the figure) is JREF. The JREF keyword is used to distinguish between fields (in different files) that share the same name. JREF identifies which file to use. For instance, if two files had a field called DATE—one date field containing the employee's date of hire and another containing the date of last salary increase—and DATE was included in the logical file layout, then JREF would have to be used to identify which file's date was to be used. To specify the file, the relative record number can be used. The logical file field specification would simply include JREF(1) or JREF(2) in the keyword area.

To create the logical file LOAD, simply save and compile member LOAD. If we were to add the information in Figure 7.15 into INSTRUCTOR and CLASS, and then looked at the logical file with QUERY/400, the result would be Figure 7.16

FIGURE 7.15

INSTRUCTOR		CLASS		
IID	Instr	Cl#	Sect#	IID
001	Galen	BIO101	96201	001
777	Beane	BUS101	96203	777
666	Hyde	PSY212	96203	666
333	Jobs	CMP101	96306	333
555	Jones	BUS101	96306	555
		ACC101	96306	777
		BUS101	96201	555

Notice that the records are in the same order as the instructor file. This is because INSTRUCTOR was defined first and is considered the primary file. The records in a join logical file will follow the arrival sequence order of the primary file.

FIGURE 7.16

```
                              Display Report
Query . . . :   MYLIBXX/LOAD               Report width . . . . . :   20
Position to line  . . . . .            Shift to column  . . . . . .
Line   ....+....1....+....2
       INSTRUCTOR     CLASS
       NAME           NUMBER
000001 Galen          BIO101
000002 Beane          BUS101
000003 Beane          ACC101
000004 Hyde           PSY212
000005 Jobs           CMP101
000006 Jones          BUS101
000007 Jones          BUS101
****** ********  End of report  ********

                                                                  Bottom
F3=Exit      F12=Cancel      F19=Left      F20=Right      F21=Split
```

If a different order is desired, a key specification can be used in the join file definition. For instance, defining instructor name as the key of the logical join file will result in an index being built. This index will be used by application programs and system functions when accessing the logical file data. For instance, defining a file KLOAD as in Figure 7.17 would result in an index being built according to the instructor's name.

FIGURE 7.17

```
 Columns . . . :    1  71            Edit                      MYLIBXX/DDSSRC
 SEU==>                                                                 KLOAD
 FMT A* .....A*. 1 ...+... 2 ...+... 3 ...+... 4 ...+... 5 ...+... 6 ...+... 7
        *************** Beginning of data ************************************
0001.00       * THIS LOGICAL FILE JOINS THE INSTRUCTOR AND CLASS FILES
0002.00       *
0003.00                R LOADFMT                 JFILE(MYLIBXX/INSTRUCTOR +
0004.00                                                 MYLIBXX/CLASS)
0005.00                                          TEXT('LOAD FORMAT')
0006.00                J                         JOIN(1 2)
0007.00                                          JFLD(IID IID)
0008.00                  INSTR
0009.00                  CL#
0010.00                K INSTR
        ****************** End of data ***************************************

 F3=Exit   F4=Prompt   F5=Refresh   F9=Retrieve   F10=Cursor
 F16=Repeat find       F17=Repeat change          F24=More keys
```

Copying that file with the CPYF command and then displaying the copied file (with the DSPPFM command) would result in Figure 7.18.

FIGURE 7.18

```
                    Display Physical File Member
File . . . . . . :  COPIED              Library  . . . . :   MYLIBXX
Member . . . . . :  KLOAD               Record . . . . . :   1
Control  . . . . .                      Column . . . . . :   1
Find . . . . . . .
*...+....1....+...
Beane       BUS101
Beane       ACC101
Galen       BIO101
Hyde        PSY212
Jobs        CMP101
Jones       BUS101
Jones       BUS101
                     ****** END OF DATA ******

                                                                  Bottom
F3=Exit   F12=Cancel   F19=Left   F20=Right   F24=More keys
```

Notice that the copy command used the index to access the records and copy them to the new file. Your application programs will also automatically use the index.

We can further control the order records will be accessed by declaring a multifield key in the logical file. The first key specification defines the primary sort field, and each succeeding key specification determines the precedence of the secondary sorts. The secondary sort fields will be used to determine the order of records that have the same value for all higher order key fields.

One limitation to join files is that all key fields must come from the primary file. So, for instance, notice that instructor Beane has two records. When accessing the logical file, the BUS101 record precedes the ACC101 record because BUS101 precedes ACC101 in the arrival sequence order of CLASS. We cannot have the Beane records in order by class name because class name is not in the primary file INSTRUCTOR and therefore cannot be a key field.

Multiple Format Logical Files

The final type of logical file is a multiple format logical file. Multiple format logical files appear to contain records from many different physical files. Unlike join files, the user does not specify individual fields. When a physical file is specified in multiple format logical file, the entire physical file record is included. The records from the various physical files, however, can appear to be mixed together.

Application programs that need information from many physical files can be greatly simplified by creating a multiple format logical file that includes the required physical files. For instance, the school employees want an application program to generate a student Class

History report that includes all student information (address, GPA, and so on), the classes each student has taken, and the grade received in each class (Figure 7.19).

FIGURE 7.19

```
              STUDENT CLASS HISTORY REPORT
STUDENT:

Fred Flintstone           Student ID :      1111111
11 Limestone Dr           Total Credits:     9
Bedrock  AZ  88888        Grade Point:       2.00

CLASSES TAKEN:

BIO101    96201   1.00    PSY212  96203     3.00
ACC101    96306   2.00

*******************************************************

STUDENT:

Wilma Flintstone          Student ID :   1234567
11 Limestone Dr           Total Credits:  12
Bedrock  AZ  88888        Grade Point:    4.00

CLASSES TAKEN:
BIO101    96201    4.00   CMP101    96306   4.00
ACC101    96306    4.00   BUS101    96306   4.00

*******************************************************

STUDENT:

Betty Rubble              Student ID :      4444444
15 Limestone Dr           Total Credits:     18
Bedrock  AZ  88888        Grade Point:       3.99

CLASSES TAKEN:


BIO101    96201    4.00   CMP101     96306  4.00
BUS101    96203    4.00   BUS201     96306  3.95
PSY212    96203    4.00   ACC101     96306  4.00

*******************************************************

STUDENT:

Barnard Rubble            Student ID :      9999999
15 Limestone Dr           Total Credits:     15
Bedrock  AZ  88888        Grade Point:       3.00

CLASSES TAKEN:

PSY212    96203    2.00   BUS201     96306  3.50
BUS101    96203    2.50   ACC101     96306  3.00
CMP101    96306    4.00

*******************************************************
```

If we had the STUDENT file from Figure 7.7 and there was a file named GRADE that had the structure defined in Figure 7.20 and the data in 7.21, we could write an application program to access the two files and build a report similar to 7.19. (To create the file GRADE, we would have to add a field GRADE to FRF with a length of three and two decimal places. The TEXT and COLHDG keywords would be set to 'GRADE'.)

The logic to retrieve the GRADE and STUDENT records would look like the following:

ReadS: Read STUDENT

If end of file Then stop

Perform print-student-info

Set KEY = STUDENT.STUDID#

ReadG: Read GRADE

If end of file

Then GoTo ReadS

Else If GRADE.STUDID# = KEY

Then Perform print-class-info

GoTo ReadG

We could decrease the number of reads performed and simplify the overall logic of the application by creating a multiple format file called STUGRD. The logical file records would appear to be

FIGURE 7.20

```
 Columns . . . :    1  71            Edit                          MYLIBXX/DDSSRC
 SEU==>                                                                     GRADE
 FMT A* .....A*. 1 ...+... 2 ...+... 3 ...+... 4 ...+... 5 ...+... 6 ...+... 7
        *************** Beginning of data ************************************
0001.00        *    THIS PHYSICAL FILE DDS DEFINITION IS FOR GRADE
0002.00        *
0003.00                                                   UNIQUE
0004.00                                                   REF(MYLIBXX/FRF)
0005.00                  R GRDFMT                         TEXT('GRADE FORMAT')
0006.00                    CL#        R
0007.00                    SECT#      R
0008.00                    STUDID#    R
0009.00                    GRADE      R
0010.00                  K CL#
0011.00                  K SECT#
0012.00                  K STUDID#
        ****************** End of data ***************************************

 F3=Exit   F4=Prompt   F5=Refresh   F9=Retrieve   F10=Cursor
 F16=Repeat find       F17=Repeat change          F24=More keys
```

FIGURE 7.21

Cl #	Sect #	STUDID#	GRADE
BIO101	96201	123456789	4.00
BIO101	96201	111111111	1.00
BIO101	96201	444444444	4.00
BUS101	96203	444444444	4.00
PSY212	96203	111111111	3.00
PSY212	96203	999999999	2.00
PSY212	96203	444444444	4.00
BUS101	96203	999999999	2.50
ACC101	96306	123456789	4.00
CMP101	96306	123456789	4.00
CMP101	96306	444444444	4.00
CMP101	96306	999999999	4.00
BUS201	96306	444444444	3.95
ACC101	96306	111111111	2.00
ACC101	96306	444444444	4.00
BUS201	96306	999999999	3.50
BUS101	96306	123456789	4.00
ACC101	96306	999999999	3.00

ordered by student id number with each STUDENT record first, followed by all the associated GRADE records. The application program logic needed to access the multiple format file would look like the following:

```
          Set KEY = null
Read:     Read STUGRD
          If end of file Then stop
          If KEY = STUDID#
          Then Perform print-class-info
          Else Perform print-student-info
               Set KEY = STUDID#
          GoTo Read
```

Notice that the second program does not have to perform an entire sequential search of the GRADE file. The multiple format logical file improves the performance of the program and simplifies the logic. The size of the program will also be decreased (since only one file is identified, opened, and read instead of many), as will the amount of programmer time needed to code and test the program. If many programs needed to access the same set of files or if a program needed to access more than two files, the savings in using a multiple format logical file would be even greater.

Creating Multiple Format Logical Files

Multiple format logical files are created the same way as physical files and the previously discussed logical files: Enter a DDS file definition into a source physical file member and compile the member. The difference with a multiple format logical file is in the definition.

Multiple format file definitions comprise the same keywords and specifications that physical and logical files use; however, there are no field specifications. Each physical file specified comes with all its fields. Furthermore, the keys defined for each physical file control how the records from the different files will be accessed. For instance, to create the multiple format logical file STUGRD, the DDS in Figure 7.22 would be entered into a member and compiled.

If we copied STUGRD into a physical file named STUFF, the records would be retrieved from STUDENT and GRADE and written to STUFF in the order shown in Figure 7.23. Notice that the STUDENT record is first followed by the GRADE records that have the same value for STUDID#. This occurs because the STUDENT file was specified before GRADE in the DDS and the primary key for both files was STUDID#. Notice also that the grade records for each student are in ascending order by section number. This is because we declared SECT# as a secondary key for the GRADE file (on line 10) and ascending is the default sequence order.

FIGURE 7.22

```
Columns . . . :    1  71           Edit                         MYLIBXX/DDSSRC
SEU==>                                                                  STUGRD
FMT A* .....A*. 1 ...+... 2 ...+... 3 ...+... 4 ...+... 5 ...+... 6 ...+... 7
       *************** Beginning of data *************************************
0001.00      *
0002.00      * THIS IS THE DDS FOR THE MULTIPLE FORMAT LOGICAL FILE
0003.00      * THAT COMBINES THE STUDENT AND GRADE FILES
0004.00      *
0005.00              R STUDREC                     PFILE(MYLIBXX/STUDENT)
0006.00              K STUDID#
0007.00
0008.00              R GRDFMT                      PFILE(MYLIBXX/GRADE)
0009.00              K STUDID#
0010.00              K SECT#
       ****************** End of data ****************************************

 F3=Exit   F4=Prompt   F5=Refresh   F9=Retrieve   F10=Cursor
 F16=Repeat find       F17=Repeat change          F24=More keys
```

FIGURE 7.23

```
                          Display Physical File Member
File . . . . . . :   STUFF                 Library  . . . . :   MYLIBXX
Member . . . . . :   STUFF                 Record . . . . . :   1
Control  . . . . .                         Column . . . . . :   1
Find . . . . . . .
*...+....1....+....2....+....3....+....4....+....5....+....6....+....7
FlintstoneFred     11 Limestone DrBedrock   AZ88888111111111 ¤ H
BIO10196201111111111
PSY21296203111111111
ACC10196306111111111
FlintstoneWilma    11 Limestone DrBedrock   AZ88888123456789   °
BIO10196201123456789
ACC10196306123456789
CMP10196306123456789
BUS10196306123456789
Rubble     Betty   15 Limestone DrBedrock   AZ88888444444444 ± ±
BIO10196201444444444
BUS10196203444444444
PSY21296203444444444
CMP10196306444444444
BUS20196306444444444¬
ACC10196306444444444
Rubble     Barnard 15 Limestone DrBedrock   AZ88888999999999 ¬
PSY21296203999999999
BUS10196203999999999
CMP10196306999999999
BUS20196306999999999
ACC10196306999999999
                        ****** END OF DATA ******
```

This "merging" of different records can occur only when the files share the same key field. For instance, let's define a file, ROSTER, to contain STUDENT and GRADE records grouped by each course. In addition, for each course, we'll include the instructor's name and id. Assuming that we have the CLASS and INSTRUCTOR files that contain the same information as shown earlier, we would create the multiple format logical file, ROSTER, with the DDS in Figure 7.24.

If we copied the logical file ROSTER into a physical file called STUFF, the records would appear as in Figure 7.25.

Notice that the STUDENT and INSTRUCTOR records appear at the bottom of the member. Since neither file shared the key fields, CL# and SECT#, their records were not merged with the CLASS and GRADE records.

Another rule regarding merging is that the shared key fields must be specified in the same order for each file. For instance, if we wanted to merge GRADE and CLASS by class and section, we could not declare CL# as the primary key and SECT# as the secondary key for GRADE. In other words, we would not declare the key fields for GRADE in this order

```
R GRDFMT                PFILE(MYLIBXX/GRADE)
K CL#
K SECT#
```

and then declare just the opposite order—SECT# first and then CL#—for CLASS

```
R CLASS                 PFILE(MYLIBXX/CLASS)
K SECT#
K CL#
```

To get the records to merge, the key fields between files must be specified in the same order. Doing otherwise will result in an error during compilation. If a file does not share a primary or earlier listed key field with the other files, the keyword *NONE must be specified in the appropriate position of the key field list (as in Figure 7.24, lines 13, 17, 18, 19, and so on.).

FIGURE 7.24

```
 Columns . . . :    1  71            Edit                          MYLIBXX/DDSSRC
 SEU==>                                                                    ROSTER
 FMT A* .....A*. 1 ...+... 2 ...+... 3 ...+... 4 ...+... 5 ...+... 6 ...+... 7
        *************** Beginning of data *************************************
0001.00       *
0002.00       *  THIS IS THE DDS FOR THE MULTIPLE FORMAT LOGICAL FILE
0003.00       *  THAT COMBINES THE STUDENT, GRADE, AND INSTRUCTOR INFO
0004.00       *
0005.00                R CLFMT                      PFILE(MYLIBXX/CLASS)
0006.00                K SECT#
0007.00                K CL#
0008.00                K IID
0009.00
0010.00                R GRDFMT                     PFILE(MYLIBXX/GRADE)
0011.00                K SECT#
0012.00                K CL#
0013.00                K *NONE
0014.00                K STUDID#
0015.00
0016.00                R STUDREC                    PFILE(MYLIBXX/STUDENT)
0017.00                K *NONE
0018.00                K *NONE
0019.00                K *NONE
0020.00                K STUDID#
0021.00
0022.00                R INSTRFMT                   PFILE(MYLIBXX/INSTRUCTOR)
0023.00                K *NONE
0024.00                K *NONE
0025.00                K IID
        ****************** End of data ***************************************

 F3=Exit   F4=Prompt   F5=Refresh   F9=Retrieve   F10=Cursor
 F16=Repeat find       F17=Repeat change          F24=More keys
```

FIGURE 7.25

```
                         Display Physical File Member
File . . . . . . :   STUFF                Library  . . . . :   MYLIBXX
Member . . . . . :   STUFF                Record . . . . . :   1
Control  . . . . .                        Column . . . . . :   1
Find . . . . . . .
*...+....1....+....2....+....3....+....4....+....5....+....6....+....7
BIO10196201001
BIO10196201111111111
BIO10196201123456789
BIO10196201444444444
BUS10196201555
BUS10196203777
BUS10196203444444444
BUS10196203999999999
PSY21296203666
PSY21296203111111111
PSY21296203444444444¬
PSY21296203999999999
ACC10196306777
ACC10196306111111111
ACC10196306123456789
ACC10196306444444444
ACC10196306999999999
BUS10196306555
BUS10196306123456789
BUS20196306444444444
BUS20196306999999999
CMP10196306333
CMP10196306123456789
CMP10196306444444444
CMP10196306999999999
FlintstoneFred     11 Limestone DrBedrock    AZ88888111111111 ¤ H
FlintstoneWilma    11 Limestone DrBedrock    AZ88888123456789   °
Rubble    Betty    15 Limestone DrBedrock    AZ88888444444444 ± ±
Rubble    Barnard 15 Limestone DrBedrock    AZ88888999999999 ¬
001Galen
333Jobs
555Jones
666Hyde
777Beane
                        ****** END OF DATA ******
                                                                  Bottom
F3=Exit   F12=Cancel   F19=Left   F20=Right   F24=More keys
```

Multiple Format versus Join Logical Files

Since ROSTER didn't supply the records in the order we wanted, a join logical file may have been the better solution. We could have created a 4 file, join logical file (as defined in Figure 7.26) that creates records as seen in Figure 7.27. Notice that all the information needed for the report is contained within the records.

There are several features demonstrated with this join file. First of all, with more than two physical files being joined, there is a need for multiple join specifications. Notice that each join specification is between different files and for different fields. For instance, the first join is based on two fields (CL# and SECT#) and is between GRADE and CLASS. Also notice that CLASS is used in two join specifications, but no fields from that file are in the join file. CLASS is simply used to tie the instructor name in INSTRUCTOR to the student's grade information from GRADE. CLASS is acting as a correlation file (a file that contains only keys from other files). Correlation files are the method for establishing many-to-many relationships between files. Finally, notice that the JREF keyword, discussed earlier, is used several times to clarify from which file the shared data field name values are to come.

FIGURE 7.26

```
 Columns . . . :    1  71            Edit                    MYLIBXX/DDSSRC
 SEU==>                                                              ROSTER1
 FMT A* .....A*. 1 ...+... 2 ...+... 3 ...+... 4 ...+... 5 ...+... 6 ...+... 7
        *************** Beginning of data *************************************
0001.00      * THIS LOGICAL FILE CONTAINS DATA FROM THE STUDENT,
0002.00      * GRADE, AND INSTRUCTOR FILES
0003.00                R R1FMT                     JFILE(MYLIBXX/CLASS +
0004.00                                                   MYLIBXX/GRADE +
0005.00                                                   MYLIBXX/STUDENT +
0006.00                                                   MYLIBXX/INSTRUCTOR)
0007.00                                            TEXT('ROSTER1 FORMAT')
0008.00                J                           JOIN(1 2)
0009.00                                            JFLD(CL# CL#)
0010.00                                            JFLD(SECT# SECT#)
0011.00                J                           JOIN(2 3)
0012.00                                            JFLD(STUDID# STUDID#)
0013.00                J                           JOIN(1 4)
0014.00                                            JFLD(IID IID)
0015.00                  CL#                       JREF(1)
0016.00                  SECT#                     JREF(1)
0017.00                  INSTR           6
0018.00                  LNAME
0019.00                  FNAME
0020.00                  STREET
0021.00                  CITY            7
0022.00                  STATE
0023.00                  ZIP
0024.00                  STUDID#                   JREF(3)
0025.00                  CREDITS
0026.00                  GRADEPT
0027.00                  GRADE
0028.00                K CL#
0029.00                K SECT#
       ****************** End of data ****************************************

 F3=Exit   F4=Prompt   F5=Refresh   F9=Retrieve   F10=Cursor
 F16=Repeat find       F17=Repeat change          F24=More keys
```

FIGURE 7.27

```
*...+....1....+....2....+....3....+....4....+....5....+....6....+....7....+...
ACC10196306Beane FlintstoneFred    11 Limestone DrBedrockAZ88888111111111 ¤ H
ACC10196306Beane FlintstoneWilma   11 Limestone DrBedrockAZ88888123456789   °
ACC10196306Beane Rubble    Betty   15 Limestone DrBedrockAZ88888444444444 ± ±
ACC10196306Beane Rubble    Barnard 15 Limestone DrBedrockAZ88888999999999 ¬
BIO10196201Galen FlintstoneFred    11 Limestone DrBedrockAZ88888111111111 ¤ H
BIO10196201Galen FlintstoneWilma   11 Limestone DrBedrockAZ88888123456789   °
BIO10196201Galen Rubble    Betty   15 Limestone DrBedrockAZ88888444444444 ± ±
BUS10196203Beane Rubble    Betty   15 Limestone DrBedrockAZ88888444444444 ± ±
BUS10196203Beane Rubble    Barnard 15 Limestone DrBedrockAZ88888999999999 ¬
BUS10196306Jones FlintstoneWilma   11 Limestone DrBedrockAZ88888123456789   °
CMP10196306Jobs  FlintstoneWilma   11 Limestone DrBedrockAZ88888123456789   °
CMP10196306Jobs  Rubble    Betty   15 Limestone DrBedrockAZ88888444444444 ± ±
CMP10196306Jobs  Rubble    Barnard 15 Limestone DrBedrockAZ88888999999999 ¬
PSY21296203Hyde  FlintstoneFred    11 Limestone DrBedrockAZ88888111111111 ¤ H
PSY21296203Hyde  Rubble    Betty   15 Limestone DrBedrockAZ88888444444444 ± ±
PSY21296203Hyde  Rubble    Barnard 15 Limestone DrBedrockAZ88888999999999 ¬
                       ****** END OF DATA ******
```

The drawback to a join file is the extra time needed to retrieve each record (due to all the duplicate STUDENT and INSTRUCTOR data between join records). However, the complicated programming and time required to access the information from four separate files or from a multiple format file where the records are not grouped together may still make the join file the best option.

Generally, a multiple format file is the best solution when the files all share (at least) the same primary key. What's more, if all the fields from each file's records are needed, the multiple format file requires less input and output processing. Using a join file to access the data results in a great deal of redundant data between records within the file (as can be seen in Figure 7.27 with address information) and increases the time needed to perform the input and output operations. However, if only a subset of fields or records is needed, there can be some considerable performance savings with a join file.

A Physical File's Relationship to Join and Multiple Format Logical Files

The AS/400 DBMS will not allow updates to data physical files through a join logical file. However, data physical files can be updated through dependent multiple format logical files. The "catch" is that the user must specify the particular file format record to be used for updating.

For instance, with DFU we can specify the multiple format logical file, STGRINSTR, as the file to update. A temporary update program will default to the first record format defined in the multiple format logical file. Any data entered will be entered into the physical file associated with that first record format.

Figure 7.27 shows that DFU defaults to the first format defined in STGRINSTR, STUDREC. The user can change the record format

FIGURE 7.28

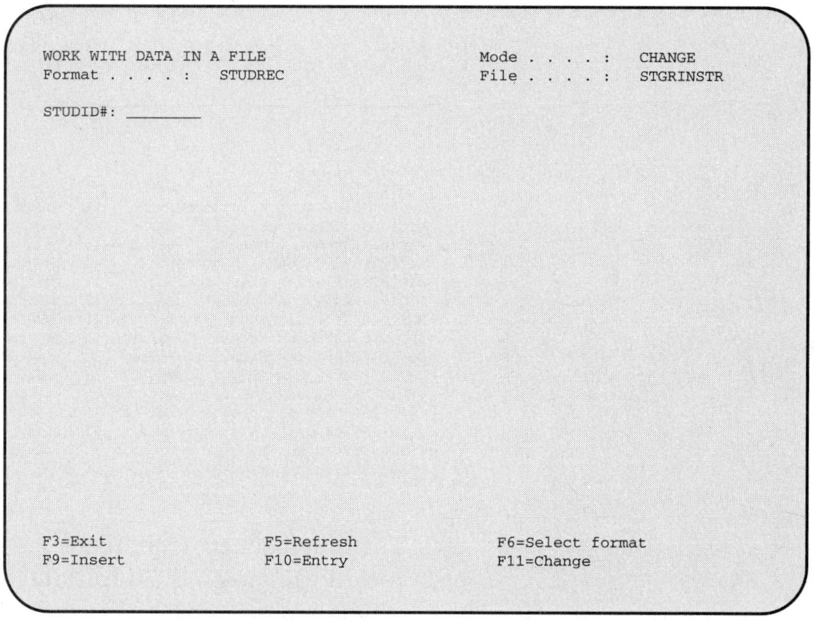

```
WORK WITH DATA IN A FILE                              Mode . . . . :    CHANGE
Format . . . . :    STUDREC                           File . . . . :    STGRINSTR

STUDID#: ________









F3=Exit                 F5=Refresh               F6=Select format
F9=Insert               F10=Entry                F11=Change
```

(and physical file) used for updating by pressing **F6**. Pressing **F6** will result in a list of the record formats specified in the multiple format logical file (Figure 7.29). The user can select one of the record formats, press **ENTER**, and the DFU update screen will reflect the chosen format. For instance, selecting INSTRFMT would result in the new DFU update screen as seen in Figure 7.30.

FIGURE 7.29

```
                         Select Record Format

Type option, press Enter.
  1=Select

Opt  Format          Description
 _   STUDREC         STUDENT RECORD
 _   GRDFMT          GRADE FORMAT
 _   CLFMT           CLASS FORMAT
 _   INSTRFMT        INSTRUCTOR FORMAT

                                                              Bottom
F3=Exit        F5=Refresh        F12=Cancel
```

FIGURE 7.30

```
WORK WITH DATA IN A FILE                     Mode . . . . :   CHANGE
Format . . . . :   INSTRFMT                  File . . . . :   STGRINSTR

INSTRUCTOR ID: ___

F3=Exit              F5=Refresh              F6=Select format
F9=Insert            F10=Entry               F11=Change
```

Again, even though the DFU update screen says that the file being updated is the multiple format logical file, in reality, the physical file associated with the chosen record format is being updated, not the logical file.

Changes to a physical file's data will be reflected in the dependent join and multiple format logical files, the same as with simple logical files. Further, the complications in deleting or changing the structure of a physical file caused by simple logical files are the same for join and multiple format logical files. No physical file can be deleted or recompiled when there are dependent join or multiple format logical files. The procedure to delete or recompile a physical file that has dependent simple logical files is also necessary for physical files with dependent join or multiple format logical files.

Summary

Usually, logical files are built to correspond to an individual user's view of the data. The three types of logical files—simple, join, and multiple format—make it easier for users to access the data. However, there is a cost for this user friendliness. When records are deleted or added in a physical file, added processing time is needed to change the logical file's access path to reflect the physical file updates. In other words, there is some performance degradation for physical file updates. Furthermore, deleting or recompiling physical files is much more complex if there are dependent logical files. The DBMS will not allow a physical file to be deleted if dependent logical files exist.

Logical files are also created to simplify program logic. Multiple format and join logical files can be created to seemingly combine information from many files. In reality, a logical file is simply a different access path through the data that the program can utilize. Multiple format logical files allow the user to access entire records from different files, whereas, join logical files provide control over individual fields. For frequently used combinations of data, these types of logical files can provide faster access to the data.

EXERCISES

1. The owners of the video store would like to view all the new consumable items. Create a logical file called CONSUM that has only those items with TYPE = "CONSUMABLE". Include in the file the item name, item number, type, and sale price. Key the file by sale price, and have the records in descending order by sale price.

2. New requirements have come to light that require changes to the database. The video store has no record of who is renting movies or whether customers are bringing them back on time. We need to create two new files CUST (customer) and TRANS (transaction) with the following layouts:

CUST File

Field Name	Text	Type	Length
Cust#	Cust number	Character	5
Cfname	Cust first name	Character	8
Clname	Cust last name	Character	10
Cstr	Cust str addr	Character	15
Ccity	Cust city addr	Character	10
Cstate	Cust state	Character	2
Czip	Cust zip code	Character	5
Cphone	Cust phone #	Character	8
Totltf	Tot late fee owed	Numeric	5.2

TRANS File

Field Name	Text	Type	Length
Trans#	Trans number	Character	9
Tdate	Trans date	Character	6
Ttime	Trans time	Character	4
Cust#	Use already existing FRF definition		
Snum	Use already existing FRF definition		
Dayspd	Days paid	Character	1
Rdate	Return date	Character	6
Rtime	Return time	Character	4
Lf	Late fee	Numeric	4.2
Lfpd	Late fee paid	Numeric	4.2

TRANS#, TDATE, TTIME, CUST#, and all fields in CUST except TOTLTF should be defined as mandatory entry fields. All new field definitions should be added to FRF.

The new physical file definitions should reference the field definitions in FRF. CUST# should be the key for the CUST file, and TRANS# should be the key for the TRANS file.

Add the following data to the new files:

CUST File

Cust#	1	2	3	4
Cfname	Adam	Eve	Sam	Archie
Clname	Able	Baker	Serpent	Gabriel
Cstr	1 Eden La	2 Eden La	3 Apple Ct	4 Gate Pkwy
Ccity	GardenCity	GardenCity	GardenCity	GardenCity
Cstate	NY	NY	NY	NY
Czip	33333	33333	33333	33333
Cphone	555-1111	555-2222	555-6666	555-3333
Totltf	500	900	109500	0

TRANS File

Trans#	1	2	3	4	5
Tdate	122594	101895	090895	070495	112295
Ttime	1623	1153	1957	1324	1814
Cust#	3	2	1	4	2
Snum	2	7	5	3	7
Dayspd	1	2	1	1	2
Rdate	122695	102195	091195	070695	112995
Rtime	1220	1543	1856	1432	1745
Lf	109500	150	500	200	750
Lfpd	0	0	0	200	0

The store employees also need a new join logical file, ACCRCV (accounts receivable), to view all customers with currently outstanding late fees and the item name(s) they were late with. Each customer's records should be grouped together, and the customers with the largest amount of late fee owed should be listed first.

To create this logical file, you will need to join CUST, TRANS, and ITEM. PRODUCT will be used as a correlation file to include the necessary ITEM fields. The join record format should be as follows:

Fname
Lname
Totlf
Iname
Tdate
Rdate
Dayspd
Lf

Select only customer records with Totlf greater than 0, and join CUST and TRANS by CUST#, TRANS and PRODUCT by SNUM, and PRODUCT and ITEM by INUM. The data, if copied from ACCRCV, would look like the following:

```
                          Display Physical File Member
File . . . . . . :   TEMP                 Library  . . . . :   MYLIBXX
Member . . . . . :   ACCRCV               Record . . . . . :   1
Control  . . . . .                        Column . . . . . :   1
Find . . . . . . .
*...+....1....+....2....+....3....+....4....+....5....+..
Sam     Serpent    n Nightmare on Elm St 1225941226951 n
Eve     Baker      ° Duck Hunt           1018951021952
Eve     Baker      ° Duck Hunt           1122951129952 ſ
Adam    Able       & Gone With the Wind  0908950911951 &
                           ****** END OF DATA ******

                                                                    Bottom
F3=Exit   F12=Cancel   F19=Left   F20=Right   F24=More Keys
```

PROGRAMMING EXERCISE

Since the CHGF file will not work if logical files are tied to the physical file being changed, update CHGF according to the steps in the chapter. In addition, modify COMCHGF with the appropriate changes to take care of logical files.

Execute CHGF and COMCHGF for the ITEM file. Make sure that the logical files (CONSUM and ACCRCV) are recreated after each program is finished.

REVIEW QUESTIONS

1. What relational functions are provided by simple logical files?
2. Where are logical file source code definitions stored?
3. What new function can the DDS keyword COMP perform in logical files?
4. When a record is added to a physical file, what is updated in the logical files that are based on that physical file?
5. What type(s) of logical file does not allow the user to exclude physical file fields from the logical file?
6. Which type(s) of logical file can be used to update the physical files they are based on?
7. What is the relationship between field reference files and logical files?
8. What is a relative file number, and how is it assigned?
9. Of the JOIN, JREF, JFLD, and JFILE keywords, which appear in the J specification?
10. Explain the relationship between a logical file and a data physical file member with no type.

DISCUSSION QUESTIONS

1. How do logical files complicate physical file structural changes?
2. What do the JOIN, JREF, JFILE, and JFLD keywords do?
3. Why are logical files used?

Query

8

Overview

The AS/400 offers many utilities to access and manipulate stored data. One of the easiest and most user friendly is QUERY/400. Through a series of easy-to-use screens and menus, QUERY/400 enables the user to select and view data. QUERY/400 also provides an extensive set of options to control and format the appearance of the output. In this chapter, we will cover how to invoke and use QUERY/400 to define, save, and change often used queries. In addition, we will review the screens and options used to define the format of a query report.

We will also explore the CL command OPNQRYF, which provides an alternative means of accessing many of the data manipulation functions explored in logical files and QUERY/400.

After finishing this chapter, you will understand

- The basic functions of a query tool
- How QUERY/400 and OPNQRYF provide these basic functions

After finishing this chapter, you will be able to

- Define, save, run, recall, and modify a query using QUERY/400
- Understand and specify the reporting options available

- Use the OPNQRYF command to manipulate data
- Use the OVRDBF and CPYFRMQRYF commands to supply OPNQRYF data to application programs

Query Packages

Database management systems are worthless if access to the data is not provided. A "query package" is one tool for accessing data. Query packages generate query programs. Most DBMS also provide a query language that allows users to write query programs and utilities to save and run the queries.

Most query packages are nonprocedural languages, a term that means menus or icons are used to define and execute query programs, not commands. Nonprocedural languages free users from remembering specific commands, keywords, and complicated syntax. After a user has finished specifying the data to be selected and its format, the query package generates the query program. An important point to remember for first-time query users is that the generated query programs read files and display information, not the query package itself.

Query packages free users from having to rely (and usually wait) on programmers to create report programs. The query package allows users to easily and quickly create their own report programs.

QUERY/400 is the AS/400's query package. QUERY/400 provides a menu-driven interface to define, modify, and execute query programs. For all the reasons listed, users generally love QUERY/400.

The AS/400 provides CL commands that can perform many of the same functions as QUERY/400 generated programs. These commands allow the users to write their own query programs.

QUERY/400

QUERY/400 provides a method to access information contained in AS/400 data files. In addition, the appearance of the data and its location on the output report can be controlled. Though QUERY/400 provides data manipulation and formatting functions, they are limited when compared to a programming language. If complex logic, calculations, or formatting is required, a high level programming language is a better choice. However, for most users, QUERY/400's capabilities will be more than sufficient.

As with most query packages, QUERY/400 is an application generator. The QUERY/400 screens allow users to define a program that will access file(s), format the retrieved data, and generate output. When a user is finished defining the query, an object with a type = *QRYDFN and attribute = QRY is created (in a user-specified library), and the query definition/program is loaded into the object. To retrieve data and generate output, the QUERY/400 generated object (called a query definition) must be run, not QUERY/400.

QUERY/400 does, however, provide an easy method to execute and recall query definitions.

Just as with most of the other AS/400 utilities, QUERY/400 has an easy-to-use screen interface. The QUERY/400 screens can be reached from the system menus, but a much quicker method is to execute the WRKQRY command. This will bring up the `Work with Queries` screen (Figure 8.1), which allows users to create a query as well as modify, run, or delete existing queries.

To begin creating a query, type **1** (Create) at the `Option` prompt. At the `Library` prompt specify the library where the query program is to be stored, and at the `Query` prompt supply a name for the query program (ROSTERQRY). Press **ENTER**, and the `Define the Query` screen will be displayed (Figure 8.2). This is the main menu for query definition. All functions and format options can be accessed from this screen.

Defining a Query

As an example, we are going to build a query that will generate class rosters from the four physical files CLASS, STUDENT, INSTRUCTOR, and GRADE. In addition, we will generate some information about each class such as the total number of students enrolled and the average grade.

FIGURE 8.1

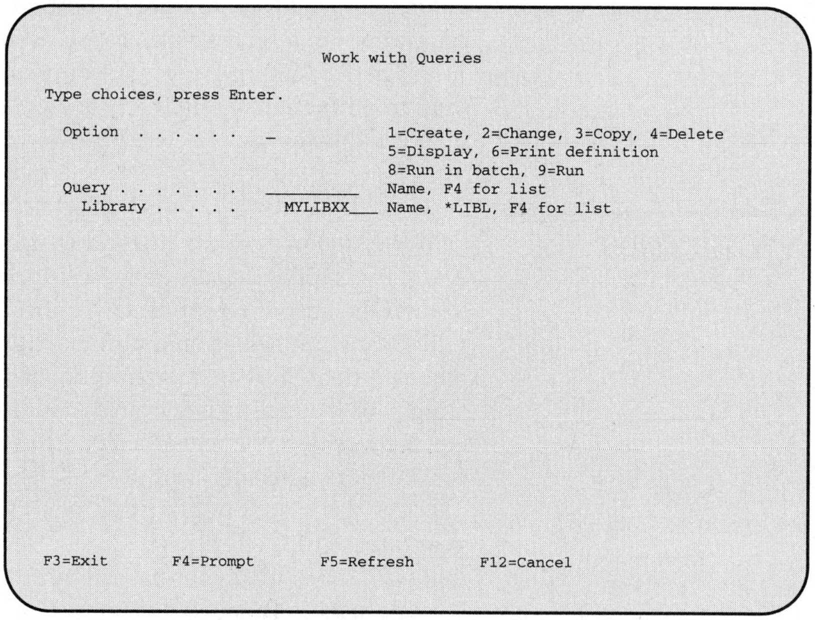

```
                          Work with Queries

Type choices, press Enter.

  Option . . . . . .  _            1=Create, 2=Change, 3=Copy, 4=Delete
                                   5=Display, 6=Print definition
                                   8=Run in batch, 9=Run
  Query . . . . . . .  __________  Name, F4 for list
    Library . . . .    MYLIBXX___  Name, *LIBL, F4 for list


F3=Exit        F4=Prompt        F5=Refresh        F12=Cancel
```

FIGURE 8.2

```
                          Define the Query

Query . . . . . . :   ROSTERQRY              Option  . . . . . :   CREATE
  Library . . . . :     MYLIBXX              CCSID . . . . . . :

Type options, press Enter.  Press F21 to select all.
  1=Select

Opt    Query Definition Option
 1     Specify file selections
 _     Define result fields
 _     Select and sequence fields
 _     Select records
 _     Select sort fields
 _     Select collating sequence
 _     Specify report column formatting
 _     Select report summary functions
 _     Define report breaks
 _     Select output type and output form
 _     Specify processing options

F3=Exit            F5=Report            F12=Cancel
F13=Layout         F18=Files            F21=Select all
```

The first and only required query definition option is the `Specify file selections` option. Notice that a 1 is already in the `Opt` field. The system automatically places a 1 in the OPT field since at least one file must be specified for a query. Pressing **ENTER** results in the `Specify File Selections` screen (Figure 8.3) being displayed. On this screen, the user specifies the library, file, and, optionally, a specific member or record format to be used in the query.

FIGURE 8.3

```
                          Specify File Selections

Type choices, press Enter.  Press F9 to specify an additional
  file selection.

  File . . . . . . . . . .      __________   Name, F4 for list
      Library  . . . . . .       MYLIBXX___  Name, *LIBL, F4 for list
  Member . . . . . . . . .      *FIRST____   Name, *FIRST, F4 for list
  Format . . . . . . . . .      *FIRST____   Name, *FIRST, F4 for list

F3=Exit              F4=Prompt             F5=Report            F9=Add file
F12=Cancel           F13=Layout            F24=More keys
```

To specify more than one file to be queried, press **F9**. A new prompt, `FILE ID`, will be added to the screen (Figure 8.4). A file id is an abbreviated method of identifying each file for the rest of the query definition process. The file id can be from one to three alphanumeric characters, and if no file id is specified, the system will use T01 and increment the digit for each additional file (for example, the second file would have an id of T02). When identifying fields in a multifile query, library and file names must also be specified. Since the AS/400 allows different files to have fields with the same name, supplying a field name alone is not enough to identify the field to be retrieved. (It's similar to trying to identify someone by first name only. There still may be some question about which Joe or Mary you are talking about.) To truly identify a field, the filename and library name of a field must also be specified. A file id saves users from having to type the library name and filename over and over when specifying fields to use as output or in calculations. (We recommend always assigning your own file ids as A, B, C, and so forth. This even saves a couple of more keystrokes than the system-assigned ids.)

After entering the first filename and file id, press **F9**. Another set of prompts for the second file will be displayed. After specifying each file and file id, keep pressing **F9** for as many files as needed. For our example, enter the CLASS, INSTRUCTOR, STUDENT, and GRADE files as seen in Figures 8.5 and 8.6, and then press **ENTER**.

FIGURE 8.4

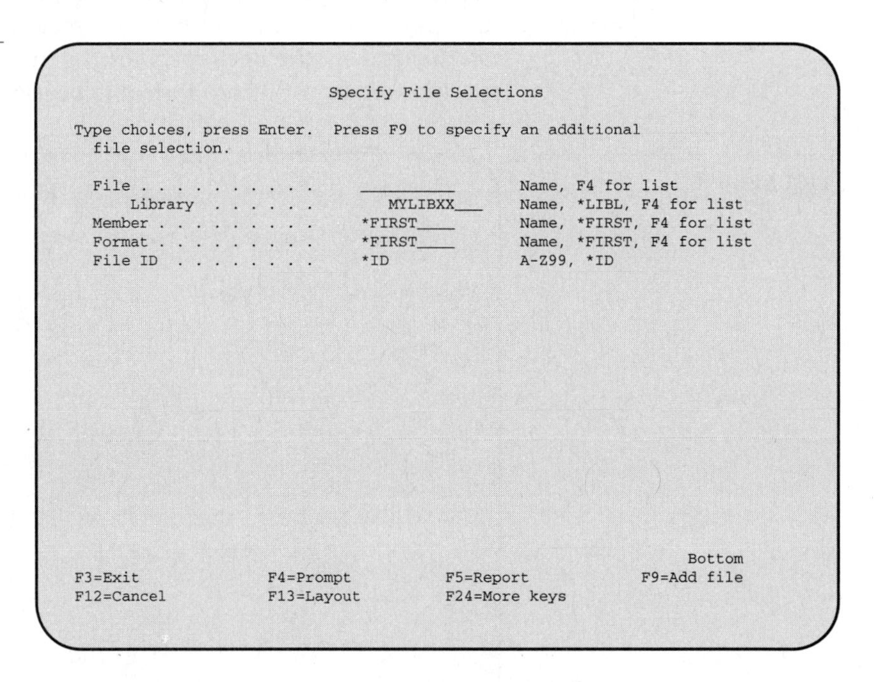

FIGURE 8.5

```
                         Specify File Selections

Type choices, press Enter.  Press F9 to specify an additional
  file selection.

  File . . . . . . . . .    CLASS            Name, F4 for list
    Library  . . . . . .      MYLIBXX        Name, *LIBL, F4 for list
  Member . . . . . . . .    *FIRST           Name, *FIRST, F4 for list
  Format . . . . . . . .    CLFMT            Name, *FIRST, F4 for list
  File ID  . . . . . . .    A                A-Z99, *ID

  File . . . . . . . . .    GRADE            Name, F4 for list
    Library  . . . . . .      MYLIBXX        Name, *LIBL, F4 for list
  Member . . . . . . . .    *FIRST           Name, *FIRST, F4 for list
  Format . . . . . . . .    GRDFMT           Name, *FIRST, F4 for list
  File ID  . . . . . . .    B                A-Z99, *ID

                                                                More. . .
F3=Exit           F4=Prompt          F5=Report            F9=Add file
F12=Cancel        F13=Layout         F24=More keys
Select file(s), or press Enter to confirm.
```

Once the files have been identified, the **join criteria** must be specified. Specifying the join criteria entails selecting a type of join and specifying the fields and arguments that will determine how the join is performed. After pressing **ENTER** on the `Specify File Selections` screen, the `Specify Type of Join` screen will be displayed (Figure 8.7). This screen displays the three QUERY/400 join options. As mentioned earlier, several types of relational joins can be performed.

FIGURE 8.6

```
                         Specify File Selections

Type choices, press Enter.  Press F9 to specify an additional
  file selection.

  File . . . . . . . . .    STUDENT          Name, F4 for list
    Library  . . . . . .      MYLIBXX        Name, *LIBL, F4 for list
  Member . . . . . . . .    *FIRST           Name, *FIRST, F4 for list
  Format . . . . . . . .    STUDREC          Name, *FIRST, F4 for list
  File ID  . . . . . . .    C                A-Z99, *ID

  File . . . . . . . . .    INSTRUCTOR       Name, F4 for list
    Library  . . . . . .      MYLIBXX        Name, *LIBL, F4 for list
  Member . . . . . . . .    *FIRST           Name, *FIRST, F4 for list
  Format . . . . . . . .    INSTRFMT         Name, *FIRST, F4 for list
  File ID  . . . . . . .    D                A-Z99, *ID

                                                                  Bottom
F3=Exit           F4=Prompt          F5=Report            F9=Add file
F12=Cancel        F13=Layout         F24=More keys
```

FIGURE 8.7

```
                              Specify Type of Join

 Type choice, press Enter.

 Type of join . . . . . . . .   1    1=Matched records
                                     2=Matched records with primary file
                                     3=Unmatched records with primary file


 F3=Exit            F5=Report           F10=Process/previous
 F12=Cancel         F13=Layout          F18=Files
```

The QUERY/400 joins are different from the standard relational joins in that fields can be selected and omitted from the join output regardless of the type of join chosen. The QUERY/400 joins control which records will be selected, not fields. Record selection is based on whether records are matched or unmatched. For instance, say we were joining three files based on a shared social security number field. If two files had a record with social security number 111-11-1111 and the other file didn't, the two records would be considered unmatched records.

The first QUERY/400 join option, the `Matched records` join, displays only records that have matches in all the join files. In our three file examples, only social security numbers that had records in all three files would be selected. The output of the matched records join is the records from each of the join files (see Figure 8.8 for results of each type of join).

The next two types of joins are concerned with matched and unmatched records but only in relation to the **primary file**. The primary file is the first file specified. In our example, CLASS was specified first, so it is considered the primary file. The second option, the `Matched records with primary file` join, displays all records in the primary file and any secondary records that match the primary records. In this case, every record in the first file plus any matching records from any of the other files would be displayed. So primary records that were matched records (records with a match in all files) would be displayed, as would primary records that were unmatched, and any matching records from the secondary files. In the case of social security number 111-11-1111, as long as one of the two files with a 111-11-1111 record were the primary file, the 111-11-1111 records from both files would be displayed.

The matched records with primary file join is the join used in multiformat logical files. Notice the data from the multiformat logical file ROSTER in Figure 7.25. There is a CLASS record for section 96201 of class BUS101 (the fifth record). Even though there was no matching student record for this class, the CLASS record was displayed. This is because CLASS was defined as the primary file, and all records from the primary file are displayed, whether they are matched or unmatched, when a matched records with primary file join is performed.

Join logical files, on the other hand, use a matched records join. Figure 7.27 proves this because all the records have information for all the fields. There are no records with partial or default information. For instance, notice that there is no record for class BUS101 section 96201. However, if a user wanted the unmatched records to be included in the join, the file level keyword JDFTVAL (join default values) would be used. This keyword directs the AS/400 DBMS to use default values (blanks and nulls unless otherwise specified) for fields not found in any of the secondary join files. This will result in a join that is the same as a matched records with primary file join in QUERY/400.

The third QUERY/400 join option, the `Unmatched records with primary file` join, selects primary records that are unmatched. This join will display the primary record and any secondary records that do match the primary file unmatched records. In our previous example, if the primary file had a record with social security number 111-11-1111, that record is unmatched because one of the secondary files does not contain a matching 111-11-1111 record. In this case, the record from the primary file and the matching record from the other secondary file would be displayed. Matched records (records with matches in all the join files) are not selected or displayed in an unmatched records with primary file join, nor would any 111-11-1111 records be displayed if File B (the file without a 111-11-1111 record) were the primary file.

Unmatched joins are often used to check a database's integrity. For instance, if an item was supposed to have a record in each file, an unmatched join would help locate some of the problem items. However, the choice of the primary file plays a key role in which items are displayed. In the school example, for instance, we might want to display classes that didn't have students or an instructor. We could do this by defining CLASS as the primary file and performing an unmatched join with STUDENT and INSTRUCTOR. Any class that did not have a matching STUDENT and INSTRUCTOR would be displayed. However, if we wanted to check for teachers that didn't have any classes, this condition would not be shown when CLASS is the primary file. To catch this condition, the INSTRUCTOR file would have to be the primary file. To do a thorough search for missing records, an unmatched join using each of the files as the primary file must be performed.

For ROSTERQRY, we'll choose a matched records join and save database integrity checking for another day.

Once the type of join has been selected, the `Specify How to Join Files` screen will be displayed. This second screen of join criteria

FIGURE 8.8

```
Files and Their Contents

    File A              File B              File C

    111-11-1111         222-22-2222         111-11-1111
    222-22-2222         333-33-3333         222-22-2222

1 - Matched records join
    Regardless of the primary file results in

    File A              File B              File C

    222-22-2222         222-22-2222         222-22-2222

2 - Matched records with primary file join
    If file A or C is primary, results in

    File A              File B              File C

    111-11-1111                             111-11-1111
    222-22-2222         222-22-2222         222-22-2222

    If file B is primary, results in

    File A              File B              File C

    222-22-2222         222-22-2222         222-22-2222
                        333-33-3333

3 - Unmatched records with primary file join
    If file A or C is primary, results in

    File A              File B              File C

    111-11-1111                             111-11-1111

    If file B is primary, results in

    File A              File B              File C

                        333-33-333
```

specification is similar to a J specification in DDS because users identify the fields on which the joins will be based. At this screen, the user specifies the common field(s) that the files share and the argument that determines how the records are joined. (This is the same information specified in the DDS JFLD keyword.) For our example, we want to join CLASS and GRADE by CL# and SECTION#, GRADE and STUDENT by STUDID#, and CLASS and INSTRUCTOR by IID (Figure 8.9) and press **ENTER**.

FIGURE 8.9

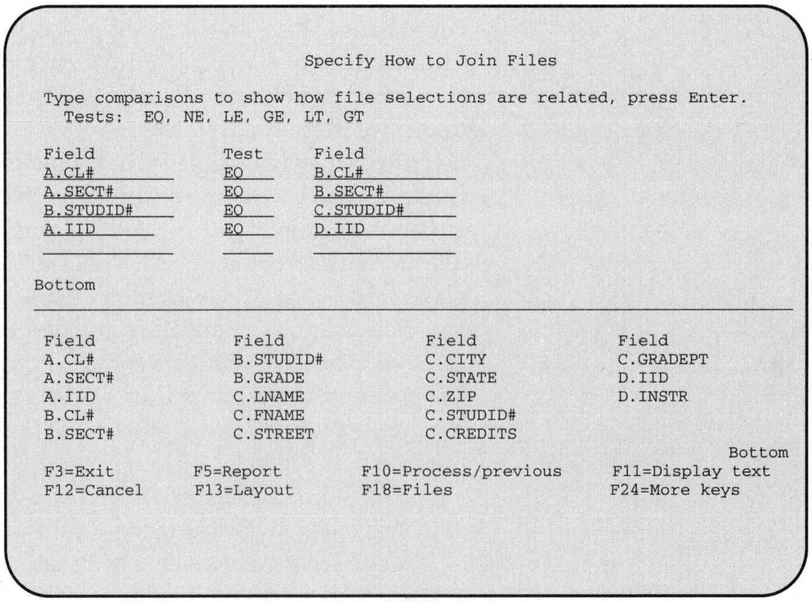

```
                          Specify How to Join Files

 Type comparisons to show how file selections are related, press Enter.
   Tests:  EQ, NE, LE, GE, LT, GT

 Field              Test     Field
 A.CL#              EQ       B.CL#
 A.SECT#            EQ       B.SECT#
 B.STUDID#          EQ       C.STUDID#
 A.IID              EQ       D.IID

Bottom
_____________________________________________________________________________

 Field                Field                Field                Field
 A.CL#                B.STUDID#            C.CITY               C.GRADEPT
 A.SECT#              B.GRADE              C.STATE              D.IID
 A.IID                C.LNAME              C.ZIP                D.INSTR
 B.CL#                C.FNAME              C.STUDID#
 B.SECT#              C.STREET             C.CREDITS
                                                                      Bottom
 F3=Exit          F5=Report         F10=Process/previous         F11=Display text
 F12=Cancel       F13=Layout        F18=Files                    F24=More keys
```

Notice how QUERY/400 places all the fields from the selected files at the bottom of the screen. This saves the user from having to leave the query definition and look up the field names or the correct spelling of the field names. Furthermore, this screen demonstrates the advantage of file ids. Instead of specifying the library names and filenames eight times, we were able to use the one-character file ids.

Field Definition, Selection, and Sequence

After specifying the files and types of joins, the `Define the Query` menu will be redisplayed. The next two options on the menu, `Define result fields` and `Select and sequence fields`, are concerned with the particular fields that will be included in the output. The `Define result fields` option lets the user create new output fields by defining how the fields will be calculated. Standard arithmetic calculations can be performed using fields from the previously specified files or constant values. In addition, string functions such as concatenation and substring can be used to define fields that will contain character information. The user can also specify some basic formatting such as the length of the new field and its column heading. Figure 8.10 shows the `Define Result Fields` screen.

The `Select and sequence fields` option allows the user to select specific fields to appear on the query output and designate the order in which they will be displayed. Until now, there have only been options that allow the user to specify groups of fields—files—for the query output. This option begins the process of fine-tuning the query to retrieve and display the exact data needed.

At the `Select and Sequence Fields` screen (Figure 8.11), all the fields from the files selected and any result fields that were defined will be displayed. A field is selected by typing a number (up to four digits) in the sequence field to the left of the field name. This sequence number both selects the field for display and indicates the field's relative left-to-right position in regard to the other selected fields. For instance, a field with sequence number 100 would be to the right of a field with sequence number 90 and to the left of a field with sequence number 110.

FIGURE 8.10

```
                          Define Result Fields

Type definitions using field names or constants and operators, press Enter.
  Operators:  +, -, *, /, SUBSTR, ||, DATE...

Field        Expression                         Column Heading        Len  Dec
__________   ________________________________   ____________________  ___  ___
             ________________________________   ____________________
             ________________________________   ____________________

__________   ________________________________   ____________________  ___  ___
             ________________________________   ____________________
             ________________________________   ____________________

                                                                      Bottom

Field              Field              Field              Field
A.CL#              B.SECT#            C.FNAME            C.ZIP
A.SECT#            B.STUDID#          C.STREET           C.STUDID#
A.IID              B.GRADE            C.CITY             C.CREDITS
B.CL#              C.LNAME            C.STATE            C.GRADEPT
                                                                   More...
F3=Exit            F5=Report          F9=Insert          F11=Display text
F12=Cancel         F13=Layout         F20=Reorganize     F24=More keys
```

FIGURE 8.11

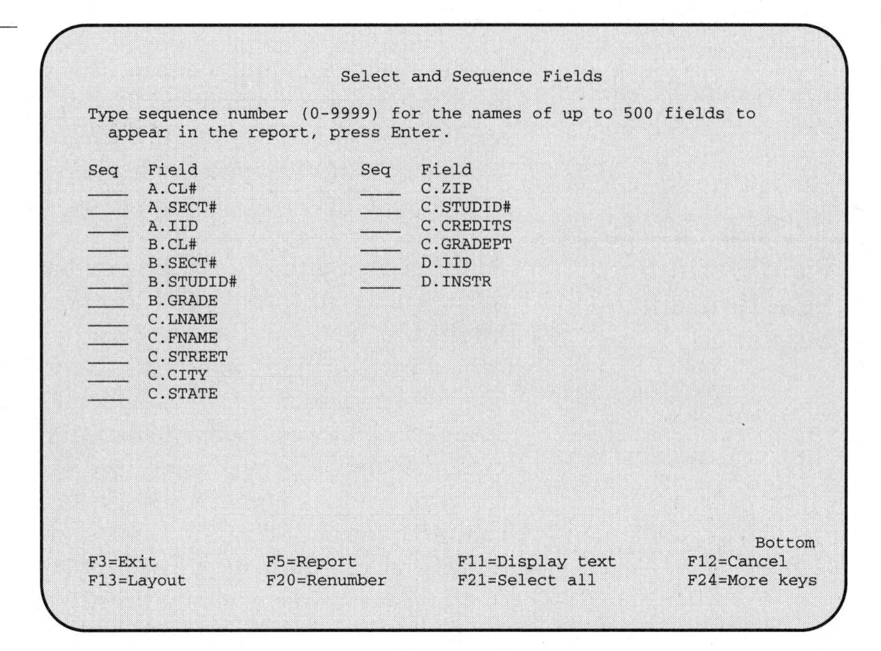

However, if there were no fields with a sequence number from 1 to 99, the field with sequence number 100 would be the leftmost field on the query output.

For our example, we would select the following fields and have them displayed in the following order by entering the sequence numbers as shown in Figure 8.12:

CL#
SECT#
INSTR
LNAME
FNAME
STREET
CITY
STATE
ZIP
STUDID#
CREDITS
GRADEPT
GRADE

After entering the data, press ENTER twice. The first time you press ENTER will sequence the fields in the order of the sequence numbers specified. The second time confirms the field's order and makes it a permanent part of the query definition.

FIGURE 8.12

```
                    Select and Sequence Fields

Type sequence number (0-9999) for the names of up to 500 fields to
  appear in the report, press Enter.

Seq   Field                 Seq   Field
____  A.CL#                 __90  C.ZIP
____  A.SECT#               _100  C.STUDID#
____  A.IID                 _110  C.CREDITS
__10  B.CL#                 _120  C.GRADEPT
__20  B.SECT#               ____  D.IID
____  B.STUDID#             __30  D.INSTR
_130  B.GRADE
__40  C.LNAME
__50  C.FNAME
__60  C.STREET
__70  C.CITY
__80  C.STATE

                                                          Bottom
F3=Exit          F5=Report          F11=Display text     F12=Cancel
F13=Layout       F20=Renumber       F21=Select all       F24=More keys
```

Selecting Records

Besides the type of joins available, QUERY/400 allows specific records to be selected based on field value tests. For instance, if we were generating a roster for only BUS101 classes, we would use the "Select Records" screen to specify the selection argument. Figure 8.13 shows the `Select Records` screen with the appropriate selection argument that will result in only BUS101 classes being included in the output.

Notice that there is another area on the `Select Records` screen with a header of `AND/OR`. This field allows the user to create a compound argument for the test. Records could be selected based on more than one value for a field or more than one fields value. For instance, if we wanted the roster for a specific section of BUS101, a second argument would be specified and the two arguments connected with an AND.

For our example, we want a roster of all classes, so we will not specify any selection arguments.

The Select Records screen is another screen where the file id comes in handy. Also notice how QUERY/400 displays a list of all the fields that can be used to select records. This includes all fields in the file(s) selected, not just the display fields selected in the previous option. In other words, fields that are not in the output can still be used as a basis for selecting records.

FIGURE 8.13

```
                              Select Records

Type comparisons, press Enter.  Specify OR to start each new group.
  Tests:  EQ, NE, LE, GE, LT, GT, RANGE, LIST, LIKE, IS, ISNOT...

AND/OR  Field            Test   Value (Field, Number, 'Characters', or ...)

        B.CL#____        EQ__   'BUS101'______________________
____    _________        ____   ______________________________
____    _________        ____   ______________________________
____    _________        ____   ______________________________
____    _________        ____   ______________________________
____    _________        ____   ______________________________
                                                                    Bottom

Field              Field              Field              Field
B.CL#              C.STREET           C.CREDITS          A.IID
B.SECT#            C.CITY             C.GRADEPT          B.STUDID#
D.INSTR            C.STATE            B.GRADE            D.IID
C.LNAME            C.ZIP              A.CL#
C.FNAME            C.STUDID#          A.SECT#

                                                                    Bottom
F3=Exit            F5=Report          F9=Insert          F11=Display text
F12=Cancel         F13=Layout         F20=Reorganize     F24=More keys
```

Sorting

After the fields and records for display have been specified, the output's appearance can begin to be defined. One of the first options is to `Select sort fields`. Choosing this option will result in the `Select Sort Fields` screen being displayed (Figure 8.14). All the fields specified on the `Select and Sequence Fields` screen will be listed and can be selected as sort fields.

FIGURE 8.14

```
                              Select Sort Fields

Type sort priority (0-999) and A (Ascending) or D (Descending) for
  the names of up to 32 fields, press Enter.

Sort                          Sort
Prty A/D  Field               Prty A/D  Field
___  _    B.CL#               ___  _    B.GRADE
___  _    B.SECT#
___  _    D.INSTR
___  _    C.LNAME
___  _    C.FNAME
___  _    C.STREET
___  _    C.CITY
___  _    C.STATE
___  _    C.ZIP
___  _    C.STUDID#
___  _    C.CREDITS
___  _    C.GRADEPT

                                                                    Bottom
F3=Exit         F5=Report       F11=Display text    F12=Cancel
F13=Layout      F18=Files       F20=Renumber        F24=More keys
```

To choose a field, type a number in the sort priority (`Sort Prty`) field to the far left of the field name. This will select the field as a sort field. The number given to the field will determine its relative importance. The smaller the number, the higher the sort priority. The field with the smallest sort priority number is the primary sort field. All other sort fields are secondary sorts, and their order of precedence matches the increasing priority number.

For instance, if C.STATE was selected with number 50, C.ZIP was selected with number 51, and the sort was in ascending order, the list of records would be in alphabetical order by student state (Alabama first, Alaska second, and so on), and records from the same state would be sorted in zip code order.

The other option that can be specified for each sort field is the order of the sort—ascending or descending. One field can be sorted in ascending order and another field in descending order. For instance, the sort based on ZIP could be in descending order by typing **D** in the `A/D` field next to the field name. In this case, the list of records would still be displayed in ascending alphabetical order by the student's state, but records with the same state value would progress from the largest zip code for that state to the smallest zip code. If A or D is not specified, ascending is assumed. For our example, let's select an ascending order by CL# then SECT# and LNAME. Do this by typing **10**, **20**, and **30** in the appropriate `Sort Prty` fields and press **ENTER** twice.

Another option available at the `Define the Query` menu can also affect sorting, `Select collating sequence`. This option gets very particular about character sorts. There are several different ways character data can be treated. For instance, should uppercase and lowercase letters be sorted together, or should lowercase come first followed by all uppercase letters? Further, a different order may be required to get foreign language words into alphabetic order. The `Select Collating Sequence` screen allows the users to choose between these options or lets them define their own character sort order. (Users who are unsure of the significance of the collating sequence can read the *QUERY/400 Users Guide* section regarding the subject or simply accept the default.)

Specifying Report Characteristics

There are three more options on the `Define the Query` screen that allow further specifications regarding the content and appearance of the query output. These options control the

Format of the report columns

Summarization processing the query is to perform

Location of report breaks

Selecting `Specify report column formatting` will bring up Figure 8.15, the `Specify Report Column Formatting` screen.

This screen allows the user to

1. Specify the spacing between columns. The number entered is the number of spaces to be skipped before the column begins. The default is 2 but to "tighten up" our report, we'll change it to 1 for all fields.

FIGURE 8.15

```
                    Specify Report Column Formatting

Type information, press Enter.
  Column headings:  *NONE, aligned text lines

                  Column
Field             Spacing       Column Heading            Len  Dec   Edit
B.CL#              0            CLASS                       6
                                NUMBER


B.SECT#            1            SECT#                       5



D.INSTR            1            INST                        6
                                NAME


                                                                  More...
F3=Exit          F5=Report     F10=Process/previous   F12=Cancel
F13=Layout       F16=Edit      F18=Files              F23=Long comment
```

2. Specify the wording of the column headings. Initially, any column heading defined in the DDS for each field is used as the default. For a query, this can be changed by simply typing over what is displayed in the `Column Heading` field for each field. We will make several modifications so that the report width is decreased.

3. Specify the size of the fields for each column. Again, the default size is the DDS-defined field. However, for reporting purposes, a user may decide to change the size of the display field. For our example, we will change the instructor name field to 6 and the CITY field to 7 (just as we did for the join logical file ROSTER1 in Chapter 7).

4. Specify formats for numeric fields. The `Edit` field at the far right of each field can be accessed for numeric fields only. Moving the cursor to this field and pressing **F16** will bring up a screen where the type of numeric formatting to be performed is defined. Initially, the user specifies whether the field is a date, time, or regular number field. Based on this answer, further options are available regarding how each type of field will be displayed. For nondate and nontime fields, display options cover whether the number should be displayed with a dollar sign, leading zeros should be shown or replaced with blanks, a comma should be used to indicate thousands, and so forth. An example of a date field format option is the ability to specify the order of day, month, and year fields.

For our example, we will accept all the default values for the numeric fields.

The `Select Report Summary Functions` screen (Figure 8.16) allows the user to specify the type of summarization functions to be performed by the query. The options available are

Calculate the sum or average

Find the minimum or maximum value

Provide a count of the number of values for a field

FIGURE 8.16

```
                    Select Report Summary Functions

Type options, press Enter.
  1=Total   2=Average   3=Minimum   4=Maximum   5=Count

---Options---    Field                    ---Options---    Field
_ _ _ _ _        B.CL#                    2 _ _ _ _        B.GRADE
_ _ _ _ _        B.SECT#
_ _ _ _ _        D.INSTR
_ _ _ _ _        C.LNAME
_ _ _ _ _        C.FNAME
_ _ _ _ _        C.STREET
_ _ _ _ _        C.CITY
_ _ _ _ _        C.STATE
_ _ _ _ _        C.ZIP
5 _ _ _ _        C.STUDID#
_ _ _ _ _        C.CREDITS
_ _ _ _ _        C.GRADEPT

                                                                Bottom
F3=Exit          F5=Report        F10=Process/previous    F11=Display text
F12=Cancel       F13=Layout       F18=Files               F23=Long comment
```

These functions are very similar to the @sum, @avg, @max, @min, and @count functions in Lotus 1-2-3 and most other spreadsheet packages. At the end of the report, the selected summary fields will be displayed for the specified columns.

For our example, let's have the query calculate the average grade and the number of students enrolled. We can do that by entering option 5 (`Count`) for the STUDID# (this will give us a count of the number of STUDID#s) and option 2 (`Average`) for the GRADE field. Pressing **ENTER** will record this information in the query definition.

The final formatting option, report breaks, groups records on the query report. Report breaks, in conjunction with the summarization options, also create subtotals for each group of records specified. However, the effectiveness of report break subtotals depends heavily on the sorted order of the records.

For instance, if the records are sorted by student name and if a report break is specified by student name, the output records will be grouped for each student. Because an average for grade has been defined, an average for each student will be generated at the break in between each group of student records.

If, however, STATE (student state of residence) was specified as the break field, each time a new state was encountered, a subtotal for all the records for that previous state would be generated. Since the records are not in state order, the subtotal figure would not include all the students from that state. In fact, the subtotal would have no meaning.

To clarify, say there were five records as follows:

Student	State
James	Texas
Jones	Texas
Lane	Texas
Smith	Colorado
West	Texas

If the query were defined to sort these records by student name, they would appear as shown in the order of James, Jones, Lane, Smith, and West. The break field, however, has been set to supplier state. When the query is ready to display the results, the first break will occur after the Lane record. Lane is from Texas, and Smith is from Colorado; therefore, since report breaks are by state, and Colorado is different from Texas, a report break will be inserted after Lane. A subtotal count field, which includes the first three records, will also be printed.

Next, the Smith record will be printed, and another report break will be inserted because the next record—West's—has a value of Texas for the state, and this is different from Smith's. Again, a subtotal field will be printed. Then, West's record will be printed, followed by a count subtotal for only West's record. Finally, a total summary field for all the records will be included. The output would appear as follows:

Supplier	State
Jones	Texas
Jones	
Lane	
	Count 3
Smith	Colorado
	Count 1
West	Texas
	Count 1
Total	count 5

Because the order of the sort is by student name but the breaks are occurring at each new occurrence of state, the subtotals have no meaning. The subtotals do not represent the number of students from each state. Therefore, be careful about the choice of your report break field. Report break fields should also be sort fields.

A nice feature of printing query output is the suppression of repeated values within a report break. For all records within a group, the value of the break field will be the same (for example, each record in the Texas group is from Texas). Therefore, a QUERY/400 query will print the value only once—in the first record of the group. However, the suppression of repeated values does not occur when data is displayed or sent to a file.

For our example, set up a report break by CL# and SECT# (as seen in Figure 8.17). Notice that the sort fields are identified on the "Define Report Breaks" screen to help you select the appropriate report break fields. After entering the break fields, press **ENTER**. The `Format Report Break` screen (Figure 8.18) provides options to suppress summary data and specify text to be printed at the end of the report. Pressing **ENTER** will result in another `Format Report Break` screen (Figure 8.19) that allows the user to specify formatting options at the first level of report breaks (CL#). Again, the user can suppress summary data and specify text. Pressing **ENTER** takes the user to each succeeding level of report breaks. (Though not shown, we will also specify some report break text for section number breaks.)

Notice also that field values can be used in the report break text by entering the field names preceded by an ampersand. In addition, the user can specify that a page should be skipped after each break.

FIGURE 8.17

```
                              Define Report Breaks

Type break level (1-6) for up to 9 field names, press Enter.
  (Use as many fields as needed for each break level.)

Break     Sort                                 Break    Sort
Level     Prty     Field                       Level    Prty     Field
  1        10      B.CL#                         _               B.GRADE
  2        20      B.SECT#
  _                D.INSTR
  _        30      C.LNAME
  _                C.FNAME
  _                C.STREET
  _                C.CITY
  _                C.STATE
  _                C.ZIP
  _                C.STUDID#
  _                C.CREDITS
  _                C.GRADEPT

                                                                         Bottom
F3=Exit         F5=Report          F10=Process/previous     F11=Display text
F12=Cancel      F13=Layout         F18=Files                F23=Long comment
```

FIGURE 8.18

```
                              Format Report Break

Break level . . . . . . . :   0

Type choices, press Enter.
  (Type &field in text to have break values inserted.)


  Suppress summaries . . . .   N              Y=Yes, N=No

  Break text . . . . . . . .   TOTALS FOR ALL CLASSES


Level   Field
  1     B.CL#
  2     B.SECT#


F3=Exit          F5=Report          F10=Process/previous     F12=Cancel
F13=Layout       F18=Files          F23=Long comment
```

FIGURE 8.19

```
                              Format Report Break

Break level . . . . . . . :   1

Type choices, press Enter.
  (Type &field in text to have break values inserted.)

  Skip to new page . . . . .  N            Y=Yes, N=No

  Suppress summaries . . . .  N            Y=Yes, N=No

  Break text . . . . . . . .  SUBTOTALS FOR &CL#


Level  Field
  1    B.CL#
  2    B.SECT#







F3=Exit          F5=Report          F10=Process/previous     F12=Cancel
F13=Layout       F18=Files          F23=Long comment
```

Selecting Output Type and Form

At the `Select Output Type and Output Form` screen (Figure 8.20), the media to be used for output is specified. The choices are sending the data to a display, a printer, or a file.

If `Database file` (option 3) is specified as the media, the library, file, and member name where the data is to be sent must be specified. Choosing `Database file` and pressing **ENTER** will result in the `Define Database File Output` screen being displayed (Figure 8.21). This screen allows the user to specify the "send to" library, file, and member. QUERY/400 also provides the capability to create the file or member to which the query output is to be sent. If this option is chosen, the public authority (the level of object control that the public will have) must also be assigned. The easiest way to assign the authority is to accept the library's public authority, *LIBCRTAUT. If the default is not wanted, a list of valid authorities can be displayed by pressing **F4**.

Another feature of choosing file as the media is that all formatting is ignored. The format specifications are saved in case the user wants to print the output at a later date. However, the appearance of the output in the file will not follow the column formatting specifications, nor will any text be included.

FIGURE 8.20

```
                    Select Output Type and Output Form

Type choices, press Enter.

  Output type . . . . . . . . . . .   1        1=Display
                                               2=Printer
                                               3=Database file

  Form of output . . . . . . . . . .  1        1=Detail
                                               2=Summary only

  Line wrapping  . . . . . . . . . .  N        Y=Yes, N=No
      Wrapping width . . . . . . . .  ___      Blank, 1-378
      Record on one page . . . . . .  N        Y=Yes, N=No


F3=Exit            F5=Report            F10=Process/previous
F12=Cancel         F13=Layout           F18=Files
```

FIGURE 8.21

```
                    Define Database File Output

Type choices, press Enter.
  (The printed definition shows the output file record layout.)

  File . . . . . . . . .   ROSTERQRYO     Name, F4 for list
    Library  . . . . . .     MYLIBXX___   Name, F4 for list
  Member . . . . . . . .   *FILE_____     Name, *FIRST, *FILE, F4 for list

  Data in file . . . . .   1              1=New file, 2=Replace file
                                          3=New member, 4=Replace member
                                          5=Add to member

  For a new file:
    Authority  . . . . .   *LIBCRTAUT     *LIBCRTAUT, *CHANGE, *ALL,
                                          *EXCLUDE, *USE,
                                          authorization list name

    Text . . . . . . . .   __________________________________________
  Print definition . . .   N               Y=Yes, N=No


F3=Exit          F4=Prompt        F5=Report        F10=Process/previous
F12=Cancel       F13=Layout       F18=Files
```

Choosing `Printer` (option 2) as the output type will require the user to either specify a specific printer, accept the default printer, or spool the file to an output queue. QUERY/400 has a screen to enable the user to specify these.

Further, on the `Select Output Type and Output Form` screen, only a summary report can be requested. By specifying `Summary only`, all detail records will be suppressed, and only the totals specified earlier will be sent. If `Detail` is selected, both detail and summary records are sent. For our example, choose `Display` (option 1) and accept the default values for all the other options.

Exiting and Saving the Query

At this point, the query has been defined. To exit the query definition function, press **F3**. The `Exit this Query` screen will be displayed (Figure 8.22), and the user can save or run the query from this screen. To save the query definition, enter a **Y** at the `Save definition prompt`. The object name and library where the query is to be stored must also be specified at the appropriate prompts. For our example, save the query as ROSTERQRY in MYLIBXX (as was specified earlier).

FIGURE 8.22

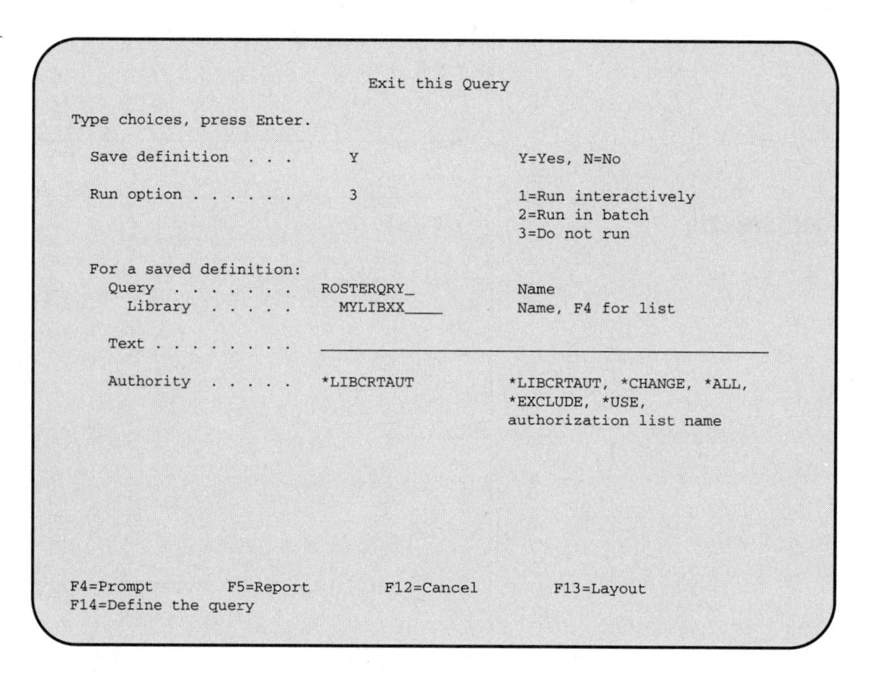

```
                         Exit this Query

Type choices, press Enter.

  Save definition  . . .      Y                     Y=Yes, N=No

  Run option . . . . . .      3                     1=Run interactively
                                                    2=Run in batch
                                                    3=Do not run

  For a saved definition:
    Query  . . . . . . .    ROSTERQRY_              Name
      Library  . . . . .      MYLIBXX____           Name, F4 for list

    Text . . . . . . . .    __________________________________________

    Authority  . . . . .    *LIBCRTAUT              *LIBCRTAUT, *CHANGE, *ALL,
                                                   *EXCLUDE, *USE,
                                                   authorization list name

F4=Prompt         F5=Report          F12=Cancel         F13=Layout
F14=Define the query
```

When the query definition is saved, an object with the query name (ROSTERQRY) will be created.

There are several ways to run a query.

1. From the `Exit this Query` screen (Figure 8.22), enter the run option number at the `Run option` prompt, and press **ENTER**.
2. From the `Work with Queries` screen (Figure 8.1), type in the name of the saved query, the run option number, and press **ENTER**.
3. From the command line, type the **RUNQRY** command, and press **F4** to prompt for the query name and other command parameters.

For our example, run the query in any of the three ways. If the output is printed, it would look like Figure 8.23; if sent to a file, it would look like Figure 8.24; and if displayed, it would look like Figure 8.25. To see the rest of the displayed report, press **F20**. This will show the rightmost portion of the query output (Figure 8.26).

FIGURE 8.23

```
                                   QUERY NAME . . . . . ROSTERQRY
                                   LIBRARY NAME . . . . MYLIBXX
                                   FILE          LIBRARY       MEMBER        FORMAT
                                   CLASS         MYLIBXX       CLASS         CLFMT
                                   GRADE         MYLIBXX       GRADE         GRDFMT
                                   STUDENT       MYLIBXX       STUDENT       STUDREC
                                   INSTRUCTOR    MYLIBXX       INSTRUCTOR    INSTRFMT
                                   DATE . . . . . . . .06/21/94
                                   TIME . . . . . . . .16:44:20
06/21/94  16:44:20                                                                     PAGE    1
CLASS  SECT# INST  LNAME      FNAME   STREET            CITY    ST ZIP   STUDID#   CR  GPA  GRD
NUMBER       NAME
ACC101 96306 Beane Flintstone Fred    11 Limestone Dr Bedrock AZ 88888 111111111  9 2.00 2.00
             Beane Flintstone Wilma   11 Limestone Dr Bedrock AZ 88888 123456789 12 4.00 4.00
             Beane Rubble     Betty   15 Limestone Dr Bedrock AZ 88888 444444444 18 3.99 4.00
             Beane Rubble     Barnard 15 Limestone Dr Bedrock AZ 88888 999999999 15 3.00 3.00
                                                                 SUBTOTALS FOR ACC101 SECTION 96306
                                                                 AVG                       3.25
                                                                 COUNT 4
                                                                 SUBTOTALS FOR ACC101
                                                                 AVG                      3.25
                                                                 COUNT 4
BIO101 96201 Galen Flintstone Fred    11 Limestone Dr Bedrock AZ 88888 111111111  9 2.00 1.00
             Galen Flintstone Wilma   11 Limestone Dr Bedrock AZ 88888 123456789 12 4.00 4.00
             Galen Rubble     Betty   15 Limestone Dr Bedrock AZ 88888 444444444 18 3.99 4.00
                                                                 SUBTOTALS FOR BIO101 SECTION 96201
                                                                 AVG                       3.00
                                                                 COUNT 3
                                                                 SUBTOTALS FOR BIO101
                                                                 AVG                       3.00
                                                                 COUNT 3
BUS101 96203 Beane Rubble     Betty   15 Limestone Dr Bedrock AZ 88888 444444444 18 3.99 4.00
             Beane Rubble     Barnard 15 Limestone Dr Bedrock AZ 88888 999999999 15 3.00 2.50
                                                                 SUBTOTALS FOR BUS101 SECTION 96203
                                                                 AVG                       3.25
                                                                 COUNT 2
       96306 Jones Flintstone Wilma   11 Limestone Dr Bedrock AZ 88888 123456789 12 4.00 4.00
                                                                 SUBTOTALS FOR BUS101 SECTION 96306
                                                                 AVG                       4.00
                                                                 COUNT 1
                                                                 SUBTOTALS FOR BUS101
                                                                 AVG                      3.50
                                                                 COUNT 3
CMP101 96306 Jobs  Flintstone Wilma   11 Limestone Dr Bedrock AZ 88888 123456789 12 4.00 4.00
             Jobs  Rubble     Betty   15 Limestone Dr Bedrock AZ 88888 444444444 18 3.99 4.00
             Jobs  Rubble     Barnard 15 Limestone Dr Bedrock AZ 88888 999999999 15 3.00 4.00
                                                                 SUBTOTALS FOR CMP101 SECTION 96306
                                                                 AVG                       4.00
                                                                 COUNT 3
06/21/94  16:44:20                                                                     PAGE    2
CLASS  SECT# INST  LNAME      FNAME   STREET            CITY    ST ZIP   STUDID# CR  GPA  GRD
NUMBER       NAME
                                                                 SUBTOTALS FOR CMP101
                                                                 AVG                      4.00
                                                                 COUNT 3
PSY212 96203 Hyde  Flintstone Fred    11 Limestone Dr Bedrock AZ 88888 111111111  9 2.00 3.00
             Hyde  Rubble     Betty   15 Limestone Dr Bedrock AZ 88888 444444444 18 3.99 4.00
             Hyde  Rubble     Barnard 15 Limestone Dr Bedrock AZ 88888 999999999 15 3.00 2.00
                                                                 SUBTOTALS FOR PSY212 SECTION 96203
                                                                 AVG                       3.00
                                                                 COUNT 3
                                                                 SUBTOTALS FOR PSY212
                                                                 AVG                        3.00
                                                                 COUNT 3
                                                                 TOTALS FOR ALL CLASSES
                                                                 AVG                        3.34
                                                                 COUNT 16
* * *  E N D  O F  R E P O R T  * * *
```

FIGURE 8.24

```
                         Display Physical File Member
File . . . . . . :   ROSTERQRYO          Library  . . . . :   MYLIBXX
Member . . . . . :   ROSTERQRYO          Record . . . . . :   1
Control  . . . . .                       Column . . . . . :   1
Find . . . . . . .
*...+....1....+....2....+....3....+....4....+....5....+....6....+....7....+...
ACC10196306Beane      FlintstoneFred     11 Limestone DrBedrock     AZ8888811111
ACC10196306Beane      FlintstoneWilma    11 Limestone DrBedrock     AZ8888812345
ACC10196306Beane      Rubble    Betty    15 Limestone DrBedrock     AZ8888844444
ACC10196306Beane      Rubble    Barnard  15 Limestone DrBedrock     AZ8888899999
BIO10196201Galen      FlintstoneFred     11 Limestone DrBedrock     AZ8888811111
BIO10196201Galen      FlintstoneWilma    11 Limestone DrBedrock     AZ8888812345
BIO10196201Galen      Rubble    Betty    15 Limestone DrBedrock     AZ8888844444
BUS10196203Beane      Rubble    Betty    15 Limestone DrBedrock     AZ8888844444
BUS10196203Beane      Rubble    Barnard  15 Limestone DrBedrock     AZ8888899999
BUS10196306Jones      FlintstoneWilma    11 Limestone DrBedrock     AZ8888812345
CMP10196306Jobs       FlintstoneWilma    11 Limestone DrBedrock     AZ8888812345
CMP10196306Jobs       Rubble    Betty    15 Limestone DrBedrock     AZ8888844444
CMP10196306Jobs       Rubble    Barnard  15 Limestone DrBedrock     AZ8888899999
PSY21296203Hyde       FlintstoneFred     11 Limestone DrBedrock     AZ8888811111
PSY21296203Hyde       Rubble    Betty    15 Limestone DrBedrock     AZ8888844444
PSY21296203Hyde       Rubble    Barnard  15 Limestone DrBedrock     AZ8888899999
                                                                         More...
F3=Exit   F12=Cancel   F19=Left   F20=Right   F24=More keys
```

FIGURE 8.25

```
                                 Display Report
Query . . . :   MYLIBXX/ROSTER                  Report width . . . . . :     126
Position to line  . . . . .                     Shift to column  . . . . . .
Line   ....+....1....+....2....+....3....+....4....+....5....+....6....+....7..
       CLASS   SECTION  INSTRUCTOR  LNAME       FNAME      STREET            CITY
       NUMBER  NUMBER   NAME
000001 ACC101   96306     Beane     Flintstone  Fred       11 Limestone Dr   Bedr
000002 ACC101   96306     Beane     Flintstone  Wilma      11 Limestone Dr   Bedr
000003 ACC101   96306     Beane     Rubble      Betty      15 Limestone Dr   Bedr
000004 ACC101   96306     Beane     Rubble      Barnard    15 Limestone Dr   Bedr
000005 BIO101   96201     Galen     Flintstone  Fred       11 Limestone Dr   Bedr
000006 BIO101   96201     Galen     Flintstone  Wilma      11 Limestone Dr   Bedr
000007 BIO101   96201     Galen     Rubble      Betty      15 Limestone Dr   Bedr
000008 BUS101   96203     Beane     Rubble      Betty      15 Limestone Dr   Bedr
000009 BUS101   96203     Beane     Rubble      Barnard    15 Limestone Dr   Bedr
000010 BUS101   96306     Jones     Flintstone  Wilma      11 Limestone Dr   Bedr
000011 CMP101   96306     Jobs      Flintstone  Wilma      11 Limestone Dr   Bedr
000012 CMP101   96306     Jobs      Rubble      Betty      15 Limestone Dr   Bedr
000013 CMP101   96306     Jobs      Rubble      Barnard    15 Limestone Dr   Bedr
000014 PSY212   96203     Hyde      Flintstone  Fred       11 Limestone Dr   Bedr
000015 PSY212   96203     Hyde      Rubble      Betty      15 Limestone Dr   Bedr
000016 PSY212   96203     Hyde      Rubble      Barnard    15 Limestone Dr   Bedr
000017
000018
000019
000020
****** ********  End of report  ********
                                                                       More...
F3=Exit      F12=Cancel      F19=Left      F20=Right      F21=Split
```

FIGURE 8.26

```
                               Display Report
Query . . . :   MYLIBXX/ROSTER               Report width . . . . . :        126
Position to line  . . . . .               Shift to column  . . . . . .
Line    +....6....+....7....+....8....+....9....+...10....+...11....+...12....+.
        EET           CITY     STATE  ZIP     STUDID#     CREDITS  GRADEPT  GRADE

000001 Limestone Dr  Bedrock   AZ    88888  111111111       9      2.00     2.00
000002 Limestone Dr  Bedrock   AZ    88888  123456789      12      4.00     4.00
000003 Limestone Dr  Bedrock   AZ    88888  444444444      18      3.99     4.00
000004 Limestone Dr  Bedrock   AZ    88888  999999999      15      3.00     3.00
000005 Limestone Dr  Bedrock   AZ    88888  111111111       9      2.00     1.00
000006 Limestone Dr  Bedrock   AZ    88888  123456789      12      4.00     4.00
000007 Limestone Dr  Bedrock   AZ    88888  444444444      18      3.99     4.00
000008 Limestone Dr  Bedrock   AZ    88888  444444444      18      3.99     4.00
000009 Limestone Dr  Bedrock   AZ    88888  999999999      15      3.00     2.50
000010 Limestone Dr  Bedrock   AZ    88888  123456789      12      4.00     4.00
000011 Limestone Dr  Bedrock   AZ    88888  123456789      12      4.00     4.00
000012 Limestone Dr  Bedrock   AZ    88888  444444444      18      3.99     4.00
000013 Limestone Dr  Bedrock   AZ    88888  999999999      15      3.00     4.00
000014 Limestone Dr  Bedrock   AZ    88888  111111111       9      2.00     3.00
000015 Limestone Dr  Bedrock   AZ    88888  444444444      18      3.99     4.00
000016 Limestone Dr  Bedrock   AZ    88888  999999999      15      3.00     2.00
000017
000018                                FINAL TOTALS
000019                                AVG                                   3.15
000020                                COUNT 17
****** ********  End of report  ********
                                                                     More...
F3=Exit       F12=Cancel       F19=Left       F20=Right       F21=Split
```

All saved queries can also be changed. At the `Work with Queries` screen, the user would specify the query to be changed, and select `Change` (option 2). This option allows the user to choose any of the query definition screens and display the values previously specified for that query. The user can change the values by simply typing over any of the existing values and exiting the screen.

QUERY/400 and Logical Files

QUERY/400 can be used by programmers to select and join data rather than building and maintaining logical files. For instance, a query could join or select data and write the results to a file. Application programs can read the query-generated file and perform any complex calculations or detailed formatting. You may be wondering why someone would use a query rather than a logical file. Logical files have a performance disadvantage in that they need to be constantly maintained. A logical file's KSAP is modified based on changes to the physical file(s) it is dependent on. If a logical file was read occasionaly (once a week or month) but the physical file was constantly being updated, creating the query file once a week or month might actually require fewer system resources than maintaining the logical file.

However, the downside to using a query is that the query will have to either build a KSAP or search sequentially through all the records to retrieve the needed data. Additional time is also spent creating the file to store the query results and writing the data to the file. Therefore, performing a query and then accessing the resulting data will probably take longer than simply accessing the data through an already existing (and constantly maintained) logical file.

The AS/400 developers realized the power of using queries in this way and improved on the process by creating a CL command to perform query functions. The OPNQRYF (open query file) command allows programmers to select and join files and easily pass the resulting data to an application program without the intermediate steps of creating and writing to a data file.

OPNQRYF

OPNQRYF can perform many of the same relational operations as DDS and QUERY/400. Like QUERY/400, it dynamically performs these operations and therefore eliminates the need to maintain KSAPs. In addition, with the use of the OVRDBF command, the query output can be directed to an application program. Application programs can process the OPNQRYF data sequentially, or OPNQRYF can create a KSAP and provide keyed access. Let's first look at the data manipulation functions provided by the OPNQRYF command and then how information can be passed to application programs.

QRYSLT

The QRYSLT keyword allows the programmer to specify the select argument. The format of the OPNQRYF command is as follows:

```
OPNQRYF FILE(library/file name) QRYSLT('select argument')
```

For instance, to select only the records that qualify for the dean's list, the OPNQRYF command would be as follows:

```
OPNQRYF FILE(mylibxx/student) QRYSLT('gradept *GE 3.5')
```

The FILE keyword identifies the file to be queried, and the QRYSLT keyword contains the argument. All the standard CL comparisons and operations (*EQ, *GT, *LT, *LE, *CAT, %SST, and so on) can be used in the QRYSLT clause.

If the argument includes a character field, the comparison value must be enclosed in double quotes. For instance, if we wanted all students from Arizona, the command would be

```
OPNQRYF FILE(mylibxx/student) QRYSLT('state *EQ "AZ"')
```

You can also create compound conditions with *AND and *OR statements as follows:

```
OPNQRYF FILE(mylibxx/student) +

      QRYSLT('gradept *GE 3.5 *AND state *EQ "AZ"')
```

Creating a Keyed Access Path

A KSAP can be defined using the KEYFLD keyword. The KEYFLD keyword identifies the field(s) to be used as the basis of the index. For instance, if we wanted to be able to access all the smart Arizonans by first name, the command would be:

```
OPNQRYF  FILE(mylibxx/student) +

         KEYFLD(fname) +

         QRYSLT('gradept *GE 3.5 *AND state *EQ "AZ"')
```

To retrieve a particular record, the application program's read command would specify the first name to be retrieved. If a program accesses the query results sequentially, the records will be retreived in key order (That is, first name order—Betty then Wilma). In the case of the dean's list, however, we would want the student records in descending order by gradept. The command to perform this would be

```
OPNQRYF  FILE(mylibxx/student) +

         KEYFLD(gradept *DESCEND) +

         QRYSLT('gradept *GE 3.5 *AND state *EQ "AZ"')
```

This would result in Wilma's record (with a grade point average of 4.0) being first and then Betty's record (with a 3.99).

Joining Files with OPNQRYF

Files can be dynamically joined with OPNQRYF through the JFLD keyword. The FILE keyword identifies the files to be joined (just like the DDS JFILE keyword), and the JFLD keyword identifies the fields that are the basis of the join (just like the DDS JFLD keyword). Before files can be joined with the OPNQRYF command, however, a record format for the join results must exist. The format is needed so that the DBMS knows what fields to include in the join and the sequence of the fields. Within the OPNQRYF command, the keyword FORMAT is used to identify the format.

For instance, to create a file similar to the ROSTER file, we would need to create a format such as that shown in Figure 8.27.

FIGURE 8.27

```
Columns . . . :   1  71           Edit                          MYLIBXX/DDSSRC
SEU==>                                                                  RSTFMT
FMT A* .....A*. 1 ...+... 2 ...+... 3 ...+... 4 ...+... 5 ...+... 6 ...+... 7
       *************** Beginning of data ************************************
0001.00       * THIS FILE PROVIDES A FORMAT FOR AN OPEN QUERY FILE DYNAMIC JOIN
0002.00       **  OF THE CLASS, STUDENT, AND INSTRUCTOR FILES.
0003.00                                              REF(MYLIBXX/FRF)
0004.00                R RSTFMT                      TEXT('ROSTER FOR OPNQRYF')
0005.00                  LNAME     R
0006.00                  FNAME     R
0007.00                  STREET    R
0008.00                  CITY      R    7
0009.00                  STATE     R
0010.00                  ZIP       R
0011.00                  STUDID#   R
0012.00                  CREDITS   R
0013.00                  GRADEPT   R
0014.00                  CL#       R
0015.00                  SECT#     R
0016.00                  GRADE     R
0017.00                  INSTR     R    6
       ****************** End of data ***************************************

F3=Exit   F4=Prompt   F5=Refresh   F9=Retrieve   F10=Cursor
F16=Repeat find       F17=Repeat change          F24=More keys
```

We would then execute the following command:

```
OPNQRYF FILE(MYLIBXX/CLASS MYLIBXX/GRADE MYLIBXX/STUDENT +
              MYLIBXX/INSTRUCTOR) +
         FORMAT(MYLIBXX/RSTFMT) +
         JFLD((CLASS/CL# GRADE/CL#) (CLASS/SECT# GRADE/SECT#) +
              (GRADE/STUDID# STUDENT/STUDID#) +
              (CLASS/IID INSTRUCTOR/IID)) +
         MAPFLD((CL# 'GRADE/CL#') (SECT# 'GRADE/SECT#') +
                (STUDID# 'STUDENT/STUDID#'))
```

The FILE keyword identifies the files to be joined, and the FORMAT keyword identifies the format to be used (Figure 8.27). The JFLD clause specifies the join criteria. (Notice how it is very similar to the JOIN and JFLD statements from the logical file ROSTER1.) Instead of filenames, the JFLD keyword can be specified using relative file numbers to qualify each field (just as with DDS). In other words, the JFLD clause could also have been coded as follows:

```
JFLD((1/CL# 2/CL#) (1/SECT# 2/SECT#) +
     (2/STUDID# 3/STUDID#) +
     (1/IID 4/IID)) +
```

Any keyword (following the FILE keyword) can substitute relative file numbers for filenames.

The type of join that OPNQRYF will perform is what QUERY/400 called a matched records join. In other words, only classes and sections that have students and an instructor will be displayed. To perform a matched records with primary file or unmatched records with primary file join, the keyword JDFTVAL must be used within the OPNQRYF command.

JDFTVAL allows the user to specify whether default values should be supplied for missing records in nonprimary files. The default value for JDFTVAL is *NO. This means that no default information will be supplied, and therefore, any unmatched primary file records will not be included in the join file since they have no matching records in the secondary files.

A JDFTVAL of *YES signifies that default data should be used for any missing secondary file records. This means a matched records with primary file join (as in QUERY/400) will be performed.

Finally, specifying *ONLYDFT will result in only unmatched primary records being selected for the join. Default information will be supplied for missing matched records, but only those primary records that need default data will be selected, joined with any matching records and default data, and displayed. Specifying *ONLYDFT within the JDFTVAL keyword produces the same result as an unmatched records with primary file join.

The new keyword MAPFLD performs a function similar to the DDS keyword JREF. Between the physical files to be joined there are fields that share the same name. The DBMS needs to know which file should supply the value for these fields. In this case, the MAPFLD keyword specifies that the GRADE file will supply the values of CL# and SECT#, and the STUDENT file will provide STUDID# (just as in ROSTERQRY created earlier).

Executing this statement would result in data as seen in Figure 8.28. This data is the same as generated by ROSTERQRY (minus the totals information) and the logical file ROSTER1 (see Figure 8.26).

FIGURE 8.28

```
                         Display Physical File Member
File . . . . . . :   RSTTEST              Library  . . . . :   MYLIBXX
Member . . . . . :   RSTTEST              Record . . . . . :   1
Control  . . . . .                        Column . . . . . :   1
Find . . . . . . .
*...+....1....+....2....+....3....+....4....+....5....+....6....+....7....+...
FlintstoneFred    11 Limestone DrBedrockAZ88888111111111 ¤ HBIO10196201  Galen
FlintstoneFred    11 Limestone DrBedrockAZ88888111111111 ¤ HPSY21296203  Hyde
FlintstoneFred    11 Limestone DrBedrockAZ88888111111111 ¤ HACC10196306  Beane
FlintstoneWilma   11 Limestone DrBedrockAZ88888123456789   °BIO10196201  Galen
FlintstoneWilma   11 Limestone DrBedrockAZ88888123456789   °ACC10196306  Beane
FlintstoneWilma   11 Limestone DrBedrockAZ88888123456789   °CMP10196306  Jobs
FlintstoneWilma   11 Limestone DrBedrockAZ88888123456789   °BUS10196306  Jones
Rubble    Betty   15 Limestone DrBedrockAZ88888444444444 ± ±BIO10196201  Galen
Rubble    Betty   15 Limestone DrBedrockAZ88888444444444 ± ±BUS10196203  Beane
Rubble    Betty   15 Limestone DrBedrockAZ88888444444444 ± ±PSY21296203  Hyde
Rubble    Betty   15 Limestone DrBedrockAZ88888444444444 ± ±CMP10196306  Jobs
Rubble    Betty   15 Limestone DrBedrockAZ88888444444444 ± ±ACC10196306  Beane
Rubble    Barnard 15 Limestone DrBedrockAZ88888999999999 ¬  PSY21296203  Hyde
Rubble    Barnard 15 Limestone DrBedrockAZ88888999999999 ¬  BUS10196203  Beane
Rubble    Barnard 15 Limestone DrBedrockAZ88888999999999 ¬  CMP10196306  Jobs
Rubble    Barnard 15 Limestone DrBedrockAZ88888999999999 ¬  ACC10196306  Beane
                         ****** END OF DATA ******



                                                                        Bottom
F3=Exit   F12=Cancel   F19=Left   F20=Right   F24=More keys
```

Notice that Figure 8.28 is actually the DSPPFM screen for a file called RSTTEST in MYLIBXX. The data from an OPNQRYF command can be written to a file with the CPYFRMQRYF (copy from query file) command. For instance, if we created, compiled, and ran the CL program seen in Figure 8.29, the file RSTTEST in MYLIBXX would be created, and the data in Figure 8.28 would be contained within RSTTEST.

FIGURE 8.29

```
FMT **  ...+... 1 ...+... 2 ...+... 3 ...+... 4 ...+... 5 ...+... 6 ...+... 7
        *************** Beginning of data ************************************
0001.00 OPNQRYF FILE(MYLIBXX/CLASS MYLIBXX/GRADE MYLIBXX/STUDENT +
0002.00              MYLIBXX/INSTRUCTOR) +
0003.00         FORMAT(MYLIBXX/RSTFMT) +
0004.00         JFLD((CLASS/CL# GRADE/CL#) (CLASS/SECT# GRADE/SECT#) +
0005.00              (GRADE/STUDID# STUDENT/STUDID#) +
0006.00              (CLASS/IID INSTRUCTOR/IID)) +
0007.00         MAPFLD((CL# 'GRADE/CL#') (SECT# 'GRADE/SECT#') +
0008.00                (STUDID# 'STUDENT/STUDID#')) +
0009.00         OPNID(TEMP)
0010.00 CPYFRMQRYF FROMOPNID(TEMP) TOFILE(MYLIBXX/RSTTEST) +
0011.00            MBROPT(*REPLACE) CRTFILE(*YES)
        ****************** End of data ***************************************
```

The CPYFRMQRYF command actually creates the new file RSTTEST. This is done by specifying MYLIBXX/RSTTEST as the "to file" and *YES within the CRTFILE keyword. If the file already existed, the CRTFILE keyword would be omitted. (The MBROPT keyword controls how information is written to already existing files—*ADD specifies that information copied to the file is added to any existing data, whereas *REPLACE overwrites all existing data. The MBROPT keyword is included only to demonstrate the syntax and is not necessary when creating the file.)

The real twist with RSTR (the CL program in Figure 8.29) is specifying the output of the OPNQRYF command as the input for the CPYFRMQRYF command. This is done through the OPNID keyword in the OPNQRYF command (see line 9 in Figure 8.29). OPNID allows the user to name the data that is produced by the OPNQRYF command. This name is then used in the FROMOPNID keyword in the CPYFRMQRYF command (see line 10 in Figure 8.29) to identify the source of the data to be copied. The CPYFRMQRYF command can also be used to print the result of an OPNQRYF command. This is done by specifying *PRINT in the TOFILE keyword.

We have shown how OPNQRYF can be used to provide alternative access paths to information just like logical files and QUERY/400 queries. The real power of OPNQRYF comes from the ability to pass that information directly to application programs.

Overriding Files

Application programs require that all files be explicitly identified. Moreover, when an input or output operation is performed, the particular file to be used must be identified. These identifications can be overridden through the CL command OVRDBF (override with database file). Within the OVRDBF command, the file to be overridden is identified in the keyword FILE, and the TOFILE keyword identifies the replacement file. The command would look like the following:

```
OVRDBF FILE(OLDFILE) TOFILE (NEWFILE) SHARE(*YES)
```

The SHARE keyword allows many programs to access the same file more efficiently and use the same "open path" to that file. In this case, we want the OPNQRYF command and the application program to both use the file created by OPNQRYF. By specifying SHARE (*YES), we ensure the file is opened to enable this.

For instance, if we were going to generate the student report in Figure 7.17 once a semester, we might consider using the OPNQRYF file rather than maintain a multiple format logical file. Since the report is generated only once a semester, is there any need for an up-to-the-minute accurate logical file? It will probably use less system resources to dynamically create a join file using OPNQRYF than building and maintaining a logical file. For instance, every time a student enrolls in the college, drops a class, or signs up for a class, the multiple format logical file would be updated. Since this is done quite frequently throughout the term, creating the index once a semester with the OPNQRYF command would probably use less system resources than maintaining the logical file.

To use the OPNQRYF command to generate the information, the program (STURPT) that generates the report would be called from a CL program. The CL program would contain the OVRDBF and OPNQRYF commands that retrieve the needed information and ensure that STURPT reads the data. Assuming that the program logic for STURPT was the following (the same logic from Chapter 7):

```
        Set KEY = null
Read:   Read STUGRD
        If end of file Then stop
        If KEY = STUDID#
        Then Perform print-class-info
        Else Perform print-student-info
             Set KEY = STUDID#
        GoTo Read
```

we would have to modify it slightly for reading a join record. The new code would look like the following:

```
        Set KEY = null
Read:   Read STUGRD
        If end of file Then stop
        If KEY = STUDID#
        Then Perform print-class-info
        Else Perform print-student-info
             Perform print-class-info
             Set KEY = STUDID#
        GoTo Read
```

The CL code to override the use of STUGRD and create the access path to the data in STUDENT and GRADE would be as follows:

```
OVRDBF    FILE(STUGRD) TOFILE(STUDENT) SHARE(*YES)
OPNQRYF   FILE(STUDENT GRADE) +
          FORMAT(JOINSG) +
          JFLD(STUDENT/STUDID# GRADE/STUDID#) +
          MAPFLD((STUDID# 'STUDENT/STUDID#'))
CALL      PGM(STURPT)
CLOF      OPNID(STUDENT)
DLTOVR    FILE(STUGRD)
```

Notice that the TOFILE is designated as the primary join file. This is because the result of the OPNQRYF join is given the primary filename. There also are a couple of new statements, CLOF and DLTOVR. When the OPNQRYF joins the files, the result file (with the primary filename) is opened. Opening a file is an internal action that the computer takes to make the file available for use. Different programming languages handle opening (and closing) files differently. Some explicitly require the programmer to open and close files, whereas others automatically open files when certain file operations are performed and close files when the program ends. CL automatically opens the result file with the OPNQRYF command but requires an explicit close with the CLOF (close file) command.

The DLTOVR command ends the override condition. Any programs called after the DLTOVR command that request the STUGRD file will get STUGRD, not the results of the OPNQRYF.

There is one condition where the results of a join OPNQRYF cannot be passed to an application program: when the application is using SQL commands for all input and output. For some reason (known only to the developers), SQL and OPNQRYF cannot share join files.

The OVRDBF can be used for nonjoin OPNQRYF results also.

Summary

QUERY/400 is a menu-driven utility that allows users to quickly and easily define query programs. These query programs can read and manipulate data from AS/400 files. In addition, query programs generate reports that can be displayed at the user's workstation, printed, or sent to a file. QUERY/400 provides basic formatting and data manipulation capability; however, any complex logic, calculations, or formatting may require a higher level programming language.

Many programmers have used QUERY/400 as a means to dynamically generate access paths to data files. By using a query the programmer creates the access path when needed and saves system resources by not having to maintain the path. The OPNQRYF command was created to make the dynamic creation of access paths easier. With a series of keywords, OPNQRYF can perform the same functions as provided by DDS and QUERY/400. Used in conjunction with the OVRDBF and CPYFRMQRYF commands, the access paths or files generated by OPNQRYF can be supplied to application programs for use in processing.

EXERCISES

1. Create a QUERY/400 query called Q4CONSUM in MYLIBXX that duplicates the function of the logical file CONSUM. Have the query write the data to a file called Q4CONSUM in MYLIBXX. If the file already exists, replace any existing records in the file.
2. Create a Query/400 query called Q4ACCRCV in MYLIBXX that duplicates the function of the logical file ACCRCV. Have the query write the data to a file called Q4ACCRCV in MYLIBXX. If the file already exists, replace any existing records in the file.

PROGRAMMING EXERCISES

1. Create a CL program called OQFCONSUM that uses the OPNQRYF command to duplicate the function of the logical file CONSUM. Create a new physical file called OQFCONSUM that contains the correct format. Use the CPYFRMQRY command to write the data generated from the OPNQRYF command to the file called OQFCONSUM.
2. Create a CL program called OQFACCRCV that uses the OPNQRYF command to duplicate the function of the logical file ACCRCV. Create a new physical file called OQFACCRCV that contains the correct format. Use the CPYFRMQRY command to write the data generated from the OPNQRYF command to the file called OQFACCRCV.

REVIEW QUESTIONS

1. What media choices does QUERY/400 provide for output?
2. Is QUERY/400 limited to displaying only stored data? If not, give an example of nonstored information that can be displayed using QUERY/400.
3. What are the advantages and disadvantages of using QUERY/400 versus application programs to generate reports?
4. Why are file ids needed for multiple file queries?
5. What are the differences between a procedural and a nonprocedural language?
6. When are access paths created and maintained for logical files versus OPNQRYF?
7. Describe the conditions where OPNQRYF would be used instead of a logical file.
8. What function does the QRYSLT keyword provide? How do QUERY/400 and DDS supply the same function?
9. Why is it preferable to use sort fields as break fields?

DISCUSSION QUESTIONS

1. Explain the three joins available with QUERY/400.
2. Discuss the QUERY/400 types of joins that are available with logical files and OPNQRYF.
3. Compare the QUERY/400 join options to DDS J specifications and keywords.
4. Compare the OPNQRYF keywords to the DDS join logical file keywords.

SQL

9

Overview

This chapter will introduce the reader to SQL/400. Many of the data definition and data manipulation functions provided by DDS and the various AS/400 utilities can be performed with SQL. We will explore interactive SQL, how SQL commands can be used with higher level programming languages and how to create and run SQL queries.

After finishing this chapter, you will understand

- The major SQL/400 components
- The implementation of the SQL/400 components as AS/400 objects
- The three ways to execute SQL commands (interactively, from within application programs, from query management queries)
- The precompiling process
- The special SQL statements required for programming
- The advantages and disadvantages of SQL/400

After finishing this chapter you will be able to

- Create tables, views, and indexes
- Manipulate and retrieve data using interactive SQL
- Create, save, and run a Query Manager query

SQL

SQL is an industrywide, standard set of relational commands that allow users to both define and manipulate data. SQL has been adopted by IBM as the common interface for relational data definition and data manipulation functions on all IBM systems. In addition, most relational DBMSs support an SQL interface, and in general, the commands are much the same between the different database packages. (After conquering one form of SQL, you will find that all others are similar and very easy to learn.)

SQL/400 is the AS/400's implementation of SQL. On the AS/400, the functions provided by DDS, DFU, QUERY/400, and OPNQRYF can also be performed with SQL/400 commands. Since we have already covered many of the relational functions (join, select, project, and so forth) and shown how the AS/400 native database implements these functions, you will probably pick up the SQL/400 commands very quickly. The difficulty lies in learning the new SQL/400 environment.

The SQL/400 Environment

There are an entirely new set of objects, such as collections and tables, in which SQL stores data. These new objects are actually implemented on the AS/400 as libraries, physical files, and logical files; however, all SQL/400 commands are issued against the SQL objects. In other words, you create a table with an SQL/400 statement even though a data physical file is actually created on the AS/400. One nice integration feature is that all the SQL objects can be accessed with PDM and CL commands. Likewise, SQL/400 commands can access AS/400 libraries and files that were created with native database functions.

SQL/400 statements can also be used to access data in application programs. Software using SQL statements can be executed on any computer system that supports the SQL interface. Because programs that reference the native AS/400 objects are limited to the AS/400 environment, SQL provides a significant portability advantage for applications.

The first new data storage entity we will discuss is a **collection.** A collection is a library with a **catalog**, **data dictionary**, **journal**, and **journal receiver**. When a user creates a collection, a library with the collection name is created on the AS/400. During the creation of the collection, SQL/400 also creates a journal, journal receiver, data dictionary, and series of physical and logical files that compose the catalog. These are all stored in the library. Collections can also contain **tables**, **views,** and **indexes**. Each of these objects is created separately with SQL/400 statements. As you can see, the collection performs the exact same function as an AS/400 library; it acts as a directory of objects.

The journal and journal receiver store information regarding updates to the SQL data. These "database transaction files" are AS/400 objects with types equal to *JRN and *JRNRCV. These objects can be used for backup and recovery of SQL data just as with native database files and will be discussed in detail in Chapter 12.

The catalog and data dictionary contain information about each table, column, index, view, and so on in the collection. The physical and logical files that make up the catalog have names that begin with the letters SYS, QSQ, and QIDCT. For instance, when a collection is created, there are files created called SYSTABLES, SYSCOLUMNS, SYSINDEXES, QSQTABLES, and QSQCOLUMNS. As mentioned, these files reside under the library or collection and either store information about the SQL data or provide a unique view of that information. In addition, an AS/400 data dictionary object (an object with type equal to *DTADCT) is created in the library. This data dictionary object contains an overview of all the SQL data.

The information contained in these objects will be updated to reflect any changes that are the result of SQL/400 commands being performed. This, of course, means added overhead for SQL/400 command processing.

Additional SQL objects such as tables, views, and indexes are the real workhorses of the SQL environment. They actually contain the data and any alternative access paths to the data required by the user.

A table is a two-dimensional array of data in rows and columns. Each row corresponds to an AS/400 record, and each column corresponds to an AS/400 field. An SQL/400 table is implemented as an AS/400 nonkeyed physical file. In other words, when a user issues the SQL/400 command to create a table within a collection, a nonkeyed physical file is created under a library that has the same name as the specified collection.

A view is implemented as a nonkeyed logical file. Views contain no data but appear to be a table. Views can contain a subset of rows or columns from a table, and these rows or columns can be in a different order than the table they are based on. In addition, views can contain rows and columns from multiple tables.

An index is an alternative access path to a table. Normally, tables are searched sequentially in arrival sequence order. Indexes can speed up the search. Indexes are implemented on the AS/400 as keyed logical files.

All these objects can be built or deleted with SQL/400 commands. The dependent indexes and views will be automatically maintained by the system when changes are made to the tables on which they are based. However, just as with logical and physical files, a large number of dependent indexes and views can affect update performance.

Executing SQL/400 Commands

SQL commands can be executed in three different ways.

From within queries

From within application programs

Interactively

An SQL/400 query is created, with the SQL/400 Query Manager utility, as a new type of object that contains only SQL statements. You can think of these queries as SQL programs.

Within application programs, SQL statements can take the place of a programming language's input and output commands such as CHAIN in RPG or READ in COBOL. However, doing this requires an added system step to "precompile" the program.

To execute SQL commands interactively, the user must activate the interactive SQL utility. Just like many of the other utilities on the AS/400, the SQL utility must be started. This is done with the STRSQL command.

For the purposes of initially learning the commands, all examples will be shown in the interactive environment. After completing a basic introduction to SQL commands, we will explore how to use the same commands in application programs and queries. At that time, we will also introduce some specialized SQL statements needed for these two alternative environments.

When starting the SQL environment there is an option to control how collections, libraries, files, tables, and so on will be identified. The user can choose to stick with the AS/400 convention of separating object names from library names with a forward slash (mylibxx/student) or opt for the SQL convention of a period (mylibxx.student). The default is the AS/400 method, and all of our examples will use that convention.

After typing **STRSQL** at any command line, the `Enter SQL Statements` screen (Figure 9.1) will be displayed. SQL commands can be typed at the prompt and executed by pressing **ENTER**. Notice that the command line consists of 17 lines. (This is the "mother of all command lines.") SQL statements can be quite long. Statements are allowed to "run over" to subsequent lines with no impact on execution.

FIGURE 9.1

```
                          Enter SQL Statements

Type SQL statement, press Enter.
===> ____________________________________________________________
     ____________________________________________________________
     ____________________________________________________________
     ____________________________________________________________
     ____________________________________________________________
     ____________________________________________________________
     ____________________________________________________________
     ____________________________________________________________
     ____________________________________________________________
     ____________________________________________________________
     ____________________________________________________________
     ____________________________________________________________
     ____________________________________________________________
     ____________________________________________________________
     ____________________________________________________________
     ____________________________________________________________
     ____________________________________________________________
                                                               Bottom
F3=Exit   F4=Prompt   F6=Insert line   F9=Retrieve   F10=Copy line
F12=Cancel            F13=Services     F24=More keys
```

Creating Tables

Before a table is created, a collection (or library) must exist. To create a collection, you must issue the CREATE COLLECTION command. For our example, we will create a collection called MYCLCXX. To create this collection, you would enter the statement **CREATE COLLECTION MYCLCXX** at the command line on the `Enter SQL Statements` screen and press **ENTER**. This command will take some time (the amount depends on the size of your machine) because SQL/400 creates all the previously mentioned objects within the collection. When processing is completed, a message will be displayed verifying that the collection was created successfully (Figure 9.2). Notice that the interactive SQL screen keeps a running record of the commands and messages. In addition, users can recall the previous command by pressing **F9**.

As mentioned earlier, creating a collection actually results in a library being created on the AS/400. If you were to use PDM to work with objects within library MYCLCXX, the display would appear as in Figure 9.3. Notice all the objects that were automatically created.

FIGURE 9.2

```
                              Enter SQL Statements

Type SQL statement, press Enter.
   > create collection myclcxx
     Collection MYCLCXX created.
===> ____________________________________________________________________
     ____________________________________________________________________
     ____________________________________________________________________
     ____________________________________________________________________
     ____________________________________________________________________
     ____________________________________________________________________
     ____________________________________________________________________
     ____________________________________________________________________
     ____________________________________________________________________
     ____________________________________________________________________
     ____________________________________________________________________
     ____________________________________________________________________
     ____________________________________________________________________
     ____________________________________________________________________
                                                                   Bottom

F3=Exit   F4=Prompt   F6=Insert line   F9=Retrieve   F10=Copy line
F12=Cancel            F13=Services     F24=More keys
```

FIGURE 9.3

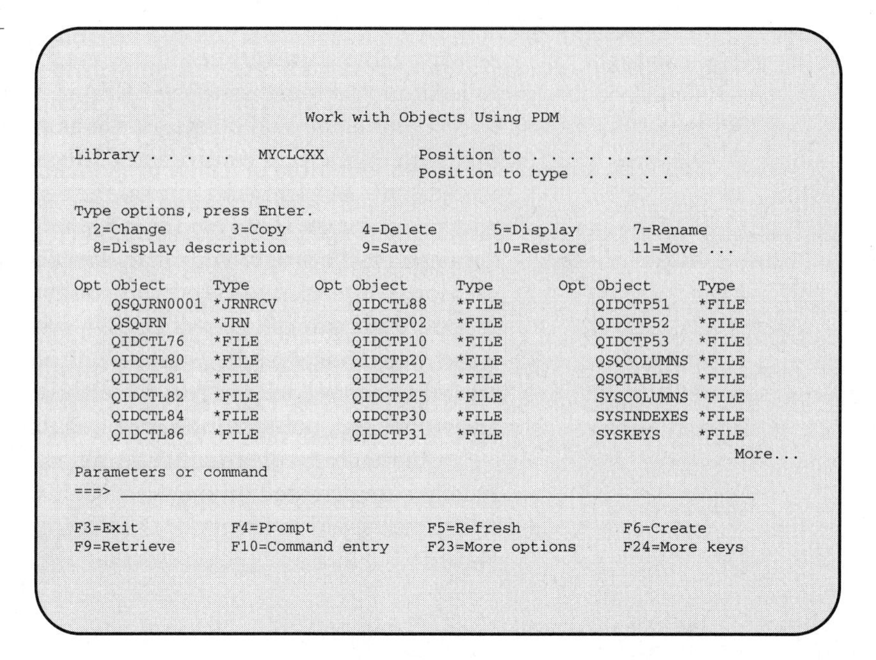
```
                         Work with Objects Using PDM

Library . . . . .   MYCLCXX          Position to . . . . . . . .
                                     Position to type  . . . . .

Type options, press Enter.
  2=Change        3=Copy        4=Delete       5=Display      7=Rename
  8=Display description         9=Save         10=Restore     11=Move ...

Opt Object      Type       Opt Object      Type       Opt Object      Type
    QSQJRN0001  *JRNRCV        QIDCTL88    *FILE          QIDCTP51    *FILE
    QSQJRN      *JRN           QIDCTP02    *FILE          QIDCTP52    *FILE
    QIDCTL76    *FILE          QIDCTP10    *FILE          QIDCTP53    *FILE
    QIDCTL80    *FILE          QIDCTP20    *FILE          QSQCOLUMNS  *FILE
    QIDCTL81    *FILE          QIDCTP21    *FILE          QSQTABLES   *FILE
    QIDCTL82    *FILE          QIDCTP25    *FILE          SYSCOLUMNS  *FILE
    QIDCTL84    *FILE          QIDCTP30    *FILE          SYSINDEXES  *FILE
    QIDCTL86    *FILE          QIDCTP31    *FILE          SYSKEYS     *FILE
                                                                    More...
Parameters or command
===> ____________________________________________________________________

F3=Exit            F4=Prompt           F5=Refresh          F6=Create
F9=Retrieve        F10=Command entry   F23=More options    F24=More keys
```

Once a collection exists, tables can be created. Creating a table will result in a data physical file and member being created. When creating a table using SQL, the structure of the table must also be defined, just as with DDS. The command to create a table is CREATE TABLE followed by

The collection that will contain the table

The table name

Each column name

The column type and size

An optional null statement

For instance, to create a table that can hold the same data as the STUDENT file, the command would be as follows (uppercase lettering denotes SQL statements and keywords):

```
CREATE TABLE myclcxx/student
            (lname    CHAR(10) NOT NULL,
             fname    CHAR(8)  NOT NULL,
             street   CHAR(15) NOT NULL,
             city     CHAR(10) NOT NULL,
             state    CHAR(2)  NOT NULL,
             zip      CHAR(5)  NOT NULL,
             studid#  CHAR(9)  NOT NULL,
             credits  DEC(3)   NOT NULL WITH DEFAULT,
             gradept  DEC(3,2) NOT NULL WITH DEFAULT)
```

Notice the keywords NOT NULL and NOT NULL WITH DEFAULT. NOT NULL performs a similar function as the DDS keyword ME (mandatory entry). Any time a row is entered into the table, a value must be entered for the columns specified as NOT NULL. Columns specified as NOT NULL WITH DEFAULT will have a value entered by the system if none is supplied. For each of the different data types, there is a different default value.

All numeric fields default to zero.

CHAR fields default to blanks.

DATE fields default to the current date.

TIME fields default to the current time.

SQL ignores extra spaces between commands, keywords, and column names and is not case sensitive. For instance, the varying number of spaces between each of the column names and the keyword CHAR are ignored. In addition, each column's definition does not have to appear on a separate line. As a matter of fact, the command could be entered as a continuous lowercase character string across five lines. Figure 9.4 shows the command with none of the "readability" spacing and the resulting message after execution.

There are several similarities and differences between DDS and the CREATE TABLE command. Certainly identifying the name of the object and defining each of the data elements is a common feature. However, SQL/400 is more limited in some of the functions and options available. For instance, SQL/400 does not allow the user to store numeric data in binary. The keyword DEC will result in the data being stored in packed decimal, and the alternative data type NUMERIC will result in zoned decimal storage. SQL does, however, support the fixed format data types of DATE and TIME. SQL also does not support text or column heading definitions, nor does it allow the user to define a default value for a column. SQL does not use record formats. On the positive side, not using record formats means there is one less thing that the user must name and remember, but this also means that multiple format files are not supported.

Defining files interactively also has some drawbacks. One major problem is that no source definition for the table is saved. To get around this problem, the user can save all commands and messages from the session to a source physical file member. This is done by pressing F13, the `Services` option, and specifying option 4, `Save session in source file`. The user will be prompted for the library, file, and member names that will hold the session. If the source physical file and member do not exist, the user can direct SQL to create them. The user would then edit the member with SEU and

FIGURE 9.4

```
                    Enter SQL Statements

Type SQL statement, press Enter.
   > create collection myclcxx
     Collection MYCLCXX created.
   > create table myclcxx/student (lname char(10) not null, fname char(8)
     not null, street char(15) not null, city char(10) not null, state c
     har(2) not null, zip char(5) not null, studid# char(9) not null, cre
     dits dec(3) not null with default, gradept dec(3,2) not null with de
     fault)
     Table STUDENT created in collection MYCLCXX.
===> ______________________________________________________________



                                                              Bottom
F3=Exit   F4=Prompt   F6=Insert line   F9=Retrieve   F10=Copy line
F12=Cancel            F13=Services     F24=More keys
```

remove any unwanted commands and messages, thereby saving the original SQL table definition. However, this is quite an effort and not very practical. If the user wants to save the SQL source statements, the table should be created with an SQL/400 Query Manager query (more about this later in the chapter).

One nice feature that interactive SQL shares with SEU is command prompting. For instance, typing the command **CREATE TABLE** and pressing **F4** would result in the `Specify CREATE TABLE Statement` screen (Figure 9.5) being displayed. The user can simply fill in the data and press **ENTER** to execute the command.

Loading Data into a Table

The SQL statement to enter a row of data into a table is INSERT INTO. The command is followed by

The names of the collection and table

The VALUES keyword

The values to be inserted into each column

All the values must be enclosed in parentheses, character data must additionally be enclosed in single quotes, and each value must be separated by a comma.

As an example, we will insert a student row for Fred Flintstone. To enter Fred's information, type the following statement at the command line, and press **ENTER**:

```
INSERT INTO myclcxx/student
VALUES ('Flintstone', 'Fred', '11 Limestone Dr', 'Bedrock', 'AZ',
       '88888', '111111111', 9, 2.00)
```

FIGURE 9.5

```
                    Specify CREATE TABLE Statement

 Type choices.

   File . . . . . . . . . . . . .  ____________      Name
     Library  . . . . . . . . . .     ___________    Name, F4 for list

 Type information, press Enter.
 Nulls:  1=NULL, 2=NOT NULL, 3=NOT NULL WITH DEFAULT
 Data:  1=BIT, 2=SBCS, 3=MIXED, 4=CCSID
 Field         Type              Length  Scale  Nulls  Data  Allocate  CCSID
 ___________   _______________   _____   ___    3      _     _____     _____
 ___________   _______________   _____   ___    3      _     _____     _____
 ___________   _______________   _____   ___    3      _     _____     _____
 ___________   _______________   _____   ___    3      _     _____     _____
 ___________   _______________   _____   ___    3      _     _____     _____
 ___________   _______________   _____   ___    3      _     _____     _____
 ___________   _______________   _____   ___    3      _     _____     _____
 ___________   _______________   _____   ___    3      _     _____     _____
                                                                       Bottom
 F3=Exit       F4=Prompt        F5=Refresh   F6=Insert line   F10=Copy line
 F12=Cancel    F14=Delete line  F21=Display statement
```

The resulting message would be `1 rows inserted in STUDENT in MYCLCXX`. This method of data entry is not very user friendly. Who can remember all the fields, their order, and whether they are character or numeric? Fortunately, prompting can help create a DFU-like environment.

Typing **INSERT INTO** and pressing **F4** would result in the `Specify INSERT Statement` screen. At this screen, the user would specify the collection and table names at the `Library` and `Into file` prompts (Figure 9.6) and press **ENTER**. A data entry screen

FIGURE 9.6

```
                        Specify INSERT Statement

 Type choices, press Enter.

   INTO file . . . . . . . . . . . .   student          Name, F4 for list
     Library . . . . . . . . . . . .     myclcxx        Name, F4 for list

   Select fields to insert INTO  . .   N                Y=Yes, N=No

   Insertion method  . . . . . . . .   1                1=Input VALUES
                                                        2=Subselect


 F3=Exit   F4=Prompt   F5=Refresh   F12=Cancel   F21=Display statement
```

with the column names and a data entry area for each column will be displayed (Figure 9.7). Unlike DFU, each data entry line is not the column length, and there is no type identifier. This information, however, can be displayed by pressing F11. The user would then enter the data (as in Figure 9.8) and press ENTER. A new row, with the data specified, would be entered into the table.

FIGURE 9.7

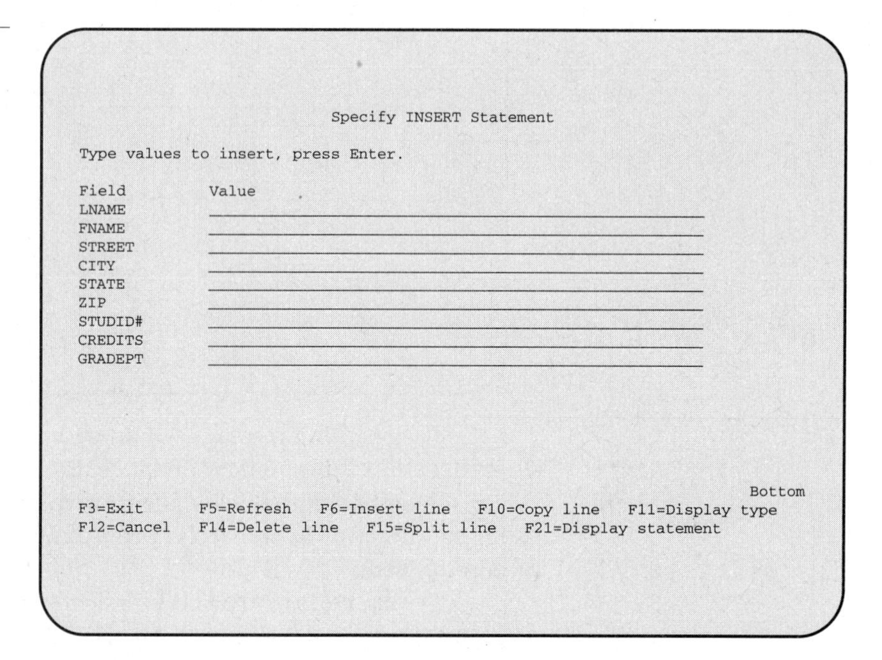

FIGURE 9.8

```
                         Specify INSERT Statement

Type values to insert, press Enter.

Field          Type              Digits  Length  Value
LNAME          CHARACTER                     10  'Flintstone'
FNAME          CHARACTER                      8  'Fred'
STREET         CHARACTER                     15  '11 Limestone Dr'
CITY           CHARACTER                     10  'Bedrock'
STATE          CHARACTER                      2  'AZ'
ZIP            CHARACTER                      5  '88888'
STUDID#        CHARACTER                      9  '111111111'
CREDITS        DECIMAL             3             9
GRADEPT        DECIMAL             3  2          2.00

                                                                  Bottom
F3=Exit      F5=Refresh   F6=Insert line   F10=Copy line   F11=Display nulls
F12=Cancel   F14=Delete line   F15=Split line   F21=Display statement
```

This method of data entry, just like DFU, is fine for a single record or two but is unmanageable if a large number of rows must be entered. If a large amount of data needs to be placed into a table or calculations need to be performed, an application program would be a better option.

If data is already in a table or member, the INSERT INTO command can also be used with the SELECT command to quickly copy a large number of rows. Let's explore the SELECT command and then show how the two can be used together.

Extracting Information with the SELECT Statement

The SQL/400 SELECT command allows the user to perform the relational functions of select and project. The user can retrieve rows and columns from a single table or multiple tables. The syntax of the SELECT statement is the SELECT keyword followed by

The column names to be retrieved

The FROM keyword

The collection and table to be accessed

The WHERE keyword

The condition by which rows are to be selected

For instance, we would retrieve the student records for the dean's list with the following SELECT command:

```
SELECT fname,lname,studid#,gradept
FROM myclcxx/student
WHERE gradept >= 3.50
```

Of course, with our current data, no records would be selected since Fred (our only student in the table) has a 2.00 grade point average. However, we can copy all the student records from the data physical file STUDENT in MYLIBXX by using the INSERT INTO and SELECT together. When the SELECT statement is used in conjunction with another statement, it is called a **subselect**. The INSERT INTO statement and subselect to perform the copy function would be as follows:

```
INSERT INTO myclcxx/student
SELECT * FROM mylibxx/student
```

The resulting message would be `4 rows inserted in STUDENT in MYCLCXX`. Notice that the subselect generates the data that will be used by the preceding SQL statement, in this case, the INSERT INTO statement. Subselects can be used in many SQL statements to enhance their power. Notice also that the subselect did not specify any column names. The token * is used to signify that all columns are to be selected.

An alternative method of entering and executing the INSERT INTO command would have been through the prompt screens. Notice in Figure 9.6 that there was an `Insertion method` prompt. Option 2 allows the user to specify a subselect. Choosing that option would have resulted in another `Specify INSERT Statement` screen where the subselect could be defined (Figure 9.9).

To verify that the data was written to the table, we can simply run a SELECT against the table with the following command:

```
SELECT * FROM myclcxx/student
```

The result can be seen in Figure 9.10. Do you see any problems with the data?

FIGURE 9.9

```
                          Specify INSERT Statement

Type subselect information.  Press F4 for a list.

  FROM files . . . . . . .   mylibxx/student
  SELECT fields  . . . . .   *
  WHERE conditions . . . .


  GROUP BY fields  . . . .
  HAVING conditions  . . .
  ORDER BY fields  . . . .



                                                                      Bottom
Type choice, press Enter.

  DISTINCT records in result file . . . . . . .  N    Y=Yes, N=No
  UNION with another SELECT . . . . . . . . . .  N    Y=Yes, N=No


F3=Exit        F4=Prompt   F5=Refresh   F6=Insert line   F9=Specify subquery
F10=Copy line  F12=Cancel   F14=Delete line   F15=Split line   F24=More keys
```

FIGURE 9.10

```
                                 Display Data
                                             Data width . . . . . . :      92
Position to line  . . . . .              Shift to column  . . . . . .
....+....1....+....2....+....3....+....4....+....5....+....6....+....7....+....
LNAME       FNAME      STREET            CITY          STATE  ZIP    STUDID#    CRE
Flintstone  Fred       11 Limestone Dr   Bedrock        AZ    88888  111111111
Flintstone  Fred       11 Limestone Dr   Bedrock        AZ    88888  111111111
Flintstone  Wilma      11 Limestone Dr   Bedrock        AZ    88888  123456789
Rubble      Betty      15 Limestone Dr   Bedrock        AZ    88888  444444444
Rubble      Barnard    15 Limestone Dr   Bedrock        AZ    88888  999999999
********  End of data  ********




                                                                      Bottom
F3=Exit       F12=Cancel      F19=Left       F20=Right      F21=Split
```

Because we entered a Fred Flintstone row first and then copied all the records from the STUDENT file, we ended up with two copies of Fred's record. Fortunately, SQL also provides data manipulation commands that allow users to modify data in a table.

Modifying Data

To solve our duplicate row problem, we would use the DELETE statement to delete the Fred rows from the table and then copy back only one Fred record from the file STUDENT. The syntax for the DELETE statement is the DELETE FROM keywords followed by

The collection and table names

The WHERE keyword

The condition that identifies the rows to be deleted

In our case, we could use the student id number field to identify the Fred Flintstone records. The statement to delete those rows would be

```
DELETE FROM myclcxx/student WHERE studid# = '111111111'
```

The resulting message would be `2 rows deleted from STUDENT in MYCLCXX`. To copy back the Fred record from the STUDENT file, we would issue the following INSERT INTO statement:

```
INSERT INTO myclcxx/student
SELECT * FROM mylibxx/student
WHERE studid# = '111111111'
```

Issuing a SELECT statement would verify that the STUDENT table contains the four student records with Fred's information in the last row.

The UPDATE statement can be used to modify data in a table. One column or many columns of a single row or multiple rows can be modified with a single UPDATE statement. The statement syntax is the UPDATE keyword followed by:

The collection and table names

The SET keyword

The column name(s) to be modified

Each column's new value

The WHERE keyword

The condition that identifies the row(s) to be modified

For instance, if the zip code changed for Bedrock, we could update all the student records with the following UPDATE statement:

```
UPDATE myclcxx/student
SET zip = '88844'
WHERE city = 'Bedrock'
```

The message returned would be `4 rows updated in STUDENT in MYCLCXX`. Multiple columns can be updated simply by specifying the other column names and their new values after the SET keyword and separating each with a comma. In addition, the WHERE condition can include AND and OR clauses. For instance, if only Bedrock residents with a zip code of 88888 should be modified, the UPDATE statement would be the following:

```
UPDATE myclcxx/student
SET zip = '88844'
WHERE city = 'Bedrock' and zip ='88888'
```

To modify every row in a table, do not specify a WHERE clause. After typing the command and pressing **ENTER**, the `Confirm Statement` screen will be displayed asking you to confirm that every row in the table should be modified. Pressing **ENTER** will confirm and execute the statement.

Tables can be deleted with the DROP command. DROP can actually be used to delete a number of SQL objects such as tables, collections, views, and indexes. The syntax is the statement DROP followed by

The type of object to be dropped

The name of the collection the object resides under

The name of the object

Of course, for collections, you do not need to specify an object name since the collection itself is being deleted. Deleting a collection will result in all objects beneath it also being deleted.

If we wished to delete the STUDENT table, the statement would be as follows:

```
DROP TABLE myclcxx/student
```

DROP can also be used to delete non-SQL objects from a library.

Views

As mentioned earlier, a view is implemented on the AS/400 as a non-keyed logical file. The view, just like a logical file, only points to data; it does not contain any information. In this case, the view provides an alternative look at data in tables.

Creating a view is very similar to creating a table. The command is CREATE VIEW followed by the particular tables, columns, and optionally, rows that are to be included in the view. For instance, we could create a view that would correspond to the dean's list. To create a dean's list view, execute the following statement:

```
CREATE VIEW myclcxx/deanslist
AS SELECT fname, lname, studid#, gradept
FROM myclcxx/student
WHERE gradept >= 3.50
```

Once again, a subselect is used. In this case, the SELECT command specifies the columns to include in the view, the FROM keyword identifies the collection and table on which to base the view, and the WHERE clause identifies the rows to be included in the view. After pressing ENTER, the system will create the appropriate access path through the data and respond with the message `View DEANSLIST created in collection MYCLCXX`. The view DEANSLIST is comparable to the simple logical file DEANSLIST created in Chapter 7.

Views can also be created with information from several tables. These types of views are the SQL/400 equivalents of joined logical files. Creating a view based on several tables requires that the FROM clause specify all tables being referenced and the WHERE clause specify how the rows should be joined. For instance, assuming we had two tables called CLASS and INSTRUCTOR (with the same layout as the files of the same name), a view called LOAD could be created that would show the instructor's name and the classes each instructor teaches. The command would be as follows:

```
CREATE VIEW myclcxx/load AS
SELECT instructor.instr, class.cl#
FROM myclcxx/class, myclcxx/instructor
WHERE instructor.iid = class.iid
```

After receiving the message stating that the view was created, we could look at the view (it sounds as if we're at the Grand Canyon) by entering the following select:

```
SELECT * FROM myclcxx/load
```

This would result in Figure 9.11, which looks exactly like the data retrieved from the DDS join logical file LOAD (see Figure 7.14).

FIGURE 9.11

```
                              Display Data
                                          Data width . . . . . . :       20
Position to line  . . . . .          Shift to column  . . . . . .
....+....1....+....2
INSTRUCTOR    CLASS
NAME          NUMBER
Galen         BIO101
Beane         BUS101
Beane         ACC101
Hyde          PSY212
Jobs          CMP101
Jones         BUS101
Jones         BUS101
********  End of data  ********

                                                                     Bottom
F3=Exit      F12=Cancel      F19=Left      F20=Right      F21=Split
```

Views can also contain columns that are calculated or the result of a function, or they can have a constant value. Calculated columns can be defined using standard mathematical functions. For instance, if we wanted to show the amount of tuition each student had paid, we could create a column that contained the number of credits multiplied by the amount of tuition per credit hour. This could be done with the following subselect in a CREATE VIEW statement:

```
SELECT fname, lname, credits, credits*140 FROM myclcxx/student
```

The data from the resulting view would appear as in Figure 9.12.

FIGURE 9.12

```
                              Display Data
                                            Data width . . . . . . :      44
Position to line  . . . . .            Shift to column  . . . . . .
....+....1....+....2....+....3....+....4....
FNAME     LNAME         CREDITS  CREDITS * 140
Wilma     Flintstone       12           1,680
Betty     Rubble           18           2,520
Barnard   Rubble           15           2,100
Fred      Flintstone        9           1,260
********  End of data  ********

                                                                          Bottom
F3=Exit      F12=Cancel      F19=Left      F20=Right      F21=Split
```

A variety of mathematical, substring, and specialty functions are available to create columns. For instance, the DAYS function will return an integer for a particular date. You can calculate the elapsed number of days between two dates with the DAYS function and a subtraction. To calculate the number of days a student has been enrolled in school, we would subtract the integer value of the current date (CURDTE) from the integer value of the enrollment date (assuming we had a field ENRDTE in the table1). The following subselect would be used:

```
SELECT lname, curdte, enrdte, DAYS(curdte) - DAYS(enrdte)
FROM clc1/table1
```

Assuming the dates (as seen in the figure), the view would appear as in Figure 9.13. (The ability to calculate elapsed days can also be done with OPNQRYF by using the MAPFLD keyword and %DAYS function.)

The final type of column available in a view is a constant value column. We could create a column in the DEANSLIST view that simply contains the text 'Deanslist'. The subselect clause would be as follows:

```
SELECT fname, lname, 'Deanslist'
FROM myclcxx/student
WHERE gradept >= 3.50
```

and the results can be seen in Figure 9.14.

Updating data can be done with views, but just as with logical files, no data in the view is actually changed—data in the table that

FIGURE 9.13

```
                                   Display Data
                                               Data width . . . . . . :        67
Position to line  . . . . .                Shift to column  . . . . . .
....+....1....+....2....+....3....+....4....+....5....+....6....+..
LNAME      CURDTE      ENRDTE       DAYS ( CURDTE ) - DAYS ( ENRDTE )
Jones      1996-10-15  1996-08-31                                45
Smith      1996-10-15  1996-06-15                               122

********  End of data  ********

                                                                       Bottom
F3=Exit      F12=Cancel      F19=Left      F20=Right      F21=Split
```

FIGURE 9.14

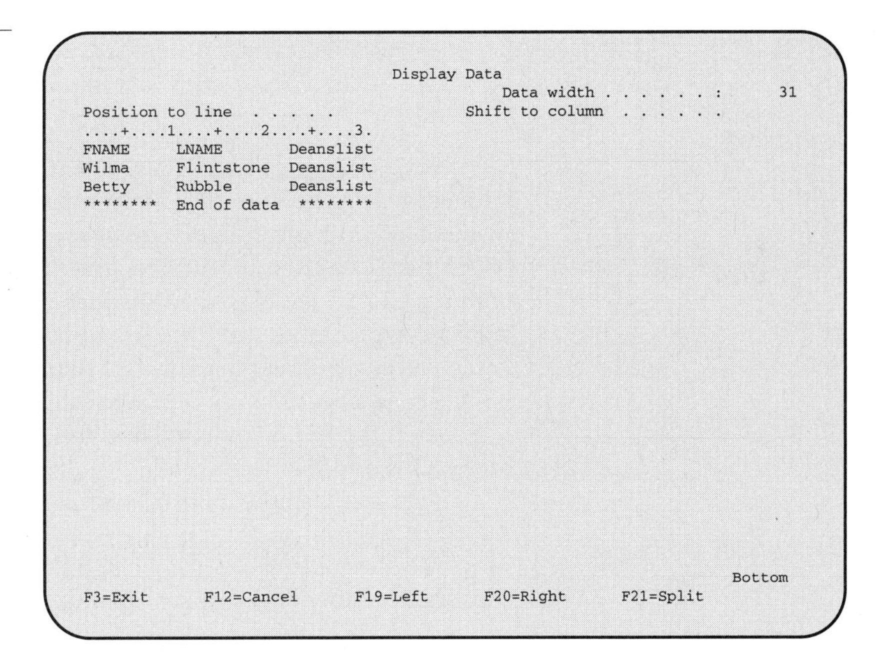

the view is based on is changed. There are, however, several restrictions for updating with views:

1. Views based on multiple tables cannot be used for updates.
2. Inserts cannot be done if the view is missing a column from a table that was defined as NO NULLS.
3. Views with a column that is a constant or that is the result of a calculation or function cannot be used to update. In other words, a view cannot be used for updating if it has a column that is not in the table.

To create a view that includes data from many files, we would specify many files in the FROM clause and use the WHERE condition to identify how to join the data. For instance, to create a VIEW that provides the same access to data as the join logical file ROSTER1, we would execute the following SQL/400 statement:

```
CREATE VIEW MYCLCXX/ROSTER1 AS
       SELECT CLASS.CL#, CLASS.SECT#, INSTR, LNAME, FNAME,
              STREET, CITY, STATE, ZIP, STUDENT.STUDID#,
              CREDITS, GRADEPT, GRADE
       FROM MYLIBXX/CLASS, MYLIBXX/GRADE, MYLIBXX/STUDENT,
            MYLIBXX/INSTRUCTOR
       WHERE CLASS.CL# = GRADE.CL# AND
             CLASS.SECT# = GRADE.SECT# AND
             GRADE.STUDID# = STUDENT.STUDID# AND
             CLASS.IID = INSTRUCTOR.IID
```

Notice that the SELECT statement identifies each field that will be included in the view. This is comparable to the field level statements in a join logical file. Fields that are in more than one file must be further identified by the filename. For instance, CL# appears in both the CLASS and GRADE file. Just as DDS requires the use of the JREF keyword to identify the file to use, SQL requires that the filename precede the field name with a period separating the two. To finish the comparisons with DDS, the FROM clause performs the same function as the JFILE keyword, and the WHERE clause does the work of the JOIN and JFLD keywords.

If we executed the following SELECT command:

```
SELECT * FROM MYCLCXX/ROSTER1
```

the resulting data display can be seen in Figure 9.15.

FIGURE 9.15

```
                                Display Data
                                        Data width . . . . . . :      131
Position to line  . . . . .            Shift to column  . . . . . .
....+....1....+....2....+....3....+....4....+....5....+....6....+....7....+....
CLASS    SECTION  INSTRUCTOR       LNAME       FNAME       STREET           CITY
NUMBER   NUMBER   NAME
BIO101    96201   Galen            Flintstone  Fred        11 Limestone Dr  Bedrock
PSY212    96203   Hyde             Flintstone  Fred        11 Limestone Dr  Bedrock
ACC101    96306   Beane            Flintstone  Fred        11 Limestone Dr  Bedrock
BIO101    96201   Galen            Flintstone  Wilma       11 Limestone Dr  Bedrock
ACC101    96306   Beane            Flintstone  Wilma       11 Limestone Dr  Bedrock
CMP101    96306   Jobs             Flintstone  Wilma       11 Limestone Dr  Bedrock
BUS101    96306   Jones            Flintstone  Wilma       11 Limestone Dr  Bedrock
BIO101    96201   Galen            Rubble      Betty       15 Limestone Dr  Bedrock
BUS101    96203   Beane            Rubble      Betty       15 Limestone Dr  Bedrock
PSY212    96203   Hyde             Rubble      Betty       15 Limestone Dr  Bedrock
CMP101    96306   Jobs             Rubble      Betty       15 Limestone Dr  Bedrock
ACC101    96306   Beane            Rubble      Betty       15 Limestone Dr  Bedrock
PSY212    96203   Hyde             Rubble      Barnard     15 Limestone Dr  Bedrock
BUS101    96203   Beane            Rubble      Barnard     15 Limestone Dr  Bedrock
CMP101    96306   Jobs             Rubble      Barnard     15 Limestone Dr  Bedrock
ACC101    96306   Beane            Rubble      Barnard     15 Limestone Dr  Bedrock
 ********  End of data  ********
                                                                       More...
F3=Exit       F12=Cancel       F19=Left        F20=Right       F21=Split
```

Indexes

Indexes are used for faster access to table data. When a SELECT is executed, a sequential search of all rows in the table(s) is performed. After each row is read, the row is checked to see if it meets the WHERE condition. If an index exists for the table, an index search will be performed to locate the correct rows instead of a sequential search of every row. By using the index, the number of data records accessed decreases and, therefore, the time it takes to perform the SELECT is less. Another nice feature of indexes is that the system will automatically check to see if an index exists before beginning a sequential search (just as with natively defined access paths).

For instance, we could create an index on the STUDENT table using STUDID# as the key field. (This would greatly speed up any selects that search for a particular student id or range of student ids.) To create this index, we would issue the following statement:

```
CREATE INDEX myclcxx/studidx ON myclcxx/student (studid#)
```

Indexes are implemented on the AS/400 as keyed logical files. In this case, a logical file STUDIDX would be created under library MYCLCXX. If data records are already in the table, the index is built when the CREATE INDEX command is issued. If there are no data records, only the index definition is stored, and when the first data record is written to the table, the index will be built.

Many indexes can be created for a single table, and all will be maintained automatically by the system. That is, whenever there are additions and deletions to the table, SQL/400 will ensure that the indexes based on that table are updated correctly. However, a large number of indexes can affect performance.

SQL Programming

SQL statements can be grouped together into SQL/400 Query Manager queries. Though they are called queries, these SQL "programs" can perform all the SQL/400 update functions previously described. As mentioned earlier, SQL queries are created through a utility called the SQL/400 Query Manager. Users can create queries with the SQL/400 Query Manager editor and directly enter SQL statements into a query object, or they can use a QUERY/400-like menu interface that allows query definition from a series of screens.

SQL can also be used with higher level programming languages (such as RPG and COBOL) to access and update data. In higher level language programs, the SQL commands take the place of the native language's input and output commands. Special commands, syntax, and procedures are required to use SQL statements with the various programming languages. We will cover some of these in a later section.

Query Manager

The command to start the SQL/400 Query Manager is STRQM. Executing this command will result in the screen shown in Figure 9.16. As mentioned, QM (query manager) allows the user to create SQL programs, which are called Query Manager queries. Option 1 provides this function.

QM also allows some basic report formatting. These report forms are defined through a menu interface and contain some of the formatting options available through QUERY/400. In general, QUERY/400 provides more control over the appearance of the data, so we will forgo any detailed discussion of the QM report forms.

QM also provides a screen to easily manipulate tables. Choosing option 3, `Work with Query Manager Tables`, will result in Figure 9.17. Notice that the `Work with Query Manager Tables` screen provides many of the same functions as the `Work with Objects using PDM` screen. You can create, copy, delete, and display, in this case, tables. Some basic table data manipulation is also provided through a series of menus that are very similar to the interactive SQL prompt screens. For these reasons, we will also bypass a detailed discussion of this option.

Choosing option 1, `Work with Query Manager queries`, results in Figure 9.18 being displayed. From this screen, we can create QM queries. We can define the program functions in two modes—PROMPT and SQL. (Notice in Figure 9.18 that the default `Query creation mode` is `PROMPT`.) If you choose to create a query at this point, a series of menus would be provided to define the type of processing to be performed and the output format.

To change from `PROMPT` mode, press **F19**. Choosing to create a query at this point will result in the `Edit Query` screen (Figure 9.19), which looks suspiciously like the SEU `Edit` screen. At this screen, SQL statements can be entered directly or prompted for by pressing **F4**.

FIGURE 9.16

```
                          SQL/400 Query Manager
                                                          System:   BRUCE
Select one of the following:

     1. Work with Query Manager queries
     2. Work with Query Manager report forms
     3. Work with Query Manager tables

    10. Work with Query Manager profiles











Selection
      __

F3=Exit   F12=Cancel   F22=QM Statement
```

FIGURE 9.17

```
                      Work with Query Manager Tables

Library . . . . . . . . . . .   MYCLCXX      Name, F4 for list

Type options, press Enter.
  1=Create table   3=Copy table      4=Delete table          5=Display table
  6=Print table    7=Rename table    8=Display definition    9=Add data
  10=Change data   11=Display data

Opt  Table          Description
__   __________
__   QIDCTP02      Data dictionary: Long comments
__   QIDCTP10      Data dictionary: Field attributes
__   QIDCTP20      Data dictionary: Format attributes
__   QIDCTP21      Data dictionary: Format contains fields
__   QIDCTP25      Data dictionary: Record ID tests
__   QIDCTP30      Data dictionary: File attributes
__   QIDCTP31      Data dictionary: File has record formats
__   QIDCTP51      Data dictionary: Record format key fields
__   QIDCTP52      Data dictionary: Record format SQL create text
                                                                      More...
F3=Exit   F4=Prompt      F5=Refresh   F11=Display table only   F12=Cancel
F16=Repeat position to   F17=Position to   F22=QM Statement
```

FIGURE 9.18

```
                    Work with Query Manager Queries

Library . . . . . . . . . . .  QGPL          Name, F4 for list
Query creation mode . . . . :  PROMPT

Type options, press Enter.
  1=Create   2=Change   3=Copy   4=Delete   5=Display   6=Print   7=Rename
  9=Run      10=Convert to SQL

Opt  Query       Type       Description
__   __________

  (Cannot find object to match specified name.)



                                                                       Bottom
F3=Exit   F4=Prompt      F5=Refresh   F11=Display query only   F12=Cancel
F16=Repeat position to   F17=Position to   F24=More keys
```

When you exit and save, an object is created in the library with a type of *QMQRY and an attribute of SQL. (If the query had been created in prompt mode, the object would have an attribute of PROMPT.) Invoking PDM, choosing the work with objects options within MYCLCXX, and paging to the end of the list would result in the `Work with Objects Using PDM` screen (Figure 9.20) being displayed. Notice the attribute and type of object SQLQRY.

FIGURE 9.19

```
                              Edit Query
Columns . . . :  1 70                                   Query . . . : SQLQRY
QM . .

Type SQL Statement
       ************************* Beginning of Data ************************
'''''''
'''''''
'''''''
'''''''
'''''''
'''''''
'''''''
'''''''
'''''''
'''''''
'''''''
'''''''
'''''''
       *************************** End of Data ***************************

F2=Alternate keys  F3=Exit  F4=Prompt    F5=Run report   F6=Run sample
F9=Retrieve        F15=Check syntax      F24=More keys
```

FIGURE 9.20

```
                         Work with Objects Using PDM

Library . . . . .   MYCLCXX          Position to . . . . . . . .
                                     Position to type  . . . . .

Type options, press Enter.
  2=Change        3=Copy        4=Delete       5=Display      7=Rename
  8=Display description         9=Save         10=Restore     11=Move ...

Opt  Object       Type        Attribute   Text
     SYSVIEWS     *FILE       LF          SQL catalog view
     MYCLCXX      *DTADCT                 COLLECTION - created by SQL
     SQLQRY       *QMQRY      SQL

                                                                   Bottom
Parameters or command
===>
F3=Exit          F4=Prompt           F5=Refresh          F6=Create
F9=Retrieve      F10=Command entry   F23=More options    F24=More keys
```

The QM query cannot be run from the PDM screen. QM must be restarted and option 9, `Run`, specified next to the query name.

High-Level Programming Languages and SQL

Using SQL statements in high-level language programs requires the added step of precompiling the program. Precompiling does not mean extra work for the programmer. Programmers simply use a different CL command to create a program object. For instance, instead of using CRTRPGPGM, CRTSQLRPG would be used on RPG source code that contained SQL statements. The CRTSQLRPG command invokes the precompiler and, after successfully precompiling the SQL statements, the RPG compiler will be started automatically.

Precompiling checks the syntax of each SQL statement and, if there are errors, will generate error messages. Each SQL statement is also "prepared" so that it can be executed. SQL statements do not undergo a normal compilation, meaning that they are not translated into machine language. Rather, when the program is executed, the command will be passed to a SQL interface program that will execute the command and pass back the results. During precompiling, the SQL statements are "prepared" so that the interface program is called and the SQL statements are passed.

The result of the precompilation process is a temporary source member that contains program language source code and the prepared SQL statements (Figure 9.21). When the program is compiled, all program language commands are translated into machine code and placed in a program object. Further, an access plan to the data is created. The access plan is the best way to access data based on the indexes available, table sizes, and so on. The process that creates the access plan is called **binding**. At run time, the access plan will be reevaluated. If the access plan is invalid (an index no longer exists), the access plan will be recreated.

The temporary source member is deleted on successful completion of the compile.

FIGURE 9.21

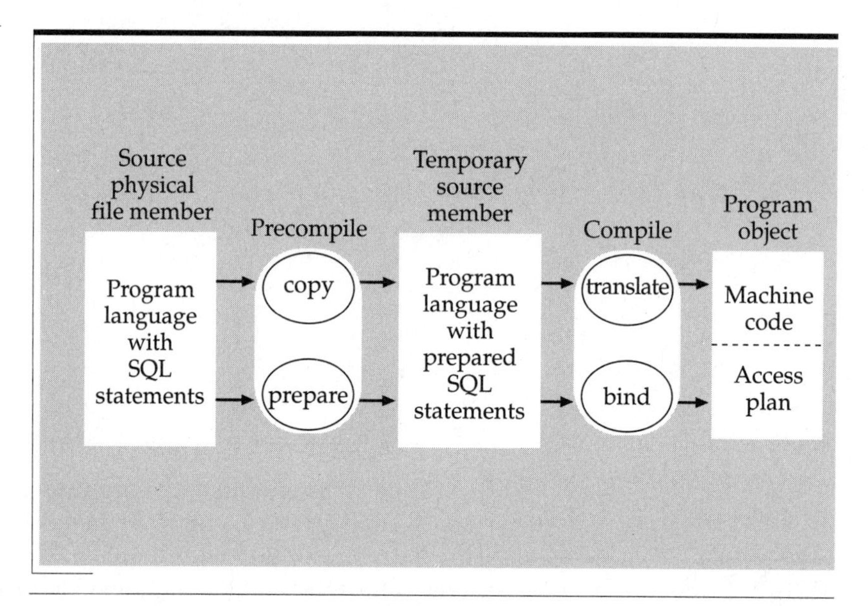

SQL Programming Statements

Because there are some significant differences in how SQL statements and most program language commands process data there are some specialized SQL programming statements. For instance, SQL statements, like UPDATE, can process many rows, and other SQL statements, like SELECT, result in a table of many rows. Most program languages, on the other hand, read and process one record or row at a time. If multiple records need to be processed, a loop is required. How can the program language commands, which process a single row of data, work with a table generated by a SELECT statement? This difference would seem to make SQL statements unusable as the data access method. This is where the specialized program statements come in.

The SQL statement FETCH will return a single row from a table that was generated by a SELECT. A FETCH will retrieve the row that the **cursor** is pointing to. A cursor points to a particular row in a table and is declared in the SELECT statement that generates the table. Initially, the cursor points to the first row in the table. For instance, the following commands:

```
DECLARE dlcursor CURSOR FOR
SELECT fname, lname, gradept
FROM myclcxx/deanslist

OPEN dlcursor

FETCH dlcursor INTO :pgmvar1, :pgmvar2 :pgmvar3
```

will result in pgmvar1 (program variable 1) being equal to Wilma, pgmvar2 being equal to Flintstone and pgmvar3 being equal to 4.00. This is because Wilma's record is the first one in the table returned by the SELECT and the cursor is initially set to the first row.

After the FETCH, the program can process the single row of information because it has been placed in program variables. If another row of data is required, the FETCH would simply be executed again. (After each FETCH, the cursor is repositioned to the next record.) This type of cursor is called a **serial cursor**. A scrollable cursor will provide more control over what is retrieved. A scrollable cursor can be created with the following:

```
DECLARE dlcursor DYNAMIC SCROLL CURSOR FOR.....
```

Scrollable cursors allow the FETCH command to specify the row to retrieve by relative row number or through a qualifying keyword. For instance, if after selecting from DEANSLIST we used the following FETCH command:

```
FETCH RELATIVE 2 FROM dlcursor INTO .......
```

Barney's row would be retrieved (assuming the cursor is positioned at the first row and Barney has pulled his grade point up and is the third record). A FETCH can also be performed with keywords such as NEXT, FIRST, and LAST. They would look like the following:

```
FETCH NEXT FROM dlcursor INTO .......
FETCH FIRST FROM dlcursor INTO .......
FETCH LAST FROM dlcursor INTO .......
```

After a result table has been processed, the cursor must be closed with the CLOSE statement as follows:

```
CLOSE dlcursor
```

Notice that SQL statements retrieve rows and then place the data into program variables. Every programming language provides a command to define variables. These program variables can be used in SQL statements and are denoted by preceding the program variable name with a colon (:).

Program variables can also be the source of data. For instance, programming language commands may handle retrieving information from a screen and placing the screen data into program variables. These variables can then be used with the INSERT INTO command to place the information into a table. For instance, if

```
pgmvar1 = Dino
pgmvar2 = Flintstone
pgmvar3 = 666666666
pgmvar4 = 2.8
```

we could insert the information into the STUDENT table using the DEANSLIST view as follows:

```
INSERT INTO myclcxx/deanslist (fname, lname, studid#, gradept)
VALUES (:pgmvar1, :pgmvar2, :pgmvar3, pgmvar4)
```

There would now be a fifth record in STUDENT with Dino's information.

There are other requirements for using SQL statements in programs. For instance, all programming languages require that the SQL statements be identified. However, each programming language has its own identification rules. All languages require that the EXEC SQL statement appear before any SQL statement or group of statements. COBOL and RPG also require that END-EXEC appear after the SQL statement(s), but FORTRAN and C don't require the END-EXEC. In addition, COBOL wants a period after the END-EXEC, and for RPG the EXEC SQL must be coded in position 8 thru 16 and preceded with a / in position 7. To fully understand each language's requirements, the *SQL/400 Programmers Guide* should be consulted. Separate chapters and appendices are dedicated to each language.

There is one final topic we should cover before leaving programming languages and SQL. Just as there are program variables for host language data manipulation, SQL requires variables in order to perform data manipulation. These variables are defined with the statement INCLUDE SQLCA (except for RPG, which automatically includes the SQLCA). SQLCA stands for SQL Communication Area and comprises a series of fields that contain information about the results of each SQL command executed. When a statement is executed, a return code is written to SQLCA, and, if something abnormal occurs, diagnostic information is also supplied. The programmer should check to see if the statement was successful before processing.

One of the variables, SQLCODE (SQLCOD in RPG), contains a return code value. For instance, when a FETCH is performed and the last row has already been retrieved, SQLCODE is set to 100. Serious errors result in SQLCODE being set to a negative number. In the program, the programmer should always check for the "end of data" condition and ensure that control passes to the next logical statement.

An easy way to check for the end of data condition is with the SQL statement WHENEVER. The WHENEVER statement can check for conditions such as NOT FOUND and SQLERROR. (These correspond to SQLCODE being equal to 100 and being negative.) There is a GO TO clause in the WHENEVER statement that identifies the program label or line number that control should be passed to. For instance,

```
WHENEVER NOT FOUND GO TO TAF
```

would pass control to a statement label named TAF (that's all folks). After a WHENEVER statement is executed, all subsequent SQL statements are subject to its conditions—meaning that when a statement triggers the NOT FOUND condition, the GO TO clause is executed, not the SQL statement or program command that follows the triggering statement.

The following pseudocode (Figure 9.22) shows the overall syntax for the SQL and program language statements. Each individual language will require different statements to define SQLCA and identify the SQL statements. However, the example gives the students a "feel" for how the SQL statements and program language commands are intermixed.

FIGURE 9.22

```
Mainline:

      EXEC SQL
           WHENEVER SQLERROR GO TO Error
           DECLARE mycursor CURSOR FOR SELECT column1, column2
           FROM clcxx/table1 WHERE col1>100
           OPEN mycursor
           WHENEVER NOT FOUND GO TO TAF
      END-EXEC
Fetch:EXEC SQL
           FETCH mycursor INTO :pgmvar1, :pgmvar2
      END-EXEC
      pgmvar3 = pgmvar1 + pgmvar2
      Print pgmvar3
      Go to Fetch

End-mainline:
Error:Print "Error occurred. Error code =", SQLCODE
TAF:  EXEC SQL
                CLOSE mycursor
      END-EXEC
      Stop
```

SQL/400 versus the AS/400 Native DBMS and Utilities

There are some definite advantages and disadvantages to using SQL. Certainly a common set of commands to perform all data definition and data manipulation is an advantage over using several different utilities to define, modify, and query data. However, a command-driven interface is not always the most user friendly. Certainly, non-programming users will find the QUERY/400 menu-driven interface easier to use and understand than a SELECT and the associated keywords and syntax. In addition, QUERY/400 provides much better control over the format of the output once the data has been retrieved. However, once mastered, the SELECT command is very effective for quick data retrieval and much easier to use than navigating the myriad QUERY/400 menus and screens.

When it comes to data definition, SQL seems easier than DDS—no column positioning or record formats to worry about and fewer keywords to remember. However, DDS provides more function and control over the data. In addition, when using DDS to define data structures, a source code definition is always saved. This is a real advantage when structural modifications are required. Instead of recreating a file definition (as would be needed with interactive SQL), modifications can be made by simply modifying the source code and recompiling. SQL/400 does offer a solution, and that is to use QM queries to define tables.

Manipulating data is where SQL really shines. SQL is a very effective way to quickly make updates. Writing a program to search for records with certain conditions and then modifying those records would take considerably longer than simply using the UPDATE command. For instance, to perform the function of one UPDATE command, most programming languages require setting up a loop around source code that

Reads a record from a file

Verifies that the record matches the update criteria

Modifies the data

Writes the record back to the file

The source code then needs to be compiled and the program executed. With SQL, the user simply types in and executes one UPDATE statement, interactively, and multiple rows of data are modified. In addition, with prompting, SQL can provide an environment as easy to use as DFU.

However, being able to change multiple records with a single command is a dangerous capability if in the wrong hands. Moreover, SQL/400 doesn't provide the same control over the data entered into tables and updates that a programming language provides. For instance, programs can be written to verify ranges of data entered and coordinate multiple table updates. SQL doesn't provide these functions with its limited set of commands.

SQL also requires added processing time and storage space to store and maintain a journal, journal receiver, data dictionary, and catalog. In addition, SQL/400 usually must be purchased separately. The native DBMS and utilities don't require SQL's overhead, and most come preloaded on the AS/400.

Summary

SQL is an industry standard set of commands for relational data definition and manipulation. Through SQL statements, users can define tables, views, and indexes, as well as enter, delete, and modify data through single commands. The AS/400 supports the SQL standard by

Providing several ways to execute SQL statements

Implementing the SQL objects as AS/400 objects

One of the ways to execute SQL statements is interactively. Just as CL commands can be executed by typing them at a command line and pressing ENTER, SQL statements can be executed through the interactive SQL utility. The AS/400 also allows SQL "programs," called QM queries, to be created through the SQL/400 Query Manager. Commonly used QM queries can be created, saved, and rerun using this utility.

SQL statements can also be used inside application programs instead of the programming language's input and output commands. Using SQL in this manner requires several special processes such as precompiling and binding that enable the SQL statements to be executed. In addition, special SQL statements are needed to

Identify the SQL statements within the program

Perform single row access and processing

Define SQL required fields

Check for errors

Using SQL in programs provides the same advantage as using any industry standard: portability across different hardware and software platforms. This means that programs using SQL will be able to function regardless of the system they are run on as long as the system supports the SQL standard. This is a powerful advantage over programming language commands and native DBMSs. In addition, compared to application programs and DDS, SQL/400 provides a powerful, simple (but often limited) method for users to define, update, and view their data.

EXERCISES

1. Create an SQL/400 view called CONSUM in MYCLCXX (if you haven't created MYCLCXX yet, create it now) that duplicates the logical file CONSUM except for ordering the records by the SPRICE field. (The ORDER BY clause cannot be used when defining a view.)

   Then display all the records in the view CONSUM in descending order by SPRICE.

2. Create an SQL/400 view called ACCRCV in MYCLCXX that duplicates the logical file ACCRCV except for ordering the records by the TOTLTF field. (The ORDER BY clause cannot be used when defining a view.)

   Then display all the records in the view ACCRCV in descending order by TOTLTF.

3. Create a QM query called SQLCONSUM in MYCLCXX that duplicates the function of the CL program OQFCONSUM (except for ordering the records). Have the QM query write the data to a file called SQLCONSUM in MYCLCXX. Create a QM query called BLDCONSUM to define and create the file SQLCONSUM.

4. Create a QM query called SQLACCRCV in MYCLCXX that duplicates the function of the CL program OQFACCRCV (except SQLACCRCV does not order the records). Have the QM query write the data to a file called SQLACCRCV in MYCLCXX. Create

a QM query called BLDACCRCV to define and create the file SQLACCRCV.

REVIEW QUESTIONS

1. What are the SQL equivalents of a nonkeyed physical file, a nonkeyed logical file, a keyed logical file, and a library?
2. What are the three ways SQL commands can be executed?
3. What is a subselect?
4. When a collection is created, what other objects are also created?
5. How are DFU and SQL/400 similar?
6. What is the major advantage of SQL/400 over the AS/400 native data manipulation utilties and programming language commands?
7. What are the type and attribute of an object that contains a QM query?
8. What is the result of the binding process?
9. What is the drawback of defining a table interactively?
10. What is an access plan?

DISCUSSION QUESTIONS

1. What is the difference between how SQL and most high-level programming languages process data? What commands and keywords does SQL/400 provide to overcome this difference, and how do they help?
2. What is precompiling?
3. Compare SQL/400 to DDS, QUERY/400, and DFU in terms of function and ease of use.

Alternative Data Structures

10

Overview

This chapter will cover nonfile methods of storing data on the AS/400. We will explain the general function and purpose of several alternative data structures and show how they are implemented on the AS/400.

After finishing this chapter, you will understand

- Linear data structures
- How queues, stacks, and linked lists function
- What a pointer is
- Why data queues and data areas are used

After finishing this chapter you will be able to

- Create data queues
- Write to and read from a data queue
- Create and manipulate data areas

Linear Data Structures

Linear data structures are storage structures that allow only sequential access. This is as opposed to nonlinear data structures that allow users to access data in a nonsequential manner. For instance, a nonkeyed file would be considered a linear structure, whereas a keyed file, because records can be accessed directly by key, is a nonlinear structure.

Unfortunately for the student, linear data structures are further defined by the terms *physical* and *logical*. Both physically linear data structures and logically linear data structures provide sequential access to the data. The difference between the two is the way in which the data is physically stored.

Physically linear data structures store data in contiguous or adjacent storage locations in some logical order, usually arrival sequence order. A **stack** is a physically linear data structure. Stacks store records one after the other in the order they are written. Access to the records in a stack is according to the **last in first out (LIFO)** method. LIFO means that when the stack is read, the last record placed on the stack is the first record read. You can think of the stack as an upside-down Dixie cup dispenser. Each cup (record) placed in the dispenser (stack) sits on top of the previously entered cup (record). When you grab a cup, you get the last one put in the dispenser. The same is true for the data stack. The last record entered is the first one retrieved.

Writing five records to a stack would result in the stack looking like Figure 10.1.

FIGURE 10.1

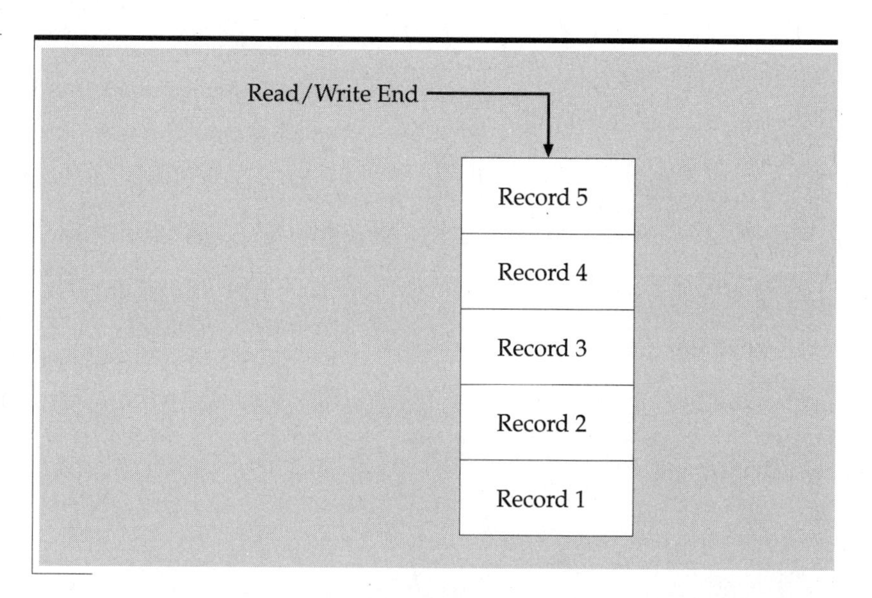

Reading two records would result in record 5 and record 4 being read (in that order) and deleted from the stack. If three more records were written after records 5 and 4 had been read, the stack would look like Figure 10.2.

FIGURE 10.2

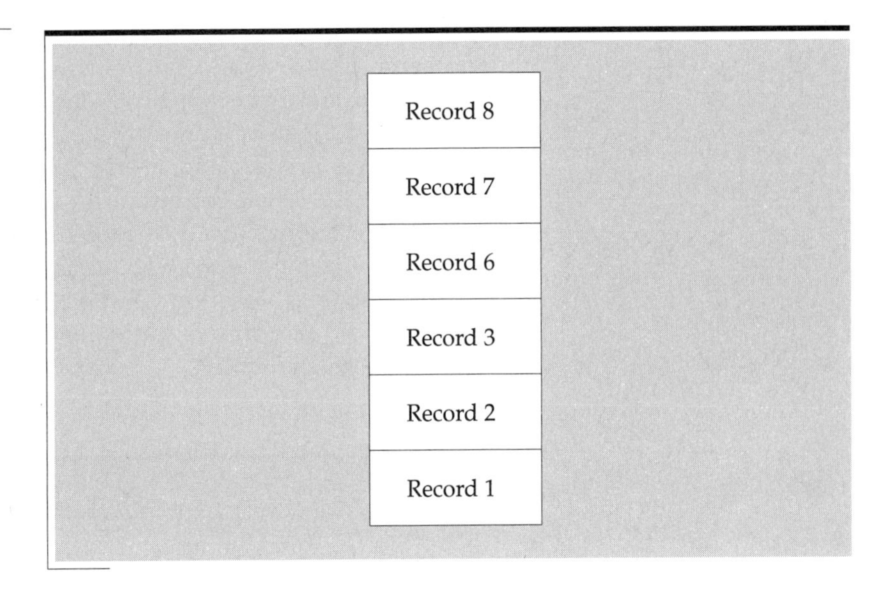

Another description of a stack is "a one-ended linear data structure." Records are written to and read from only one end. This is as opposed to a **queue**. Queues are two-ended linear data structures. Records are written to one end and read from the other. Therefore, the records are accessed in a **first in first out (FIFO)** manner.

Writing five records to a queue would result in Figure 10.3.

FIGURE 10.3

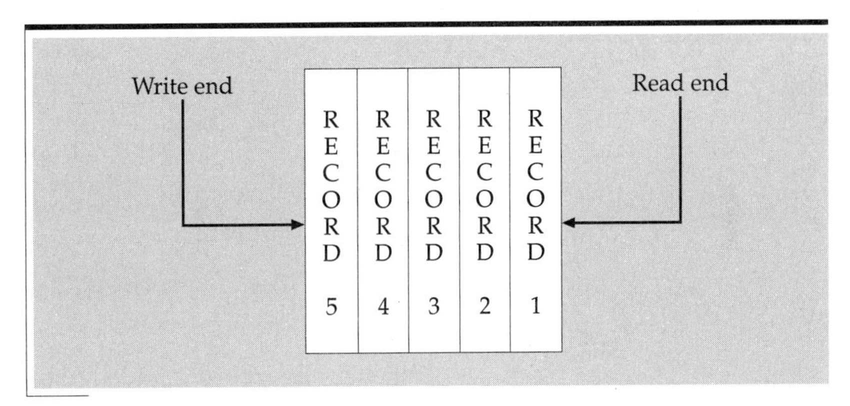

A program reading two records would get records 1 and 2 (in that order), and the two records would be deleted from the queue. If three more records were then written, the queue would look like Figure 10.4.

FIGURE 10.4

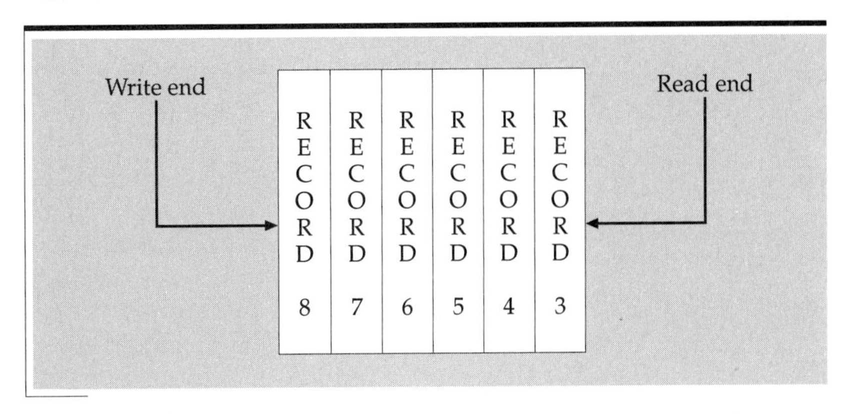

Just as logical files seem to store data, logically linear data structures seem to store data sequentially but in reality do not. For instance, a **linked list** is a logically linear data structure. In this case, the records are not stored next to each other. Rather, they are stored wherever there is space and a series of pointers is used to keep track of the sequential order. For instance, say the storage area consisted of ten storage locations named A through J (Figure 10.5). As long as the database management system kept track of where the first record was stored (in this case, location G), the DBMS retrieval program could simply follow the pointers to the locations indicated and read the records in sequential order.

FIGURE 10.5

Location	Data records	Pointer
A	Record 3	D
B		
C	Record 5	
D	Record 4	C
E		
F		
G	Record 1	I
H		
I	Record 2	A
J		

When a new record is added, the last logically sequential record must be updated. If record 6 were written to storage location B, record 5's pointer would have to be updated to reflect the change (Figure 10.6).

In addition (or should we say, in deletion), if a record is erased, the associated pointers must also be updated. If record 3 were deleted, record 2's pointer would have to be changed to point to the next logically sequential record—record 4. This would result in the linked list looking like Figure 10.7.

FIGURE 10.6

Location	Data records	Pointer
A	Record 3	D
B	Record 6	
C	Record 5	B
D	Record 4	C
E		
F		
G	Record 1	I
H		
I	Record 2	A
J		

So with logically linear structures, such as linked lists, the data appears to be stored linearly but actually is not. A Data Management System, however, will provide sequential access to the linked list data just like a physically linear structure.

FIGURE 10.7

Location	Data records	Pointer
A		
B	Record 6	
C	Record 5	B
D	Record 4	C
E		
F		
G	Record 1	I
H		
I	Record 2	D
J		

AS/400 Linear Data Structures

The AS/400 employs stacks and queues throughout the system. For instance, if you have programmed on the AS/400 and used the DEBUG tool, you've heard of the DEBUG stack. It keeps track of up to ten program names that are in debug mode.

The AS/400 also makes extensive use of queues. For instance, there are output queues and job queues. Output queues hold spool files, and job queues contain user requests for the system to perform work. (Have you ever noticed when you submit a compile that the message states that the job has been submitted to the QBATCH job queue? Compilation requests are written to this queue, and when the subsystem QBATCH is ready to perform more work, requests from the job queue will be read and processed.)

The AS/400 does not limit the user to accessing queues in a FIFO manner. There are screens (`Work with Output Queue`, `Work with Job Queue`, and so forth) that list the spool files or jobs in FIFO order but allow individual file or job processing. So, even when a simple data structure like a queue is used, the AS/400 makes the structure easier to work with and more user friendly.

There is another important queue on the AS/400, a **data queue**.

Data Queues

Data queues are used to temporarily store data. Usually, queues reside in main memory. This means accessing data in a queue is faster than if the data were stored in a file (which is on slower disk memory). However, if the system "goes down" and main memory is erased, all queue data is lost. On the AS/400, queues can be forced to disk storage; however, this will slow retrieval performance.

Since queues use volatile main memory, programmers usually store nonpermanent data in queues. Two examples of nonpermanent data are data that is transferred between two programs and data that is temporarily stored before it is used to permanently update a file. For instance, many organizations have disbursement systems that employees access to retrieve items from inventory. Employees enter the item numbers they want into a program, and the program prints out the location of each item and decrements the quantity in stock. Most systems, however, also have a limit on the total dollar value of the items being removed from inventory. As the employee enters each item number, the program should not make the permanent inventory file updates until all the items have been entered and the total value is checked. This is a perfect situation for a data queue. As each item and quantity is entered, the program can keep track of the total amount of items requested so far, and a record of each order and its cost would be written to a data queue. When the employee is finished entering all the items, the program checks the total value against the cutoff value. If the total value is less than the cutoff, the program reads the data queue and makes the permanent file updates. If the total is more than the cutoff value, the program will read the data queue, display all the orders on a screen, and allow the user to eliminate any items from the request.

Data queues as implemented on the AS/400 are more versatile than the standard definition of a queue. For instance, AS/400 queues can be created to act as stacks. Further, AS/400 queues can be keyed, and individual records retrieved from the queue by key value.

Creating a Data Queue

The CL command CRTDTAQ allows users to create a data queue on the AS/400. Executing this command will result in an object with a type of *DTAQ being created. An additional parameter can be specified that determines how records will be retrieved from the queue. This parameter's keyword is SEQ, and the default value is FIFO—meaning the queue will work as a "normal" queue. Specifying LIFO will result in the queue acting as a stack.

When creating a queue, the only required parameters are a queue name and the maximum length of any "record" into the queue. Since the queue is not defined by DDS, it doesn't really have fields or a record definition. As a matter of fact, different length entries with different data and formats can be written to a queue. This is useful when information from multiple files needs to be stored. Because there is no record format, only one queue needs to be created to hold the different information.

The command syntax to create a data queue is as follows:

```
CRTDTAQ DTAQ(library/queuename) MAXLEN(#####)
```

The maximum length that can be specified is 64,512. To define a stack, the CRTDTAQ command would be as follows:

```
CRTDTAQ DTAQ(library/queuename) MAXLEN(#####) SEQ(LIFO)
```

Working with a Data Queue

Reading from and writing to a data queue is a little complicated. No CL commands can be executed to write or retrieve data directly from a data queue. Instead, an **API (application program interface)** program must be called. The API program actually updates queues.

The AS/400 developers have supplied API programs to perform certain system functions that would be difficult or impossible to perform from application programs. Besides providing a specific system function, the advantage to an API program is that it can be called from any higher level language program. If you want to write to a data queue from an RPG, COBOL, or CL program, the same API program will always be called. By providing this function with an API program rather than a CL command, access to data queues is not restricted to CL programs. If a CL command had been created to write to queues, the command could not be incorporated into a program written in RPG, COBOL, or any other high-level language except CL.

The program that writes to data queues is QSNDDTAQ. When invoking QSNDDTAQ, the application program must supply the following information:

The name of the data queue

The library containing the data queue

The length of the data being sent

The program variable containing the data to be sent

The syntax for calling the program and writing an entry to the data queue is as follows:

```
CALL PGM(QSNDDTAQ) PARM(qname qlib varlength varname)
```

To retrieve an entry from a data queue, the QRCVDTAQ program would be called. This program requires the application program to specify

The name of the data queue

The library containing the data queue

A variable name to hold the length of the data being read

A variable name to hold the data being read

The amount of time to wait for an entry

The amount of time to wait is an interesting variable. If a negative number is specified, the API program will wait until there is an entry to the data queue. If a zero is specified and there is not an entry, the application program will be immediately restarted, and the length of the data being returned will be set to zero. If the wait value is a positive number, it represents the number of seconds the API program is to wait until an entry arrives on the queue. All the other variables are similar to the QSNDDTAQ variables.

There is one other important data queue CL command—DLTDTAQ. This command will delete an existing data queue. The parameters passed with the command are the queue name and library. The syntax of the command is as follows:

```
DLTDTAQ DTAQ(library/qname)
```

Because of the way data queues use space, they should be periodically deleted and recreated. As entries are made to a data queue, the data queue increases in size (more space is allocated to the queue). However, when an entry is read (and, therefore, deleted) the space is not "de-allocated." The space will be reused by the queue if a record is written, but the queue size will never decrease because of a read. In other words, the queue is always the size of the maximum number of entries it ever contained.

Data Areas

Another storage structure on the AS/400 is a data area. Data areas are more limited than data queues. They contain a single entry and are used to

Store a permanent piece of information

Pass a small amount of information between programs

For instance, in our school example, there is a program that enrolls students into the school and assigns a student number. A data area would be useful to keep track of the last student number assigned. Each time the enrollment program runs, it would

Read the data area

Increase the student id number by one

Assign that student number to the enrolling student by writing his or her information and student id to the STUDENT file

Rewrite the data area to reflect the last student id number assigned

In this way, the data area and program ensure that all numbers are being used and that duplicate numbers are not being assigned.

Using Data Areas

To create a data area, use the CRTDTAARA command. The only required parameters are the data area name and library and the type of data to be stored in the data area. The two primary types are *CHAR and *DEC, which define the data as character or numeric.

The syntax of the command is

```
CRTDTAARA DTAARA(library/areaname) TYPE(value)
```

When specifying either type, an optional LEN parameter can be used to set the length of the data being stored. Maximums are 2,000 characters and 24 digits (with 9 decimal places), and the default values are 32 characters and 15 digits (with 5 decimal places). There is also an optional parameter on the CRTDTAARA command that allows the user to define an initial value for the data area at creation time. The keyword to do this is VALUE.

When the CRTDTAARA command is executed, a new object with a type of *DTAARA is created under the library. Once a data area has been created, its contents can be manipulated with the CHGDTAARA command. CHGDTAARA allows the user to change the value of the data area or, in the case of character data, allows manipulation of portions of the character string. The basic syntax is

```
CHGDTAARA DTAARA(library/areaname)
          VALUE(value or variable)
```

If the data area has been defined as character and the value specified in the VALUE keyword is made up of numeric characters, the numeric characters must be enclosed in single quotes.

As mentioned, the CHGDTAARA command can be used to change substrings within the data area. For instance, in Chapter 4, we talked about building a table containing the number of days in each month to help improve our date edit function. A data area could be used to store 12, 2-digit numbers that correspond to each month's number of days. However, every 4 years, we would need to change the number of days for February from '28' to '29'. Initially, we would create the data area and the appropriate initial values with the following command:

```
CRTDTAARA DTAARA(MYLIBXX/DAYS)
          TYPE(*CHAR)
          VALUE('312831303130313130313031')
```

When leap year rolls around, we would want to change the 3rd and 4th characters to '29'. The substring to be changed is specified with two new parameters that specify the starting location of the substring and the length of the substring. They would be specified in the CHGDTAARA command as follows:

```
CHGDTAARA DTAARA(MYLIBXX/DAYS (3 2)) VALUE('29')
```

To verify that the data has been updated, we could display the contents of the data area. This is done with the DSPDTAARA command. The syntax is as follows:

```
DSPDTAARA DTAARA(MYLIBXX/DAYS)
```

The resulting screen would look like Figure 10.8

FIGURE 10.8

```
                          Display Data Area
                                                        System:   BRUCE
Data area . . . . . . . :   DAYS
  Library . . . . . . . :     MYLIBXX
Type  . . . . . . . . . :   *CHAR
Length  . . . . . . . . :   24
Text  . . . . . . . . . :

           Value
Offset      *...+....1....+....2....+....3....+....4....+....5
    0      '312931303130313130313031'

                                                              Bottom
Press Enter to continue.

F3=Exit   F12=Cancel
```

CL programs can retrieve the value of a data area with the RTVDTAARA. Substrings can also be specified and retrieved using the same format as in the change command. For instance, a CL program could retrieve the correct number of days in February by issuing the RTVDTAARA command as follows:

```
RTVDTAARA DTAARA(MYLIBXX/DAYS (3 2)) RTNVAR(&DAYS)
```

The most important difference between the RTVDTAARA and CHGDTAARA commands is the RTNVAR parameter. The RTNVAR keyword identifies the program variable name that will hold the value returned by the RTVDTAARA command. After the RTVDTAARA command, the application program can use the variable &DAYS.

Summary

Files and databases are not the only types of data structures. Several structures—stacks, queues, and linked lists—store data and allow sequential access to the data. These linear data structures are usually used to store temporary information and pass information between programs. Generally, queues provide faster access to the data than files or databases. This is because they reside in main memory. Files and databases are stored on secondary storage, which takes longer to access.

The AS/400 supports queues and stacks with an object called a data queue. This object can be created and deleted with the CL commands CRTDTAQ and DLTDTAQ. Access to a data queue is provided by two API programs—QSNDDTAQ, which writes to a data queue, and QRCVDTAQ, which reads from a data queue. Both of these API programs can be called from application programs to perform their respective function.

Another type of data structure on the AS/400 is a data area. Data areas are used to store a small amount of data that is relatively permanent or that is to be passed between programs. Data areas, unlike data queues, can be created, deleted, and manipulated through a series of CL commands.

PROGRAMMING EXERCISES

A data area would be useful in the ADD program. Currently, there are no restrictions on assigning item or serial numbers. Users can pick any number they want, and there is no way of knowing if a number has been used or not (except for trial and error).

We want to create two data areas for the highest item and serial numbers. In addition, we will create two data queues to hold any deleted item or serial number. Two new programs should be written to erase item and serial records. Any deleted (and therefore, reusable) item or serial number should be written to the appropriate data queue.

The ADD program should be modified so that when any new items or products are added, the appropriate data queue is read for the new item or serial numbers. If there is a number on the queue, it should be the number assigned. If the queue is empty, the data area should be read for the next number. The ADD program will also have to add 1 to the data area value and rewrite the data area.

This assignment consists of the following:

1. Create two new data queues called ITEMDTAQ and PRODDTAQ. Define them as FIFO, numeric, and large enough to hold the appropriate number.
2. Create two data areas called ITEMDTAA and PRODDTAA. Define them as numeric and large enough to hold the appropriate number. Set the initial value of ITEMDTAA equal to 17 and PRODDTA equal to 20.

3. Modify the `Add New Item` and `Add New Serial` screens so that the item number and serial number fields are output only.

4. Modify the ADD program to use the new data areas and queues as described. The changes to the pseudocode would be as follows:

```
ADD

            Start: Display Add Items and Serials menu
                   If option 1
                   Then Call AddItm
                   Else If option 2
                        Then Call AddSer
                        Else If option 3
                             Then End program
                   Goto Start

            AddItm
NEW==>             IDTAA = N
NEW==>             Read ITEMDTAQ
NEW==>             If read unsuccessful
NEW==>             Then IDTAA = Y
NEW==>                   Read ITEMDTAA
NEW==>             Move item number to screen.item number
            Disp:  Display Add New Item screen
DELETE==>          Read ITEM file using screen.item number as the key
DELETE==>          If item number in ITEM file
DELETE==>          Then Send message "Item already exists."
DELETE==>                Goto Start
                   If Type not equal "CONSUMABLE" and MEDIA is blank
                   Then Send message "Must fill in MEDIA."
                         Goto Disp
                   Move screen data to ITEM record
                   Write to ITEM file
                   If Serial = Y
                   Then fill in item number on Add New Serial screen
                         Call AddSer
NEW==>             If IDTAA = Y
NEW==>             Then add one to item number
NEW==>                   Write item number to ITEMDTAA
             EndAddItm

             AddSer
NEW==>             PDTAA = N
NEW==>             Read PRODDTAQ
NEW==>             If read unsuccessful
NEW==>             Then PDTAA = Y
NEW==>                   Read PRODDTAA
NEW==>             Move serial number to screen.serial number
```

```
        Disp1: Display Add New Serial screen
               Read ITEM file using screen.item number as the key
               If item number in ITEM file
               Then Move screen data to PRODUCT record
                    Set Status = A
                    Set Rent# = 0
                    Write to PRODUCT file
NEW==>              If PDTAA = Y
NEW==>              Then add one to serial number
NEW==>                   Write serial number to PRODDTAA
DELETE==> Else  fill in item number on Add New Item screen
DELETE==>           Call AddItm
NEW==>         Else Send message "Can't add serial.  Item doesn't
NEW==>                   exist."
NEW==>              If Serial = Y
NEW==>              Then Goto Disp1
         EndAddSer
```

5. Create a new logical file called KPROD that uses INUM as a key to PRODUCT.

6. Create two new delete programs called DELITEM and DEL-PROD in MYLIBXX. DELITEM will delete an item record and all associated product records for that item. DELPROD will delete a single record. Both programs will write out the deleted item and serial numbers to the appropriate data queue.

   The pseudocode for the programs would be as follows:

```
DELITEM
         Receive item number for deletion
         Delete record in ITEM for item number
         If delete successful
         Then Write item number to ITEMDTAQ
              Read record in KPROD for item number
              Do while read successful
                  Delete record in KPROD for item number
                  If Delete successful
                  Then Write serial number to PRODDTAQ
                  Read record in KPROD for item number
              Enddo
ENDELITEM

DELSER
         Receive serial number for deletion
         Delete record in PRODUCT for serial number
         If delete successful
         Then Write serial number to PRODDTAQ
ENDDELSER
```

7. Verify that the programs worked by deleting item 2 and adding the following new items:

INAME	Cashews	Paths of Glory
TYPE	Consumable	War
MEDIA		VD
RPRICE		2.50
SPRICE	5.75	69.95
SERIAL	N	Y

Enter one new serial record into the PRODUCT file for the new movie "Paths of Glory."

8. If the program worked correctly the following should occur:
   - Item "Cashews" should have an item number of 2.
   - Item "Paths of Glory" should have the highest item number in the file—17.
   - One product record with a serial number of 4 should be in the product file, and there should not be a serial number 12 in the product file
   - The PRODUCT record for serial 4 should have an item number equal to 17.
   - The data area ITEMDTAA should contain the value 18.
   - The data area PRODDTAA should contain the value 20.
   - The data queue ITEMDTAQ should be empty, and the data queue PRODDTAQ should have a single entry equal to 12.

REVIEW QUESTIONS

1. Explain what a linear data structure is.
2. What is the difference between physically linear data structures and logically linear data structures?
3. What do stacks and queues have in common, and how are they different?
4. What object does the AS/400 use to implement stacks and queues?
5. What is the difference between AS/400 data queues and data areas?

DISCUSSION QUESTIONS

1. What are the advantages and disadvantages of storing data on a queue versus a file?
2. Explain how data queues are updated from application programs and the versatility of this method.

Data Control

11

Overview

The purpose of this chapter is to introduce the concepts behind data security and the necessity of data control. We will cover how the AS/400 provides both access and functional control over data. We will also discuss specialized objects that the AS/400 uses to provide these controls.

After finishing this chapter, you will understand

- Why controls are necessary
- The different authorities that can be granted to data files
- The different levels of data control and how the AS/400 helps provide these controls

After finishing this chapter, you will be able to

- Manipulate library and file authority
- Control data update capability
- Establish record and field level control
- Create alternative user environments

What Are Controls?

In any system, whether manual or computer, monitoring and control are essential for orderly operations and error prevention. There are controls in almost every aspect of society, and you are exposed to many different controls every day. For instance, traffic lights control the flow of motor vehicles. For some (constantly in a hurry) drivers, traffic lights aren't effective. That is why there are police who monitor traffic and issue tickets. Traffic police are a second control system over the flow of traffic. If these two control systems don't work on certain motor vehicle operators, the court system becomes involved. The court can revoke licenses and, if some drivers persist in violating traffic laws, the ultimate control—jail—can be exercised. As you can see, there are many control systems in everyday life, even several for as common an activity as driving a car. Imagine how many controls are necessary to ensure that a more complicated process (such as maintaining and updating millions of data records) is performed correctly and accurately.

Though controls can sound ominous, they are instituted so that actions and procedures are the safest and in the best interest of all. Without controls, chaos would result. For instance, imagine New York City traffic without lights to govern who stops and who goes. (As it is, some would say that NYC traffic lights don't govern much traffic. So maybe *some* chaos is part of any system and a better description is that *more* chaos would result without controls.)

Data Controls

Organizations will use computer systems only if functional controls ensure data accuracy and the confidentiality of data can be assured through restricted access. In other words, if people cannot count on accurate, confidential information, they will not use a computer.

One common method to decrease errors is to limit access to data and the functions that can be used to modify data. Only personnel who have received proper training on how to manage data and use the system are given authority to access and modify the data. All computer systems supply utilities that provide the framework to establish access and functional control over data.

In terms of functional control of data, there are several key "times" when control should be exercised.

1. When the information is entered. People make mistakes, press the wrong keys, there are data transmission errors, and so forth.

2. When data is updated. Any data processing that takes place must be accurate and authorized. For example, decrementing inventory should be accurately reflected in all data. In addition, a record should be kept of all transactions.

3. When data is deleted. Only unneeded data should be deleted. If data is mistakenly deleted, backup and recovery procedures should be in place to recreate the missing data.

Errors can be reduced during each "event" by allowing only authorized personnel (those trained in the correct procedures for entering, updating, and deleting information and, therefore, the people who will make fewer mistakes) to perform these functions. In addition, program controls should ensure that data being entered is accurate, updates are processed correctly, and deletions to be performed are valid.

As an example of a program control, consider a bank that has three files containing customer, checking, and savings account information. Before deleting any customer records, the program that deletes customer records should read the savings and checking files and make sure the customer has no accounts currently open. (It stands to reason that if a customer has active accounts, the bank does not want to lose the customer information.) This type of program check ensures that if a customer number is mistakenly entered, the customer information is not deleted. Program controls, like these, need to be performed at each of the three critical data events in order to protect data integrity.

Access control certainly helps with data accuracy by limiting the data that a user can access and perform functions against. If someone is denied access to data, he or she cannot perform any function. More important, access controls help ensure that data is confidential.

Confidentiality requires controlling access to files, as well as individual records and fields. For instance, bank customers should be able to access the account files, but access should be restricted to the records regarding their accounts; access to all other records should be denied. Proper access controls help control access to files, records, and fields.

In most computer systems, access and function controls are supplied through the operating system, the database management system, and specialized security programs. The AS/400 is no exception. The AS/400 supplies these controls through its combined database management and operating systems, and a set of specialized security and authorization commands and objects.

Control Levels

Controls specify which data and functions can or cannot be used. However, access to data or a function is not a simple yes or no condition. Controls need to be exercised at many different levels for both data and functions. Someone may have access to a function but can use it only on a small subsection of data. Or someone may have access to an entire file but can perform only a limited set of functions (such as move and copy but not delete) against that file. The complexity of the control system will depend on how well the data organization matches the business functions and the degree of security required.

Data Levels

Traditionally, data has to be controlled at three levels: file, record, and field.

In most systems, users need different files or portions of the database to do their jobs. For instance, a manufacturing employee may need to look at inventory location information so that he can get raw materials from the stockroom to the manufacturing line. The shipping manager also needs to see the inventory locations so that she can find parts to ship to the customers. In addition, before shipping any parts, the customer's payment history must be checked. Therefore, the shipping manager also needs access to the accounts receivable file. This business requires file level control that allows both employees access to the inventory information but only the shipping manager access to the payment data.

Record level security provides a second, finer level of access control. In many instances, people require access to files but do not need everything in the file. For instance, the manufacturing employee works on the razor blade manufacturing line. The inventory location file contains information about stockrooms across the manufacturing site that contain toolkits, batteries, precious metals, hazardous materials, and so on. The razor blade manufacturing line employee has no business need to access any of that information. In fact, it may lead to temptation if he knows where the gold and platinum are stored. Restricting access to only those inventory parts that he uses would solve this problem. Record level control accomplishes this.

Field level control provides further data control within the record. If access to a particular record is granted, control can still be maintained over which fields can be accessed. For instance, our shipping manager also needs to access the employee file. There is record level control such that the shipping manager can access only his employee's records. However, even within each employee's file, there is medical information that only the company's medical department should see. In this case, field level control is necessary.

AS/400 File Level Access and Function Control

These three levels of data security (file, record, and field) are all handled by the AS/400. Since files are stored as objects on the AS/400, file level access is controlled by restricting or granting the user access to **object functions**—read, copy, edit, delete, and so on. As soon as users are granted any object function, they have file level access. Access to object functions on the AS/400 is grouped into three types of authority.

1. Object management authority—the authority to work with the object as a whole
2. Object operational authority—the ability to manipulate an object's contents
3. Object existence authority—the authority to delete the object

Users who are granted authority to the object as a whole (users with object management authority) can perform such functions as copying, renaming, and moving the object to a different library. This type of authority, however, does not provide the capability to go inside the object and change its contents. Only object operational authority allows the contents of an object to be changed.

These authorities can be granted only by someone with **object authority**. Object authority is the ability to perform all object functions and transfer ownership of the object to another user. The two users who always have object authority are the owner of the object and the system security officer.

The owner of the object is the user who creates the object or someone to whom ownership has been transferred. (Remember, transferring ownership is a function that users with object authority can perform.) In other words, users have object authority over a data file if they create the file.

A security officer is someone in the organization who is responsible for all system security. On the AS/400, a special signon id (QSECOFR) is given to that person. QSECOFR has object authority for all objects on the system. (QSECOFR has access and control over just about everything in the system.)

As an example, say three sisters worked in the information systems department of the manufacturing company mentioned earlier. Megan Byte is the programmer who created the inventory location data file used by the shipping manager and manufacturing employee. As the object creator, Megan automatically had object authority. She granted her sister Gigi, a system operator, object management authority. Part of Gigi Bytes's job is to make sure all data is copied onto backup tapes (in case of a disaster). However, as a system operator, Gigi does not need to change the contents of the file. With object management authority, she can copy the data file, but she cannot change the data.

Meanwhile, Ursala Ser, needs content control because she is responsible for receiving deliveries to the stockroom and updating stock quantities in the file. Tara Byte, who is security officer for the company, grants U. Ser object operational authority. As the system security officer, Tara also has object authority and the ability to grant authority to the file. When Megan gets a new job, it will be Tara's job to transfer ownership (another capability of users with object authority) to the programmer taking over Megan's responsibilities.

Working with Object Authorities

The CL command that allows the owner or QSECOFR to grant the various authorities to another user is the GRTOBJAUT (grant object authority) command. Within the GRTOBJAUT command, the owner (or QSECOFR) can control the functions that the new user will be able to perform by specifying up to eight of the following values in the AUT parameter:

OBJOPR (object operational authority)—allows viewing of the object's description and further specification of the content control functions

OBJMGT (object management authority)—allows a user to move, copy, rename, and grant authority to the object

OBJEXIST (object existence authority)—allows a user to delete and save an object

For content control functions (in conjunction with OBJOPR authority), the following can be specified:

READ—enables the user to look at data in file members

ADD—allows the user to insert new information

UPDATE—lets the user modify existing information

DELETE—allows information to be erased, not the entire object

Other values can be specified that provide a combination of the preceding authorities.

*EXCLUDE—denies all access to the object

*USE—provides OBJOPR control and read-only capability

*CHANGE—gives OBJOPR control and all content control functions

*ALL—grants object MGT, OPR, and EXIST control and all content control

The syntax for the GRTOBJAUT command is as follows:

```
GRTOBJAUT OBJ(libname objname) OBJTYPE(objtype)
USER(userid) AUT(up to 8 of the above values)
```

Executing this command provides the access specified in the AUT parameter to the object specified in the OBJ and OBJTYPE parameters for the signon id specified in the USER parameter. What actually occurs is that the signon id and authority specified in the GRTOBJAUT command are added to the **authorization list** for that object. When an object is created, an authorization list is created for that object. The authorization list is used to identify the object owner and who has access to the object. Only the owner of the object or the QSECOFR can grant authority or manipulate authorization lists.

Another way to change the authorization list is with the EDTOBJAUT command. Typing **EDTOBJAUT** and pressing **F4** will bring up the `Edit Object Authority(EDTOBJAUT)` screen where the user would specify the object name, library, and type (Figure 11.1) and then press **ENTER.** This will bring up the `Edit Object Authority` screen (Figure 11.2). To add new users, you would press **F6** at this screen. To change a user's authority, just type over the current object authority value.

FIGURE 11.1

```
                    Edit Object Authority (EDTOBJAUT)

 Type choices, press Enter.

 Object . . . . . . . . . . .   MYLIBXX       Name
   Library  . . . . . . . . .     QSYS        Name, *LIBL, *CURLIB
 Object type  . . . . . . . .   *LIB          *ALRTBL, *AUTL, *CFGL...

                                                                    Bottom
 F3=Exit   F4=Prompt   F5=Refresh   F12=Cancel   F13=How to use this display
 F24=More keys
```

FIGURE 11.2

```
                         Edit Object Authority

Object . . . . . . . :   MYLIBXX          Object type  . . . . :   *LIB
  Library . . . . . :      QSYS          Owner  . . . . . . . :   BIGSHOT

Type changes to current authorities, press Enter.

  Object secured by authorization list  . . . . . . . . . . . .   *NONE

               Object
User           Authority
BIGSHOT        *ALL
*PUBLIC        *CHANGE

                                                                     Bottom
F3=Exit   F5=Refresh   F6=Add new users   F10=Grant with reference object
F11=Display detail     F12=Cancel         F17=Top    F18=Bottom
```

The EDTOBJAUT command displays all current authorities and enables object owners to easily assign authorities. On the `Edit Object Authority` screen, pressing **F11** (`Display detail`) will result in the screen seen in Figure 11.3 being displayed. Notice that each authority (`*CHANGE`, `*ALL`) is broken down into its constituent security keywords (`Opr`, `Mgt`, `Add`, and so on). The user can also modify authorities by blanking out or adding Xs for any keyword and create any combination of authorities. Authority combinations specified that are not predefined on the system will be labeled "user defined."

FIGURE 11.3

```
                         Edit Object Authority

Object . . . . . . . :   MYLIBXX          Object type  . . . . :   *LIB
  Library . . . . . :      QSYS          Owner  . . . . . . . :   BIGSHOT

Type changes to current authorities, press Enter.

  Object secured by authorization list  . . . . . . . . . . . .   *NONE_____

               Object     ----Object-----   ----------Data-----------
User           Authority  Opr  Mgt  Exist   Read  Add  Update  Delete
BIGSHOT        *ALL        X    X     X      X     X     X       X
*PUBLIC        *CHANGE     X    _     _      X     X     X       X

                                                                     Bottom
F3=Exit   F5=Refresh      F6=Add new users   F10=Grant with reference object
F11=Nondisplay detail     F12=Cancel         F17=Top    F18=Bottom
```

To take away authority to an object, the RVKOBJAUT (revoke object authority) command is used. This command removes a userid from the authorization list.

In our earlier example regarding the shipping manager and the manufacturing line employee, the QSECOFR would execute the GRTOBJAUT command for the inventory location file and specify OBJOPR authority for both the manager and the manufacturing line employee. For the accounts receivable file, she would specify OBJOPR for the shipping manager and *EXCLUDE for the manufacturing employee. Before these authorization list changes are made, the system checks to make sure that QSECOFR has the authority to perform these changes for the inventory location and accounts receivable objects. QSECOFR does, so the authorization lists would be updated. Next time the shipping manager tries to access either of these objects (through either a menu or CL command), the authorization list will be checked. If the shipping manager tries to update either data file, the request will be rejected. If the manager's actions are within the granted authority—such as reading the data—access will be allowed. The same holds for the manufacturing employee. Any access to the accounts receivable object will be denied, but trying to view the inventory location object will be allowed.

AS/400 Record and Field Level Security

Record and field level control are handled through logical files. Since logical files offer an alternative view of physical files, we can build logical files to include only certain records and fields. Because logical files are also objects, authority to only specified records and fields can be granted with the previously discussed authority commands.

The special relationship between logical and physical files also has an impact on authorization. For instance, when granting authority to a logical file, object operational authority cannot be further defined with the read, add, update, and delete authorities. If you grant users operational authority to a nonjoined logical file, they get all content control (add, update, and delete) over the records in the physical file. They will be able to access only the records and fields specified in the logical file, but all content control functions can be performed against the data in those fields. This could pose a problem. For instance, allowing people to view DEANSLIST would also mean they have the ability to change the fields. Using DFU, a user could change someone's GPA in DEANSLIST, and the physical file that the logical file is based on would be updated. This would happen even if the user is explicitly excluded from the physical file. Excluding users from the physical file will stop direct updates to physical files or executing commands such as DSPPFM against the physical file, but it does not prevent access through logical files.

Therefore, logical files can control access to records and fields, but we still have not been able to totally control the functions that can be performed against the data. To adequately protect the data, further control over the functions that can be performed must exist.

Controlling Other AS/400 Data Objects

Control over other data objects such as data queues and data areas is also achieved with object control. Just like physical files, users can be granted any combination of authorities to data queues and data areas.

Data objects can also be controlled at the library level. Authority to a library must be granted in order for the user to have any access to the objects. For instance, if a user was excluded from MYLIBXX, he or she could not access any of the objects within the library regardless of the authority granted to individual objects such as STUDENT and DEANSLIST.

If object management and object existence authority were granted, the user could manipulate the library as a whole but still could not access the individual objects. Only if a user is given object operational authority can the objects be accessed. Note that ADD and DELETE library object operational authorities control whether objects can be added or deleted within the library, not whether records can be added or deleted to all the objects within the library. If any level of object operational authority is granted for the library, each object's authority list controls access to the object.

Functional Control Levels

There are a variety of different levels of functional control. For instance, the ability to update data can be controlled at the system level by not giving someone a userid and password. This level of control prevents someone from updating any data and from performing any function.

Most organizations need a finer level of functional control than system level control. One such control is at the object level. An organization can restrict updating to certain files, records, and fields. However, updating information through an application program is completely different from updating with DFU. The chances for error are much greater with DFU than with an application program that performs data edits and audits. Therefore, object level control (and its simple yes or no control over content functions) is not enough because control over *how* updating is done is needed. In other words, to provide better data integrity and accuracy, control over what "tool" is used to perform functions against data must exist. This means controlling who can use application programs, utilities, and operating system functions.

Program Control

Application programs are usually created to perform additions, deletions, and changes to data files. Programs are the preferred method because they can ensure better data integrity. For instance, whenever our shipping manager, mentioned earlier, ships an item, the following needs to be done:

Decrease the inventory quantity in the inventory file

Write a shipping record to the shipping file

Update the customer order status as SHIPPED in the customer order file

DFU could be used to manipulate the different files. With proper authority, this method would be possible but not very fast or safe. For instance, the shipping manager will, once in a while, type in the wrong information (make a subtraction error when entering the new inventory quantity or transpose numbers when filling in the date of shipment). Because of the need for data integrity and efficiency, a specialized program is usually created to perform these functions. The shipping manager only has to call the program and enter the customer order number being shipped. The program will read the order file (for the amount being shipped) and update all the appropriate files. This solution does not eliminate all chances of human error (for instance, the customer order number could still be entered incorrectly), but it does cut down on the number of opportunities for entering incorrect information.

If the user who called the program does not have authority to the files, file level security prevents the program from performing any of the updates. The same holds for DFU. However, if we wanted the employee to be able to modify the file with the program but not with DFU, CL commands, or any other application programs, file authorities will not help. In this case, access to the functions needs to be restricted.

Object security works for restricting access to programs. Since programs are just another type of object, all the object controls previously discussed can be exercised against application programs. However, files can also be manipulated with CL commands and system utilities like DFU and SQL/400. Since these are not objects, object control does not help control these functions. Security officers can, however, stop users from executing CL commands and accessing utilities by creating an alternative user environment.

Alternative User Environments

An alternative user environment consists of menus and screens with limited options and no command line. Users are then restricted to using only these screens and menus. Access to the AS/400-supplied menus, CL commands, and therefore, any method to invoke system functions or utilities is denied to the user. By limiting access to only presented options, the security officer has created a new environment for the user to work in.

The first thing needed to set up an alternative programming environment is the screen(s) or menu(s) to which the user will be restricted. For instance, if we wanted to set up an alternative user environment for our shipping personnel, we could use DDS or SDA to create a screen, SHIP, as seen in Figure 11.4. This screen would provide only two options—run the shipping program or signoff. Notice that there is no command line, nor do any of the function keys activate any system utilities such as PDM or DFU. The trick is making this menu appear whenever a shipper signs on to the system. This can be accomplished with the use of an object called a **user profile**.

When a userid is created, a user profile (an object with type equal to *USRPRF) is created in the library QSYS. This new object has the same name as the userid and contains information about the userid—such as the initial program to run, the default output queue, and so on. We could create a simple CL program called SHIP that displays the `SHIP screen`, reads the user's selection, and then either activates the shipping program or logs the user off the system. Whenever the shipping program finishes, the SHIP screen will be redisplayed. We would then set the "initial program to run" parameter in the user profile to SHIP and the library to MYLIBXX. The prompt `Initial program to call` in Figure 11.5 is where the CL program name and the library are specified. Figure 11.6 shows the CL source code for the program. After the user profile is modified, whenever the shipper signs on, the SHIP program will be invoked, and the SHIP screen will be displayed. In this way, the user will be restricted to this newly created "shipper's environment."

FIGURE 11.4

```
SHIP                                    SHIP screen

Select one of the following:

     1. Ship an item
     2. Signoff









Selection _
```

FIGURE 11.5

```
                         Change User Profile (CHGUSRPRF)

Type choices, press Enter.

User profile . . . . . . . . . . > SHIPPER1       Name
User password  . . . . . . . . .   *SAME          Name, *SAME, *NONE
Set password to expired  . . . .   *NO            *SAME, *NO, *YES
Status . . . . . . . . . . . . .   *ENABLED       *SAME, *ENABLED, *DISABLED
User class . . . . . . . . . . .   *PGMR          *SAME, *USER, *SYSOPR...
Assistance level . . . . . . . .   *SYSVAL        *SAME, *SYSVAL, *BASIC...
Current library  . . . . . . . .   *CRTDFT        Name, *SAME, *CRTDFT
Initial program to call  . . . .   SHIP           Name, *SAME, *NONE
  Library  . . . . . . . . . . .     MYLIBXX      Name, *LIBL, *CURLIB
Initial menu . . . . . . . . . .   *NONE          Name, *SAME, *SIGNOFF
  Library  . . . . . . . . . . .                  Name, *LIBL, *CURLIB
Limit capabilities . . . . . . .   *NO            *SAME, *NO, *PARTIAL, *YES
Text 'description' . . . . . . .   *BLANK




                                                                    More...
F3=Exit   F4=Prompt   F5=Refresh   F12=Cancel   F13=How to use this display
F24=More keys
```

FIGURE 11.6

```
        *************** Beginning of data ************************************
0001.00 /*********************************************************************
0002.00 /* THIS LIMITS SHIPPERS TO ONLY THE SHIPPING FUNCTION.
0003.00 /* THE PROGRAM INITIALLY DISPLAYS THE SHIP SCREEN AND READS THE
0004.00 /* USER SELECTION.  IF THE USER SELECTS "1" THE PROGRAM CALLS THE
0005.00 /* SHIP PROGRAM.  IF THE USER SELECTS "2" THEN THE SIGNOFF COMMAND IS
0006.00 /* EXECUTED.
0007.00 /*********************************************************************
0008.00 START:       PGM
0009.00              DCLF       FILE(MYLIBXX/SHIP) RCDFMT(SHIP)
0010.00 LOOP:        SNDRCVF RCDFMT(SHIP)
0011.00              IF COND(&FLD001 *EQ '1') +
0012.00              THEN(DO)
0013.00                   CALL MYLIBXX/SHIP
0014.00                   ENDDO
0015.00              IF COND(&FLD001 *EQ '2') +
0016.00              THEN(DO)
0017.00                   SIGNOFF
0018.00                   ENDDO
0019.00              GOTO LOOP
0020.00 END:         ENDPGM
        ****************** End of data ***************************************
```

Summary

Controls are required for all systems whether they are manual or computer systems. The AS/400 provides extensive functional and data level control capabilities. Through its object-oriented approach, it is able to provide access control to multiple levels of data, object functions, and user application functions. Though most systems provide this, the AS/400's object-oriented architecture—treating all data and programs as objects—allows control through the same command set and utilities. Normally, there are separate commands, functions, and systems for data and application program control, and most computer systems require a separate database management system if record or field level control is needed.

The AS/400 architecture also provides several methods to restrict access to system functions and utilities. One of the most popular is the ability to create alternative user environments. Through the user profile, a userid can be restricted to certain screens, menus, application programs, system functions, and utilities. This restricted set of functions or alternative user environment enables security officers to exert functional control over individual CL commands and system utilities.

As with all AS/400 commands and functions, the security and authorization functions are supported with prompts, screens, and online help to facilitate their use and understanding. All security functions can be accessed through the extensive menu system or directly with CL commands.

PROGRAMMING EXERCISE

Many of the video store employees have been using DFU and SQL to update the ITEM and PRODUCT files rather than application programs. To prevent this, we need to create an alternative user environment for the video store employees. This environment will provide access to the application programs and QUERY/400 queries they need to do their jobs but will not allow them to perform CL commands or access other utilities such as DFU or SQL/400.

To create the alternative user environment, we must first create a screen that looks like the following:

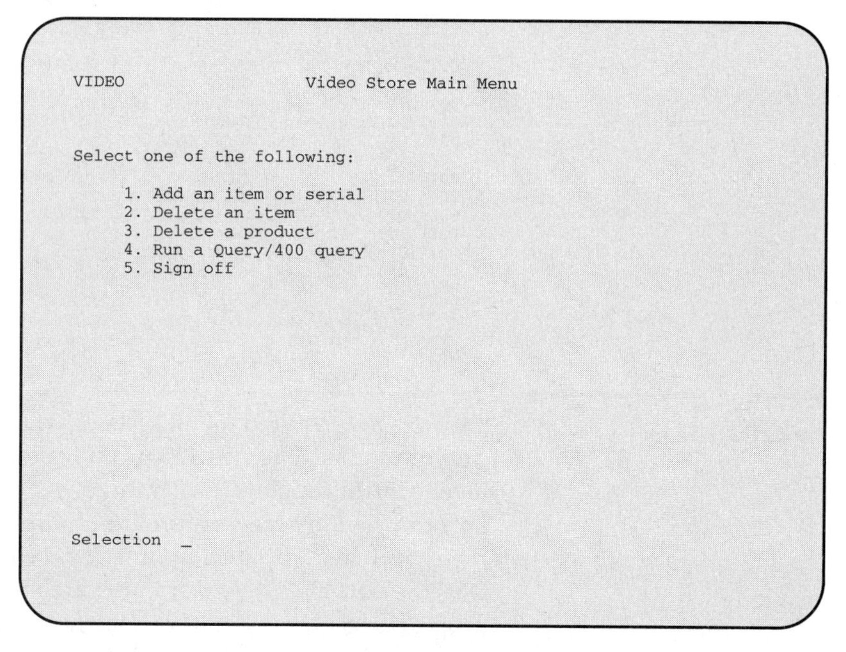

VIDEO
Video Store Main Menu
Select one of the following:
1. Add an item or serial
2. Delete an item
3. Delete a product
4. Run a Query/400 query
5. Sign off
Selection _

Use DDS or SDA to create the screen and store the source code in a member called VIDEO in MYLIBXX/DDSSRC. Create a display file called VIDEO within MYLIBXX by compiling the DDS source.

We will also create three new screens that will make the deletion programs easier to use (by prompting for deletion information) and enable users to specify and run QUERY/400 queries. The screens should look like the following:

```
DELITM                         Delete Item

Enter the item number to be deleted

     Item number: _______
```

```
DELPRD                              Delete Product


Enter the item number and serial number of the product to be deleted

        Item number: _______

      Serial number: _______
```

```
ACTQRY                         Activate Query/400 query

Enter the library and query name of the query to be run


         Library: __________

           Query: __________
```

Store the screen source code definitions in members called DELITM, DELPRD, and ACTQRY within DDSSRC in MYLIBXX. Create display files with the same names within MYLIBXX by compiling the source code members.

The CL programs DELITEM and DELSER need to be modified to use the new screens. The program changes would be as follows:

DELITEM

DELETE==> Receive item number for deletion
NEW==> Display DELITM screen

```
CHANGE==>  Delete record in ITEM for screen.INUM
           If Delete successful
           Then Write item number to ITEMDTAQ
CHANGE==>        Read record in KPROD for screen.INUM
                 Do while read successful
CHANGE==>            Delete record in KPROD for screen.INUM
                     If Delete successful
                     Then Write serial number to PRODDTAQ
CHANGE==>            Read record in KPROD for INUM
                 Enddo
        ENDELITEM

        DELSER
NEW==>     Display DELPRD screen
CHANGE==>  Delete record in PRODUCT for screen.SNUM
           If Delete successful
CHANGE==>  Then Write screen.SNUM to PRODDTAQ
NEW==>     Else Send message "Could not delete serial."
        ENDDELSER
```

A new program ACTQRY needs to be created in MYLIBXX to display the ACTQRY screen and activate the query specified. The CL source code for ACTQRY is the following:

```
START:  PGM
        DCLF     FILE(MYLIBXX/ACTQRY) RCDFMT(ACTQRY)
        SNDRCVF  RCDFMT(ACTQRY)
        RUNQRY   QRY(&FLD001/&FLD002) OUTTYPE(*DISPLAY)
END:    ENDPGM
```

Notice the OUTTYPE parameter in the RUNQRY command. Certain query parameters can be overridden in the RUNQRY command. The OUTTYPE parameter allows the programmer to control where the output will go. In this case, we have specified that the output should go to the display terminal instead of a file being built and the query results being written to the file.

Finally, a CL program named VIDEO within MYLIBXX needs to be created to display the VIDEO screen and process the requests. The following is the CL source code for VIDEO:

```
        PGM
        DCLF    FILE(MYLIBXX/VIDEO) RCDFMT(VIDEO)
START:  SNDRCVF RCDFMT(VIDEO)
        IF COND(&FLD001 *EQ '1') THEN(CALL PGM(MYLIBXX/ADD))
        IF COND(&FLD001 *EQ '2') THEN(CALL PGM(MYLIBXX/DELITEM))
        IF COND(&FLD001 *EQ '3') THEN(CALL PGM(MYLIBXX/DELPRD))
        IF COND(&FLD001 *EQ '4') THEN(CALL PGM(MYLIBXX/ACTQRY))
        IF COND(&FLD001 *EQ '5') THEN(SIGNOFF)
        GOTO START
END:    ENDPGM
```

Enter the CL source for the two new programs into member VIDEO and ACTQRY in CLSRC within MYLIBXX. Create the programs VIDEO and ACTQRY in MYLIBXX by compiling the source code.

To verify that the programs work correctly, perform the following steps:

1. Invoke the program VIDEO.
2. Choose option 1.
3. Add an item and serial.
4. Choose option 3.
5. Delete the serial just added.
6. Choose option 2.
7. Delete the item just added.
8. Choose option 4.
9. Run the Q$CONSUM query in MYLIBXX. (The results should be displayed.)
10. Choose option 5.

You should be signed off the system. Executing the DSPPFM command against the ITEM and PRODUCT files should show that no new item or product has been added to the files.

REVIEW QUESTIONS

1. Who has object authority?
2. What is an authorization list?
3. Explain how logical files help with data control.
4. How are user-written applications controlled on the AS/400?
5. How can system functions be controlled?
6. Describe the scope of authority granted to the QSECOFR userid.
7. What is the difference between the GRTOBJAUT and EDTOBJAUT commands?
8. Explain how control is exercised over data queues and data areas.

DISCUSSION QUESTIONS

1. Explain the different levels of data control, and give reasons why each level would be needed.
2. Explain what functions can be performed if a user has *ALL authority to a logical file but *EXCLUDE to the physical file it is based on.
3. What are alternative user environments, and how can they help with data accuracy and integrity?

Data Backup and Recovery

12

Overview

This chapter will cover basic strategies to protect against data loss. We will explain how data can be "lost" or corrupted at the transaction, file, disk, and system level and show the impact on an organization's operations. We will then explore strategies and functions that enable the timely recovery of data at all levels of failure.

After finishing this chapter, you will understand

- The impact of data loss
- Standard procedures for backup and recovery
- The function of journals and journal receivers
- COMMIT and ROLLBACK
- Save files
- ASPs
- Mirroring
- The advantages and disadvantages of saving information on different storage media

After finishing this chapter, you will be able to:

- Create a journal and journal receiver
- Start journaling for a physical file
- Execute the COMMIT and ROLLBACK functions
- Create a save file
- Save files to a save file
- Restore a data file from a save file
- Recover transaction data using the journal and journal receiver

Recovery

When a catastrophe like an earthquake or a hurricane strikes, restoring a computer system is a nightmare. Getting new hardware, restoring data and software, finding alternative sources of power, and even transporting personnel to the data processing location may be required to restore normal system operations. Because of the complexity involved in system recovery, recovery plans are created long before any mishaps occur. These plans try to anticipate all problems and include procedures to restore any lost system resources. Recovering data is an essential part of any complete recovery plan, but it is only one piece of the recovery puzzle. For instance, if after a disaster, data was recovered but none of the programs that access and use the data were available, the data would still be of no use to the organization.

Even though AS/400 commands and utilities are available for "nondata" recovery, we will confine our discussion to the procedures and methods that enable the fast recovery of data and the programming methods to prevent data errors. All the examples will deal with data, but the problems and procedures are applicable to the other aspects of system recovery. We will not explore recovering these other system essentials because of the unique concerns and timing factors that must be thoroughly understood (for instance, with software, saving source code versus machine language code). These special problems are clearly not within the scope of this book—AS/400 data management.

Data Loss and Protection

As the first chapter pointed out, most organizations use computers to improve efficiency and provide functions that would not be possible manually (for example, quickly locating an item in a large warehouse). Computer systems have become so integral that most organizations would not be able to function for long if their systems were unavailable. For instance, could the local convenience store have supplies delivered if their computerized ordering system was unavailable? If their supplier's names and phone numbers were stored on the computer, they couldn't even find out who to order from. Even if they could find the names, they probably wouldn't have the manpower available to implement a manual system to order the goods, keep track of receipts, and make payments to the suppliers. Because of this reliance on computer systems, being able to protect data and recover from errors and data loss has become a vital part of all business planning.

The causes of data loss can range from someone inadvertently hitting a "power off" button to the natural disasters mentioned earlier. However, whether a single update transaction fails or an entire file, disk, or system is lost, the key to protecting and recovering data is duplication. Just as redundant data (and the extra storage space it requires) help with system performance, duplicate data also protects organizations from data loss. In this case, duplicate data helps because a copy of a data file is just as valuable as the original (too bad other assets like gold, jewelry, or money aren't more like data).

Another advantage data has over other assets is that copies of data can be made quickly. Because of these unique characteristics, protecting data against the different levels of loss can be looked at as "simply" a matter of what data is copied and where the copied data is stored. However, this "simple matter" of how to copy, store and retrieve data, where to store the data and how much data to store will be the focus of the rest of this chapter.

Transaction Errors

Every business and organization functions by performing a variety of transactions. The convenience store orders goods, receives those goods, sells merchandise and, of course, pays employees. Each one of these processes is a business transaction.

Every transaction can be broken down into a series of smaller steps. For instance, the sales transaction actually comprises many manual and computerized actions. First, the convenience store employee enters the items and quantities being sold. The computer looks up the prices and then calculates and displays the total purchase amount. The employee then enters the amount paid. If necessary, the computer calculates the amount of change that should be given. Next, the computer decrements each item's "quantity in stock" field (contained in the inventory file) by the quantity sold, and then the general ledger file is updated by increasing the "cash on hand" and "total sales" amount fields by the purchase amount.

Because every transaction comprises many steps, there is a chance that an interruption during processing could result in an error or loss of information. For instance, what would happen if there was a electrical outage right after the inventory file was updated but before the general ledger file was updated? Unfortunately, the answer largely depends on the data management system and the backup and recovery utilities that are being employed. In our example, if no precautions have been taken, the general ledger file will not be updated, and the amount of cash on hand and total sales figures will be incorrect.

Now, if you were the attendant or even owner of the store, missing a couple of slurpie sales might not sound like a big deal. However, the accounting firm that performs the yearly audit will not think so lightly of a company that cannot accurately keep track of business. As a matter of fact, a bad audit rating can result in a higher interest rate being charged for loans to the company (due to the company's uncertain finances), or in a worst case scenario, a total physical audit can be mandated. Total physical audits require that every asset—nickel, dime, corn dog, soda cup, and so forth—be counted and inventoried because the computer files cannot be trusted to accurately reflect the state of the business. This generally means an incredible added cost to the company, if not necessitating the business to close during the audit.

As you can imagine, system developers are extremely concerned with transaction integrity. This is such a common and important concern that most DBMSs provide a **commit** and **rollback** function to ensure that transactions are performed completely. A commit function allows programmers to specify that updates to a file are to be committed (permanently in place) only after all related updates are successful. If a problem arises during a transaction, a rollback (or undo) of all uncommitted updates can be performed. On the AS/400 these functions are performed with the use of two new objects—**journals** and **journal receivers**.

Journals and Journal Receivers

A journal and journal receiver are used to record actions against a file. The actions recorded include additions, deletions, and modifications, as well as nonupdate actions such as opening or saving a file. Journal entries record the type of action that was performed, what job performed the action, and the time the action took place. Update journal entries also include the data that was involved in the modification. For instance, any time a record is added or deleted, a journal entry is written that contains the data added or deleted and the time of the addition or deletion. For data modifications, an image of the data record before and after the modification can be stored.

The rollback function uses the duplicate data in the journal to reverse changes; that is, if a rollback is issued, the uncommitted journal entries are applied in reverse to the data—additions are deleted, deletions are added. For change transactions, the before image replaces the after image. However, when a programmer issues a commit, all entries are marked as committed and cannot be rolled back. This means that a rollback will restore file data to the point in time when the last commit was issued. RPG, COBOL, CL, PL/1, and SQL/400 all support the commit and rollback functions with their own commands.

Commit and rollback allow the programmer to avoid the convenience store problem. Encoding the program so that a commit command was issued only after both the inventory and general ledger files were updated successfully would enable a rollback to be performed if the general ledger update failed. The rollback would reverse the inventory update (because it was not committed) and restore the data to its last correct state (its condition prior to the transaction).

Using rollback and commit commands in a program, however, does not prevent the data errors that would result from an electrical outage. If there is an electrical outage, main memory is erased, and the computer stops executing all program statements. In this case, the encoded rollback commands would never be executed. Fortunately, a general system feature helps with this problem. If the entire system ends abnormally (such as when the electricity is shut off), an IPL (initial program load) must be performed. When an IPL is performed after an abnormal system end, a systemwide rollback is performed (all uncommitted changes against all files are reversed). This would result in the inventory update being rolled back even though the program instruction wasn't executed.

Rollbacks are also automatically performed if a program ends (normally or not) and there are uncommitted updates.

Journaling a File

File transactions are not automatically recorded in journals. The file to be journaled, the information to be recorded, and the specific journal and journal receiver that will hold the transaction information must all be specified by the user. In addition, users must create journals and journal receivers and attach journal receivers to specific journals. A journal receiver(s) is attached to a journal when the journal is created. Therefore, a journal receiver must be created before the journal is created.

Journal receivers (and journals) are simply another type of object. The CRTJRNRCV command will create a journal receiver object under a specific library. Issuing the following command:

```
CRTJRNRCV JRNRCV(MYLIBXX/MYJRCV)
```

will create an object with a type of *JRNRCV in MYLIBXX.

After a journal receiver has been created, a journal can be created. The CRTJRN command will create a journal within a library. The following command will create a journal called MYJRN within MYLIBXX and attach the journal receiver MYJRCV to MYJRN:

```
CRTJRN JRN(MYLIBXX/MYJRN) JRNRCV(MYLIBXX/MYJRCV)
```

Going to the `Work with Objects using PDM` screen would show the two new objects within MYLIBXX (Figure 12.1).

FIGURE 12.1

```
                      Work with Objects Using PDM

Library . . . . .   MYLIBXX          Position to . . . . . . . .
                                     Position to type  . . . . .

Type options, press Enter.
  2=Change        3=Copy         4=Delete       5=Display       7=Rename
  8=Display description          9=Save         10=Restore      11=Move ...

Opt  Object      Type          Attribute    Text
 _   MYJRCV      *JRNRCV
 _   MYJRN       *JRN

                                                                More...
Parameters or command
===>
F3=Exit          F4=Prompt           F5=Refresh          F6=Create
F9=Retrieve      F10=Command entry   F23=More options    F24=More keys
```

Creating the journal and journal receivers does not automatically start journaling. The files to be journaled and the journal to hold the entries must be identified. The STRJRNPF (start journal physical files) command is used to identify the two objects and activate the journaling function for the file. The following STRJRNPF command identifies STUDENT as the file to be journaled, MYJRN as the journal to store the information, and starts the journaling function for the STUDENT file:

```
STRJRNPF FILE(MYLIBXX/STUDENT) JRN(MYLIBXX/MYJRN) IMAGES(*BOTH)
```

Notice the parameter *BOTH specified within the keyword IMAGES. *BOTH tells the system to include both a before and after image of the record in the journal whenever a record is modified. (The two images are not recorded for additions or deletions, only for changes.) As mentioned earlier, with both images recorded in the journal, file changes can be rolled back.

COMMIT and ROLLBACK

To demonstrate the commit and rollback functions, we'll use the program in Figure 12.2 to update the STUDENT file. This RPG program (which uses very little RPG but a lot of SQL statements) will demonstrate the rollback and commit functions by performing two additions to the file. One record addition is committed, and the other is not. Both update transactions are also followed by a ROLLBACK command. If the commit and rollback work as discussed, only one transaction will be reflected in the file when the program finishes.

If we were to stop the program at line 7 (after the first insert), the STUDENT file would look like Figure 12.3.

FIGURE 12.2

```
        *************** Beginning of data *************************************
0001.00      H
0002.00      C/EXEC SQL
0003.00      C+ INSERT INTO MYLIBXX/STUDENT VALUES ('Smart', 'Max',
0004.00      C+ '86 Control Lane', 'Washington', 'DC', '22222', '868686868', 6,
0005.00      C+ 086)
0006.00      C/END-EXEC
0007.00      C*
0008.00      C/EXEC SQL ROLLBACK
0009.00      C/END-EXEC
0010.00      C*
0011.00      C/EXEC SQL
0012.00      C+ INSERT INTO MYLIBXX/STUDENT VALUES ('99', 'none',
0013.00      C+ '99 Control Lane', 'Washington', 'DC', '22222', '099099099', 9,
0014.00      C+ 099)
0015.00      C/END-EXEC
0016.00      C*
0017.00      C/EXEC SQL COMMIT
0018.00      C/END-EXEC
0019.00      C/EXEC SQL ROLLBACK
0020.00      C/END-EXEC
0021.00      C*
0022.00      C                    SETON                        LR
        ****************** End of data ***************************************
```

FIGURE 12.3

```
                        Display Physical File Member
File . . . . . . :   STUDENT              Library  . . . . :   MYLIBXX
Member . . . . . :   STUDENT              Record . . . . . :   1
Control  . . . . .                        Column . . . . . :   1
Find . . . . . . .
*...+....1....+....2....+....3....+....4....+....5....+....6...
FlintstoneFred     11 Limestone DrBedrock    AZ88888111111111 ¤ H
FlintstoneWilma    11 Limestone DrBedrock    AZ88888123456789   ·
Rubble    Betty    15 Limestone DrBedrock    AZ88888444444444 ± ±
Rubble    Bernard 15 Limestone DrBedrock     AZ88888999999999 ¬
Smart     Max      86 Control LaneWashingtonDC21212868686868 ? q

                          ****** END OF DATA ******

                                                                       Bottom
F3=Exit   F12=Cancel    F19=Left    F20=Right    F24=More keys
```

Executing the ROLLBACK statement on line 8, however, will reverse the Max Smart record insert. The second update, however, is followed by a COMMIT statement. Notice on line 12, the program writes a second record. This is followed by a COMMIT statement on line 17 and a ROLLBACK statement on line 19. Displaying the file after the program finished would result in the data as seen in Figure 12.4. This shows that only the second update was permanently recorded.

FIGURE 12.4

```
                        Display Physical File Member
File . . . . . . :   STUDENT                    Library  . . . . :   MYLIBXX
Member . . . . . :   STUDENT                    Record . . . . . :   1
Control  . . . . .                              Column . . . . . :   1
Find . . . . . . .
*...+....1....+....2....+....3....+....4....+....5....+....6...
FlintstoneFred     11 Limestone DrBedrock   AZ88888111111111 ¤ H
FlintstoneWilma    11 Limestone DrBedrock   AZ88888123456789   ˙
Rubble    Betty    15 Limestone DrBedrock   AZ88888444444444 ± ±
Rubble    Bernard 15 Limestone DrBedrock   AZ88888999999999 ¬
99        none     99 Control LaneWashingtonDC22222343434343 ¤ Đ
                       ****** END OF DATA ******

                                                                     Bottom
F3=Exit   F12=Cancel   F19=Left   F20=Right   F24=More keys
```

Even without stopping the program, we can prove that the Max Smart record was in the file at one point by displaying the file description. Displaying the description and paging to the bottom would result in a screen as seen in Figure 12.5. Notice that the total number of records is five (which correlates with the number of data records in Figure 12.4) and that one record was deleted. This deleted record was the Max Smart record.

A more complete accounting of file changes can be seen by looking at the journal entries directly. This can be done with the following command:

```
DSPJRN JRN(MYLIBXX/MYJRN)
```

Executing the DSPJRN (display journal) command for MYJRN would result in the `Display Journal Entries` screen (Figure 12.6). This display lists all the transactions performed against the STUDENT file since journaling was started with the STRJRNPF command. Remember that in addition to changes to the file, events such as opening and closing the file are included.

To easily identify the transactions, each is assigned a code and a type. For instance, a code equal to R means that a specific record was modified. A type of PT means that a record was added. To see more detail about the event, type a 5 in the option field to the left of the journal

FIGURE 12.5

```
                          Display Spooled File
File . . . . . :   QPDSPFD                          Page/Line   3/2
Control . . . . .                                   Columns     1 - 78
Find . . . . . .
*...+....1....+....2....+....3....+....4....+....5....+....6....+....7....+...
    Text . . . . . . . . . . . . . . . . . . . . :            STUDENT RECORD
  Total number of formats . . . . . . . . . . . :            1
  Total number of fields . . . . . . . . . . . . :           9
  Total record length  . . . . . . . . . . . . :           63
 Member List
                          Source Creation     Last Change                  Dele
  Member           Size    Type  Date        Date     Time       Records    Reco
  STUDENT          15360         02/24/94 05/11/94 12:37:43           5
    Text:
  Total number of members . . . . . . . . . . . :                 1
  Total records . . . . . . . . . . . . . . . . :                 5
  Total deleted records . . . . . . . . . . . . :                 1
  Total of member sizes . . . . . . . . . . . . :             15360

                                                                        Bottom
F3=Exit   F12=Cancel   F19=Left   F20=Right   F24=More keys
```

FIGURE 12.6

```
                         Display Journal Entries

Journal . . . . . . :   MYJRN          Library . . . . . . :   MYLIBXX

Type options, press Enter.
  5=Display entire entry

Opt   Sequence  Code  Type  Object       Library     Job         Time
 _           1   J     PR                            SF20101S1   15:35:42
 _           5   F     JM   STUDENT      MYLIBXX     SF20101S1   15:42:25
 _           6   F     OP   STUDENT      MYLIBXX     SF20101S1   12:37:37
 _           7   C     BC                            SF20101S1   12:37:38
 _           8   C     SC                            SF20101S1   12:37:38
 _           9   R     PT   STUDENT      MYLIBXX     SF20101S1   12:37:39
 _          10   F     CL   STUDENT      MYLIBXX     SF20101S1   12:37:40
 _          11   R     DR   STUDENT      MYLIBXX     SF20101S1   12:37:41
 _          12   C     RB                            SF20101S1   12:37:41
 _          13   F     OP   STUDENT      MYLIBXX     SF20101S1   12:37:42

F3=Exit   F12=Cancel
```

entries sequence number. This will result in the more detailed journal entry display seen in Figure 12.7.

Notice in Figure 12.7 how all the data that was added to the file is duplicated in the journal entry. This is the information used for performing the rollback.

The COMMIT and ROLLBACK commands are good protection against data loss and integrity problems caused by an incomplete transaction. However, if a file has been erased, such as the general ledger file in our earlier example, the COMMIT and ROLLBACK statements will prevent all file updates from occurring.

FIGURE 12.7

```
                          Display Journal Entry

Object . . . . . . . :   STUDENT          Library  . . . . . . :   MYLIBXX
Member . . . . . . . :   STUDENT          Sequence . . . . . . :   9
Code . . . . . . . . :   R  - Operation on specific record
Type . . . . . . . . :   PT - Record added

          Entry specific data
Column    *...+....1....+....2....+....3....+....4....+....5
00001     'Smart      Max      86 Control LaneWashingtonDC21212'
00051     '868686868 ? q'

                                                                   Bottom
Press Enter to continue.

F3=Exit   F6=Display only entry specific data
F10=Display only entry details   F12=Cancel   F24=More keys
```

This means no business transactions can be processed. In this case, the COMMIT and ROLLBACK commands do prevent the files from becoming "out of sync," but they do not help solve the problem of the lost file.

Fortunately, the AS/400 does provide several methods to save a file or group of files and recreate them if they are lost.

Object Loss

Anyone who has worked with a PC knows that one of the first "safety" lessons taught is "back up your files." (The second is "don't use diskettes as drink coasters.") As mentioned earlier, copying valuable information provides protection from loss because duplicate data is just as good as original data. Because of this, all computers provide methods to quickly copy and store data. On the AS/400, several "save" commands allow the user to easily copy and store data and "restore" commands allow the user to retrieve the saved data. Therefore, the same rule applies to the AS/400—"back up your files!"

The first save command we will cover is the SAVOBJ (save object) command. SAVOBJ allows users to save a duplicate data file(s) to tape, diskette, or disk. Typing **SAVOBJ** and pressing **F4** will result in the `Save Object (SAVOBJ)` screen being displayed (Figure 12.8). On this screen, the user can specify a single object or many objects to be saved. For instance, to save all files within a library, you would enter the library name at the `Library` prompt, the value *ALL at the `Objects` prompt, and *FILE at the `Object types` prompt (Figure 12.9).

The user must also specify were the copied file should be placed—tape, diskette, or disk. If the file is being saved to tape or diskette, the device name (for example, **TAP001**) is entered at the `Device` prompt. If the object is being saved to disk, the user enters the value ***SAVF** (save file) and presses **ENTER**. The `Save Object(SAVOBJ) Screen`

FIGURE 12.8

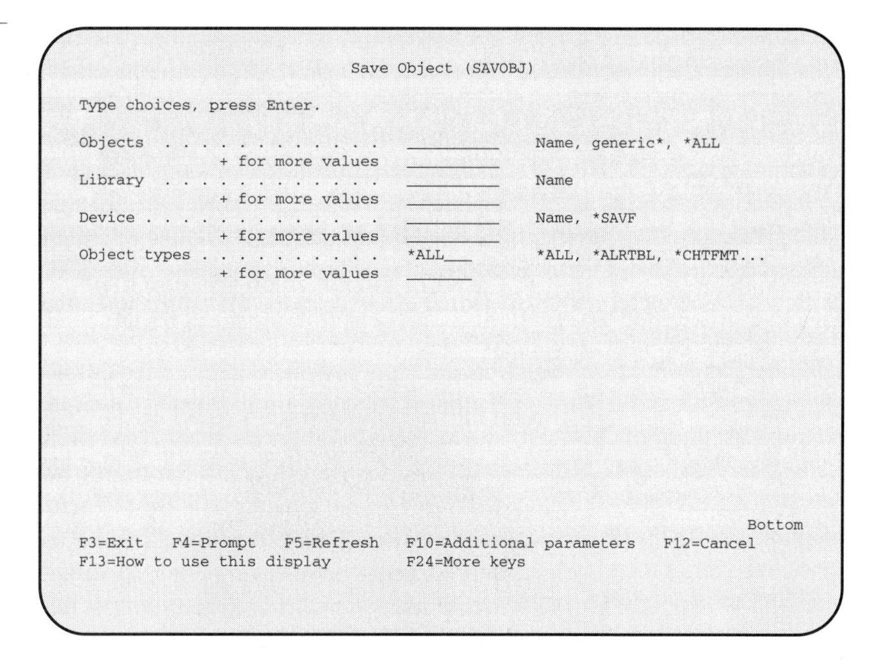

FIGURE 12.9

```
                         Save Object (SAVOBJ)

 Type choices, press Enter.

 Objects  . . . . . . . . . . . > *ALL______    Name, generic*, *ALL
                + for more values _________
 Library  . . . . . . . . . . . > MYLIBXX___    Name
                + for more values _________
 Device . . . . . . . . . . . . > *SAVF_____    Name, *SAVF
                + for more values _________
 Object types . . . . . . . . .   *FILE_____    *ALL, *ALRTBL, *CHTFMT...
                + for more values _________
 Save file  . . . . . . . . . . > BACKUPFILE    Name
   Library  . . . . . . . . . . >   BACKUPLIB   Name, *LIBL, *CURLIB
 Update history . . . . . . . .   *YES          *YES, *NO

                                                                  Bottom
 F3=Exit   F4=Prompt   F5=Refresh   F10=Additional parameters   F12=Cancel
 F13=How to use this display        F24=More keys
```

will then add prompts for the name of the save file and library to be used. The save file must be created before saving an object. The command to create a save file called BACKUPFILE in BACKUPLIB is

```
CRTSAVF FILE(BACKUPFILE/BACKUPLIB)
```

After entering the information on the `Save Object(SAVOBJ)` screen, press ENTER. All specified objects will be copied to the save file.

Save files (files with an attribute equal to *SAVF) serve a very different function than source physical files and data physical files.

Save files are used exclusively to store backup data in case of data loss. Information in save files should not be accessed and modified. There are some built-in system guards to protect against this. For instance, if you were to bring up the `Work with Objects using PDM` screen for BACKUPLIB and try to use option 18 (`Change using DFU`), an error message saying the option is invalid would be displayed. (The same is true for QUERY/400.) However, application programs can read and write to the file. The only way to stop these updates is to ensure that proper object control is exercised for the save file. For instance, the system operator(s) responsible for backup and recovery should be the only ones authorized to the save files.

Besides the SAVOBJ command, several other "save" commands will save many objects at a time (including objects other than files). For instance, SAVLIB saves all the objects within a specified library, and SAVSTG saves everything in auxiliary storage and the LIC. There are restore commands to retrieve the information at these levels also.

Finally, two storage options are available when saving objects that minimize the storage space used. The two options are data compression and data compaction.

Pressing **F10** at the `Save Object (SAVOBJ)` screen makes additional option screens available. Paging down through these screens will bring up the screen seen in Figure 12.10. Notice the two options—`Data compression` and `Data compaction`—towards the bottom of the figure.

FIGURE 12.10

```
                          Save Object (SAVOBJ)

Type choices, press Enter.

Object pre-check . . . . . . . .   *NO            *NO, *YES
Save active  . . . . . . . . . .   *NO            *NO, *LIB, *SYSDFN
Save active wait time  . . . . .   120            0-99999, *NOMAX
Save active message queue  . . .   *NONE          Name, *NONE, *WRKSTN
  Library  . . . . . . . . . . .     *LIBL        Name, *LIBL, *CURLIB
File member:
  File . . . . . . . . . . . . .   *ALL           Name, *ALL
  Member . . . . . . . . . . . .   *ALL           Name, generic*, *ALL, *NONE
              + for more values
            + for more values
Save access paths  . . . . . . .   *NO            *NO, *YES
Save file data . . . . . . . . .   *YES           *YES, *NO
Storage  . . . . . . . . . . . .   *KEEP          *KEEP, *FREE
Data compression . . . . . . . .   *DEV           *DEV, *NO, *YES
Data compaction  . . . . . . . .   *DEV           *DEV, *NO
Output . . . . . . . . . . . . .   *NONE          *NONE, *PRINT, *OUTFILE

                                                                   More...
F3=Exit   F4=Prompt   F5=Refresh   F12=Cancel   F13=How to use this display
F24=More keys
```

Data compression is a technique that reduces the number of repeating characters stored in a save file. (Data compression is also widely used in industry to cut down on the amount of data that is transferred over networks, thereby reducing telecommunication costs.) For instance, if fields were defined to hold an employee's address, one field would hold the city in which the employee resides. The CITY field would have to be long enough to hold city names such as Philadelphia, Jacksonville, and Poughkeepsie, yet for cities such as Boston or Enid, the CITY field would have as many blanks as characters. Compression on the AS/400 takes many repeating fields (such as blanks) and reduces them to 1 or 2 bytes. This byte(s) contains a code signifying that the data is compressed and, in the case of nonblank repeating characters, also contains the EBCDIC representation of the repeated character. Obviously, reducing 60 repeating characters to 2 bytes provides significant storage savings.

Data compaction is a hardware option available on certain tape units that better utilizes tape space. (Check with the system programmer to see if data compaction is available on your system.)

Both techniques, compression and compaction, allow users to store more information in less space, but of course, there is a catch—less space means a loss in performance. In the case of compression, writing and reading the data requires the added step of compressing and decompressing the data. For files that are constantly updated, the time delay caused by compression and compaction would make timely access impossible. However, for save files (which will be written only once and ideally never read), both options are desirable for their storage savings.

Another performance consideration is the relative speed of the various devices and media. In general, saving and restoring to disk will be faster than tape or diskette. Therefore, if a single file is lost, disk would be the best option for restoring the data quickly. But what if an entire disk is lost?

Disk Failure

Though not common, disk failures do occur. With age and constant use, the chance of disk failure increases. Saving backup data to tape or diskette and then moving them to a safe location will solve this problem. However, the ability to quickly retrieve the information is lost when the saved data is physically removed from the system location. Therefore, the AS/400 developers have provided two other options to help protect against disk failure and still allow users to store all backup data on disk.

The first feature is **auxiliary storage pools (ASPs)**. An ASP consists of a single disk or group of disks as specified by the user. In other words, when users create ASPs, they assign specific storage units to the ASP. (There is a system ASP—ASP1—that is used to store to system objects and is already created. Users, however, can create up to 15 additional ASPs numbered 2 through 16.) When the user creates ASPs, one can be used exclusively for storing backup data. All libraries and data files would be located in the system ASP or user ASPs other than the backup ASP. All save files, journals, and journal receivers, however, would be located on the designated backup ASP. To put these objects on a specific ASP, the user must specify the ASP when creating the objects. For instance, on the `Create Save File (CRTSAVF)` screen (Figure 12.11) notice the `Auxiliary storage pool ID` prompt in the `Additional Parameters` section of the screen.

With the data arranged as described, if there is a disk failure on one of the nonbackup user ASPs or the system ASP, the data can be quickly restored from the backup ASP. If any of the disks in the backup ASP fails, all data should be saved immediately either to another backup ASP, tape, or diskette. In either case, with a single disk failure, no data will be lost.

FIGURE 12.11

```
                         Create Save File (CRTSAVF)

 Type choices, press Enter.

 Save file . . . . . . . . . .   __________    Name
   Library . . . . . . . . . .     *CURLIB     Name, *CURLIB
 Text 'description' . . . . . .  *BLANK

                          Additional Parameters

 Maximum records . . . . . . . .  *NOMAX       1-536854528, *NOMAX
 Auxiliary storage pool ID . . .  *LIBASP      1-16, *LIBASP
 Maximum file wait time . . . . . *IMMED       Seconds, *IMMED, *CLS
 Share open data path . . . . . . *NO          *NO, *YES
 Authority . . . . . . . . . . .  *EXCLUDE     Name, *EXCLUDE, *ALL...

                                                                     Bottom
 F3=Exit   F4=Prompt   F5=Refresh   F12=Cancel   F13=How to use this display
 F24=More keys
```

The second option that keeps backup data on disk is called **mirroring**. Mirroring duplicates all information at the ASP level. In other words, mirroring "pairs" ASPs. Each ASP in the pair will contain exactly the same data. When updates are performed, both copies of the data are updated. When reads are performed, the faster ASP is accessed. The double updates are hidden from the user; however, the impact on performance will be apparent on jobs performing many updates.

The advantage to mirroring is that if a disk is lost, the system can continue processing. Mirroring provides a backup copy of the data that can be accessed immediately. The mirrored data doesn't have to be retrieved, decompressed, or uncompacted. Without mirroring, the user must wait until the data is restored (which may even depend on fixing or replacing the failed disk). Of course, the downside to mirroring is the extensive duplication of data and the expense of the extra storage hardware.

Both ASPs and mirroring are useful for data backup and recovering from disk failures. However, what if there is a fire? A save file and data physical file stored on different ASPs will both be lost if the system goes up in flames. Just backing up the data isn't the solution. Where the backup data is stored is equally important.

When files are saved to tape or diskette, they can be moved and stored in a different room or building. In the case of system loss, the copied data will be safe; however, retrieving the data will take a little longer because of the physical distance from the system.

What happens if more than the system is lost? What about a hurricane? What about a meteor hurtling from the sky and devastating a 25-square-mile area? (The meteor example may be a little melodramatic, but we need it to keep the subject matter lively.) What steps should we take to protect our data and business from the possibility of a fiery death from the heavens?

Catastrophic Loss

Protecting against catastrophic loss encompasses many areas and could fill an entire book of its own. To protect data, the cheapest method is to save to tape or diskette and store the data in a safe location. Determining whether a location is safe depends on the catastrophe being avoided. Storing the data remotely (several hundred miles away) will provide adequate coverage for most natural disasters, and many companies specialize in providing storage areas for sensitive media. However, safety is only one aspect of a good location. The ability to quickly retrieve the stored data is as important as its safety.

As we have already learned, having information but not being able to access it is just as bad as not having the data at all. For instance, if a company's disaster recovery procedure is to collect 350 backup tapes each week, and this is accomplished by stopping at 50 different locations each day of the week for one tape, how long will it take to get delivery after a disaster? Some locations will get their tape in one day, others in seven and that assumes that the roads are passable. (The California earthquake in 1994 showed how unreliable that assumption is.) Many disaster recovery specialists have been overwhelmed when disaster strikes because their resources support only the timely collection of backup data, not the timely supply of data in adverse conditions. To be useful, organizations must be sure that data can be supplied in a timely manner after a disaster.

An alternative to backup tapes and diskettes is a duplicate system. Two AS/400 systems, on the same network, with duplicate copies of all files, would allow a business to function if one system were lost. Even if a system was lost and communication lines were cut, the information can be downloaded to tape or diskette and flown, driven, or "rickshawed" to the disaster location. Usually, however, communication lines are reestablished long before new computer systems can be supplied. So the business can run on the backup system until the primary system is fixed or replaced. When the replacement system is ready, the information can be transferred via the network and the dual system environment reestablished.

Though duplicate systems are the safest method, there are daunting complications and costs. For instance, keeping the data updated on two separate systems is a real juggling act. What happens if communication with one of the machines is lost for an hour? Procedures must be in place to mark transactions that have been applied to only one system and, when communications are reestablished, make sure that the transactions are applied to the other system. Should transactions be rolled back if they fail on one system but not the other? What about discrepancies between system files?

Besides the added complexity with coordinating updates, there is the considerable added cost of duplicating all hardware and software. Not only is the cost of purchasing the computer hardware and software greater, but there are increased support costs such as personnel, electricity, and rent on the building space to house the equipment.

Restoring Saved Data

With any loss, there are many more considerations than just restoring the data from the saved files or tapes. Natural disasters bring a host of other problems to reestablishing normal operations. However, once normal hardware operations have been established and the backed up data is available, restore procedures can be exercised to recreate the lost data.

The command to retrieve saved objects is RSTOBJ (restore object). For instance, if the logical file DEANSLIST had been mistakenly deleted from library MYLIBXX, we could restore the file with the RSTOBJ command. Typing the command and pressing **F4** results in the `Restore Object (RSTOBJ)` screen (Figure 12.12). At this screen, you would identify the object to be restored by entering the object name (DEANSLIST) and the library (MYLIBXX). In addition, the save file must be identified. This is done at the bottom of the screen, and in this case, BACKUPFILE and its library, BACKUPLIB, would be specified. Pressing **ENTER** after typing the information would result in a new object DEANSLIST being created under MYLIBXX. Moreover, the saved information (the KSAP) would be decompressed and loaded into DEANSLIST. After successfully restoring the object, the system will respond with the message, `1 objects restored from MYLIBXX to MYLIBXX at MM/DD/YY HH:MM:SS`.

FIGURE 12.12

```
                         Restore Object (RSTOBJ)

Type choices, press Enter.

Objects . . . . . . . . . . . > DEANLIST      Name, generic*, *ALL
              + for more values
Saved library . . . . . . . . > MYLIBXX       Name
Device . . . . . . . . . . . . > *SAVF         Name, *SAVF
              + for more values
Object types . . . . . . . . .   *ALL          *ALL, *ALRTBL, *CFGL...
              + for more values
Save file . . . . . . . . . . > BACKUPFILE    Name
  Library . . . . . . . . . . >   BACKUPLIB   Name, *LIBL, *CURLIB

                                                                    Bottom
F3=Exit   F4=Prompt   F5=Refresh   F10=Additional parameters   F12=Cancel
F13=How to use this display        F24=More keys
```

Earlier we had compared data with other assets and found that a real advantage to data was that it could be easily duplicated and that a duplicate file was as good as an original. However, another not so convenient aspect of data is that it is constantly changing. Unlike most assets that are fairly permanent (such as a building, inventory, and money), data is changing by the second. Information that was saved two days ago may be of no use to a business if it bears no resemblance to the current state of the business. For instance, a supermarket's inventory file that was saved on Wednesday night is grossly inaccurate by Saturday. Trying to reorder products based on inventory figures from Wednesday is a guessing game at best. This fact brings some problems to our recovery procedure. If the inventory file was lost on Saturday, what good would restoring Wednesday's data be?

There are two solutions to this problem. The first is to perform backups more frequently. If the data is changing rapidly, maybe daily or hourly backups are necessary. Of course, constantly backing up the data will take its toll on system performance.

A second alternative is to stick with the infrequent file backups and simply reapply journal entries against restored files. The journal and journal receiver contain copies of all the data involved in each file transaction and the AS/400 provides a method to reexecute these transactions. In other words, if a file is saved once a week on Wednesday, and on Saturday the file is mistakenly erased, when the Wednesday save file is restored all journal transactions (since the save) can be applied against the restored data, thereby bringing the data up to date. In the case of object loss, the file can always be recovered to the most recent level as long as journaling is being performed. What about system loss?

In the case of system loss, the journals and journal receivers must also be saved. Saving journal information rather than the data file could also provide considerable savings in time. (This, of course, depends on the size of the files versus the size of the journal information. The size of the journal file, in turn, is greatly determined by the activity rate against the file.)

For instance, if a business is trying to protect a small file with a lot of activity, saving the small file frequently is as good as if not better than infrequent file saves and frequent journal saves. If, however, there is a large file (a million or more records) with relatively little activity (100,000 transactions a day), it would be better for system performance to save the smaller journal more frequently than the larger file. How often the journals should be saved depends on the amount of activity and the importance of the data.

As before, the safest method would be to duplicate the files and journals on a separate system. This would eliminate the need for any saving or restoring. However, the cost of this solution usually prevents its implementation. All the previous discussion regarding media and the location of saved data holds for saving the journal information as well.

Applying Journal Changes

Once a file has been restored, journal transactions can be applied with the APYJRNCHG (apply journal changes) command. Applying journal transactions means performing the transactions again. If there is a journal transaction for a record addition, applying that journal transaction means that the record will be added to the file.

Let's simulate the time lapse problem mentioned earlier by performing a save on the STUDENT file (while it contains only the four Flintstone and Rubble records) and then adding two student records (Max Smart and 99) to the file.

The files and journals would then contain the following information:

> STUDENT in MYLIBXX has six records containing information on the Flintstones, Rubbles, Max, and 99.
>
> STUDENT in save file BACKUPFILE in library BACKUPLIB has four records containing information on the Flintstones and Rubbles.
>
> MYJRN and MYJRCV in MYLIBXX have two file update transactions, one containing information on Max and the other on 99.

If the STUDENT file in MYLIBXX were erased, we would restore the object with the RSTOBJ command. At this point, STUDENT in MYLIBXX would contain the four student records with information on the Flintstones and Rubbles. To apply the journal changes, you would type **APYJRNCHG** and press **F4**. The `Apply Journaled Changes (APYJRNCHG)` screen would be displayed (Figure 12.13).

FIGURE 12.13

```
                  Apply Journaled Changes (APYJRNCHG)

Type choices, press Enter.

Journal . . . . . . . . . . .   MYJRN          Name
  Library . . . . . . . . . .     MYLIBXX      Name, *LIBL, *CURLIB
Journaled physical file:       _
  Journaled physical file  . . . STUDENT       Name, *ALL
    Library . . . . . . . . .     MYLIBXX      Name, *LIBL, *CURLIB
  Member . . . . . . . . . . .  *FIRST         Name, *FIRST, *ALL
             + for more values _
Range of journal receivers:
  Starting journal receiver  . . *LASTSAVE     Name, *LASTSAVE, *CURRENT
    Library . . . . . . . . .     __________   Name, *LIBL, *CURLIB
  Ending journal receiver  . . . __________    Name, *CURRENT
    Library . . . . . . . . .     __________   Name, *LIBL, *CURLIB
Starting sequence number . . . . *LASTSAVE     Number, *LASTSAVE, *FIRST
Ending sequence number . . . . . *LASTRST      Number, *LASTRST, *LAST




                                                                  More...
F3=Exit   F4=Prompt   F5=Refresh   F12=Cancel   F13=How to use this display
F24=More keys
```

On this screen, the user would specify the journal and physical files involved in the apply operation: in this case, MYJRN in MYLIBXX and STUDENT in MYLIBXX. In addition, the user must specify what journal entries are to be applied. The range of journal entries to be applied can be specified by journal entry sequence numbers. (Figure 12.6 shows the sequence numbers on the `Display Journal Entries` screen.) The user would specify the range of journal entries at the `Starting sequence number` and `Ending sequence number` prompts on the bottom of the `Apply Journaled Changes (APYJRNCHG)` screen.

Besides sequence numbers, the system allows the user to specify the journal entries to be applied as "all entries from the last save" until the "last restore." This can be done by specifying the variable names *LASTSAVE and *LASTRST at the prompts.

After the options have been typed, pressing ENTER will result in the data file being updated from the journal information.

Summary

Data recovery is contingent on successfully backing up (copying and saving) vital information and being able to quickly access the copied data in the event of data loss. The AS/400 provides a variety of "save" and "restore" commands that provide these capabilities at many levels of storage. The AS/400 also allows the data to be saved to disk, tape, or diskette. There are advantages and disadvantages to each media regarding the level of loss they protect against and the speed of saving and restoring the data. For instance, saving to different ASPs or instituting mirroring provides protection against object loss or disk failure and the fastest recovery. For system or catastrophic loss, disk does not provide the needed protection. Saving data to tape and diskette allows backup data to be physically moved to a safe location away from the system. Though tape and diskette provide protection against large-scale loss, these media require more time to save and restore data.

Making copies of files at one point in time is not always enough to ensure accurate backup data. Since data is constantly being updated, saved data is accurate only until the first file update transaction occurs after the save. Fortunately, a record of all update transactions can be kept. These duplicate transactions are stored in a journal and journal receiver. When data is restored, the file can be brought "up to date" by applying the journal entries.

Journals and journal receivers are also used to perform COMMIT and ROLLBACK commands. These two functions help programmers ensure data integrity at the transaction level.

EXERCISES

In this exercise, we will provide better protection for our customer's database by

Modifying the application programs to include commitment control for multiple updates

Instituting a regular backup procedure

Creating a journal and journal receiver

Beginning journaling

We will then test our new backup and recovery procedures by simulating transaction abends (abnormal ends) and a file loss. To perform any commits and rollbacks, journaling must be active. Before we can begin journaling, a journal and journal receiver must be created.

1. Create a journal receiver called JRNRCV and a journal called JRN in MYLIBXX.

   The CL commands to create the journal and journal receiver are the following:

   ```
   CRTJRNRCV JRNRCV(MYLIBXX/JRNRCV)
   CRTJRN JRN(MYLIBXX/JRN) JRNRCV(MYLIBXX/JRNRCV)
   ```

2. Start journaling for the ITEM and PRODUCT files.

   The CL commands to start journaling for the ITEM and PRODUCT files are the following:

   ```
   STRJRNPF FILE(MYLIBXX/ITEM) JRN(MYLIBXX/JRN) IMAGES(*BOTH)
   STRJRNPF FILE(MYLIBXX/PRODUCT) JRN(MYLIBXX/JRN) IMAGES(*BOTH)
   ```

3. Create a library called BACKUPXX (where XX is your unique two-digit number). Within BACKUPXX, create save files called ITEMBU and PRODUCTBU.

   The CL command to create the library BACKUPXX is

   ```
   CRTLIB LIB(BACKUPXX)
   ```

   The CL commands to create the save files are

   ```
   CRTSAVF FILE(BACKUPXX/ITEMBU)
   CRTSAVF FILE(BACKUPXX/PRODUCTBU)
   ```

4. Save the ITEM and PRODUCT files to save files called ITEMBU and PRODUCTBU in BACKUPXX.

   The CL commands to save ITEM and PRODUCT to the save files ITEMBU and PRODUCTBU are

   ```
   SAVOBJ OBJ(ITEM) LIB(MYLIBXX) DEV(*SAVF) OBJTYPE(*FILE)
          SAVF(BACKUPXX/ITEMBU)

   SAVOBJ OBJ(PRODUCT) LIB(MYLIBXX) DEV(*SAVF) OBJTYPE(*FILE)
          SAVF(BACKUPXX/PRODUCTBU)
   ```

5. Modify the ADD and DELITEM programs so that changes to the ITEM file are backed out if there is a failure in adding or deleting PRODUCT records. The modification to the pseudocode would be as follows:

<u>ADD</u>

```
Start: Display Add Items and Serials menu
    If option 1
    Then Call AddItm
    Else If option 2
        Then Call AddSer
```

```
                Else If option 3
                    Then End program
            Goto Start

          AddItm

NEW==>        NEWITEM = N
              IDTAA = N
              Read ITEMDTAQ
              If read unsuccessful
              Then IDTAA = Y
                   Read ITEMDTAA
              Move item number to screen.item number
        Disp: Display Add New Item screen
              If Type not equal "CONSUMABLE" and MEDIA is
              blank
              Then Send message "Must fill in MEDIA."
                   Goto Disp
              Move screen data to ITEM record
              Write to ITEM file
              If Serial = Y
              Then fill in item number on Add New Serial screen
NEW==>             NEWITEM = Y
                   Call AddSer
              If IDTAA = Y
              Then add one to item number
                   Write item number to ITEMDTAA

        EndAddItm

        AddSer

              PDTAA = N
              Read PRODDTAQ
              If read unsuccessful
              Then PDTAA = Y
                   Read PRODDTAA
              Move serial number to screen.serial number
        Disp1: Display Add New Serial screen
              Read ITEM file using screen.item number as the key
              If item number in ITEM file
              Then Move screen data to PRODUCT record
                   Set Status = A
                   Set Rent# = 0
                   Write to PRODUCT file
NEW==>             If write successful
NEW==>             Then COMMIT
CHANGE==>               If PDTAA = Y
                        Then add one to serial number
                        Write serial number to PRODDTAA
NEW==>             Else If NEWITEM = Y
NEW==>                  Then ROLLBACK
```

```
NEW==>                  Send message "Item and product not
NEW==>                     added. Could not add serial to
NEW==>                     PRODUCT."
NEW==>                  If IDTAA = N
NEW==>                  Then Write item number to ITEMDTAQ
NEW==>              Else Send message "Could not add serial
NEW==>                     to PRODUCT."
NEW==>              If PDTAA = N
NEW==>              Then Write serial number to PRODDTAQ
          Else Send message "Can't add serial.  Item doesn't
                    exist."
CHANGE==> If NEWITEM = Y
          Then Goto Disp1

  EndAddSer

  DELITEM

            Display DELITM screen
            Delete record in ITEM for screen.INUM
            If Delete successful
DELETE==>   Then Write item number to ITEMDTAQ
CHANGE==>   Then Read record in KPROD for screen.INUM
                 Do while read successful
                    Delete record in KPROD for screen.INUM
                    If Delete successful
                    Then Write serial number to PRODDTAQ
NEW==>              Else ROLLBACK
NEW==>                  Send message "Failed item deletion for
NEW==>                  item ",INUM,". Couldn't delete serials
NEW==>                  from PRODUCT.  PRODDTAQ may
NEW==>                  have serial numbers that are still in use,
NEW==>                  the serial numbers must be deleted from
NEW==>                  PRODDTAQ."
NEW==>                  End program
                    Read record in KPROD for item number
                 Enddo
NEW==>           COMMIT
NEW==>           Write item number to ITEMDTAQ
NEW==>           Send message "Item and serials deleted."
NEW==>      Else Send message "Could not delete item from
NEW==>      ITEM file."
  ENDELITEM
```

Notice that if the write to the PRODUCT file fails, the ADD program corrects the data queue information. Because only files can be journaled, ROLLBACK does not affect data queues and data areas. The programmer must ensure that nonfile information (such as information in data areas and data queues) is correctly maintained and corrected when errors occur.

In the DELITEM program, the program ensures accurate data is on the ITEMDTAQ data queue but not PRODDTAQ.

ITEMDTAQ was protected by writing the item number to ITEMDTAQ after the PRODUCT record(s) were successfully deleted. In other words, an item number doesn't have to be removed from ITEMDTAQ if a product record deletion fails.

PRODDTAQ is another matter. PRODDTAQ is updated multiple times if more than one serial is deleted. The serial numbers that were deleted from PRODUCT (and added to PRODDTAQ) are not stored in a journal. Therefore, if one serial deletion fails, the program cannot remove the serial numbers that were added to PRODDTAQ because no record was kept of which serial numbers were added. (One solution is for the program to create another data queue to temporarily store the serial numbers, and then if there is a problem there would be a record.) For this exercise, we have simply sent a message stating which item number failed. The programmer would then search the PRODUCT file for all serial numbers for that item number and delete those serial numbers from PRODDTAQ.

6. Add the following data to the files:

INAME	Sno-caps	Jeremiah Johnson
TYPE	Consumable	Drama
MEDIA		VHS
RPRICE		2.25
SPRICE	2.25	79.95
SERIAL	N	Y

Enter two new serial records into the PRODUCT file for the new movie "Jeremiah Johnson."

The ITEM and PRODUCT files should look like the following:

```
                          Display Physical File Member
File . . . . . . :   ITEM                   Library  . . . . :   MYLIBXX
Member . . . . . :   ITEM                   Record . . . . . :   1
Control  . . . . .                          Column . . . . . :   1
Find . . . . . . .
*...+....1....+....2....+....3....+....4....+.
1       Gone With the Wind  Romance    VD     r¬Y
2       Cashews             CONSUMABLE        ï¬N
3       Super Mario Bros IIIGame       CRT    ß¬Y
4       E.T.                Sci-Fi     VHS    r¬Y
5       Duck Hunt           Game       CRT      Y
6       Nightmare on Elm St Horror     VHS    r¬Y
7       Popcorn             CONSUMABLE         ¬N
8       Jujubes             CONSUMABLE          N
9       Milk Duds           CONSUMABLE         ¬N
10      Citizen Kane        Drama      VD     r¬Y
11      Fireball            CONSUMABLE          N
12      VCR                 SONY       VHSø   ˙ Y
13      VCR                 RCA        VHSø   ˙ Y
14      Citizen Kane        Drama      VHS    i¬Y
15      Licorice            CONSUMABLE          N
16      Peanuts             CONSUMABLE         ¬N
17      Paths of Glory      War        VD     r¬Y
18      Sno-caps            CONSUMABLE         ¬N     <===== New item 18
19      Jeremiah Johnson    Drama      VHS ¬ r¬Y     <===== New item 19

                           ****** END OF DATA ******
```

```
                     Display Physical File Member
File . . . . . . :   PRODUCT               Library  . . . . :    MYLIBXX
Member . . . . . :   PRODUCT               Record . . . . . :    1
Control  . . . . .                         Column . . . . . :    1
Find . . . . . . .
*...+....1....+..
1      6      Aå
2      6      O ?
3      4      AÏ"
4      17     A
5      1      O
6      3      Oè¬
7      5      A
8      3      Oã"
9      3      O
10     4      Oà|
11     1      A "
13     10     A
14     12     A
15     13     A
16     14     A
17     12     A
18     13     A
19     14     A
12     19     A     <==== New item 12
20     19     A     <==== New item 20
                       ****** END OF DATA ******
```

7. Delete the PRODUCT file to create an object loss situation. Before deleting PRODUCT, make a copy of the file just in case you made a mistake in any of the previous steps. Further, execute the DSPDBR command to find all PRODUCT's dependent logical files. The dependent logical files must be deleted before deleting PRODUCT.

8. Using the DELITEM program, try to delete the ITEM "Jeremiah Johnson" added in step 6.

   An error message should be sent saying the PRODDTAQ may be in error and that the item wasn't deleted.

9. Using the ADD program, add the following movie to the ITEM file:

INAME	HUD
TYPE	DRAMA
MEDIA	VD
RPRICE	2.50
SPRICE	65.75
SERIAL	Y

   Try to enter a serial record into the PRODUCT file for the new movie "HUD."

   An error message should be sent saying the item and product couldn't be added.

10. Restore the PRODUCT file from the save file PRODUCTBU.

The command to restore PRODUCT from the save file PRODUCTBU in BACKUPXX is

```
RSTOBJ OBJ(PRODUCT) SAVLIB(MYLIBXX) DEV(*SAVF)
 SAVF(BACKUPXX/PRODUCTBU)
```

After the restore, the data in the file PRODUCT should look like the following:

```
                              Display Physical File Member
File . . . . . . :   PRODUCT               Library  . . . . :   MYLIBXX
Member . . . . . :   PRODUCT               Record . . . . . :   1
Control  . . . . .                         Column . . . . . :   1
Find . . . . . . .
*...+....1....+..
1       6       Aå
2       6       O ?
3       4       AÏ"
4       17      A
5       1       O
6       3       Oè¬
7       5       A
8       3       Oã"
9       3       O
10      4       Oà|
11      1       A "
13      10      A
14      12      A
15      13      A
16      14      A
17      12      A
18      13      A
19      14      A
                              ****** END OF DATA ******
                                                                   Bottom
F3=Exit   F12=Cancel   F19=Left   F20=Right   F24=More keys
```

Notice that there is no serial 12 or 20. This is because both serials were added after PRODUCT was saved to the save file PRODUCTBU.

11. Apply the journal changes to PRODUCT to recapture the serial numbers that were added to PRODUCT after it was saved to PRODUCTBU.

    The CL command to apply the journal changes is the following:

    ```
    APYJRNCHG JRN(MYLIBXX/JRN) FILE((MYLIBXX/PRODUCT))
    ```

    The system should return a message saying that it cannot execute one of the changes. This is the deletion of the data file you executed in step 7 to simulate the object loss situation.

12. Verify that the PRODUCT file has been recreated with serial numbers 12 and 20.

The data in PRODUCT should look like the following:

```
                    Display Physical File Member
File . . . . . . :   PRODUCT              Library . . . . :   MYLIBXX
Member . . . . . :   PRODUCT              Record . . . . . :  1
Control  . . . . .                        Column . . . . . :  1
Find . . . . . . .
*...+....1....+..
1        6        Aå
2        6        O ?
3        4        AÏ"
4        17       A
5        1        O
6        3        Oè¬
7        5        A
8        3        Oã"
9        3        O
10       4        Oà|
11       1        A "
13       10       A
14       12       A
15       13       A
16       14       A
17       12       A
18       13       A
19       14       A
12       19       A
20       19       A
                    ****** END OF DATA ******

                                                                  Bottom
F3=Exit   F12=Cancel   F19=Left   F20=Right   F24=More keys
```

Notice that serials 12 and 20 have been restored at the end of the file.

REVIEW QUESTIONS

1. What does the ROLLBACK function do?
2. What type of information do journals and journal receivers contain?
3. What level of data loss do the COMMIT and ROLLBACK functions help protect against?
4. How does journaling help with data integrity and recovery?
5. What is a save file, and what is its purpose?
6. What is data compression?
7. What does "restoring" an object actually do?
8. Name two other levels at which objects can be saved.
9. What does applying journal changes actually do?

DISCUSSION QUESTIONS

1. Explain why the "simple" decision of what data to store and where to store it is not so simple.
2. What are the advantages and disadvantages regarding backup and recovery with a dual system environment?
3. What is an ASP, and how is it used to protect against disk failure?
4. How is data similar and dissimilar to other assets, and how does this affect backup and recovery?

Database Design

13

Overview

In this chapter, we will cover the procedure for designing an efficient and effective relational database. We will start with an overview of the software design process and then explore how to determine the most efficient storage organization using the data normalization process. We will also highlight some normalization rules that are especially relevant for relational databases and discuss performance and data integrity considerations in AS/400 database design.

After finishing this chapter, you will understand

- The four normalized forms of data
- The Boyce-Codd normal form of data
- Performance reasons for using redundant data and inefficient data structures
- Distributed data and distributed processing
- Physical file constraints

After finishing this chapter, you will be able to

- Organize data efficiently using normalization
- Create DDM files
- Update the distributed relational database directory
- Generate gross size estimates for AS/400 files

System Design

Like money, application systems do not grow on trees. Software is built like any physical object such as a dishwasher, car, or computer. The difference with many applications is that they are one of a kind and not mass-produced. Building a system is more like building a skyscraper or a spacecraft than a kitchen appliance. Application systems, like each new building or each succeeding spacecraft, share characteristics and parts with its predecessors; however, each new creation requires extensive design before a single screw is turned or line of code is written.

The purpose of system design is to fully understand the customer's requirements and design the most efficient system to meet those requirements. Efficient, unfortunately, is not an exact term when used to describe computer systems. A system can have many different measures of efficiency—CPU utilization, cost effectiveness, response time, effect on business revenue, and so on. The system design process tries to achieve overall maximum efficiency. But as anyone who has tried to shave time off a long drive knows, increasing speed will get you to the destination faster, but gas mileage suffers. Computer systems are much the same. Improvements in one measurement usually will adversely affect others (for example, increasing CPU utilization will adversely affect response time).

The design process, therefore, entails a series of tradeoff decisions. Because of this, one of the first things a designer does is extensively analyze the business. Through the analysis process, the designer tries to gain total knowledge of the business area. As a matter of fact, at the end of analysis the designer often knows more about the business than any customer. It's from this base of knowledge that the analyst can make the multitude of tradeoff decisions that result in the best overall system design.

One piece of system design is data design. Data design is highly dependent on the processing needs of the customer and, in turn, directly affects how processing is performed. For instance, in our school example, when our customers wanted to see a dean's list, we created a logical file DEANSLIST. Our customer's requirement directly affected our database structure. Database design will also directly affect overall system performance. Therefore, organizing the data to "fit" the system is extremely important.

To stress the importance of good database design (and stretch an analogy as far as it can go), you can think of database design as designing the fuel system for the space shuttle. NASA and the taxpayers (customers) have requirements for the space shuttle (the overall system). These overall requirements are translated into individual system (program) requirements, such as environmental controls, the radio telescope, and a grappling arm, which together dictate an overall shuttle size (storage space) and amount of lift (response time) required. These requirements will determine the size of the engine (CPU) and the fuel (data) needed. The functional requirements of the individual systems "drive" the design of the fuel (database) system. The design of the fuel (database) system includes not only identifying the fuel that will be used (defining the data) but how the fuel will be stored (how data will be organized) and how the fuel will be delivered to the engine (how data will be accessed). When the fuel (database) system is finally designed, changes in the individual systems (programs) designs regarding how they get power (data) may be needed. As a matter of fact, the fuel system decisions will affect all personnel involved with the design and operation of the shuttle. Similarly, making a decision on where and how data is stored affects every program and how each user will perform his or her job.

Database Design

The purpose of database design is to determine the optimal organization of data. The optimal design does not take up the least amount of storage space, nor does it provide the fastest response time. As we have seen many times, there is always a tradeoff between space and performance. When the final design is chosen, there will always be some organizations that provide more efficient storage with worse performance and others that have better response time but waste a large amount of space and use more redundant data.

In the time-honored business tradition of allocating the least amount of an expensive resource and then requiring justification for any additional allocations, database design starts with the global design that requires the least amount of storage space but still meets all the customer's data storage and access requirements. To create the optimal organization, the designer must determine the performance provided by that data organization and then, if needed, add space and redundant data to improve performance.

Normalization is the process that yields the most space-efficient and easily maintained organization. The "normalized" data is then used as the starting point for the tradeoff process. Adding space and redundant data to the normalized data is permitted only when it helps the overall system operate at the customer-required performance levels.

Data Normalization

Normalization is a series of steps that a designer follows to highlight and correct inefficient data organizations. For each inefficient organization, normalization specifies the structural changes that will resolve the inefficiencies. Organizations are identified as inefficient based on the "relationships" between data fields. Because normalization is based on the relationships between data, it is essential that the designer have a thorough understanding of the data and how the data is used by the customer.

The normalization process was introduced by the father of the relational database, E. Codd, in 1972, but good programmers had been intuitively using many of the techniques for years. Codd, however, provided a structured approach and formal terminology (as demonstrated with terms like "update anomalies") that pinpointed various problems that arise in data organizations and specified exactly what should be done to rectify those problems.

Another important aspect of normalization is that it can be used for general data analysis and design. Normalization does not dictate a particular data model or DBMS; therefore, most explanations of normalization avoid any specific DBMS terminology. Because normalization tries to be technology nonspecific, the terminology adopted for normalization is completely different from any DBMS. Normalization talks about "data entities" and "multivalued attributes" rather than files and fields. This terminology, of course, makes normalization more difficult to learn but greatly expands the scope of application. You'll be happy to hear that since this book is concerned specifically with the AS/400, the terms used to describe normalization will correspond to the AS/400's native database system.

We'll start with a simple, noncomputer example of data organization. The two forms in Figure 13.1 make up a student's record. The Student form is filled out once when the student is admitted to the school, and a Class History form is filled out for each class the student completes. If you were put in charge of maintaining the forms for all students, would you have any opinions about the data stored on each form?

FIGURE 13.1

Student	Class History
Student Name	Student Name
Phone #	Social Security #
Student #	Class #
Social Security #	Class Name
Marital Status	Section #
Age	Grade
GPA	Instructor
Date of Birth	Instructor ID #

Let's hope you have spoken up and demanded a school policy of not allowing anyone to get married and change his or her name. If you haven't, then whenever a student changes his or her name, you will have to change every Class History form for that student. Further, doesn't it seem like a waste of paper and ink (and your time) to rewrite the student, class, and instructor name on every Class History form? For classes with 500 students, this would mean writing the instructor's name 500 times—once for each student in the class!

Though this may not sound like high-level analysis, these two observations have hit on one of the major problems with bad design—redundant data. Redundant data not only wastes space but also increases processing time and the chance of **update anomalies**. Update anomalies is a fancy way of saying update errors. Many data organizations greatly increase the potential for data error and loss. These organizations are said to have a greater chance of update anomalies. These same organizations, because of redundant data, also require extra processing to maintain or modify the data. For instance, when entering the instructor's name for the 500 students who took Introduction to Biology, you are bound to make spelling errors. The chance of this update error (anomaly) occurring is much greater because of the poor data organization that causes the instructor's name to be repeated on many forms. The extra processing time caused by redundant data is illustrated by imagining how long it would take to modify an instructor's name if he or she married. The name would have to be updated on every Class History form. For the Biology class alone, this would mean updating the name 500 times. With a good organization, the instructor's name would be written only once, resulting in much faster updating and less chance of errors.

Normalization is the process that yields the least redundant organization of data.

First Normal Form

The "normal forms" refer to how data is organized after a normalization "step" has been performed. For instance, one record layout (organization) for implementing the Class History form as a file can be seen in Figure 13.2.

FIGURE 13.2

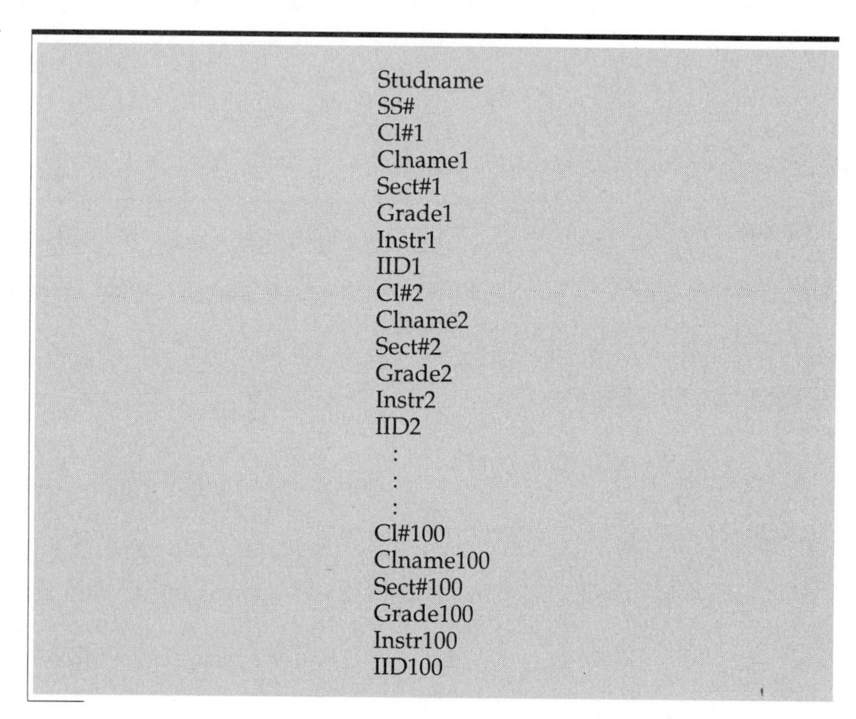

Studname
SS#
Cl#1
Clname1
Sect#1
Grade1
Instr1
IID1
Cl#2
Clname2
Sect#2
Grade2
Instr2
IID2
:
:
:
Cl#100
Clname100
Sect#100
Grade100
Instr100
IID100

The first step in normalization is to identify and eliminate repeating data fields within an organization. By eliminate, we do not mean erase the data; rather, we need to eliminate the wasted space caused by repeating data fields. To demonstrate how this organization wastes space, imagine that the file was built as in Figure 13.2. Notice that we allocated space for each student to take 100 classes. From your personal experience, how many people take 100 classes in their college careers? Not many (unless you're hanging out with a very nerdy crowd). Student records for people like Frank Freshman, who hasn't completed a single class, or Sally Sophomore, who has taken only ten classes, would be predominantly empty. Since 90 percent of all alumni took only 40 classes to graduate but we built the database to accommodate Joe Genius, who took 100 classes back in the 1950s, this file organization results in an incredible amount of wasted space.

There are two ways to eliminate the repeating fields. The first is shown in Figure 13.3. This solution changes the file structure such that the repeating fields appear only once. However, this solution also requires that a separate record be entered into the file for each class a student completes. In other words, CLASSHISTORY holds multiple records for each student, and each record contains information regarding one class that the student has taken. This method to solve the inefficiency can be generally stated as follows:

FIGURE 13.3

CLASSHISTORY

Studname	SS#	Cl#	Clname	Sect#	Grade	Instr	IID
Genius, Jill	999999999	BIO101	Intro to Bio	96201	A	Galen	001
Genius, Jill	999999999	BUS101	Intro to Bus	96203	A	Beane	777
Genius, Jill	999999999	PSY212	DeviantPsych	96203	A	Hyde	666
Sewso, Samuel	555555555	CMP101	Intro to Comp	96306	B	Jobs	333
Sewso, Samuel	555555555	BUS101	Intro to Bus	96201	C	Jones	555
Sewso, Samuel	555555555	ACC101	Intro to Acct	96306	B	Beane	777
Dreags, Don	111111111	BUS101	Intro to Bus	96201	I	Jones	555
Dreags,Don	111111111	BIO101	Intro to Bio	96201	D	Galen	111
Dreags,Don	111111111	CMP101	Intro to Comp	96306	F	Jobs	999
Dreags,Don	111111111	CMP101	Intro to Comp	96401	C	Jobs	999

Change the original structure to include only one occurrence of the repeating fields.

Create a separate record for each occurrence of the repeating data.

The second method of eliminating repeating fields is to remove the fields from the original file and create a new file that contains one occurrence of the repeating fields. This solution uses two files to hold all the information. In this case, CLGRADE has a single record for each class completed, and STUDENT contains one record for each student. The alternative organization that eliminates the repeating fields can be seen in Figure 13.4.

FIGURE 13.4

CLGRADE

SS#	Cl#	Clname	Sect#	Grade	Instr	IID
999999999	BIO101	Intro to Bio	96201	A	Galen	001
999999999	BUS101	Intro to Bus	96203	A	Beane	777
999999999	PSY212	Deviant Psych	96203	A	Hyde	666
555555555	CMP101	Intro to Comp	96306	B	Jobs	333
555555555	BUS101	Intro to Bus	96306	C	Jones	555
555555555	ACC101	Intro to Acct	96306	B	Beane	777
111111111	BUS101	Intro to Bus	96201	I	Jones	555
111111111	BIO101	Intro to Bio	96201	D	Galen	001
111111111	CMP101	Intro to Comp	96306	F	Jobs	999
111111111	CMP101	Intro to Comp	96401	C	Jobs	999

STUDENT

Studname	SS#
Genius, Jill	999999999
Sewso, Samuel	555555555
Dreags, Don	111111111

This second method of eliminating repeating fields can be generally stated as follows:

Create a new structure containing the repeating fields.

Eliminate the repeating fields from the original structure.

Both methods of eliminating repeating fields put the data into first normal form (1NF). However, just by looking at the two organizations, you should be able to tell that Figure 13.4 is more efficient. The two files CLGRADE and STUDENT seem to take up less space than the single CLASSHISTORY file in Figure 13.3. This is because the second method (and the results in Figure 13.4) eliminate some inefficiencies that are dealt with in the second normal form of data.

Notice also in Figure 13.4 that when we used two files to hold all the data, the ability to join the data records in the different files was maintained by having the student social security number in both files. One important aspect of normalization is that when creating any new structures, all the data should be able to be retrieved through a joined logical file. In this case, placing SS# in CLGRADE satisfied this requirement.

You may be wondering why did social security number go into CLGRADE? Couldn't we have incorporated Cl# in STUDENT? Yes, we could have taken the second option, but to store all the class numbers a student takes in the STUDENT record would mean that multiple CL# fields would have to be incorporated into the STUDENT file. This means that a repeating field would be in STUDENT, and therefore, STUDENT would no longer be in first normal form. To explain this situation, let's look a little more closely at the relationship between CLGRADE and STUDENT data.

CLGRADE and STUDENT have a one-to-many relationship—that is, a particular grade is for only *one* student, but a student can be associated with *many* grades. This relationship is shown with an arrow diagram as follows:

```
STUDENT <------------->> CLGRADE
```

A one-to-many relationship is implemented in a relational database by putting the key of the "one file" (STUDENT) record into each record of the "many file" (CLGRADE)—in other words, putting the key of STUDENT, SS#, into CLGRADE. If we did it the other way around, placed all the many file (CLGRADE) keys in each one file (STUDENT) record, we would have had to design the STUDENT file to hold up to 100 CLGRADE keys. The CLGRADE keys would constitute a repeating field, and the STUDENT file would no longer be in first normal form. Therefore, to implement a one-to-many relationship, the many file is modified to include a foreign key (the one file key field(s)).

Many-to-many relationships are a little more difficult to implement. With a many-to-many relationship, placing a foreign key into either of the files would result in repeating fields. Relational data-base designers use a correlation file to maintain a many-to-many relationship.

The correlation file contains the key fields from each file, and each correlation file record has one unique combination of key values.

For instance, if the school implemented team teaching for classes, each class could have multiple teachers, and each teacher would have multiple classes. The relationship would look like the following:

```
Instructor <<------------------->> Class
```

To capture the fact that multiple instructors can teach a class, we could create multiple instructor fields in CLGRADE. However, this would mean CLGRADE was no longer in first normal form. The best solution for many-to-many relationships is to create a correlation file with the keys of the two files that have the many-to-many relationship. In this case, the correlation file would include CL#, SECT#, and IID. Each class is uniquely identified by CL# and SECT#, and each instructor is identified by IID. The correlation file's key would comprise all three fields, and there would be a correlation file record for each instructor teaching any portion of a class. The resulting file relationships would look like the following:

```
Instructor <------->> Correlation file <<-------> CLGRADE
```

Each instructor or CLGRADE record can be associated with many correlation file records. But each correlation record is associated with only one Instructor record and one CLGRADE record.

So our second method for eliminating repeating fields should have a third step to ensure that the new file(s) can be joined to the original file. The third step will depend on the type of relationship between the two files.

For one-to-many relationships, introduce a foreign key by duplicating the key of the one file in the many file.

For many-to-many relationships, create a correlation file containing the keys of the two files.

For simplicity's sake, we will assume that there is no team teaching in our future examples.

Second Normal Form

After all the repeating fields have been removed, the designer is ready to move on to the second step. The second normal form of data eliminates any partial dependencies on the key.

"Dependent" has a special meaning in normalization. A field is dependent on another field when its value can be determined or is directly related to the other field. For instance, STUDNAME is dependent on SS# because the SS# dictates the name. Only one name is associated with each SS#. A field can still be dependent on the key (or another field) even though it cannot be determined by the key value. For instance, a particular grade is assigned to a student for each class taken. Though the grades for different classes and different students can be the same, a specific grade is associated with each student and class.

If a file's key is made up of many fields (the file has a multifield key), the designer wants to make sure that all fields within the record are fully dependent on the key. In other words, the designer wants to eliminate any fields that are dependent on only part of the key. This "partial dependency" condition is inefficient because it results in redundant data between records. For instance, notice in CLGRADE that information, such as class name, is repeated on many data records. This repetition occurs because the field CLNAME is not fully dependent on the file's key, which is made up of the fields SS#, CL#, and SECT#. The value in the CLNAME field is dependent only on the value in CL#. Or in other words, CLNAME is said to be partially dependent on the key.

Once the partially dependent fields are identified, normalization tells the designer to create a new file containing the partially dependent fields and the key fields on which they are dependent. The portion of the key (on which the fields are dependent) is not removed from the original file; rather, those fields are duplicated in the new file. The fields are duplicated so that the files can be joined through a logical file.

This procedure eliminates the redundant data, thereby reducing the amount of space needed and decreasing the chance of update anomalies. Our school example will illustrate this better. Because CLNAME is dependent only on CL#, we would remove CLNAME from CLGRADE and create a new file called CLASS that contains the CL# and CLNAME fields. The data and files would look like Figure 13.5.

FIGURE 13.5

CLGRADE

SS#	Cl#	Sect#	Grade	Instr	IID
999999999	BIO101	96201	A	Galen	001
999999999	BUS101	96203	A	Beane	777
999999999	PSY212	96203	A	Hyde	666
555555555	CMP101	96306	B	Jobs	333
555555555	BUS101	96306	C	Jones	555
555555555	ACC101	96306	B	Beane	777
111111111	BUS101	96201	I	Jones	555
111111111	BIO101	96201	D	Galen	001
111111111	CMP101	96306	F	Jobs	333
111111111	CMP101	96401	C	Jobs	333

CLASS

Cl#	Clname
BIO101	Intro to Bio
BUS101	Intro to Bus
PSY212	Deviant Psych
CMP101	Intro to Comp
ACC101	Intro to Acct

CLSTUD

Studname	SS#
Genius, Jill	999999999
Sewso, Samuel	555555555
Dreags, Don	111111111

Notice the savings in space in the database because we eliminated the partial dependency. (This database has only three students; imagine the savings if there were 80,000 students.) Besides space savings, this organization decreases the chance of update anomalies mentioned earlier. For instance, when the data was in 1NF, we had to enter the class name for each student taking the class. The old file organization (and the 500 students each semester taking Introduction to Biology) gave us 500 chances to make an error. With the new file structures, the name of the class is entered only once, no matter how many students take the class.

Another update anomaly was possible when the data was in 1NF. Entering information about a new class meant entering a record into CLGRADE that contained "dummy" student information. Since no student could take a course until it is entered into CLGRADE, the only way to get the class information into the file was by creating false student information or leaving the student information blank. This could cause several processing problems. First, incorrect data is being entered by putting in a false SS# or blanks. If we try to join CLGRADE and STUDENT, there will be no matching SS# for a false or blank social security number in the STUDENT file. In addition, when a student finally does enroll in the class, the "dummy record" is no longer needed and must be eliminated (otherwise, reports will be generated listing the dummy student information). If we kept the files in 1NF, programs would have to be written to check for these conditions and perform the deletions. With a separate structure for CLASS, new class data can be entered without entering any dummy student information. Updating and maintaining data in 2NF is simpler, the chance of errors is decreased, and space is saved.

Our structure, however, is still not in 2NF. A designer (with complete understanding of the data and its relationships) would also know that the instructor and instructor id are not fully dependent on the key. Instructor information is dependent only on CLASS# and SECT#. The instructor is not dependent on which student takes the class. (That is, regardless of the student, the instructor will always be the same.) The instructor information's partial dependency on the key is also evident by the fact that the instructor names and ids repeat between records. According to normalization, to get the data into second normal form, we need to remove the partially dependent fields from the file and create a new file containing the partially dependent fields and the key fields on which they are dependent. In this case, it means creating a new file called SECTION, which contains the instructor data (Instr and

IID) and the key fields on which it is dependent (CLASS# and SECT#). The new organization can be seen in Figure 13.6.

FIGURE 13.6

CLGRADE

SS#	Cl#	Sect#	Grade
999999999	BIO101	96201	A
999999999	BUS101	96203	A
999999999	PSY212	96203	A
555555555	CMP101	96306	B
555555555	BUS101	96306	C
555555555	ACC101	96306	B
111111111	BUS101	96201	I
111111111	BIO101	96201	D
111111111	CMP101	96306	F
111111111	CMP101	96401	C

CLASS

Cl#	Clname
BIO101	Intro to Bio
BUS101	Intro to Bus
PSY212	Deviant Psych
CMP101	Intro to Comp
ACC101	Intro to Acct

STUDENT

Studname	SS#
Genius, Jill	99999999
Sewso, Samuel	555555555
Dreags, Don	111111111

SECTION

Cl#	Sect#	Instr	IID
BIO101	96201	Galen	001
BUS101	96203	Beane	777
PSY212	96203	Hyde	666
CMP101	96306	Jobs	333
BUS101	96306	Jones	555
ACC101	96306	Beane	777
BUS101	96201	Jones	555

Third Normal Form

The second normal form identified fields that were partially dependent on the key. The third normal form removes fields that are not dependent *at all* on the key. Some fields appear to be dependent on the key but in actuality are dependent on another nonkey field within the record. These fields are said to have a **transitive dependency**. The first step toward organizing the data into third normal form is to identify fields that are dependent on a nonkey field(s).

In our class example, instructor name in SECTION seems to be dependent on the key field Sect#. However, instructor name is actually dependent on the instructor id. Instructor name and instructor id have a dependent relationship. Because instructor name is only transitively dependent on the key, the instructor name is duplicated throughout the database. The duplicated instructor name has the same space and updating problems as duplicated data resulting from partially dependent fields. To eliminate these problems (and put the data into 3NF), we need to create a new file that contains the transitively dependent field(s) and the field(s) it is dependent on. In this case, we create a file for instructor name and id as seen in Figure 13.7.

FIGURE 13.7

CLGRADE

SS#	Cl#	Sect#	Grade
999999999	BIO101	96201	A
999999999	BUS101	96203	A
999999999	PSY212	96203	A
555555555	CMP101	96306	B
555555555	BUS101	96306	C
555555555	ACC101	96306	B
111111111	BUS101	96201	I
111111111	BIO101	96201	D
111111111	CMP101	96306	F
111111111	CMP101	96401	C

CLASS

Cl#	Clname
BIO101	Intro to Bio
BUS101	Intro to Bus
PSY212	Deviant Psych
CMP101	Intro to Comp
ACC101	Intro to Acct

STUDENT

Studname	SS#
Genius, Jill	999999999
Sewso, Samuel	555555555
Dreags, Don	111111111

SECTION

Cl#	Sect#	IID
BIO101	96201	001
BUS101	96203	777
PSY212	96203	666
CMP101	96306	333
BUS101	96306	555
ACC101	96306	777
BUS101	96201	555

INSTRUCTOR

IID	Instr
001	Galen
777	Beane
666	Hyde
333	Jobs
555	Jones

Once again, the justification for creating the new structure is space savings and ease of updating. In 2NF, any updates to a instructor name or id would have required multiple updates to SECTION records (see Figure 13.6). Furthermore, whenever a new section was created, the instructor's name would have to be reentered. Because the name is entered multiple times, the chances for misspelling or not matching the name to the correct IID are much greater.

Another update anomaly with the old organization was that instructor information could not be added unless there was section data. Dummy section numbers and class numbers could be used; however, just as before, this would mean that the application programs must be aware that there are no matches in CLASS for the dummy class information and that the dummy record should be removed as soon as a real entry is made.

Boyce-Codd Normal Form

Usually, a designer doesn't have to go any further than the third normal form of data. However, several other normal forms deal with special situations. Each specialized normal form results in an organization that provides even further space savings and less chance of update anomalies. However, there are fewer situations where these specialized normal forms come into play, and therefore, there is not as much benefit from normalizing to this extent. We will deal with just two other normal forms: the Boyce-Codd normal form (BCNF) and the fourth normal form. These are both particularly appropriate for relational databases.

BCNF deals with the special case where a multifield key is partially dependent on a nonkey field. 3NF ensured that all fields were dependent on the key fields. Any transitive dependencies were eliminated by creating new structures, but 3NF did not deal with any key field dependencies. 3NF allowed a key field to be dependent on a nonkey field. BCNF does not allow this condition to exist.

If we had three fields (as in Figure 13.8) where fields 1 and 2 made up the key, field 2 could be dependent on field 3 and the file would still be in 3NF (because field 3 is also dependent on the key of field 1 and field 2).

FIGURE 13.8

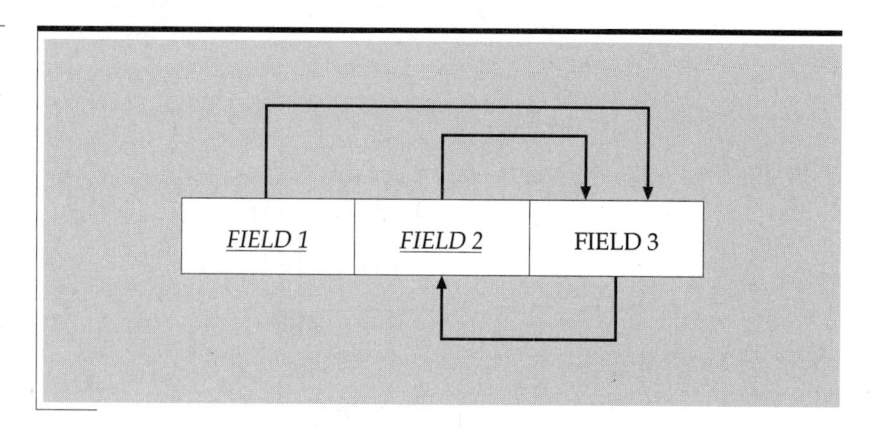

To better illustrate the problem, imagine that a computer store sells a variety of computers. (which shouldn't be to hard to imagine). Inventory information regarding each computer, such as the model number, the size of the hard drive, and so on is stored in a file called inventory. This file's key is the manufacturer's serial number and manufacturer name. The file structure and sample data records look like Figure 13.9.

FIGURE 13.9

INVENTORY

MSN	*MANFCT*	MODNUM	HDSIZE	other data
0001	IBM	PS2/50	120	XXXXXXXXXX
0001	APPLE	PM7100	250	XXXXXXXXXX
0002	IBM	PS2/90	240	XXXXXXXXXX
0003	IBM	PS2/50	180	XXXXXXXXXX
0004	IBM	PS2/50	120	XXXXXXXXXX
0005	IBM	PS2/50	120	XXXXXXXXXX
0004	APPLE	PM7100	180	XXXXXXXXXX
0007	IBM	PS2/90	180	XXXXXXXXXX

This structure is in 3NF because all the fields are dependent on the key. However, there is also a dependency between MODNUM and MANFCT. Given the model number, you can always tell the manufacturer (only IBM manufactures PS2/50s, only APPLE manufactures 7100s, and so on). Therefore, part of the key (MANFCT) is dependent on a nonkey field (MODNUM).

The problems with this type of dependency are the same as all the others: redundant data resulting in wasted space and complex updating. The BCNF solution is to move the dependent key field and the nonkey field it is dependent on into a different file. In terms of Figure 13.9, we would create a new file called MODEL and remove MANFCT and MODNUM from INVENTORY. BCNF also dictates that the key of the original file should now include the nonkey field. In our example, we would replace MANFCT in the INVENTORY file key with MODNUM (Figure 13.10). Notice that this also allows the two files to be joined.

FIGURE 13.10

INVENTORY

MSN	*MODNUM*	HDSIZE	other data
0001	PS2/50	120	XXXXXXXXXX
0001	PM7100	250	XXXXXXXXXX
0002	PS2/90	240	XXXXXXXXXX
0003	PS2/50	180	XXXXXXXXXX
0004	PS2/50	120	XXXXXXXXXX
0005	PS2/50	120	XXXXXXXXXX
0004	PM7100	180	XXXXXXXXXX
0007	PS2/90	180	XXXXXXXXXX

MODEL

MODNUM	*MANFCT*
PS2/50	IBM
PS2/90	IBM
PM7100	APPLE

INVENTORY would now be keyed by MSN and MODNUM, and the repeating values of IBM and APPLE would be eliminated from the file INVENTORY.

Fourth Normal Form

4NF is concerned with multifield keys that have many-to-many relationships between the individual fields that make up the key. (How's that for a mouthful of definition.) The many-to-many relationships between key fields result in repeating values between records or empty space. For instance, our instructors also advise students, and students can have multiple advisors. In addition, instructors are advisors to student activities such as the school paper, honor societies, and various clubs. To keep track of each student and activity for which an instructor is responsible, we could modify the INSTRUCT file as seen in Figure 13.11 and define the key as IID, SS#, and ACTCODE. (These fields will provide a unique value for each record.)

FIGURE 13.11

IID	SS#	ACTCODE	INSTR
001	999999999	paper	Galen
001	555555555	paper	Galen
777	111111111	chess	Beane
666	999999999	paper	Hyde
333	555555555	pbk	Jobs
333	111111111	chess	Jobs
555	333333333		Jones

The relationships between the fields would look like the following:

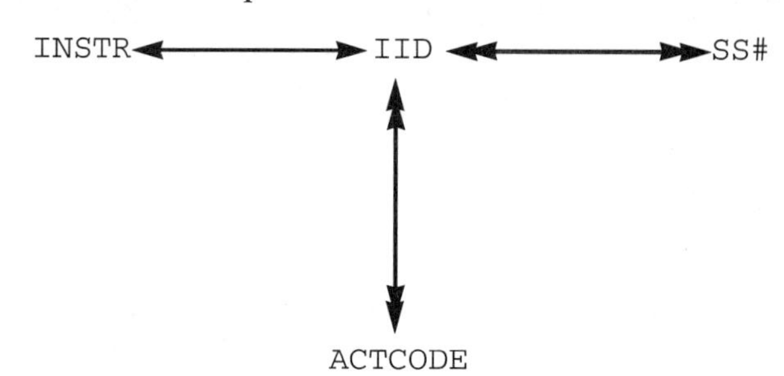

When we try to bring the structure into second normal form, we would remove INSTR because it is dependent on only part of the key, IID. This would leave us with Figure 13.12, with all the remaining fields making up the key.

FIGURE 13.12

IID	SS#	ACTCODE
001	999999999	paper
001	555555555	paper
777	111111111	chess
666	999999999	paper
333	555555555	pbk
333	111111111	chess
555	333333333	

Notice that this file structure leaves us with some problems that we have seen before. Updating an instructor's activities may require changing many records. For instance, if Galen, IID = 001, decides not to be the faculty advisor for the paper, we need to update multiple records. Moreover, if instructor 333 no longer advises student 555555555 and we delete the record, we will lose the information that he is the faculty advisor to the Phi Beta Kappa honor society. Instead of deleting the entire record, we could simply blank out the student id; however, this would result in a record with empty space.

The root of these problems is the many-to-many relationships between instructor and student and between instructor and activity. To bring the data into 4NF, we need to create two separate files to clearly delineate the many-to-many relationships (Figure 13.13).

Now, if instructor 333 no longer counsels student 555555555, the ADVISORS record can be erased, and no instructor activity information will be lost. Further, if an instructor advises a student, a single ADVISORS record would be entered into the ADVISORS file. No dummy activity data or blanks would have to be entered in the files, nor would any special maintenance programs need to be written.

FIGURE 13.13

ADVISORS

IID	SS#
001	999999999
001	555555555
777	111111111
666	999999999
333	555555555
333	111111111
555	333333333

ACTIVITIES

IID	ACTCODE
001	paper
777	chess
666	paper
333	pbk
333	chess

Over-Normalizing

As with all good things, sometimes too much is not so good. There is a point where creating separate structures doesn't make sense. The purpose of creating new structures is to save space and group data logically so that updating is simpler. The pursuit of space savings can sometimes go too far and result in "unnatural" grouping of data or the creation of fields that are "data processing constructs."

For instance, a close look at the grade and section numbers in CLGRADE could result in the conclusion that there are many repeating values. Section numbers repeat between classes, and there are only seven possible grade outcomes (A, B, C, D, F, I, W). We could create a structure called OUTCOME that has a record for each section number and grade combination. Each OUTCOME record would have a unique id (OID, outcome id), as seen in Figure 13.14.

The question the designer needs to ask is "What is the data in OUTCOME?" Does it relate to anything in our customers' business? The data contained in OUTCOME has no logical connection, nor does it relate to anything our customer would want to see. These are both signs of over-normalizing.

Another test for over-normalization is "Does the new structure

FIGURE 13.14

CLGRADE

SS#	Cl#	OID
999999999	BIO101	1
999999999	BUS101	8
999999999	PSY212	8
555555555	CMP101	142
555555555	BUS101	143
555555555	ACC101	142
111111111	BUS101	7
111111111	BIO101	4
111111111	CMP101	146
111111111	CMP101	248

OUTCOME

OID	SECT#	GRADE
1	96201	A
2	96201	B
3	96201	C
4	96201	D
5	96201	E
6	96201	F
7	96201	I
8	96203	A
9	96203	B
10	96203	C
:	:	:
252	96401	I

solve any update problems?" Was there a chance that we would have an inconsistency in data, as with the computer manufacturer and model number? Again the answer is no. A course's section number has no bearing on the grade that is assigned. We removed model number and manufacturer (from our earlier example) to a separate file to reduce the chance of putting in an erroneous manufacturer for a particular model. Separating section number and grade does not serve a similar purpose.

Other Levels of Database Design

Once normalization is complete, the designer will have a global view of all the data. The term *global view* means that all the data fields have been identified, the fields have been grouped into files, and the file relationships have been documented. Two other levels of design need to be addressed, the **user** and **physical design**. User design means defining all the individual views of data that users need to perform their jobs. On the AS/400, these "user views" would translate into logical files, SQL views, or query programs.

Another important function of user design is that it "double checks" the global design. The overall design should support all the user views. This means the global design should store all the necessary data to support the views and provide the means to join or access the data as the user desires. For instance, the designer may find that the school employees need to retrieve lists of classes for a particular discipline (business, biology, psychology). The designer needs to ensure that the global design is built to support this view. Looking at our class numbers, we see that they are made up of a three-character discipline code and a three-digit class number. Our customer's view of the data (classes grouped by discipline) would be better supported if we broke the class number into two fields, DISCIPLINE and NUMBER. This would enable the user to access all the classes by the DISCIPLINE field. User design will usually uncover even more fundamental problems such as missing data fields. (So don't feel bad the first time you perform user design and see how many things you missed during global design.)

The final phase, the physical design, is usually done by a specialist in the particular hardware and software adopted for data management. For the AS/400, only a few areas of physical design can be controlled, such as the order of the records within a file or the location of data on specific storage devices. Both of these physical issues are not trivial. They can directly affect performance and the ability to recover lost data. With the increasing popularity of distributed processing, the actual geographic location or particular machine on which the data will reside is also part of the physical design. With OS/400 Version 3, there will be many enhancements to the database that support distributed processing, or as it is more popularly known, **client–server processing**. The next section will discuss current features of the AS/400 that help with distributed databases and client–server processing.

Database design also includes defining data queues and data areas. Certain information will be better suited to these data structures than files. Identifying critical data for backup and recovery and designing the backup and recovery procedures are also both integral parts of the data design process. No database can be considered properly defined until all these issues are resolved.

Distributed Data and Distributed Processing

Distributed data, distributed processing, and client–server processing are all hot buzzwords. As with all buzzwords, a precise definition is needed to understand the implementation requirements.

Distributed data is a concept that advocates placing data at the location where it will be used. For instance, a companywide inventory file for a retail organization such as Wal-Mart or Sears would contain information regarding each store location's inventory (for instance, the number of washing machines in the Muncie, Indiana, store). In a nondistributed data environment (also called a centralized data environment), all information is in one database at one physical location. Whenever users in Muncie want to look at inventory, they must access the data at the central location. This type of processing takes time and incurs large telecommunication costs.

One distributed implementation of the inventory file would be to place each store's inventory data at the store location (for instance, the Muncie, Indiana, data would reside on a computer in the Muncie store). Distributing data has its advantages. For example, users can access the store information faster, and no telecommunications costs are incurred. Moreover, if telecommunications lines are disrupted or the main computer is offline, users can still access the local information.

There are, however, disadvantages to not having a central location for all information. For instance, if access to companywide inventory records is needed, all communication lines and local systems must be up. If there are 10,000 stores, the chances are pretty good that some will be inaccessible. In addition, distributing data requires that someone at each location be responsible for the data. With centralized data, one backup program can save all the inventory data. With distributed data, 10,000 separate backup programs must be run. What do you think the chances are that every store will diligently back up their data? In general, distributed data is more difficult to control and access in its entirety than centralized data.

Distributed processing is concerned with where application programs are run. Where the data is located will have a big impact on this decision. For instance, if the data is centrally located, running a program on the Muncie machine to search the data on the central computer (which is miles away) would not be very efficient. If the distributed program were searching the centralized inventory file for the number of washing machines in the Muncie store, each record in the inventory file would have to be sent to the Muncie machine. The program on the Muncie machine would then check each record to see if it contained Muncie washing machine data. Obviously, in the case of centralized data, it would be better to run a program on the central machine to search the database and then send the appropriate Muncie washing machine data to the Muncie machine. This is an example of centralized data with a central computer acting as a **file server**.

If the inventory data were distributed, however, it would make more sense to run the search program on a local machine. In this case, the search program would run on the Muncie machine and search the Muncie inventory data for washing machine data.

There are pluses and minuses to distributed versus centralized processing. Certainly, centralized processing and data or distributed processing and data are better than centralized data and distributed processing or distributed data and centralized processing. (Think about that.) However, a totally centralized or distributed environment will probably not be best for an entire organization or complex application. Some blend of both centralized and distributed processing and data is generally required. This blend is called a client–server environment. For instance, we might keep the data centralized but distribute data on request for processing at distributed locations. If a user wanted to calculate the total value of inventory for the Muncie store, a program on the central computer would be run to select all the Muncie data. The data would be passed to the local computer where a program would calculate the total inventory value. Notice that data is distributed (when requested) and processing occurs both at the central and local locations.

AS/400 Distributed Data Support

Decisions regarding the physical location of data have an immediate impact for AS/400 database designers. The AS/400 currently has two tools that support distributed data. DDM (distributed data management) supports native access to AS/400 files and SQL tables. The RDBD (relational database directory) supports SQL/400 access to distributed SQL tables. AS/400 database designers need to create DDM files or add entries to the RDBD to access distributed native DB files or remote SQL tables.

DDM files are created with the CRTDDMF (create DDM file) command. The DDM file acts as a path to the distributed file. In other words, DDM files contain no data. DDM files contain "directions" to a remote file that contains data. When a DDM file is created, the user must at least specify the name of the DDM file, name of the remote file, and system on which the remote file resides.

For our store example, if the inventory data were distributed to each store, each store would hold the data in a library called INV and a file called OURS. To access the data on the Muncie AS/400, we would have to create a DDM file on our AS/400 that identified the Muncie file. We could create the DDM file as follows:

```
CRTDDMF FILE(INV/MUNCIE) RMTLOCNAME(MUNCIE)
        RMTFILE(INV/OURS)
```

If a program or query needed Muncie data, the programmer would simply "read" the DDM file INV/MUNCIE. When the request for data from INV/MUNCIE is passed to the operating system, OS/400 will read the DDM file and initiate a communication session with the remote system identified by the DDM file (that is, Muncie). An operating system program is started on the Muncie AS/400, which retrieves and sends the data back to the requesting system. OS/400 then supplies the data to the requesting program or query. All this is done without the programmer having to worry about where the data is physically located or how to access it. (Of course, several networking prerequisites need to be filled to successfully use DDM files. However, these concerns are outside the scope of this book and should be handled by the system network administrator.)

If the remote data is stored in an SQL table, the table can be accessed through a DDM file in the same manner as described for native files. However, remote tables can also be accessed if they are identified in the **relational database directory**. The RDBD acts as a single source of "directions" to all remote SQL databases. When users want to access a remote table, they simply connect to the remote database and, using SQL statements, identify the particular collection and table to be accessed.

To access a remote table through the directory, the user needs to first add a directory entry. This is done with the ADDRDBDIRE (add relational database directory entry) command. (There are individual CL commands to add, delete, change, or display directory entries. There is also a work command that provides access to all these functions.) For instance, to identify the Muncie database, the command would be as follows:

```
ADDRDBDIRE RDB(MUNCIE) RMTLOCNAME(MUNCIE)
```

This would create a directory entry on our computer for the Muncie database.

To access the Muncie data, the user has to connect to the remote database. This is done with the CONNECT TO statement. After connecting to the database, SQL commands such as SELECT and JOIN would be used to identify the remote collection and table that contains the data. SQL commands accessing remote data can be issued interactively, from a query management query or from an application program.

To see the Muncie inventory quantity for part number 11111, the user would issue the following SQL statements:

```
CONNECT TO MUNCIE
SELECT QTY FROM INV/OURS WHERE PART# = '11111'
```

If we wanted to then find the quantity of the part in Santa Fe (assuming a directory entry existed for Santa Fe), we would enter:

```
CONNECT TO SANTAFE
SELECT QTY FROM INV/OURS WHERE PART# = '11111'
```

Our directory entries would include entries for Muncie, Santa Fe, and our own local database. If we issued the DSPRDBDIRE (display relational database directory entries) command, the screen would look like Figure 13.15.

FIGURE 13.15

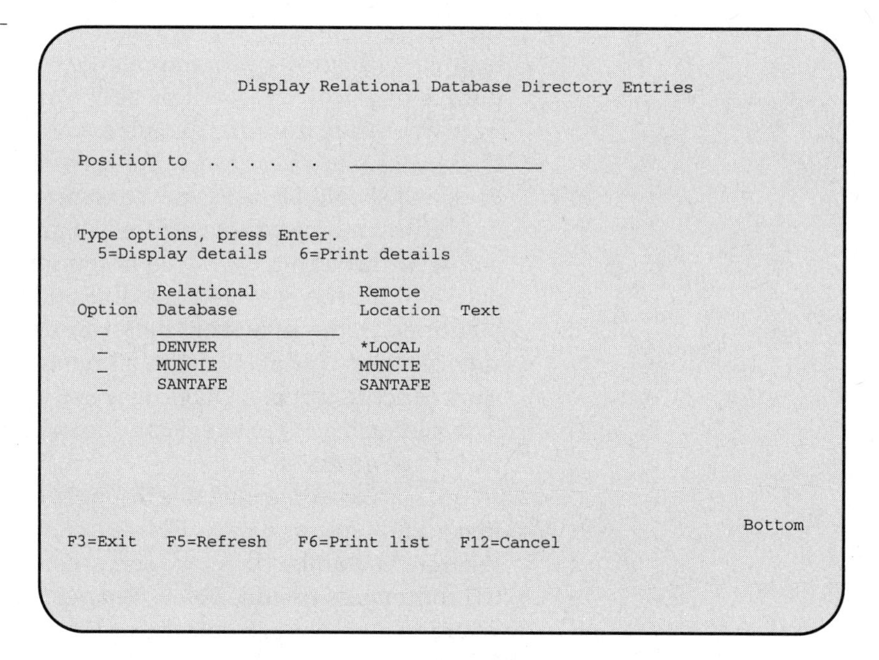

```
                Display Relational Database Directory Entries

Position to . . . . . .   ________________

Type options, press Enter.
  5=Display details   6=Print details

        Relational           Remote
Option  Database             Location  Text
  _     ________________
  _     DENVER               *LOCAL
  _     MUNCIE               MUNCIE
  _     SANTAFE              SANTAFE

                                                              Bottom
F3=Exit   F5=Refresh   F6=Print list   F12=Cancel
```

Both Muncie and Santa Fe would also have RDBD entries for all three locations. The difference would be that each location would specify their locations' database as *LOCAL.

The AS/400 developers are enhancing and creating system functions to further facilitate client–server processing. The ability to create client applications that can execute programs on the server is provided in OS/400 Version 3 through **stored procedures**. Stored procedures are user-created programs on a server computer (AS/400) that can be called by programs running on local machines (PCs). In addition, system utilities to quickly create and propagate copies of data will be included in the OS/400 Version 3 family of releases.

Relational Database Integrity

Because redundant data is used to join tables in relational databases, maintaining data is more difficult. Update anomalies can occur whenever data is changed, deleted, or inserted. For instance, what happens to our school database if a course number changes? If the customers tell us that all CLGRADE records should also be changed, a program is needed to change all the records that contain the course number.

(A program would be used to reduce the chances of any update anomalies.) What about when an instructor leaves? Erasing the instructor record would also create an anomaly. Some SECTION records would have no matching IID number in the INSTRUCTOR file.

What about inserts? Earlier we talked about how inserts to data in 1NF could cause anomalies (the need for dummy data when inserting records). Even with fully normalized data, inserts can cause anomalies. For instance, a CLGRADE record should not be inserted if it contains a SS# that does not exist in the CLSTUD file. The same is true if the values of CL# and SECT# don't exist in the SECTION file. Furthermore, SECTION records should not be inserted if a matching CLASS record does not exist.

The business rules regarding data maintenance are usually very complex and closely tied to the relationships between files. Because the maintenance rules are based on file relationships, it is important that during the DB design process all relationships between files be thoroughly understood and documented. When this has been done, determining the rules for inserting, updating, and deleting will be easier.

As we said, the relationships between files will determine the integrity rules for updating, inserting, and deleting. As an example, general rules for updating, inserting, and deleting should be determined for all files that have a one-to-many relationship:

> Should updates to a parent records' key value be reflected in the child records?
>
> For child record insertions, should a matching parent record exist?
>
> Should parent record deletions be allowed if a child record exists, or should the deletion of a parent record cascade to the child file (should all the children records be deleted)?

Once the rules are determined, they are normally enforced in application programs. Whenever an insert, update, or delete occurs, the application program must include and check the appropriate rules. Using tools such as SQL or DFU on the AS/400, however, will circumvent the rules in the application programs. The AS/400 developers are aware of this problem and have announced that DB2/400 (Version 3 of the AS/400 DBMS) will support trigger programs (which we discussed in Chapter 4) and **referential integrity constraints**. Both tools can be used to enforce business rules that ensure data integrity.

Trigger programs can be tied to a particular file such that whenever an update, insert, or deletion occurs, a trigger program is activated. Trigger programs can include integrity rules. Having trigger programs enforce the rules avoids duplicating the rule program logic in many application programs, and it ensures that the rules are enforced for all updating, whether from user applications or system utilities like DFU.

Referential integrity constraints will be part of the OS/400 Version 3 family of releases. A constraint is defined by the CL command ADDPFCST (add physical file constraint). This command allows the user to specify the:

- Type of constraint (referential, delete, update)
- Files that share a relationship
- Fields the constraint is based on
- Rules of the constraint

The rules of a constraint can be:

- Restrict—Do not allow the action if child records exist.
- No Action—Enforce the constraint only after all updating is complete.
- Cascade—Perform the action against all child records.
- Set Default—Set the identified child record fields to their default value.
- Set Null—Set the identified child record fields to null.

For instance, if we defined a deletion constraint between instructors and classes, we might specify the rule as Set Null. Defining the rule as Set Null means that when an instructor record is deleted, any classes that are being offered with that instructor should have their instructor field set to blanks. Of course, if the database can't accept nulls in the instructor field, we might have to set the constraint to Restrict. This would mean that if any Class records contained the instructor id being deleted, the instructor record deletion would not be allowed. In order to delete the instructor record, the Class records would have to be modified first. (New instructors would have to be assigned to the classes.)

Constraints are independent of any program or utility and are tied directly to a file. Constraints defined for a file will be enforced regardless of the utility or program that is making the change.

OS/400 Version 3 Release 1 will fully support deletion constraints but has limited support for update constraints. (The only rules supported are Restrict and No Action.) Insert and nonsupported update constraints will have to be handled with trigger programs or application code.

AS/400 Database Design Considerations

Every data management system has its own strengths and weaknesses. One key area the designer should be aware of is the storage space required to support each file and user view. Even when normalization dictates a new file, sometimes the space overhead of a new file negates any gains from eliminating duplicate data. In addition, organizing data in separate files will adversely affect data retrieval performance, possibly to an unacceptable level. File overhead and performance are the two major reasons to put data in a nonnormalized form. However, you shouldn't rush out and justify inefficient structures too hastily. Don't forget the disadvantages of nonnormalized data: extra storage space and update anomalies.

Since these space and performance effects are directly tied to the individual data management package being used, the designer does not consider them during the normalization process. These factors are considered only after the normalization process is completed and the data is in a normalized form. The AS/400 database designer, however, should be aware of the storage overhead for AS/400 physical and logical files.

Besides the space required to store data in a physical file, overhead space is required for information regarding:

The file

Each member of the file

Each record in the file

The KSAP

For instance, a rough approximation of the storage overhead involved in a physical file can be calculated with the following sizing guidelines.

The static space (overhead) associated with a physical file is 1,048 bytes. In other words, if you create a physical file without any data or members, the file will take up 1,048 bytes. For each member in the file, an additional 5,120 bytes are required. For each record in the file, an additional 2 bytes are needed.

So for a file with 80,000 records and one member, the overhead is:

```
1,048 + 5,120 + 2 × 80,000 = 166,168 bytes
```

If the file is keyed, the KSAP also takes up storage space. The static amount is 4,096 bytes. In addition, the KSAP stores each key plus 8 bytes and then needs approximately 48 percent more space per key. So for our file STUDENT, with unique SS# values that are 9 bytes in length, the amount of overhead space would be:

```
4,096 + ((9 + 8) × 80,000 × 1.48) = 2,016,896
```

A logical file, even though it contains no data, also takes up space. Each logical file requires a static 1,024 bytes. If the logical file is keyed, it will take up the same amount of additional space as a physical file KSAP. If the logical file uses a unique format, there is an additional space requirement of 512 bytes plus 75 bytes per field. Moreover, if a physical file has logical files based on it, an additional 272 bytes are needed in the physical file plus 16 bytes per logical file. So a logical keyed file with selected fields could be quite "expensive" in terms of space.

Most designers do not get down to the individual byte level because their time is too valuable to waste worrying about a couple of thousand bytes. In addition, these formulas are all approximations and highly dependent on the individual file characteristics—the number of fields, size of keys, number of records, and so on. The best way to find out the size is to create the file and fill it with data or, if the file already exists, display the file definition.

The point of the formulas is to show that creating separate files does not come without cost. In many instances, the amount of space saved by normalization needs to be balanced against the space requirements of the physical files needed to support the normalized organization. In addition, don't forget that nonnormalized organizations may provide faster retrieval performance. However, the faster retrieval is achieved through redundant data, and update performance will be affected. In addition, the chance of update anomalies is much greater with redundant data.

Before creating logical files, the AS/400 database designer should also consider other alternatives for providing the user with his or her required data. User views of the data can be implemented with queries or the OPNQRYF command instead of logical files. Having a program generate the data on request saves the space and maintenance processing that would be "spent" on logical files. However, using QUERY/400 or OPNQRYF to access data will generally be slower than using already existing logical files. This is because each of these tools must locate or even dynamically create a KSAP to access the data for the required user view.

Summary

Data design is one piece of overall system design. The process of data design is highly dependent on the user requirements and cannot be done in a vacuum. The data base designer must be aware of all processing and access requirements to design the best overall data organization.

Most database design starts with some preliminary data organization that originates from either the current system or program design. The designer then normalizes the data. Normalizing data yields the most space-efficient organization and provides the best protection against update anomalies. There are many different types or forms of normalization, and most designers consider the 3NF sufficient. However, several other normal forms can provide further savings.

Once the data is normalized, the designer begins the process of ensuring that access time requirements are met. Retrieval performance can sometimes be improved by placing data in nonnormalized forms. Furthermore, since every DBMS has overhead storage for files, the designer must balance the benefits of normalization against the "real-world" costs of separate files.

Data design also includes designing all the individual user views and ensuring that the global design supports the individual views needed. In addition, the designer must make physical design decisions such as what ASP a file should reside on, which files should be journaled, and, in the growing world of distributed data, even what computer the data will reside on.

The AS/400 has utilities to help with distributed data such DDM files and the RDBD (relational database directory). Future releases of the AS/400 DBMS will be called DB2/400. DB2/400 will also include more distributed data functions (such as a data propagator) and client–server utilities (such as stored procedures). In addition, maintaining database integrity will be easier and more efficient through trigger programs and referential integrity constraints.

EXERCISE

Given the following organization for our customer's database:

Customer File	Inventory File	Serial File
CUST#	INUM	SNUM
CCITY	SNUM	INUM
CFNAME	MEDIA	INAME
CLNAME	RENT#	
CSTATE	RPRICE	
CSTR	SERIAL	
CZIP	SPRICE	
CPHONE	STATUS	
TOTLTF	TYPE	
TRANS#1		
SNUM1		
TDATE1		
TTIME1		
DAYSPD1		
RDATE1		
RTIME1		
LF1		
LFPD1		
: :		
: :		
TRANS#99		
SNUM99		
TDATE99		
TTIME99		
DAYSPD99		
RDATE99		
RTIME99		
LF99		
LFPD99		

normalize the video store's data. Show the data in the first, second, and third normal forms. Explain the advantages of the differences between the normalized data and the ITEM, PRODUCT, CUST, and TRANS files we have used so far.

PROGRAMMING EXERCISE

Major modifications to the databases such as the conversion to a normal form from a nonnormalized form can have significant repercussions throughout an application system. For instance, for our customer's database, not only must the physical files be modified, but the application programs, logical files, backup procedures, journaling and data screens also have to be changed. In addition, conversion programs will have to be written to transfer the data to the new structures and security established to ensure proper access capability. This significant amount of work to change a database is one good reason for performing data design before creating a database. Of course, in any dynamic business environment, change is a fact of life. However, by thoroughly analyzing and properly normalizing data, extensive database modifications can be minimized.

For this exercise, change the video store's system so that the database is in 3NF. To put the video store database into 3NF, the programmer will have to:

Create new Inventory, Price, and Serial files.

Change each logical file's source code (for logical files based on ITEM and PRODUCT) to reflect the new physical files.

Write and execute a conversion program to move the data from the old ITEM and PRODUCT files to the new files.

Delete the old logical and physical files.

Create the new logical files.

Change the application programs and screens that add and delete items and products to reflect the new physical files.

Ensure that the new files are backed up and regularly journaled.

To perform the conversion, two new logical files will be helpful. Create one logical file called NAME that is based on the file ITEM, has all the ITEM fields, and has a key of INAME. Create another logical file called SINUM that is based on the file SERIAL, has the INUM and SNUM fields, and has a key of INUM.

The pseudocode for the conversion programs using the new logical files is as follows:

```
Convert-Serial
Read: Read PRODUCT
      If end of file Then Go to End
      Move PRODUCT data to SERIAL record
      Read ITEM where INUM = PRODUCT.INUM
      Move ITEM.MEDIA to SERIAL.MEDIA
      Write Serial record
      Go to Read
End:  End program


Convert-Inv-and-Price

      ITEMNUMBER = 0
      PREVNAME = " "
Read: Read NAME
      If end of file Then Go to End
      If PREVNAME not equal NAME.INAME
      Then Write NAME data to INVENTORY record
           Write NAME data to PRICE record
```

```
                ITEMNUMBER = NAME.INUM
                PREVNAME = NAME.INAME
           Else Write NAME data to INVENTORY record
                Write NAME data to PRICE record
                INVENTORY.INUM = ITEMNUMBER
                PRICE.INUM = ITEMNUMBER
   ReadS:       Read SINUM where INUM = NAME.INUM
                If read successful
                Then SINUM.INUM = ITEMNUMBER
                      Write SINUM
                      Go to ReadS
                Write NAME.INUM to ITEMDTAQ
           Write INVENTORY
           Write PRICE
           Go to Read
End:       End program
```

The pseudocode to modify the applications is as follows:

<u>ADD</u>

```
Start: Display "Add Items and Serials" menu
       If option 1
       Then Call AddItm
       Else If option 2
              Then Call AddSer
              Else If option 3
                     Then End program
       Goto Start

AddItm
                NEWITEM = N
                IDTAA = N
                Read ITEMDTAQ
                If read unsuccessful
                Then IDTAA = Y
                     Read ITEMDTAA
                Move item number to screen.item number
       Disp:    Display "Add New Item" screen
                If Type not equal "CONSUMABLE" and MEDIA is blank
                Then Goto Disp
CHANGE==>       Move screen data to INVENTORY record
CHANGE==>       Write to INVENTORY file
NEW==>          If Write successful
NEW==>          Then For each Media
NEW==>                    Move screen data to PRICE record
NEW==>                    Write to PRICE file
NEW==>                    If Write unsuccessful
NEW==>                    Then ROLLBACK
NEW==>                         Send message "Item not added. Could
NEW==>                            not write to PRICE."
```

```
NEW==>                       End program
              If Serial = Y
              Then fill in item number on "Add New Serial" screen
                     NEWITEM = Y
                     Call AddSer
              If IDTAA = Y
              Then add one to item number
                     Write item number to ITEMDTAA

         EndAddItm

         AddSer

              PDTAA = N
              Read PRODDTAQ
              If read unsuccessful
              Then PDTAA = Y
                     Read PRODDTAA
              Move serial number to screen.serial number
         Disp1: Display "Add New Serial" screen
CHANGE==>     Read PRICE file using screen.item number and
CHANGE==>            screen.media as the key
CHANGE==>     If read successful
CHANGE==>     Then Move screen data to SERIAL record
                     Set Status = A
                     Set Rent# = 0
CHANGE==>            Write to SERIAL file
                     If write successful
                     Then COMMIT
                            If PDTAA = Y
                            Then add one to serial number
                                   Write serial number to PRODDTAA
                     Else If NEWITEM = Y
                           Then  ROLLBACK
                                   Send message "Item and product not
                                        added. Could not add serial to
                                        PRODUCT."
                                   If IDTAA = N
                                   Then Write item number to ITEMDTAQ
                          Else Send message "Could not add serial
                                 to PRODUCT."
                          If PDTAA = N
                          Then Write serial number to PRODDTAQ
             Else Send message "Can't add serial.  Item doesn't
                          exist."
                  If NEWITEM = Y
                  Then Goto Disp1
```

```
             EndAddSer

            DELITEM

             Display DELITM screen
CHANGE==>    Delete record in INVENTORY for screen.INUM
             If Delete successful
NEW==>       Then Read record in KPRICE for screen.INUM
NEW==>            Do while read successful
NEW==>                Delete record in KPRICE for screen.INUM
NEW==>                If delete successful
NEW==>                Then Read record in KPRICE for screen.INUM
NEW==>                Else ROLLBACK
NEW==>                    Send message "Item number ", INUM," not
NEW==>                      deleted. Could not delete item from PRICE"
NEW==>                    End program
NEW==>            Enddo
CHANGE==>         Read record in KSERIAL for screen.INUM
                  Do while read successful
CHANGE==>             Delete record in KSERIAL for screen.INUM
                      If delete successful
                      Then Write serial number to PRODDTAQ
                      Else ROLLBACK
                          Send message "Failed item deletion for
                            item ",INUM,". Couldn't delete serials
                            from PRODUCT. PRODDTAQ may have serial
                            numbers that are still in use, the serial
                            numbers must be deleted from PRODDTAQ."
                          End program
                      Read record in KSERIAL for item number
                  Enddo
                  COMMIT
                  Write item number to ITEMDTAQ
                  Send message "Item and serials deleted."
             Else Send message "Could not delete item from ITEM
                               file."

            ENDDELITEM

            DELSER

                  Display DELPRD screen
CHANGE==>         Delete record in SERIAL for screen.SNUM
                  If delete successful
                  Then Write screen.SNUM to PRODDTAQ
                  Else Send message "Could not delete serial."

            ENDDELSER
```

In addition to modifying the programs, a new logical file KSERIAL will have to be created to take the place of KPROD. KSERIAL will be based on SERIAL but have a key of INUM. Moreover, a new logical file KPRICE will have to be created that is based on PRICE but has a key of INUM.

The "Add New Serial" and "Add New Item" screens have to be modified too. The "Add New Serial" screen must include the field MEDIA, and the "Add New Item" screen must accommodate multiple media and prices. The screens should look like the following:

```
                    Add New Item screen

Item number:  _______
Item name:    ____________________
Type of item: __________
Serial:       _

Media:         ___    Media:         ___    Media:         ___
Rental price:  ____   Rental price:  ____   Rental price:  ____
Sales price:   ______ Sales price:   ______ Sales price:   ______

            Change item number and press Enter
                           or
            Enter item data and press Enter
```

```
                  Add New Serial screen

Serial number: _______


  Item number: _______


        Media: ___



Fill in serial number, item number and media then press Enter
```

REVIEW QUESTIONS

1. What is the purpose of system design?
2. Normalizing data provides what two major advantages?
3. Which normal form eliminates repeating data fields within a structure?
4. What are the three levels of data design?
5. What is meant by update anomalies?
6. How are update anomalies related to normalization?
7. What is contained in a correlation file, and what purpose does a correlation file serve?
8. Where is the foreign key placed when two files have a one-to-many relationship and why?
9. Why are foreign keys introduced during normalization?

DISCUSSION QUESTIONS

1. Explain the relationship between system design and data design and the requirements it places on the system designer.
2. Give some reasons data should not be stored in a fully normalized form.

Index